More Than a Game

Why North Carolina Basketball
Means So Much to So Many

THAD WILLIAMSON

Economic Affairs Bureau
Cambridge, Massachusetts

MORE THAN A GAME: WHY NORTH CAROLINA BASKETBALL MEANS SO MUCH TO SO MANY
Thad Williamson

Copyright © 2001 by Thad Williamson

ISBN 1-878585-21-5

The Economic Affairs Bureau publishes *Dollars & Sense*, a bimonthly magazine. *D&S* explains the workings of the U.S. and international economies and provides a progressive perspective on current economic affairs. It is edited and produced by a collective of economists, journalists, and activists who are committed to social justice and economic democracy.

For more information, contact:

Dollars and Sense
740 Cambridge Street
Cambridge, MA 02141
www.dollarsandsense.org

Cover by Alison Strickler
Photography by Michelle Hillison (cover), Adria Scharf, and Sam Williamson

Manufactured by Transcontinental Printing
Printed in Canada

In memory of two great Tar Heels, Neil Jacobson and Mebane Pritchett;

In thanksgiving for the life of one new Tar Heel, my nephew Robert Wallace Brown;

And with hope that he may grow up in a peaceful world.

Contents

Introduction

I don't know the exact date or even year I became a Carolina basketball fan (though I think it was 1974). I do remember where and how it happened, however.

It happened at 706 Churchill Drive in the Briarcliff neighborhood of Chapel Hill, about one-quarter of a mile from Ephesus Road Elementary School. My parents were set to go to Raleigh for the evening one winter weeknight—leaving my older brother George, older sister Treeby, and me with a babysitter. They were going to Reynolds Coliseum to see North Carolina play North Carolina State in basketball.

Somehow I blurted out to my older brother that I hoped North Carolina State would win the game. "Why?" George asked incredulously. Well, I said in my 4-year-old voice (a voice that had such a hard time saying "r"s and several other consonants that I couldn't even say my own brother's name very well), North Carolina State represents the whole state of North Carolina, whereas the University of North Carolina only represents the university, so clearly the state is more important than just the university and therefore the state—N.C. State—should win the game. My brother's response was pretty direct: "No, that's wrong. We all root for UNC. That's who we are and that's who you have to root for. You actually want UNC to win, not State."

George could not have been more accurate with respect to the family identity—our father was a tenured member of the history faculty at UNC–Chapel Hill. And George was already in fourth grade up the street at Ephesus, which as I would in time find out firsthand, is full of little kids who love UNC and regard its basketball players as nothing short of real-life angels.

But George also imparted a valuable and lasting lesson about the value of particularity ("we all root for UNC") as opposed to a diffuse wish for the aggregate common good (the notion that the "state" would be somehow more important than just the "university"). Both attachments to particularity and a general wish for the greater good are important human values, important habits of thought and living. But only one is capable of constituting an individual's identity in a deep, inescapable sense, in a way that shapes your very perceptions of reality and touches the deepest wellsprings of the heart.

And so it was that I became a Carolina fan, at that very moment. George's lesson sunk in immediately. I was actually disheartened to learn the next morning that Carolina had in fact lost.

That moment of conversion—which ended up in time affecting such a substantial portion of my subsequent thoughts, emotions, and actions—had nothing to do with a convincing rational argument by my brother or a reflective rational choice on my part. It had everything to do with the accident of happenstance, the fact that my family had left Cambridge, Massachusetts and come to Chapel Hill and not some other college town—and perhaps also with the fact that it was not until age 9 or 10 that I reached the intellectual breakthrough that not everything my five-year-older brother told me was necessarily 100% true.

The upshot is that being a Carolina basketball fan has been constitutive of my identity for almost as long as I can remember. It was constitutive of the identity to greater and lesser degrees of most of the people I spent the first 18 years of my life with, as well as the communal identity of most of the institutions in the town I grew up in. And it has been constitutive of the identity of the several thousand Carolina basketball fans I happened to have corresponded with, mostly electronically, in the past six years.

What is the substance of this attachment to Carolina basketball shared by so many? Is it on balance a healthy thing? What are its better and worse aspects? Is it healthy that so many people are capable of being so moved by games played by people they for the most part don't know? How does a college basketball team fit into the everyday lives of its supporters? In the end, what do the thousands of hours spent by hundreds of thousands of people following the team's fortunes amount to? And what (if anything) does this devotion of fans to their team tell us about the society we live in?

*

This book will explore those questions. Whether satisfactory answers emerge remains to be seen and for the reader to judge. The best way to start, however, is by looking at people's stories showing how North Carolina basketball fits within their lives—both the big moments they readily recall and the smaller flashes of memory that may be more difficult to communicate.

Since Dean Smith became the head coach of the men's basketball program in 1961, just over 200 players have lettered for the Tar Heels. Another 70 or so have been managers. Including coaches and other support staff, perhaps 300 people in the last 40 years have actually been a member of a North Carolina Tar Heel basketball team.

I'm not one of those people. I have had, over two separate stretches of time, the chance to observe those people at very close range—first as a kid with the best unpaid job in Chapel Hill, then as a moonlighting journalist taking advantage of the doors opened by the "new media." And I have had, quite by chance, the opportunity to be in close proximity to a handful of those key people, close enough to have a sense of who they are as human beings, not just figures on the television screen. But I have never been a beat writer covering the Carolina basketball team night in and night out, or a radio or television commentator, or a confidante of a coach or player.

Likewise, this book is not simply another attempt to tell the story of those 300 select people and their many exploits and accomplishments—although the pages that follow necessarily touch on those accomplishments and their impact on me and on other fans. I cannot tell the Dean Smith story, the Bill Guthridge story, or the Ed Cota story. Those stories (as Smith has already shown) are best told by the principals themselves, not the interested bystander.

On the other hand, my sense of what Carolina basketball is all about is irrevocably shaped by the way I've seen these people conduct themselves firsthand under the glare of bright lights, the interviews I've conducted in joyous and distraught locker rooms, the interactions among players and coaches I've glimpsed. Having an on-target understanding of what Carolina basketball is all about and what those 300 or so people have been up to all these many years is critical to understanding why Carolina basketball has touched so many people so deeply.

So one eye in this inquiry is focused, as it should be, on the accomplishments of the 300 or so people who have been part of the Carolina program. The other eye, however, is trained on a second group of people: the 600-plus individuals who took 30–45 minutes each to respond to an 86-question survey regarding their personal relationship to Carolina basketball. Most of these people are not (and never have been) close friends with any former Carolina player or coach.

Adequately understanding the phenomenon of Carolina basketball means paying attention to the experiences and viewpoints of those 600-plus people—for the simple reason that the vast majority of human beings who care about Carolina basketball fall into this latter camp, not the small group of people who have been inside the program. This book tries to understand how people relate Carolina basketball to their own lives, drawing on original, unprecedented data about the values and habits of serious North Carolina basketball fans, as well as on some of the compelling stories and anecdotes told by those fans.

But no social science tool, no survey, no statistical analysis can capture the texture of how allegiance to a sports team fits into one's life quite so well as a single well-expressed story. The fan story I am best equipped to tell is my own—although that story is intertwined with the stories of many other fans and of the community and social networks in which I grew up. Part One of this book, then, tells that story—picking up where we just left off, sometime back in 1974 or 1975, and continuing in the first two chapters until roughly 1995. Interspersed with my own memories of the events on and off the basketball court that shaped my experience as a fan will be some of the hundreds of stories I have collected illustrating how other fans of different ages and in different places have been touched by Carolina basketball.

Chapter Three of the book shifts focus to a different time frame and a different perspective: the eventful five-year period during which I covered North Carolina basketball as a journalist and columnist, from 1995 to 2000. That period coincided with two head coaching changes, as well as a sharp increase in media attention given to the program, fueled both by the Internet and by the boundless appetite of hard-core fans for recruiting news and other inside information. And that period also happened to coincide with the appointment of someone I had known most of my life as a family friend to the head coaching job at Carolina. My journalistic work is the primary source for this part of the book, complemented by the memories of both observers of and participants in the varied events of that period.

Part Two takes a step back from story-telling and journalistic observation to take up more directly three central questions: How does Carolina basketball fit into the lives of its fans and their communities? Is this "fit" between fans and their passion on balance a good thing—either for the fans or for society? And are there any broader lessons to be drawn from this close look at North Carolina fans?

Chapter Four digs into these issues by asking "what's good" and "what's bad" about the phenomenon of North Carolina basketball and the impact it has on fans' lives. Chapter Four also develops the idea that there are better and worse ways to be both a sports fan in general and a fan of North Carolina basketball in particular. The discussion in this chapter draws upon my own observations about Carolina basketball, as well as upon my own research on the impact of sports fanhood upon civic and social well-being in the United States.

Chapter Five turns from this theoretical discussion to a concrete look at how Carolina fans actually think and behave, using as evidence detailed "fan diaries" kept by 15 Carolina supporters during the 2000–01 campaign.

Chapters Six, Seven, and Eight examine in detail the second major source of evidence used in this book: the 606 responses to the North Carolina Basketball Fan Survey. Those responses provide evidence on everything from what Carolina fans really think about Duke to how many UNC supporters plan on raising their children as little Tar Heels to the values Carolina fans associate with the program.

Finally, in the Conclusion, I attempt to tie together the themes of the book, with special emphasis on two questions: Is the attachment of North Carolina fans to their team on balance a good thing? And what, if anything, does this deep attachment say about our society? That concluding discussion reflects my own judgments as both a committed Carolina fan and as a student of ethics and social thought—as well as the process of critical self-reflection that has brought this book to life.

Readers will correctly note that in many ways this book has a dual personality. On the one hand, I express my own views about Carolina basketball and give an account of how I came to hold them. On the other hand, I attempt to step back from my experience to examine and critically evaluate the experiences and attitudes of UNC fans in general. The book is organized so as to first, provide one highly specific account of how being a fan fit into my own life and that of the community I grew up in; second, move to a somewhat broader level of generality by tracking the experiences of 15 ardent UNC supporters over the course of a single season; and finally, consider the experiences of the much broader range of fans represented in the North Carolina Basketball Fan Survey.

Similarly, the narrative of the book progresses from storytelling to several different levels of analysis: analysis of the Carolina basketball program on its own terms (with special reference to the period between 1995 and 2000); analysis of the pros and cons involved in being a Carolina fan; and analysis of the actual habits of North Carolina basketball fans. In short, this book brings to bear multiple perspectives on the central questions at hand, with the full consciousness that the shifts from one perspective to another may be jarring to readers. That jarring effect is deliberate, in the sense that if I did not believe that human beings with passionate, even irrational commitments to certain sports teams were not also capable of stepping back and examining their own attachments to those teams with a critical eye, there would be no reason to write this book.

Most of the time, when the ball is in play, there isn't a great deal of time to think reflectively on the basketball court, especially at the fast-moving ACC level. Locker room interviews rarely provide appropriate moments to ask really big, macro-level questions about the meaning of all these games—although on occasion coaches' press conferences held by Dean Smith and Bill Guthridge did touch on just such questions. Internet message boards and mailing lists have helped Carolina fans in different places hold conversations with each other in ways unimaginable 10 years ago, but are rarely the source of deep insight or sustained thought. Next-day newspaper columns in the sports section often reflect snap judgments on what just happened the day or week before.

But none of these facts should lead one to the stereotypical conclusion that sports fans, athletes, and coaches can't think beyond the present moment and ask bigger-picture questions. They can, and most in fact do. I hope that this book can contribute to such thought, and inspire not only moments of nodding recognition, but also moments of critical self-reflection in the Carolina fans (and others) who read these pages. Critical thought should not be made the enemy of loyal fanhood. It is my conviction that we can all become better fans by occasionally reflecting on the difficult and perhaps unanswerable questions raised in the pages to come.

1

The Socialization and Education of a Carolina Basketball Fan, 1976–1988

1975–76

My first three years of schooling—two years of pre-kindergarten and then kindergarten itself—took place at the Church of the Holy Family in Chapel Hill, located off the 15–501 Bypass, about two miles from where the Smith Center now sits. I remain in touch with two of my fellow students from Holy Family to this day. The first is David Simpson, who starting at that young age became my best childhood friend. David lived a couple of blocks from me, on Eden Lane. At some point his mom and my mom met and they hit it off. Before long we all—Sam, Joan, George, Treeby and Thad Williamson, and David, Suzanne, David, and Laura Simpson—became lasting family friends. Like us, the Simpsons also belonged as members to Holy Family, an Episcopalian church, as they do to this day.

My friendship with David at that age wasn't based on basketball or on being fans of the same team, and in fact it never has been (even though David grew up a Carolina fan, is a UNC graduate, and still likes to go to Carolina games when he's on leave from the Navy). Our friendship was based rather on a spirit of mutual complementarity, I think—in one episode of lasting fame, we allegedly made an agreement that I would help David with his reading if he would teach me to tie my shoes. (Decades later, friends who heard about this bargain sometimes pointed to my oft-untied laces and wondered whether David had ever learned to read.) David was more naturally athletic than I was, but didn't memorize the rules to sports as fast as I did—in one unpleasant episode from around age six, about which I still feel a little guilty, I threw a fit because David didn't yet know that you couldn't take two steps without dribbling.

So David wasn't the most precocious basketball fanatic in the Holy Family class of 1976. Thing is, I'm not sure I was, either. Also present in that class was a girl named Michelle Donohue, who was to my knowledge the only other kid in the class who knew exactly who Mitch Kupchack was. "Mitch Cupcake" we would call him and laugh. "Mich" also delighted in pointing out the similarity between her own nickname and that of the Tar Heel All-American. Like me, Mich was a kid who had caught the Carolina bug early.

The truth is, though, that I caught the basketball bug probably just a little bit earlier than the Carolina bug. The family archive has a home movie of me stuffing a ball into a box at around age four, and of dribbling a basketball at the kindergarten talent show at Holy Family in 1976. While there already was a 10-foot goal in the back yard, sometime around that year my dad installed a second, adjustable-height goal so I could shoot away, as I immediately did for hours. (The goal is still there nearly a quarter century later at 706 Churchill, though I haven't snuck back there to take a few shots in over a decade.) I shot a lot by myself as a little kid—and might have shot (and more important, run) more if I had known just how tall I would turn out to be. In my case, at least, the love of basketball slightly preceded my affection for the young men in light blue and white shorts who played the game not too far away from Churchill Drive.

Nevertheless, by the 1975–76 season, I had a clear understanding of the notion of "Tar Heels," and by the time the 1976 Olympics rolled around, I knew exactly who Phil Ford, Tom LaGarde, Walter Davis, Dean Smith and Bill Guthridge were, as well as Kupchack. Kupchack held a special place in my very early experience as a fan, however, not only because of his seemingly edible last name, but because of his basket against Virginia which produced a 73–71 victory in Carmichael Auditorium that February.

That was the first Carolina game I ever attended, watching alongside my father. All I can really remember from that early game was the excitement of the crowd and how happy I was to be there—but then the suddenly nervous feeling that it was a close game. "Carolina can't lose," I thought to myself, "that's just not possible."

After a late Virginia basket to tie it up, the crowd around me wasn't so sure. But Kupchack broke free for the lay-up just before the buzzer and Carolina had a win as the crowd broke into ju-

---

ONE WINTER NIGHT IN CARMICHAEL AUDITORIUM

"After watching a six-point lead slip through their hands over the last 2:46 of the contest, the Tar Heels suddenly found themselves tied with the tenacious Cavaliers 71–71 when a hot-handed Billy Langloh dropped in an 18-footer with just 19 seconds showing on the Carmichael clock. Instead of calling time immediately, the Tar Heels threw the ball in, ran the clock down to seven seconds and then elected to stop action and devise their strategy. The plan had John Kuester throwing the ball in to Walter Davis down in the corner, and the smooth junior forward penetrated slightly to his left before releasing a 15-footer. The ball really never had much chance, but fortunately for UNC the rebound bounced long and into Kupchak's waiting hands. Immediately the 6-10 center put the ball back on the board and through the hoop, to release an arena of frustration."

—Dan Collins, writing in *The Chapel Hill Newspaper,* February 22, 1976

bilation. I don't remember anyone being unhappy that it had been such a close game against a less talented opponent. The important thing was, they won. I was hooked.

If that was a stirring introduction to the highs of basketball fandom, the next few weeks also brought my very first taste of the lows. While I'm sure I had seen parts of Carolina games before, the first two games which I remember deliberately sitting down in front of the television with my family to watch came in the ACC Tournament and the NCAAs that year. The ACC Final against Virginia was played on a Saturday night. I think we had pizza for dinner, and we watched the game more or less as a family. "They're going to lose tonight," my dad said with a grimace with a few minutes to go, and he was right, as Carolina fell to 26–3 on the year with a 75–69 defeat. However, my dad also explained, it was O.K., Carolina would still go to the NCAA Tournament.

A week later, Carolina played Alabama in their first-round NCAA Tournament game. The Tar Heels were beaten badly. The play I remember that astonished me most was when a Tar Heel player got called for a double-dribble. I couldn't believe it. Everyone knows you can't double dribble! How could a Carolina player do that?

"As a little kid, I used to examine my life after each loss to try to determine what sin caused the Heels to lose. I knew it must have been my fault, because I couldn't believe that Coach Smith or his players could have made any mistakes!"   —Marshall Thomason, 43, data administrator in Cary

Dazed and disappointed, I wandered outside to the backyard. Still plenty of Saturday afternoon left. I picked up the basketball. Dad was out there too, doing yardwork of some kind I think. Probably realizing my unhappy state, Dad simply said, "There are a lot of sad people in Chapel Hill right now." Somehow that thought did in fact make me a feel a little better. Dad then continued with the yardwork.

1976–77

We all watched the Olympics that summer on TV of course, Jim McKay's head filling the screen. Everyone was talking about the four Tar Heels on the United States basketball team, and how Dean managed to get away with that. Even then I was media-conscious enough to know that Smith had pointed out that he had nothing to do with selecting the team other than asking for team-oriented players. The U.S. beat Yugoslavia handily in the final to reclaim the gold medal, and posters of the four Carolina players plus Smith became a hot item in Chapel Hill.

1976–77 was the Williamson family's lost year in terms of Carolina basketball. While the Tar Heels overcame the loss to injury of senior center Tom LaGarde to win the ACC title and string together an incredible NCAA run, we were thousands of miles away in Cambridge, England. Sabbatical time for the history professor, and research to do at Churchill College. I liked that year abroad, liked going to first grade in England at the same school as my sister Treeby, liked the apartment complex where we lived, which had plenty of kids from a lot of different countries. I missed basketball some, but not too intensely for the most part. Two exceptions stand out: Once, on a side trip to Yugoslavia (not an inappropriate place to visit for a World War I historian and his family), we saw a full-court basketball game being played outside in Dubrovnik, which made me very emotional.

The second exception was when word came back via phone from the States that North Carolina had made it to the NCAA finals. Somehow along the way my grandmother Frances in Springhill, Louisiana had caught on to the Carolina basketball and Dean Smith thing, and she became a big Smith fan the rest of her life. "I can't believe they made it to the finals the one year we went away," said brother George with some indignation. A day or two passed, and then we found out they had lost. "They were so close," our grandmother related.

A few days later, we were able to read all about it in the *Sports Illustrated* that came across the Atlantic every week. The real story came, however, via a letter to George from his best friend Jonathan Broun. Jonathan described the new t-shirt in Chapel Hill that he had just gotten, pertaining to that 1976–77 season. "First in the ACC, First in the Eastern Region, First in Our Hearts, and First in the Nation.... Almost!"

1977–78

August 1977 saw the death of Elvis, the second month of the "Star Wars" craze, and also the month we returned to Chapel Hill. George was now at Phillips Junior High, Treeby and I at Ephesus Road School. David Simpson was in my second grade class, and we—and pretty much everyone we knew—played Rainbow Soccer that year. My dad started teaching again at Carolina, but now in a new job—that of Dean of Arts and Sciences.

The 1977–78 season was the first year I very consciously followed Carolina's basketball progress from game to game the entire season. One day, Dad came home with what in later days would come to be known as a "media guide," but which I knew first as simply the "Blue Book." It had four full pages devoted to national player of the year candidate Phil Ford, two pages of which consisted of a "Phil Ford: What They're Saying" section. Led by its senior point guard, Carolina started off with back-to-back games against Oregon State, an odd and never repeated arrangement, and was ranked No. 1 after beating Duke and State to win the Big Four Tournament. But then came a stunning loss to William and Mary on the road. I recall Jonathan Broun being particularly baffled by that one.

January saw Carolina fall to Duke 92–84 in Cameron, a game I watched over at the Simpsons.' That was the first time I really saw the Duke fans in their full glory—they were absolutely nuts at that game. Another memorable game was against Wake Forest on Super Bowl Sunday, a close Carolina win, the only time Carolina bested Rod Griffin and the Deacons in 1978. I remember Phil Ford gracefully helping pick a Wake player off the floor after a mid-court collision. On my birthday

(January 27th), I was the happy recipient of a miniature toy basketball with the North Carolina logo on it and the signatures of most of the team, including Ford's. The next day, I got to go to my one game of the season, to see Carolina put its annual Chapel Hill whipping on Clemson, 98–64. That was exciting because Ford scored his 2,000th point as a Tar Heel in that game, and the crowd knew it, letting out a big roar. Two days later, my sister Treeby got to go to her one game of the year—a supposed-to-be blowout against Mercer. Carolina won only 73–70. I later heard that Jonathan had problems finishing his homework that night because he had planned to turn off the radio and start it only after Carolina pulled away, which never happened. (For her part, Treeby reported that she saw lots of her school friends at the game—this was evidently the one game of the '78 season that faculty members saw fit to bring their daughters to.)

At some point in early February, the realization hit me like a Geff Crompton pick that Ford's days as a Carolina player were numbered. In a few weeks, it would all be over. There was still plenty of time to go, but it would end. It wasn't going to last forever. I don't think I was the only Chapel Hillian with similar feelings in February 1978. Everything was pointing emotionally to the day Carolina would say goodbye to its most beloved—and best—player ever.

Carolina had a couple of rocky patches on the way—a stunning loss to Furman, and then a close loss to Providence, as Mike O'Koren got injured, in a nationally televised Sunday game that I watched with great disappointment. But Carolina bounced back, led by Ford, to beat Virginia handily the following Saturday. Ford had 30 points and was absolutely brilliant. The next day in Sunday school, we were given the assignment of drawing pictures with the crayons, and I proudly showed my buddies David Simpson and Paul Pritchett a crude but well-intentioned portrayal of Ford walking off the court with his arm wrapped around Virginia freshman Jeff Lamp, saying, "Don't worry Jeff, you'll still get ACC Rookie of the Year."

Carolina lost to State in midweek, with an injured Ford sitting out, leading the Carolina fans in Reynolds in cheers from the bench. Fortunately, Ford and O'Koren would make their returns for the final game against Duke, with the ACC regular season title on the line.

That final game was memorable for lots of reasons. In our household, it was most memorable because it was linked with one of the defining stories of the Williamson family of the late 1970s. Mom and Dad got two tickets to basketball games by virtue of the teaching position. For some reason, Mom had a long-planned day trip on the date of Ford's last game. So one of the three kids would get to go in her spot. George was a big Carolina fan and huge Phil Ford fan. Treeby perhaps wasn't quite so much a Carolina hoops fan, but was a Phil Ford fan and wanted to go just as much. And by now you can imagine how I felt.

Rather than have to announce a choice among the three of us, leaving two of us upset and resentful, my parents came up with the following Solomonesque procedure: A name would be drawn from a hat to determine who would get to go to the game with Dad. About three days before the game, we gathered around the kitchen table to conduct the drawing. This was a high-stakes deal. And when the name drawn was George's, it was better than Christmas for my big brother.

Treeby came in second—and made a claim that she should get to go to the Duke game next year. Hearing that, I immediately put in a claim for the Duke game in 1980, which, I quickly added, would be Mike O'Koren's last home game and hence perhaps almost as exciting an event. (That didn't happen—my parents hastened to explain that's not the way the deal worked.)

At least four years passed from that date in February 1978 before I was informed that my parents had rigged the drawing in George's favor.

So Saturday afternoon came, and away Dad and George went to the game. Treeby and I were left at home to watch the game on TV. I'm not sure Treeby even watched the game. I watched the first half downstairs, which didn't go well for the Tar Heels. At halftime, I went outside, and kept saying to myself, "We have to win, we have to win." And then I shot baskets, whipping myself into a frenzy, getting completely fired up and excited that Carolina could come back and win. I just kept shooting and shooting and shooting. In fact, I kept shooting so long and so intensely that almost half the second half had been played before it struck me, "Hey, the game's back on by now." When I realized that, I dropped the ball and ran back inside.

It was on, but Carolina was still down. Then good things started to happen. Mike O'Koren made big play after big play, including a huge dunk on which he was called for a technical for hanging on the rim and trying to avoid an injury. And Ford was unreal, piling up 34 points. Carolina pulled ahead, and with less than 10 seconds to play Ford was sent to the line to shoot the game-clinching free throws. He bounced the ball, stuck his tongue out just above his lips, cocked the ball behind his head, and hit the first free throw. And then the second. Duke, which had gotten 20-point-plus performances from all three of its big guns—Jim Spanarkel, Mike Gminksi, and Gene Banks—failed to score, and Carmichael erupted into absolute pandemonium, the likes of which have not been seen in the nearly quarter century since. O'Koren picked up Ford and carried him around. There was a massive mob scene at mid-court as students stormed the floor. My father and brother waited with the crowd as they kept chanting, "We want Ford," until the Rocky Mount product re-emerged from the locker room to acknowledge the crowd.

> "It was the greatest outpouring of love for a single player I have ever seen. And I think love *is* the correct word."   —George Williamson, recalling Phil Ford's last home game

George came home acting as if he had just seen a glimpse of Valhalla. He brought back a Carolina blue cloth ribbon, the kind that had been handed out to all fans before the game in honor of the occasion, as his memento—and put that ribbon on his bulletin board, where it remained, its hue slowly fading, for over a decade as a happy reminder of that day. The next morning I read every article *The Chapel Hill Newspaper* had about the game, and kept looking at the incredible color photograph the paper ran of the mid-court celebration at the end of the game.

"The older I get, the more I think about things like that. Like the Olympics, the older I get, the more winning a gold medal means. The older I get, the more the camaraderie of playing here at North Carolina, being a student-athlete at North Carolina, means. I remember telling Walter Davis, who graduated the year before me, we had a bet, he bet me that I would cry, and I bet him that I wouldn't cry, and I think I was standing out there at midcourt for maybe five seconds before the tears came down. It was a sad day, but it was a good day. As a team, in the four years we had won some games, I had become a better basketball player, and I was on track to receive my degree in business administration. But I knew I would never be wearing a Carolina uniform again in Carmichael Auditorium. That was kind of nostalgic, but we were fortunate to pull out a good win over a very good Duke basketball team."

—Phil Ford

At that point, I was as in to Carolina basketball as any eight-year-old could possibly be. But that didn't mean my parents were willing to waive any of the duties befitting an eight-year-old. In other words, I wasn't yet allowed to stay up to watch the late games. That meant I missed seeing Carolina's loss (after a first round bye) in the ACC Tournament Semifinals against Wake Forest the following Thursday.

I didn't miss, however, Carolina's opener in the NCAA Tournament, a matchup in the West Region against Bill Cartwright and San Francisco on a Saturday afternoon. Earlier in the day Dad was out working in the backyard, and I asked him what he was doing. "A lot of people in Chapel Hill are outside working right now," he said. "So they can watch the game later." Those who watched saw a close game, but an intensely frustrating one for the Tar Heels, one where they couldn't quite get over the hump at the end despite some valiant last-ditch efforts by Ford. Carolina lost 68–64. Heavily disappointed at the loss and devastated by the end to Ford's career, I had a few tears. I then walked outside again to the backyard.

Still plenty of Saturday afternoon left. And not for the first time on a Saturday in March, a lot of sad people in Chapel Hill, too.

1978–79

Every grade we advanced in elementary school, Carolina basketball grew just a little bit larger as a common thread holding my classmates together. By age eight or nine, just about every kid my age that I knew well liked Carolina. Many frequently wore Carolina blue. At that young age, Carolina football also was very prominent, mainly because it was far more likely that a small kid would get to go to a football game in Kenan Stadium than make it into Carmichael.

The fall of 1978 saw my first experience on a team sport in which winning was actually taken seriously (as opposed to the relatively noncompetitive attitude of Rainbow Soccer at its youngest levels). This was the Cowboys little league football team in Chapel Hill, which I joined as a two-way lineman. Several of my friends, including David Simpson and David Moreau, had played for the Cowboys the year before, and I had gone to their championship game against the Patriots. Paul Pritchett was also on the team, and Martin and Brian Baucom, sons of the coach, started at quarterback and wide receiver. Jonathan Wagoner, fleet of foot and capable of breaking long runs, was the backup quarterback. The best player on the team (and the only African-American) was William Burnette, our tailback and linebacker. Most of our plays consisted of fullback Moreau blocking for Burnette. We had a good team and a good time.

But I doubt that many people on that team actually cared more about winning a little league football game than we would have about a Carolina–Duke basketball game. I certainly didn't. The day before our season-ending showdown with the feared Giants, a game we needed to win to avenge our one loss and earn a share of the league title, I complimented our coach, Ladd Baucom, on the preview he had written of the '78–'79 Tar Heels for the *ACC Basketball Handbook*. The lead of that article had talked about life after Phil Ford and somehow found a way to get "Twinkies" and "Geff Crompton" into the same sentence when discussing the Heels' departed seniors. Mr. Baucom thanked me, but then quickly reminded me to be sure I knew what was going on with the new play we were going to use the next day. I did, and much more important, we got great games from Burnette and Wagoner, and also scored a touchdown on a Baucom-to-Baucom trick play to beat the Giants, 24–20. That was an intoxicating moment. It was also the end of my football career—the town of Chapel Hill abandoned recreation football leagues for kids the next year.

It was also intoxicating a few weeks later when Amos Lawrence capped an even bigger miracle in Kenan, as Carolina rallied from a late 15–3 deficit to topple Duke and finish Dick Crum's first year on a winning note. I always had cared about basketball more, but I didn't then fully get it that it was no good expecting as much out of the football team as the basketball Heels, that it was a completely different deal (and in fact still is). Even so, that comeback in Kenan was certainly a memorable moment as a Carolina fan. Fact is, those of us who were true sports fans, like Jonathan and Dan Broun, and David Moreau and Paul Pritchett, and my brother, and many more, could get excited about Carolina doing well in anything. David Simpson and I saw Carolina capture its first women's soccer national title, the AIAW crown of 1981, in Kenan. George and I listened to the radio account of Carolina winning the lacrosse national championship that same year, 1981, and went crazy when Carolina won. Paul Pritchett went to so many home baseball games that he could have taken out a mortgage on Boshamer Stadium. I was in the stands there too when the Yankees came to town in 1979, and in 1981 when Carolina blew a ninth inning lead to lose the ACC Tournament to future major leaguer Jimmy Key and Clemson.

It would be misleading to say, then, that Carolina basketball was the only sport we cared about as kids. There was almost always something going on in Chapel Hill involving people wearing light blue uniforms, and we were interested in most of it. But it would not be misleading to say that Carolina basketball was at a completely different level in terms of how much we cared, how much we knew, how much we expected, how much we talked about it.

And one of the neatest things about living in Chapel Hill as a budding nine or 10-year-old fan was the fact that it was actually possible every so often to bump into a Carolina player. Every year elementary school students in Chapel Hill were bused up to Memorial Hall on campus for a children's concert performed by the North Carolina Symphony—one year Treeby reported that Phil Ford strolled up to the window during the concert and waved at the thrilled kids. I saw Dudley Bradley in person three separate times around 1978—once at the Ephesus Road school fair, once at a YMCA summer league game I was playing in (I made a steal in the backcourt in his honor, but then went on to blow the lay-up), and once when he spoke to our third grade class at Ephesus. That occasion was actually slightly depressing—Bradley emphasized the sacrifices it takes to make it as a player at Carolina, how hard he had to work, and the fact they had to cut back on eating sweets and things like that. My sweet-toothed heart sank a little at that report, but it was still something else to have a real Tar Heel come talk to a classroom of 25 kids for 15 minutes.

As usual, Jonathan Broun had the best of this sort of story in the circle I knew. Sometime in 1976, he learned that through a university program for kids with learning disabilities, he was going to be part of a special basketball clinic with Mitch Kupchack. Then the word came, as relayed through George, that the clinic was also going to feature Walter Davis. Finally the clinic came and went, and Jonathan reported to George that Mitch Kupchack, Walter Davis, AND Phil Ford had all been there! Still, that kind of thing was not uncommon for kids in Chapel Hill—George later went to a clinic of his own with Mike O'Koren. I don't think any of these sorts of interactions had a particularly profound effect on me or on my peers. But it did help me at least have some sense early on that the athletes I cheered for on the television screen and on occasion in Carmichael were real people.

*

Dudley Bradley, of course, became the central figure in the 1978–79 season. Expectations were lower with Ford gone, and I'm not sure how well today's Carolina fans could handle the uncertainty of going into a season knowing that odds are at best 50–50 to make the NCAA Tournament, as Carolina did that year. (In fact, Carolina didn't guarantee a claim to one of the two NCAA spots available to the ACC in 1979 until the conference tournament.) No one was much surprised early when Carolina lost to Duke by 10 in the Big Four tournament in December, although the fact that the game was tight until Al Wood fouled out was encouraging.

I got to see Carolina blow out Detroit and Jacksonville in Carmichael that December, the only real highlight being when the PA announcer mistakenly referred to Jacksonville coach Tates Locke as still being Clemson's coach after Locke picked up a technical foul.

That winter stands out most in my mind, however, as the winter I most relied on Woody Durham's every word over the radio. George got to see Carolina play Earvin Johnson and highly rated Michigan State on December 16. Bradley stole the ball from Johnson for a dunk in the first half, the trademark play of this Carolina team, and harassed Johnson into eight turnovers overall. Carolina hung on in the final minute to win 70–69.

The next game was also dramatic—George and I listened together in his room nervously as Carolina pulled out a close one at Cincinnati, 62–59. A couple of weeks later we were literally bouncing off the walls as an excited Durham called Carolina's double-overtime home win over Virginia. And a few weeks after that, all the Williamsons listened in disbelief as the Tar Heels passed up a chance to move to No. 1 in the national polls by losing at Clemson. That loss hurt a little extra because it came on my birthday.

In between came what most people regard as the most memorable moment of 1979, the crazy game at Reynolds in which Carolina roared to a 40–19 lead over N.C. State, lost all of the lead, then got it back on Bradley's steal from State guard Clyde Austin and subsequent dunk. Remembered by everyone but me—I was still on the no late game bedtime rule. I was as usual the first the next morning to run out and get *The News and Observer,* and the banner headline told me the story. I didn't miss an equally dramatic, if less-remembered game, a few days later, when Carolina battled Maryland on the road in a classic, pre-shot-clock battle that matched the wills of the coaches as much as those of the players. Down one with less than a minute to play, Carolina waited until less than five seconds remained before Al Wood drained a 17-footer on the right side of the court to give Carolina a 54–53 lead. After an apparent out-of-bounds infraction on the inbounds pass to half court went uncalled, Maryland got a good shot off to win. But Greg Manning missed from the baseline, and Carolina had its second crucial away victory in a week. The next day at Holy Family, Paul Pritchett and I recounted the final plays of the Maryland game endlessly. Paul was still upset that Maryland hadn't been called for stepping out of bounds.

The bizarre game against Duke in 1979 at Cameron to end the regular season—when Carolina used a delay game the entire first half—doesn't require a recounting here. The thing about it that made the most impression on me was former Tar Heel Walter Davis going on the radio with Woody at halftime and saying that Dean Smith would be no different in the locker room at halftime down 7–0 than if the score were 37–30. That was an interesting observation.

The other thing of note is simply that it never occurred to me (or to George, or to anyone I talked to at that age) that there was anything wrong with Smith's stall ball strategy. He did it—and we assumed he knew what he was doing. We remembered that just a year earlier Carolina had used the four corners extensively in the first half of a home win over Virginia when the Heels got a lead and were playing without O'Koren, and went on to score 71 points and win by 17. Although the fact that Carolina went on to play Duke on even terms in the second half perhaps put the wisdom of the strategy at Cameron in doubt, that didn't cause a great deal of angst. Indeed, while Smith did hear it from the critics over that decision, he didn't hear it from Carolina fans. It's hard to imagine that would be true if something like that happened today. As it was, I thought it was kind of cool to see a stall basketball game.

In any case, all that was over and forgotten a week later, when Carolina brought home the ACC Tournament championship from Greensboro. The Heels had won a draw with co-champion Duke and gotten the first round bye, and had to beat Maryland in the semifinal to guarantee a spot in the NCAA Tournament—if neither Duke nor Carolina won the tournament, Duke would likely have gotten the at-large bid based on taking two of three from the Tar Heels during the regular season. My parents went to the game, leaving us with pizza money. Before going, Mom informed George, Treeby and me that we were each officially authorized to use the word "hell" once per each night of the tournament while watching the games. That authorization got us fired up! But as it was, such expressions were hardly necessary against Maryland, as the Tar Heels played probably their best game of the year in running away from the Terps, 102–79.

Duke held off N.C. State in a classic semifinal game, setting up round four between Duke and Carolina, slated for Saturday night. Point guard Bob Bender missed the game for Duke, but the Devils still had capable backup John Harrell. Carolina played well to take a 31–25 halftime lead, as George, Treeby and I watched excitedly together. By the end of the game, we were jumping up and down like nobody's business. Dave Colescott hit his jumpers, Rich Yonakor was perfect from the baseline, and then Bradley took over in the four corners with two fantastic dunks to put the game away. It was a convincing win, one that capped a season much stronger than Ladd Baucom or anyone else would have dared to predict the previous fall. And it was a night I still recall as one of unmitigated happiness: watching the game with my brother and sister, being excited, and then getting to relive it all again when Mom and Dad came got back from Greensboro.

That elation turned to disbelief and the tears of March a week later, after Carolina lost on "Black Sunday" in Raleigh to Penn, 72–71. The only two plays I can recall from that game are Bradley stepping out of bounds after making a steal in the open court that would have set up a dunk, a play that typified the day's frustration, and then Carolina scoring a lay-up to cut it to one with time almost gone. I felt utter despair as the last ounce of hope, so difficult to let go of (and from experience, so unwise to give up), faded away. My mom tried to offer some consolation, but I wasn't having much of it as the game ended.

The fact that Duke lost the same day undoubtedly made the next couple of weeks more bearable (although I had actually mildly cheered for Duke in '78 when they made their big run after Carolina was out). Even so, for that Sunday afternoon, it was the same old story—walk outside, try to come to terms with what happened, just swallow it, try to think about what a good season it had been, try to think about next year. Even though I could tell Carolina hadn't played very well against Penn, the thought of casting blame or getting mad about it didn't enter my head. Losing was something you just had to take with the good, and it didn't change one's opinion of the Smith system or the coaches or the players. Losing was just a cause for sadness, that's all.

"The inevitable disappointment which comes with each year's loss in the Tournament provides more emotional feeling than any other event of the year. Understanding that it must happen, yet feeling the abject terminal disappointment as well as the dozens of sub-disappointments during the game gives a feeling unique to sports. Coming from 15 back for the last-second win is like a drug in comparison, great and then gone."   —44-year-old alumnus in Ontario

1979–80

It's difficult to imagine today North Carolina choosing to open its season by playing N.C. State and Duke on back-to-back nights. But that's exactly what happened to start the 1979–80 season, and Carolina again finished second in the Big Four Tournament. It was a mild surprise three weeks later when O'Koren led Carolina to a win against Indiana in Assembly Hall. In the first of many such conflicts in the coming years, I missed seeing that game to play in a recreation league game of my own; but of course someone brought a black and white TV to the gym at Lincoln Center in Carrboro to keep us apprised.

In January, the new decade started badly with a blowout loss to a really good Clemson team and me listening on the radio. Frustration grew when Carolina lost at Virginia in the next game. "North Carolina is 0–2 in the ACC," the announcers said. "Can you believe it?" But then Carolina came back with four straight league wins, including a memorable 15-point victory over Duke after Dean Smith had announced to the papers that Carolina should be favored to lose by 27 (since the Heels had lost to 17 at Clemson whereas Duke had taken the Tigers to overtime before losing, plus 10 points for the home court advantage). I again missed the game due to a rec ball conflict—but got back in time to see O'Koren leading a happy Tar Heel team off the court at Cameron. A few nights later, I fell asleep listening to the radio broadcast of Carolina's game against conference newcomer Georgia Tech. I awoke the next morning to learn that Carolina had won only because the Jackets' best player, Lenny Horton, had missed a lay-up at the buzzer. "Luck of the Irish," my dad called it. To me, it was only fair.

The defining point of the season came in a bad home loss to Maryland on a Sunday afternoon in January that was made a whole lot worse by freshman James Worthy's breaking his leg. My brother, who had already adopted Worthy as his favorite player, watched it at home with me. (George liked James so much that in one of his many fibs to me over the years, he called me into his room one time to hear this "song a guy from Chapel Hill wrote about James Worthy," which turned out to be "Sweet Baby James," by James Taylor.) The injury ended any serious national aspirations for the 1980 team.

Yet for a season in which Carolina failed to meet either its ACC or national aspirations, 1980 still had its share of interesting moments. One was listening to Woody's call of Mike Pepper coming off the bench to score 11 points in garbage time in a game against Furman in the North-South doubleheader. That outburst was followed by a 12-point night against Yale in Chapel Hill in which Smith gave the junior guard 28 minutes of playing time. Pepper had been something of a team mascot his first two years, and "We want Pepper" became a popular chant in Carmichael at the end of lopsided wins. One of my dad's students at Carolina explained to me that Pepper was well-liked because the ordinary student could relate to him and his less-than-overwhelming body type. And then lo and behold, over the course of 1980, on a team that seemed to have plenty of depth at guard, Pepper became a contributor, noted more for his good shooting form than his hairless legs. Woody was thrilled when Pepper came up with the two double-figure nights, and so was I.

A second interesting moment was the bitter, epic defeat in the rematch against Maryland in College Park. Carolina played one of its better games of the year to stay in it, yet trailed 70–67 after two Terrapin free throws with only seconds remaining. But Yonakor hit Al Wood with a perfect baseball pass past a napping Maryland defense for a lay-up to cut the lead to one, and Carolina used a timeout. Maryland threw it away on the inbounds pass, and suddenly Carolina had a chance to win. Maryland appeared to hold senior forward John Virgil as the Tar Heels tried to run an inbounds set, but there was no call, and the Heels didn't get a shot off. Dean Smith said afterwards that he expected Carolina to win after they had gotten the ball back. Somehow, that bold statement made me feel better about it—we could have won, we could have won. I wasn't happy about the loss, but I was proud of how the team had played—probably the first time I felt that particular combination of emotions. Meanwhile, George and Jonathan Broun had a quite different experience of the game. As ninth graders, they had to attend an open house at Chapel Hill High School that night to give them a taste of their future school's environs. The orientation session took place with Woody's commentary piped through the school PA system. People in the Chapel Hill city schools knew that accommodation to the local passion was a wise move. And the relevant administrators almost certainly cared about the game, too.

As in 1978, Carolina finished the regular season with emotional home wins over Virginia and Duke, sandwiched around a tough loss at State, this one marked by Clyde Austin's bounce pass assist through a Tar Heel's legs to Hawkeye Whitney for a dunk. The Virginia win was the famous "Jeff Wolf" game, when the offense-averse senior center played a tremendous game against Ralph Sampson on both ends of the court, and capped the day with two late dunks out of the four corners. The game against Duke saw Carolina start five seniors—Colescott, O'Koren, Wolf, Yonakor, and Virgil—whom one sentimental Chapel Hillian had named as their all-ACC team in a reader ballot held by *The Chapel Hill Newspaper*. The Tar Heels romped past Duke with ridiculous ease, 96–71.

But Duke turned the tables six days later en route to winning the ACC Tournament in snowy Greensboro, Mike Gminksi hitting jumper after jumper as Carolina fell by 14 points. In the subsequent snow-filled week, the Williamson family moved from Churchill Drive into a new house in a new neighborhood off Cleland Drive, close to the Chapel Hill Country Club golf course, but also close to Rainbow Soccer and the Church of the Holy Family. It was at 18 Kendall Drive that I watched Carolina lose a double-overtime heartbreaker to Texas A&M, as Jimmy Black missed a potential game-winning shot and Carolina fell behind in the second overtime. A desperate Dean Smith refused to give up and had his team keep fouling until the final margin was pushed to 17. A tough way for O'Koren and company to go, and the third straight year Carolina had failed to make it into the second week of tournament play.

But help was on its way, in the form of Sam Perkins and Matt Doherty, as well as a recovered James Worthy. It would be 14 years before I or any other Carolina fan had to look at the Sweet 16 brackets knowing Carolina's season was already over.

1980–81

I continued to attend Ephesus Road Elementary School for the remainder of fourth grade in 1980, even though we had moved to a different school district. I wasn't completely reconciled to our new address until the basketball court and goal were finally erected at the end of April after what seemed like weeks of torturous deprivation without a hoop to shoot at. (There weren't any backdoor hoops nearby to shoot at either, in sharp contrast to the situation on Churchill Drive.) On one of her visits, my grandmother Frances told me as pointedly as she could to stop grousing about it—life wasn't so bad.

And of course it wasn't. In time, the goal went up, and I started shooting at it. Before long, I began playing through the upcoming 1980–81 Carolina season in imaginary games. The basic scenario would be for the action to pick up with about two and half minutes to play and Carolina down by two or three. I would then shoot for both teams the rest of the game with running commentary in my head. The shots consisted of long jumpers (which I had become pretty proficient at after years of shooting over George), or turnaround shots, or moves to the basket. Sometimes I surprised and disappointed myself by taking a really tough shot, playing as Virginia or some other opponent, only to see the shot go in and have to live with the consequences. Most of the time, these imaginary games came down to me, as a Carolina player, having to hit a wide-open shot from about 15 feet to win the game at the buzzer.

It was around 1980 that I first began to take note of the concept of recruiting in a sustained way. *The Chapel Hill Newspaper* had reported that the new players on the 1981 Tar Heels would include Sam Perkins, Matt Doherty, Cecil Exum, Dean Shaffer, and a Finnish center named Timo Makkonen. One late summer day in 1980 I played through a fantasy game, this one a Carolina blowout, and managed to score imaginary baskets for all the new players as well as those on the existing roster—with one nagging exception. Everyone had scored—Pepper and Pete Budko, Braddock and Black—but someone was missing. I sat and thought for about 20 seconds knowing something was awry in my imaginary Tar Heel game. Then it hit me—I'd forgotten Al Wood! The most important player of all for 1981! I felt a little guilty and stupid for a few moments, then put some time back on my imaginary clock so that Wood could get a few baskets.

It was also around this time that I became more aware that the top assistant basketball coach at UNC attended our church at Holy Family. I had known that for a couple of years and had said hello or some such to Bill Guthridge as a real little kid a couple of times. But one day around 1980, my dad told me that if I wanted to ask Guthridge a question about Carolina basketball some time after church, I could do that. I said "sure." The next Sunday came, and standing outside after church I asked Guthridge in front of about four other adults about the accuracy of a *Chapel Hill Newspaper* article saying that with Cecil Exum signed, Carolina now had the inside track on his high school teammate, Lynwood Robinson. Guthridge, not at all alarmed that a 10-year-old kid had asked such a detailed question, said, "Sorry, Thad, I can't answer that. We don't talk about recruiting in public." My face fell a little bit, I think. But I accepted Guthridge's reply, and absorbed a pretty good lesson on the boundaries and ethics relevant to Carolina basketball in the process. (It turned out later, of course, that *The Chapel Hill Newspaper* had been on to something.)

The fall of 1980 saw George start at Chapel Hill High School, my sister start ninth grade at Phillips Junior High, and me enter fifth grade at the elementary school in our new district, Glenwood. I knew exactly one kid when I started at Glenwood—Paul Pritchett. And Paul's mom, Betsy, knew enough about Glenwood to put in a special request for Paul to be placed in Dixie Wier's fifth grade class—and to tell my mom to do the same for me. The day before school started, the class lists were posted on the outside of the school, and Paul and I both had indeed been put in Mrs. Wier's class. And everyone, I was told, should want to be in Mrs. Wier's class. The veteran teacher from Nebraska had an awesome reputation.

I don't think it's unfair to say that I learned more in that one single year from one great teacher than I did in any other year I spent in the Chapel Hill public schools, in terms of both substance and how to study. Mrs. Wier taught us the concept of how to make outlines about what we were reading to use as study guides, insisted that we memorize dates in American history (starting with 1492), gave us weekly vocabulary tests, made us do monthly book reports, and assigned homework four nights a week. (Weekends were off.) I felt like we were being worked hard, and so did everyone else. Over the course of the year, a great spirit of class solidarity emerged, encompassing really everyone in the class.

Mrs. Wier also made a point of making sure I became friends with another kid in the class with heavy interests in history, math and everything else, Tom Williams. Also in our class was Michelle Donohue, last seen in kindergarten and still a Carolina fan. By the end of the year, pretty much everyone in the class knew each other quite well. We bonded mainly because of the experiences we went through in the class, the discipline and the class projects. But the common assumption of a love for things UNC helped in that bonding too, and in my social adjustment in particular. Mrs. Wier was fully aware of how much people loved basketball in Chapel Hill. Each morning, just after the Pledge of Allegiance, we would raise our hands and tell the class a piece of "news." Mrs. Wier accepted that invariably someone would report the score of the UNC football or basketball game during this time if there had been one the day or weekend before. She wanted us to talk about current events or really interesting things that had happened at home, too, but saw no harm in acknowledging explicitly what was already in the air anyway. At some point, I imagine, Mrs. Wier probably reckoned it was better to get out into the open what was on our minds early in the day so as to get over it or get beyond it, whether it was a win or a loss.

Glenwood School, I thought, was a better set-up than Ephesus in many ways, at least in terms of bonding with other students. I rode a school bus for the first time, and it always got to school about 20 minutes early, before the first bell. That usually meant 20 minutes to play basketball in what was then a very ample, large chunk of black asphalt, equivalent to a football field plus a basketball court, with four hoops available to shoot on. For the sake of quick organization and maximizing available time, teams were chosen quickly in the morning and not limited to five on five. It was a fun way to start the day, and I got to appreciate firsthand the athletic talents of new friends like Tom Kerby and Jeff Jones.

Another good thing was, unlike at Ephesus, there was a guaranteed recess period every day for fifth and sixth graders. And unlike at Ephesus, in which recess was minimally supervised and kids organized themselves—leaving ample room for some kids to be insiders and some to be outsiders—Glenwood recess consisted of an organized activity, usually a game like dodge ball or kickball, involving the whole class. Another chance to play, and another chance to earn the respect of and make friends with new classmates via athletic expression. It was something to look forward to every day.

But with Mrs. Wier, there was something to look forward to every night, too: a very substantial amount of homework. Monday nights were the heaviest workload—math, a new set of vocabulary words, and usually something else as well. One Monday night in the middle of the year, I was sort of grousing my way through the work and took a break, not quite done with my work, at about 9 p.m. and turned on the TV. Just then the phone rang. I was the only one home, so I answered it. It was Bill Guthridge calling, trying to reach my dad. (This was not a frequent event.) When he heard it was me, the first thing he said was "Are you doing your homework?" "I'm just taking a break right now, but I've been doing it," I said slightly guiltily, knowing it was not all done yet. Still, I was pleased he asked. By then I knew he was probably aware of my habit at church of being the first kid to answer the questions our rector, the Reverend Gary Fulton, asked of us youngsters during the weekly homily. (During one immortal episode, Gary asked us during a Palm Sunday homily what was different about church that week. With a helpful prod from my brother, I answered, "The church is full.") In any case, it was nice to know that Guthridge was keeping tabs on me and my cohort.

But the call made me feel especially guilty and stressed out the next morning when I accidentally left at home some of my vocabulary cards. (Mrs. Wier let me off the hook very gently on that occasion and told me not to get upset.) Many years later, I often thought about that brief phone conversation when trying to juggle graduate school and going off somewhere to cover Carolina or spending time writing a column; and inevitably I would conclude that getting the homework done had to be the top priority. Fortunately, however, there is a lot more leeway to fit it all in when you are no longer bound to go to bed by 10 or at the latest 11 p.m., as I was back in 1980.

As always, November and December finally came in 1980. I actually watched the second night of the Big Four tournament (Carolina lost to Wake Forest in the final) while spending the night with another new friend from Glenwood, David Bresenham, who was a committed Duke fan (for reasons that still escape me). David was probably my first real friend across enemy lines, as it were; but he had a sense of humor about it and Duke wasn't very good that year anyway. (Carolina had beaten Coach K's first team the night before.) The highlight of December was another superb win over Indiana, this time in Carmichael, that George got to go to as the home game closest to his December 15 birthday.

ONE DECEMBER AFTERNOON IN 1980

When I moved to Chapel Hill in 1980, I went to my first game in Carmichael, UNC–Indiana in December. I still get chills thinking about it.

Two things struck me. One was how loud the place was, of course. I've seen lots of games at Cameron, and Carmichael was just as loud. The other thing was the quality of play on both sides. Both teams played SO smart and SO disciplined, yet in very different ways. Carolina used to switch defenses a lot back then, sometimes each trip down the court. Jimmy Black called them and the team seemed to switch effortlessly and instantly. And while IU played all man and Carolina played a fair amount of zone, both played it so well. Those were pre-shot clock days, and both teams showed incredible patience on offense; something you'd never see nowadays. At the half I was amazed. I knew and expected to see great athletes, and I knew these were two great coaches. But still, the level of team play and effort and discipline just stunned me.

IU led by about five for three-quarters of the game. Then at about the 10- or 12-minute mark of the second half, IU's patience on offense led to a very long possession. As they kept working the crowd, the crowd noise started to build. They were cheering for the defense, something I'd never seen at a game before. After about a 60-second possession, the crowd was deafening, as if there'd been a huge dunk or game-winning play. But all that was happening was that IU couldn't seem to get a clear shot. Then one of the Carolina defenders stepped into a passing lane, fast break, dunk. Instantly Carolina was in the press, though I don't recall anyone calling it out from the bench. Boom, another turnover and basket. Then another. My wife, who was sitting next to me and had never seen a big-time game before, was screeching uncontrollably.

Suddenly it was a five-point Carolina lead, which they never relinquished. I came away from that game amazed that any two teams could play at that level. From that point on I became a Dean Smith fan, something that took on even more meaning for me as I learned more about the off-the-court aspects of the program and about Dean himself. But that game got me started.

—David Spence, 42, college professor in Austin, TX

1980–81 was a very topsy-turvy year for Carolina, the first roller coaster season I experienced. Carolina got beaten over the holidays pretty soundly by Minnesota, a game not on television, and then they lost to Kansas by one point in a game that was on the tube in Chapel Hill. I got so upset during that game that my dad told me that I had to behave better if I wanted to see more games, the one and only time he said anything like that to me. A little bit later came a heartbreaking loss at Virginia after Carolina had taken a double-digit second-half lead. I was totally convinced watching that game that Carolina would win, and then the Cavaliers took it away.

But mixed in with those losses were some really good performances: an easy win over Duke, a good win at State in which the Reynolds crowd yelled every time Matt Doherty touched the ball, and a 100–60 laugher over Georgia Tech (another "Treeby game"). In that game, down 98–58, Georgia Tech's reserves went into a stall in the last minute to try to stop Carolina from breaking the century mark. Freshman guard Dean Shaffer (to Dean Smith's chagrin) went out and fouled a Tech player at mid-court: after the free throws, Cecil Exum came down and hit a jumper at the buzzer to send the crowd into a frenzy. A few months later at Chapel Hill High School's Junior Follies, a skit had supposedly bored young Chapel Hillians complaining "the only time we ever see the circus is when Georgia Tech comes to town to play basketball."

The emotional peak of the regular season, however, was the rematch against Virginia in Carmichael. Everyone in Chapel Hill was pumped up for this game. Carolina fans knew all too well that 7-4 center Ralph Sampson, a *Sports Illustrated* cover boy as a high school senior, had picked the Wahoos over Chapel Hill. No one particularly liked Virginia's backcourt of Othell Wilson and Ricky Stokes. At one game, George told me, an elderly female Carolina fan uttered the phrase, "That little Ricky Stokes, he's like a little devil!" And it wasn't hard to come up with derogatory chants that rhymed with Othell, even though those chants would never find collective public expression as long as Dean Smith was coach.

Carolina played brilliantly over the first 30 minutes in building a double-digit lead. Freshman Sam Perkins was terrific, holding his own against Sampson and using a clever move to sneak under Sampson's arms for a lay-up in the first half in one of the memorable moments of the game. But then with nine or ten minutes to play, Virginia put a run together and cut a 16-point deficit in half. At that point, over the radio (we were listening to WCHL while watching on TV), Woody Durham said, "shades of Charlottesville," a comment that greatly irritated me. "No way!" I thought.

Way. Virginia battled all the way back and tied the game on a Jeff Lamp jumper with just seconds to play. On the ensuing possession, Carolina got a top-of-the-key jumper from Jimmy Black in transition at the buzzer. After recovering from a serious auto accident in the off-season, Black was a much improved player as a junior starter, and whereas I hadn't had much confidence that he would have hit the shot against Texas A&M the previous March, this shot looked destined to go in. The players and managers on the Carolina bench thought so too, jumping in the air in anticipation. But the ball spun tantalizingly out, and it was overtime.

Virginia finally pulled ahead for good in the second overtime, and though Al Wood scored to cut the lead to the final margin of 80–79 in the final seconds, time ran out. At the buzzer, Doherty and Wilson got into a scrape that would probably be considered mild today, but seemed a big deal at the time—I hadn't seen that sort of thing before (not being able to remember some of the tussles that took place on the court between Carolina and Duke in the 1960s). But after that incident was broken up, reality began to set in: Carmichael Auditorium had just seen one of the epic games in its history, and Carolina had lost it. It was a supremely disappointing moment. For the last time that I can remember, I actually cried when the game was over, and stayed up in bed in the dark, looking over at the digital clock/radio, thinking of all the different ways Carolina might have won the game, and how great it would have been if only Black had hit that shot.

The rest of the regular season seemed to me almost an afterthought after that game. I did finally get to go to a senior game, for Al Wood, Mike Pepper, and Pete Budko, as Carolina easily beat Clemson. However, I missed the broadcast of the Carolina–Duke season finale to be at Tom Williams' birthday party. As was the style of the time, the party went downtown for pizza and to play video games. The game was a little on my mind, and when we got back to Tom's house, I called home to find out we had lost. Worthy hadn't played due to injury, so it didn't seem like a major blow, though I'm glad that I caught the highlights show on TV the next day to be able to see the Gene Banks shot that Duke fans keep talking about.

Next came the tournaments—and a truly magical March for Carolina, the first I directly experienced. The Tar Heels played really well in beating State for the third time in the first round of the ACC Tournament. Then came the fourth game against Wake Forest. Both teams played well in a back-and-forth game, highlighted by a crazy scramble by all 10 players all over the court for a loose ball with under a minute to play, a ball Carolina eventually came up with. In the final moments, Carolina got the ball down by a point. Mike Pepper buried a jumper from about 18 feet out on the left, not too far away from the court spot that a high school senior watching in Wilmington would soon make famous. Wake had a last shot, but Frank Johnson missed, and Carolina was through to the tournament final. I was ecstatic, and especially happy for Pepper. The next morning, Saturday morning, my rec basketball team had a game, and I talked with anyone who would listen about it. That night, Carolina topped Maryland 61–60 in a final that was only slightly less thrilling.

March was just getting started, however. Carolina got sent out to the West Region, where the Tar Heels finally broke their NCAA Tournament losing streak with a 17-point win over Pittsburgh in a dominating performance, capped in the closing minutes by an gorgeous drive to the basket for a three-point play by Matt Doherty.

In its next game, Carolina was matched up against Utah, on Utah's home court. Utah had two excellent forwards in Tom Chambers and Danny Vranes, and Ute head coach Jerry Pimm had made some comment to the effect that Carolina might have a hard time with that combination. For Paul Pritchett and me, that comment became a rallying cry all week at Glenwood: "Eat your words, Jerry Pimm!" The Pritchetts had a grown-ups party scheduled the Thursday night of the game to which my parents were invited, so I went along with them and watched the game with Paul in his parents' bedroom, while the adults had their party and kept tabs on the game. (There's little doubt that Paul's father, Mebane, a former Morehead Scholar and director of the Morehead Foundation, would probably have liked to have been able to focus totally on the game as well.) Carolina had a small lead at halftime, then pulled away in the second half for a convincing victory. It was another terrific performance. And Paul and I said "Eat your words, Jerry Pimm" all night long.

In the next game, Carolina beat Bill Guthridge's alma mater, Kansas State, to advance to the Final Four. Kansas State had done Carolina a huge favor by knocking out top seed Oregon State in the round of 32 on a Rolando Blackman jumpshot at the buzzer. But Carolina was in control of the regional final throughout, and on its way to Philadelphia—and another rematch with Virginia.

Some years, making the Final Four is cause for joy in itself, regardless of what happens next. George and I and all the other Carolina fans I knew were excited to be in the Final Four, but knew that Carolina just had to beat Virginia. Virginia, Virginia, Virginia—that's all we talked about, barely even broaching the subject of whether Carolina could actually win the NCAA title. The New York Yankees came to town to play a baseball exhibition against Carolina the week before the game, and bumper stickers were distributed outside of Boshamer Stadium parodying the famous "Virginia is for Lovers" bumper sticker: this was a blue and white bumper sticker saying "Virginia is for Losers" and showing a broken heart. *The Chapel Hill Newspaper* made a bet with the Charlottesville daily paper that if Carolina lost the game, it would run its masthead the following day in burnt orange, whereas the Charlottesville paper would run its masthead in Carolina blue, if the Tar Heels won. Meanwhile, my parents got ready to travel to Philadelphia to see the Final Four, as part of the school entourage.

Finally, Saturday came. The game tipped off, and Al Wood went wild. The senior eventually hit for 39 points—none of his shots were forced, he simply had a hot hand, and his teammates kept looking for him. It was a superb team performance. And unlike in Charlottesville or Chapel Hill, Carolina never gave Virginia a way back into the game. Wood just kept scoring. The final was 78–65. Carolina had beaten Virginia and made it to the national championship game! Carolina would be playing on Monday night! George and I sat there in our father's study for about an hour afterwards, talking about the game, all the contributions made by the different players, all the implications. I felt just this whole glow in my body and brain, like we had been lifted to a different plane of consciousness. We didn't even watch the second game, Indiana–LSU. Who cared?

Monday morning, all the kids at Glenwood were stoked. We played the usual morning basketball, but with a much higher level of intensity. Everyone was running hard, going at it full bore, all completely excited. Tom Williams had been taken by his father to the downtown celebrations on Franklin Street after the Virginia game, and he had a full report about that, about being lifted onto his dad's shoulders so he could see everything. Carolina's win was the top agenda item in the morning news with Mrs. Wier. (There were a lot of huge, lifelong Carolina fans in that class: Tom Kerby, Michelle Donohue, Tom Williams, Paul, and myself. Indeed, pretty much everyone in the class was interested in it by that point.) We were on the brink of the promised land.

As usual, the bell rang at 2:40 p.m., I got on Bus 80, and went home. As I got home, the television was on and I learned that Ronald Reagan had been shot outside the Hilton in Washington. I was being raised as a good little liberal and wasn't a big fan of Mr. Reagan, but the news was staggering—so much so that I immediately went into the little prayer stool in my dad's office and asked forgiveness for some rather un-Christian thoughts I had had about the new president prior to the shooting. At some point in the afternoon, my parents called home to check on me. Word came through the television that the president was going to survive his gunshot wound. Authorities with the NCAA in Philadelphia decided that the championship game between Indiana and Carolina could and would be played.

So, as per the original plan, George and I went over to the Brouns' house to watch the game with Jonathan and Dan. Donald Boulton, a university official and ordained minister whom my dad knew well and whom I had met, gave an invocation before the start of the game praying for the president's health. The game tapped off, and things went badly for Carolina almost from the start: James Worthy got into early foul trouble, a big blow, as no one seriously expected Wood to score another 39 points against Indiana.

At halftime it was close, but we were all pessimistic as we walked the Brouns' dog outside. Dan was poised to blame it on me, since I hadn't come over to their house for a Carolina game before—I must have been the jinx. (I knew he wasn't being serious—or at least not too serious. Dan and Jonathan later came up with a list of "official excuses" for each season Carolina didn't win the NCAA title, most of which were farcical.)

After halftime, Isiah Thomas, who had been in foul trouble in the game at Chapel Hill in December, simply took over the game, repeatedly getting the best of Jimmy Black. Carolina fell behind and couldn't put together a run to get back into it. Indiana was clearly the better team. Margie Broun came downstairs late in the game to check on us and said she was impressed by how well we were taking the loss. There wasn't any crying that night on my part.

Paul Pritchett and I commiserated the next morning before Mrs. Wier's class (Paul had had some tears). But the basketball game outside went on as it did every morning, and there was a definite "wait till next year" spirit among us kids. The "news" section with Mrs. Wier was evenly divided between the game and the shooting. One classmate suggested that Carolina might have been upset by the shooting, thus accounting for their relatively poor play. Mrs. Wier cut that line of thought off at the pass, and forcefully insisted that we all admit the real reason Carolina had lost: they had been beaten by a better team. No excuses allowed by Mrs. Wier. And no feeling sorry for ourselves, either. Bill Guthridge couldn't have said it any better than his fellow Midwesterner did that morning.

I can't really remember just how down or unhappy I was during the school day after the loss. But whatever disappointment I had was largely washed out that afternoon: I got taken by Mom (already back from Philly) up to Carmichael to see the Tar Heels return from the Final Four. I was there at the side entrance to Carmichael as the team bus rolled in and the players got off—there were at least a thousand people there to meet them, all cheering appreciatively. The players smiled as they got off. The band played a little and Carolina blue pompoms were handed out. Standing on the edge of the end zone seats inside Carmichael, I watched Al Wood, in his suit and tie, speak to a local TV station, and dropped a pompom right below to where the interview was taking place (Wood didn't seem to notice). It was a good scene, and good therapy for the night before. Al Wood, sadly, would not be back for next year. But we all knew a darn good team would be.

1982

1981–82 was a good year for the Tar Heels, but it wasn't for my personal athletic career. My taste for playing soccer soured in 1981 as a direct result of attending Duke Soccer Camp. I had been a pretty good 10-year-old goalie in Rainbow Soccer and attended the goalkeeper's school part of the Duke camp. I just couldn't learn the techniques they were teaching about how to get low to stop the ball, I lost confidence, started thinking instead of playing by instinct as I had before, and basically completely lost it as a goalkeeper, losing the job even on my Rainbow team that fall after a few games. It wasn't a great year for me in rec basketball either—after being a major player and probably the leading scorer on losing teams the previous two years, I got put on the second string by a new coach, playing behind other kids I had been ahead of the year before. I was pretty tall and could shoot the ball really well for a 12-year-old and had good ballhandling skills, but was basically out of shape—about 10 pounds overweight, with a lot of energy but not much aerobic endurance and little or no muscle. That bad year as a sixth grader had lasting consequences, because afterward I didn't have the confidence that I was good enough to try out for soccer or basketball in junior high.

At the same time, though, other interests were developing. I got interested in politics and the Cold War and all, and was told by my brother that reading George Orwell's *Animal Farm* would be a good way to understand the Soviet Union, so I read that and liked it so much I read it again. I also got more interested in church stuff and theological matters, and started reading writers like C.S. Lewis. Still, most of my reading at this time consisted of sports books or "Doctor Who" novels (an interest derived from our year in England and kept alive by the sci-fi types in Chapel Hill who ponied up enough donations every year to get the program aired on WUNC-TV). By age 11 or 12, I had read dozens of sports books—biographies of Willie Mays, Bob Cousy, Tom Seaver, Pete Rose, Hank Aaron, an English novel called *Goalkeepers Are Different* that I really liked, and on and on.

Then, in 1981, a book that was seminal for my brother and me appeared: Thad Mumau's *Dean Smith: More Than a Coach*. I read that book cover to cover as soon as it showed up. Apart from the basketball stuff, two things about the book immediately stood out for me: First, how cool it was that Dean had been a ping-pong champion as a kid, since I loved table tennis too. Second, Smith's interest in Christian theology. That interest signaled to me, the 11-year-old reader, that theology was a worthwhile subject, and perhaps unconsciously, that Carolina basketball itself was not a religion, despite our reverence for the Tar Heels.

Or was it? That question is one that our minister at Holy Family, Gary Fulton, tried to address a couple of times in what to me were quite memorable homilies. During one children's homily in the fall of 1981, the day after football tailback Kelvin Bryant and UNC had run wild in beating Furman in a September game, Gary asked us kids what the two most significant things going on that weekend were. Paul raised his hand and mentioned the football game. The congregation chuckled a bit but Gary said yes, that's right. What was the second thing? There was a long pause. I suspected Gary meant the church service, but wasn't sure. Gary finally gave the answer: It was the church service. What was the difference between the football game and church, Gary asked? Paul answered that at church the object is not to tackle each other to the ground. That reply got a laugh, and Gary agreed, but then went on to the point of his homily, which is that football games are essentially spectator events, but church is not supposed to be. Church involves the participation of the congregation in worshipping God, and we don't go to church to "watch."

On another occasion, Gary tried to describe the passion and love present in the early church. Gary described how members of the earliest Christian churches would be so excited to see each other that they would greet each other with hugs. And they had a passion for God. "Do we know what passion is?" he asked. Yes, we do—think of the passion present at a Carolina basketball game. That is the sort of passion the early church had. And think, Gary added wistfully, what the church could be if we had the same passion in church we showed for basketball?

Gary went on to say that there was nothing wrong with a passion for basketball, but his point was clear: As important as basketball was in the town of Chapel Hill, commitment to church should be even more important. That may not sound like a terribly prophetic message to the outside observer, but in the social context of Chapel Hill, it hit home, or at least it did to my ears.

Another interest that I began nurturing around ages 10 and 11 was music. After a couple of years taking beginner piano lessons, a space opened up for me with my brother and sister's teacher, Pearl Seymour, who was very well regarded. Having us all at one piano teacher made life easier for my mom, and she thought I would like Mrs. Seymour.

I did like her—though only partly for her skill in teaching piano. Pearl Seymour was the organist at Binkley Baptist Church in Chapel Hill, where her husband, Bob, was the pastor, and Dean Smith was the best-known congregant. Rev. Robert Seymour had been a leader in civil rights activity in Chapel Hill 20 years earlier, and had called on Smith to help integrate the town by entering a restaurant with a black man in a now-famous episode. I was dimly aware of all this when I started taking lessons with Mrs. Seymour, but probably didn't really grasp it until a long *Sports Illustrated* article came out prior to the 1981–82 season talking about Smith and mentioning the Seymours and the civil rights era.

What I figured out a lot sooner was that Pearl Seymour was a really big Carolina basketball fan. She was perhaps the biggest fan in Chapel Hill, a fixture at home games (even on Sunday afternoons) and a frequent traveler to away games and tournaments. Unlike my siblings, who performed in festivals, concerto contests, and that sort of thing, I was a pretty average piano student: I had a slight gift for sight-reading new pieces, but that was a double-edged sword, as the lack of improvement in how I played a piece the week after sight-reading it betrayed how little I had practiced (the two days before the lesson, and perhaps one other time).

But despite my somewhat glacial progress, lessons were usually fun—and often ended with five minutes or so of talking about Carolina basketball while we waited for my ride to arrive at Greenwood Road. Whatever was in the newspaper most recently, we would talk about. In the fall of 1981, one item of note was Dean Shaffer being suspended from the basketball team for academic reasons. Mrs. Seymour expressed regret that this had happened, but then added, "The thing

Jimmy Black at the New Orleans airport the day after winning the 1982 national title.

is, Dean would have done the same thing if it had been James Worthy or Sam Perkins." While by that time the idea that Dean Smith is someone who does the right thing was firmly established in my mind, I hadn't thought about the Shaffer incident in that light, and that comment by Smith's close friend stuck with me.

*

At this point, however, piano and all other activities still ranked far behind my preferred free-time pursuit: shooting baskets outside, whether alone in the backyard or against other kids, or against George and any friends he brought along, or playing HORSE against my dad. The most frequent scenario was still to shoot by myself, however, and play out the Carolina games. Before every Carolina game, sometime on the day of the game, I would perform a little ritual George had taught me: the "Carolina lay-up." Basically meaning, you would take a lay-up, and if you made it, Carolina would win that day. If you missed...well, you weren't supposed to miss. I was later pleased to read somewhere that Tar Heel reserve Cecil Exum had a similar superstition—he would take a little four-footer as his last shot in warm-ups before going to the bench and make sure he drained it every time as good luck.

Sixth grade at Glenwood presented a slightly different cast of characters in Mrs. Tyson's class, and it was another pretty good year school-wise. Tom Williams was still in my class and sat right ahead of me, lending pieces of paper to me day after day. Tom Kerby was usually the kid to beat playing basketball or dodgeball or anything else, and we got along well. The most popular girl in the class, Laney Abernethy, happened to catch bus 80 to Glenwood at the same stop as me, and we chatted regularly (she was a Carolina fan too). Then I had three newer friends who lived near Paul in the Greenwood Road neighborhood: Jeff Jones, David Pearsall, and Don Liner. Jeff and David were into the basketball stuff big time and were pretty good players, so I was over in that neighborhood more often. Just about all the kids I spent any time with at this age followed Carolina, some more fervently than others.

And it was an article of faith among us that 1981–82 would be the year that Carolina finally won it all. Dean Smith and the four returning starters were on the cover of *Sports Illustrated* to start the season, confirming our optimism. A freshman from Wilmington named Mike Jordan scored the first basket of the season against Kansas State on a little baseline jumper. (No kidding, even at that moment I thought, "What if he also makes the last basket of the season?") A *Chapel Hill Newspaper* columnist wrote that this Jordan kid, while he had a lot to learn, could be a good player for the Tar Heels. With the Big Four Tournament gone the way of the old Dixie Classic, the most memorable December game was the matchup of No. 1 vs. No. 2, Carolina against Kentucky, in the Meadowlands. Belying the delay-game offense and low scores that marked most of the season, Carolina ran and ran on Kentucky to an 82–69 win. As became our habit that season, I watched downstairs while my brother watched alone in his room on a small television. Already at that point, George had a habit of watching games with relentless pessimism, and I had a habit of watching games with relentless optimism. We were each happier watching in our own individual zone, dealing with the tension in our own way, and then celebrating or commiserating afterward without having gotten on each other's nerves during the game itself.

If you look back at the scores from 1981–82, most of the ACC games were relatively close, but only a handful seemed tense as the games were being played. An eight-point lead meant more in the days before rushed, off-balance jumpers to beat the shot clock and the three-point shot. And Carolina had an incredibly disciplined, veteran team that could pass the ball around at will and was very, very unlikely to give up a quick 10–0 run. If Carolina had a second-half lead that year, there wasn't much to worry about.

The most memorable regular season game was again at home to Virginia, in January this time. Carolina trailed in the second half before rallying to a four-point victory. The defining moment of the game came when Matt Doherty drove in for a lay-up, then hustled back to intercept a Cavalier pass and save it back to a Tar Heel. Our rec basketball coach made a point of talking about that play in our next practice. The other noteworthy moment came when Dean Smith took the center court microphone and asked students to end the use of profanity. I thought I'd had a pretty good time watching at home on a sunny Saturday afternoon, but I was jealous to learn at school on Monday that Jeff Jones (the Glenwood student, not the Cavalier) had successfully sneaked into the game.

James Worthy the day after winning the 1982 title. In the foreground on the right is Joan Williamson; at left (partially hidden) is Bill Guthridge.

As is often the case among Carolina fans, losses seem to loom larger in the memory more than all but the biggest wins. The two losses in 1981–82 were no different. The first defeat came at home to Wake Forest with Sam Perkins sick in the hospital. James Worthy was absolutely brilliant to start the game, as Carolina got off to a nice lead, but Wake came back by halftime and ended up winning 55–49, as Carolina's offense was stymied in the late stages.

That game sticks out in Williamson family lore by virtue of the fact that my brother got to go to the game. Why was this a big deal? Well, George had been convicted by the family legal structure of a sin committed several months earlier at the Clemson football game in Kenan, the one Carolina lost 10–8 when both teams were in the Top 10. Basically, George, Treeby and I all had gotten into a fight at the end of the game, and George was considered to have committed the worst single act. The penalty was that he was going to miss seeing a Carolina basketball game—he could go to the nonconference game nearest his birthday in December, but not to an ACC game. Well, word of this incident made its way to the Broun household, and Ken Broun, a UNC law professor, and Margie Broun both thought that this punishment was entirely too severe, too draconian. The Brouns' view was that losing a Carolina basketball game could only possibly be a just punishment for a first- or second-degree felony, not for a misdemeanor. And so they did nothing to stop Jonathan from using their tickets one night and inviting George to come. (My parents gave in at this point and didn't stop George from accepting the ticket.) That game happened to be the loss to Wake Forest. Trust me, George was happier that he got to go the game than he was sad that Carolina had lost it. Especially with Perkins out, it was viewed as an entirely acceptable loss with no long-term consequences.

Three games later, Carolina had its second loss of the season, at Virginia, by 17 points. That was one of those games where the only surviving image is of Virginia players making jumper after jumper and Ralph Sampson coming down on the break and dunking. I watched the game with Paul at his house: we had a rec basketball game earlier in the night, and our team had won by exactly 17 points. Paul's mom, Betsy, pointed this out near the end of the game as if to say, well it all balanced out in the end, but Paul didn't like that line of reasoning at all (and I didn't either, though I bit my tongue).

Having gotten to see Carolina beat Clemson (again) on my birthday, for some reason I got to go to a second game that year, which turned out to be the home game against Georgia Tech. I sort of liked Tech player Brook Steppe, especially after reading a newspaper article talking about some of his Chapel Hill connections. But Tech's other quality player, Lee Goza, stole the show by scoring for Carolina to open the second half. Goza took the inbounds pass, went to the same basket he had shot at in the first half, and laid it in. Worthy started to block his shot, then stopped. The crowd was stunned for a split second, then roared in delight. Goza later said his mother had always dreamed that someday he would score for Carolina.

Sometime that winter, a brief but significant conversation took place in our household: My dad asked me if I had noticed the boys who toweled up the sweat on the court in Carmichael Auditorium, and whether I would like to be one. I thought this must be an entirely hypothetical question, and my first reaction was nervousness and shyness. I remembered during a summer league UNC baseball game I had gone to with Paul, how Paul and I were given the job of chasing down foul balls hit behind the plate and out of Boshamer Stadium, and how I had sat nervously through the game, terrified of doing something wrong. So I gave sort of a noncommittal answer. But Treeby was there and saw through this and said, "Of course you'd really want to do it, wouldn't you Thad?" And I had to admit, yes I would. Dad sort of grinned and left, and that was the last I heard of it for a while.

The season finale against Duke was the day the lights went out in Carmichael, two minutes into the game. I was listening at home to WCHL, which kept broadcasting after the TV screen went dark. There was a 30- or 40-minute delay, my dad called home to check on me, and then the lights came back. Carolina beat the stuffing out of Duke that day, with senior Chris Brust skying for two dunks in the second half. My favorite play, though, was when a Duke big man threw two head fakes on Worthy before taking it up for a lay-up, and then Worthy blocked his shot anyway. If history teaches us anything, it's that beating Duke emphatically in the regular season finale is a prerequisite for Carolina winning a national title, and that's what Carolina did that day. (I don't think

Sam Perkins, James Worthy, Matt Doherty, Jimmy Black, and former assistant coach John Lotz congregate with UNC supporters in New Orleans before flying back to North Carolina.

Mike Krzyzewski has forgotten it, either.) The next day at church, I bumped into Bill Guthridge and asked him, "Who taught Brust how to dunk?" Guthridge replied directly, "He always could dunk, Thad, it was just a matter of getting the opportunities." Not for the last time, elation and excitement got in the way of my asking an intelligent question of someone in Carolina basketball, but Guthridge smiled anyway.

Carolina played Friday afternoon in the ACC Tournament, while school was in session. Mrs. Tyson arranged for a TV to be brought into the classroom with the idea that we could see the last few minutes of the game against Tech—but the timing was a little off, and all we saw was the final score and maybe some of the final minute. No matter, I appreciated the thought. Carolina beat State handily in the semifinal, setting up the rubber match against Virginia.

Both my parents and the Pritchetts went to the game in Greensboro on Sunday, so Paul came home with us after church (my brother and sister could both drive by this point) to see the game at our house. He was absolutely bouncing off the wall as we went to get lunch, completely riled up. Paul was only wearing on his sleeve what George and I felt inside: this was a huge day, a game between possibly the best two teams in the country to see who would have ACC superiority and all the confidence going into the NCAAs. Perkins tapped the ball to Worthy for a dunk to start the game, and it was a brilliantly played first half, both teams playing at the highest level, Carolina's best proving to be just a little bit better than Virginia's. Then came the second half Four Corners slowdown, with Carolina nursing a one-point lead and Virginia refusing to chase the ball as the last eight minutes ticked away. The media ripped both coaches after the game for letting it happen, but again, questioning Smith's tactics was the furthest thing from my mind as the game was being played. I just wanted Carolina to win, and the tension was palpable. In the final seconds, after Matt Doherty hit one of two free throws to leave the door open, Virginia turned the ball over on their chance to tie. Doherty then hit two free throws to seal it. A huge win, and another signal that this might be the year.

In 1981, I had just wanted Carolina to do something in the NCAAs for a change. In 1982, everyone knew that anything short of a national championship would be a huge disappointment. I remember staring at the NCAA brackets the Monday before the tournament started, sitting in the office of the "eye doctor" in Durham (I wore glasses until age 15), not quite praying but using all my powers of wishful thinking to will that Carolina win it all. Somehow I felt like it would happen, but I wasn't sure—who could be? The first game, against James Madison, was in some ways the most tense, but Carolina got a crucial three-point play from Worthy with about a minute to go to preserve a narrow victory.

The regionals were played in Raleigh. Dad managed to get hold of three tickets, and I got to go to both games. In each contest, against Alabama and Villanova, Carolina was in control throughout, with brilliant team play and great passing leading to dunks for Worthy and Perkins. Carolina really wasn't ahead by very much in either game, but the team's confidence never wavered, and neither did the confidence of this fan. It was an incredible scene when the buzzer sounded against Villanova and Carolina advanced to the Final Four. I can't imagine what the car ride back to Chapel Hill would have been like had either of those games turned out differently. As it was, we drove back contentedly, listening to Woody's post-game show, thrilled with what we saw.

And greedy for more. Mom and Dad, native Louisianans—my dad played for the 1954 Springhill High School state basketball champions—had talked about going to New Orleans for the Final Four since the middle of the season. They again went as part of the official university entourage, flying on the plane with the team and collecting autographs. I honestly don't remember a huge amount about the buildup during the week, other than a *Chapel Hill Newspaper* retrospective on Smith's previous Final Four appearances. In the Williamson household, we were confident, hopeful, and unwilling to think that another disappointment could lie ahead. My parents left on Friday morning, and just as I was waking up to go to school, Dad came in to say good-bye and tell me that they were going to "bring back the bacon."

We were left with Tom Conner, a doctoral student in history at Carolina working with my father, for the weekend. We all liked Tom a lot, and he was a huge Carolina basketball fan too, so that was certainly fine. The day of the semifinal against Houston, I went over to visit Tom Williams and watched at his house as Carolina put on an incredible spurt in the opening minutes, only to have a good Cougar team battle back to make it a game again by halftime. Tom and I went out at halftime on a mild sunny afternoon and shot baskets at a nearby goal. It was a few minutes' walk to the goal, and we ended up being late to see the start of the second half. Carolina maintained command in the second half against Houston's great athletes, winning in a fashion much more convincing than the five-point final margin indicated.

Another special Monday, then. Again at Glenwood School in the morning, the pre-bell basketball was played with manic intensity, the 11- and 12-year-olds applying our passion for Carolina to our own playground ball. The day came and went, and this time the afternoon before the game was uneventful. I just shot a few baskets outside and waited for 9 p.m. to come.

To avoid jinxing the Tar Heels in another title game, it was decided that this year the Brouns would watch at their house and the Williamsons at theirs, but that we would meet up after the game if Carolina won. Tom and I watched downstairs, George took to his room, and Treeby wandered back and forth between television sets.

The game started strangely of course, with all those goaltends by Patrick Ewing. It soon evolved into an incredibly tense game between two well-prepared teams with great competitors on each side. James Worthy had clearly brought something special for the occasion, which was encouraging, but Carolina still trailed by a point at halftime. Tom weighed in on Carolina's chances with a dose of his own characteristic pessimism. I considered going outside to shoot, but instead played a Pac-Man rip-off on our spanking new Apple II-plus computer during halftime, which soothed the nerves a little bit. Tom yelled for me when the game started again.

With years of videotape watching, and more recently the constant replays on ESPN Classic, many Carolina fans by now can almost recite possession-for-possession what happened in the second half of that game. Until the final minute, the only plays I can honestly say I remember from the moment they happened—and not subsequent replay watching—are the pass from Buzz Peterson to Worthy for a stuff over Sleepy Floyd, the quick pass from Matt Doherty to Worthy for another dunk, and then Jordan's lay-up over Patrick Ewing to give Carolina a 61–58 lead. (Jonathan Broun later declared that when Jordan went up for that shot he was "Mike," but when he came down he had become "Michael.")

I thought Matt Doherty would hit his one-and-one with over a minute to play and the score 61–60, but Tom didn't have a great feeling about it. This time, Tom's pessimism was right, Doherty missed, and Floyd hit a nice 15-foot jumper to give Georgetown the lead. Carolina had played to its highest possible level as a team, probably its best game of the year, and it still would come down to the final play. North Carolina fans have never had the luxury of winning a national title in a game they played sloppily—the satisfaction of winning it all has always been mixed with the satisfaction of seeing a great team play at its very best, and perhaps even a little above themselves.

Carolina in-bounded the ball with 32 seconds to go, couldn't get the ball inside, and then went to Doherty just beneath the top of the key. Doherty threw it to Black, who then pushed a swing pass over the top of the zone to Jordan, who took the jumper from just about his maximum freshman-year range. Swish. I was sitting on the floor but sort of jumped up a little bit. Tom and I heard a huge whoop from upstairs.

No timeout called. Georgetown got the ball to Fred Brown. I was scared to death of Floyd getting another shot. Then, for a few moments, time stood still. The human mind is capable of thinking and feeling an enormous array of thoughts and emotions in a very quick time span. When James Worthy gambled to try to steal an anticipated Brown pass, a pass that Brown didn't throw, I immediately thought to myself, "how great would it be if Worthy had stolen that pass, that would have been awesome." Tom sort of groaned. And then, a split-second later, Brown did throw the ball to Worthy! Worthy, to recall, had already seen it all that year with the Lee Goza lay-up into the wrong basket, so with only the slightest hesitation he took off to the other end. Tom and I now heard a much louder yell from upstairs combined with a very large stomping of a foot on the floor. Worthy was fouled, and Georgetown used its last timeout to try to regroup emotionally.

Worthy missed both free throws, but a couple of Tar Heels stood in Floyd's way, and his halfcourt heave, though not far offline, was well short. (In the endless recitation of these events that subsequently took place, I think it was Dan Broun who first suggested, what if when Perkins caught the miss and tossed it in the air it had gone in Georgetown's basket?) That was it! High-fiving galore, George came tumbling down the stairs, and we all watched the post-game hoopla together.

Just about every Carolina fan who was alive that day remembers whom they saw the game with and what their reaction was. But for me, and for many of the Tar Heel fans surveyed for this book, the single moment that endured as the most powerful image of March 29, 1982, was not Jordan's shot, and it was not Fred Brown's mistaken pass to James Worthy. It was the sight of senior point guard Jimmy Black hugging Dean Smith on the Superdome floor.

"Jimmy Black and Coach Smith hugging and crying after the 1982 championship really transcended basketball. Where else would one see a 22-year-old black kid from the Bronx, hugging a fifty-something white man from Emporia, Kansas? Two people from different backgrounds coming together for one common cause. I tear up every time I think about it."
—Jon Sasser, 28, television producer in Virginia Beach

After a phone call to the Brouns, we headed over there and made the 10-minute walk from Whitehead Circle and Mason Farm Road to Franklin Street. A mass of Carolina blue humanity, yelling, blue paint, people climbing on trees and telephone polls, toilet paper on every available limb, a bonfire. My sister reported the next day that she had been kissed by a random passing stranger. It was that kind of night.

After maybe an hour up on Franklin Street, the Broun-Williamson-Conner contingent started walking home. All the Brouns were convinced that the next day should be a holiday from school. That didn't turn out to be the case, and I got into bed staring at my clock/radio at about 1 a.m, and sat there eyes wide open, completely happy, thinking about what had happened. I woke up once in the middle of the night briefly, which was great because I immediately remembered everything.

The next day at school, someone in Glenwood had gotten word of when the Tar Heels would return from New Orleans, and so at about 2 p.m. the class walked from school out to the intersection at Glen Lennox where the Tar Heel bus was expected to roll by on the way from the airport before going up Raleigh Road to Carmichael. We had a congratulatory/welcome back banner, and at some point, a bus did come rolling by, although no one was completely sure whether that was really the team bus. It was a warm, sunny day, and a welcome-home rally was scheduled at Kenan Stadium for 3 p.m. Jeff Jones and David Pearsall thought if we hustled on our bikes, we could make it up there before it ended. So I got off the bus home from school, wrote a note on the chalkboard by the phone to Mom and Dad telling them I had taken off for Kenan Stadium, and pedaled with all my might the two miles or so from Kendall Drive to the intersection of Raleigh Road and Greenwood Road, where David, Don Liner, and Jeff were waiting. We had a hard time making it up that hill, but finally got to Kenan Stadium—just as the crowds were starting to leave. We had missed it.

No matter. I was extremely thirsty after all that biking and went and bought a Coke from the concession stand inside Kenan, which I figured counted as a form of participation in the celebration event. We walked our bikes back across the intramural fields to Raleigh Road. Jeff and I were talking about the three possible scenarios for next year, two of which we liked very much. One scenario was that both Ralph Sampson and Worthy would stay in school. We'd still be better than Virginia. The second scenario was that Sampson would leave and Worthy would stay. That would be incredible. The third possibility, Sampson staying and Worthy leaving, we didn't talk about that much. Jeff and David then went on to imagine what Carolina's players would be up to the rest of the day after getting home, and there was a consensus that R-rated material would be involved. (This is what 12-year-old boys talk about, after all.)

I got home, and Mom was waiting, happy to see me and not excessively perturbed that I had taken off on my own on the bike. Dad had gone into the office for an hour or so, and then we all traded stories about our respective experiences of the weekend. In a few days, Dad's pictures were developed, and I got a glimpse of the players on the airplane, the scene inside the Superdome, the nervous-looking Carolina crowd.

Jonathan Broun said shortly after the 1982 title that he felt like there should never be another college basketball game played. I certainly understood the feeling. The ultimate telos of following a college basketball team, in competitive terms, had been reached. Already in my short tenure as a fan I had seen a lot of disappointment, which made the victory sweeter. "Carolina 63, Georgetown 62" resonated throughout the spring and the rest of the school year, in the appearance of merchandise as diverse as the first 1982 title T-Shirts and the Carolina-blue commemorative cans of Coke (I drank a couple and saved one). It also resonated in the form of this astonishingly great, unambiguously happy memory that could be played back if you ever needed cheering up or just something to think about while walking to school or doing a chore one day. And, amazingly, what happened in late March 1982 continues to resonate to this day for many, many Carolina fans—this one included.

"My son was sophomore manager when we won our National Championship in 1982, and when the watches were given out he was not in line for one. Coach Guthridge told him that they would order a duplicate for him when they returned to Chapel Hill. A few days later Coach Smith called him into his office and told him he wanted him to have his watch instead. This was Dean's first championship, but he gave his watch to a manager!"   —Richard Hart, 70, alumnus in Arden, NC

1982–83

No one I know cites junior high school as the happiest time of his or her life. I definitely do not either. I sort of naively thought that going into seventh grade I should be in good shape socially, since at Culbreth Junior High I would have friends there from both elementary schools I had attended, which both fed into Culbreth. It didn't quite work out that way. I didn't realize the extent to which the social cocoon provided by all-day togetherness with the same group of kids would be gone, and that I'd be facing a social environment at the same time much larger and much more fragmented than anything I'd experienced. And what counted as cool had changed too, not in ways favorable to the characteristics I happened to have at that particular time. As the three years wore on, I adopted an identity as a rebel against what I portrayed in my head as a structure of cliques (none of which I really fit into). I wouldn't say I was a social outcast, but I was lonely a lot, the kind of kid who didn't have a regular group of people to have lunch with everyday and in time didn't want one either. I got picked on some, though never physically threatened or anything like that. It was in many ways an unpleasant, awkward time.

But there were a lot of sources of solace. First, there was the example of my older brother and sister, both in high school when I entered seventh grade, and both of whom had faced social difficulties of their own in junior high. Treeby in particular assured me several times that high school would be much better than junior high, and that the value structure of junior high was not to be taken seriously. George and Treeby also helped me get turned on to rock'n'roll and pop music in general, the salve of every teenager's angst, and I had a habit of coming home from school and putting Bob Dylan's greatest hits or Stevie Wonder's "Musiquarium" or a Beatles record on Treeby's turntable and turning it up loud.

Second, most of the stronger friendships I had from before continued. Tom Williams, David Simpson, and David Moreau all were in my Latin class for two years, by far my favorite subject. I also saw David Simpson along with Paul Pritchett at a minimum every Sunday night at "EYC," the youth group at Holy Family. And perhaps most significantly in terms of total time, David Moreau moved next door in the spring of 1982, probably the one person in my age group who liked the idea of a game just as much as I did. Sometimes we played tennis or ping-pong or hacked around the golf course, but mostly it was basketball. David was just a little bit better than me in hoops (as with every other sport we ever played together), but not so much so that it wasn't competitive. Very competitive. And those hours were an important antidote to early teenage loneliness.

The third thing I had going for me was the development of two skills that became an important source of self-confidence: playing trombone and writing. My mom had played trombone in high school in Louisiana in the 1950s, and to this day can give a mean performance of "When the Saints Go Marching In." My brother played as well and was by this time quite good. That I picked trombone to play—I knew I wanted to play something—resulted from the fact that the day the junior high band director came to talk to Glenwood sixth graders about band, everyone's hand shot up when the band director asked who wanted to play saxophone (my first choice). That turned me off, so I didn't raise my hand. Almost no one raised a hand for trombone, so I thought, what the heck, and put mine up. That decision probably saved my parents a couple of hundred bucks in the short run, since I wouldn't have to obtain a new instrument but could use Mom's old high school horn.

But the long-run consequences turned out to be far more significant. For instance, I soon got to meet Bruce Reinoso, George's trombone teacher, a UNC graduate and composer/teacher/trombonist who became a major influence on me. I had my first lesson with Bruce before school even started in seventh grade, which meant that while the other new trombonists were still learning the seven slide positions the first week of school, I could already play, and being just a little bit better at the beginning gave me confidence to keep getting better and eventually make the instrument a major part of my life.

Bruce was very smart, very charismatic, and a very tough teacher. He taught a wide range of students, from junior high band types like me to conservatory-bound prodigies. He had four students in Chapel Hill, and he would drive over from Raleigh every Saturday afternoon to make the rounds, stopping at our house to teach first George (until he left for college) and then me. I was a little intimidated by Bruce at first, but soon grew to like him a lot. And what makes him especially significant in this story is that he was one of the first adults/teachers I knew well who just didn't care about college basketball or sports in general. It's not that he was oblivious to the whole thing—he was well aware of how much people cared about it in Chapel Hill, and at one point he allowed that he in fact had watched the 1982 title game.

But Bruce's philosophy was that life should be about your own accomplishments, not watching somebody else's. And Bruce emphasized that meaningful accomplishments in music required serious dedication. He would tell me about UNC undergrad music majors he knew who would be in the practice hall by 8 a.m. every day in order to find time to put in their four hours of daily practice. Or he might tell me, as he did before I went to music camp one summer, not to goof around much but act like a professional musician and spend a couple of hours practicing drills on my own every day on top of the rehearsal schedule. In short, Bruce imparted a sense of what dedication to a craft looked like, and the commitment it required. Bruce knew that George and I were sports fans, and didn't knock it directly—although one day, before George headed off one Saturday morning from youth orchestra rehearsal at Hill Hall to Kenan Stadium, Bruce told my brother, "Unlike most football fans, you look like you have a gleam of intelligence." Bruce showed me, at an age I'm not sure I really knew it, that look, there was this whole other universe of life and learning out there—in music—that was rewarding, demanding, and had absolutely nothing to do with dominant popular culture (including the culture of college basketball in the Triangle).

So trombone became an important outlet, the thing that I "did," which was significant, since I wasn't playing school sports, unlike many of my elementary school friends. The other skill that started to come out was writing. As a seventh grader, I wrote for the school paper and got a rather morbid poem published in the literary magazine. As an eighth grader, I was on the staff of the magazine and the sports editor of the school paper. After I wrote about an eight-paragraph account of a fumble-filled Culbreth–Phillips football game, the faculty adviser to the paper, Sharon Burney, told me that the article made her feel like she was at the game, which was a nice boost. In ninth grade I edited the literary magazine and wrote an essay about Martin Luther King, Jr. for a contest sponsored by the Orange County Rainbow Coalition that got published in *The Chapel Hill Newspaper*. Writing certainly didn't bring me any great social standing and it really didn't take up much of my time or energy either, but it was another source of resistance against teenage anomie.

Lastly, there was still Carolina basketball—and more significantly, the fact that my interaction with Carolina basketball got ratcheted up to an altogether higher plateau. The somewhat cryptic conversation I had had with my parents the previous winter about being a towel boy in Carmichael had panned out: at some point in early fall, I learned that I was going to be taken on for a job at the games, either wiping up the floor or helping turn the wooden scoreboard at the end of the Carolina bench. My parents didn't tell me exactly how it came about, but I had an inkling that it probably had involved a conversation between my dad and Bill Guthridge. I still have never inquired into the details, preferring to view it as just this remarkable stroke of good fortune. The job fit the definition of a totally unearned privilege, but I had no intentions of giving it back on that account.

Even so, I don't recall being overly excited or worked up about it until the day of the first preseason game in the fall of 1982. It was a Blue–White game played on a football Saturday. Dad and I walked over from Kenan to the media entrance to Carmichael, and lo and behold, my name was indeed on the list. Dad walked in with me, and saw David Folds, a high school sophomore who was a veteran at the job, and asked him to show me the ropes. David judged that since they already had two guys to wipe the sweat off the court, I should join him and Matt Karres, another high school student, in turning the flip scoreboard. Then Coach Guthridge turned up, said hello to Dad and made sure everything was squared away. Dad took off and wished me well.

The set-up at the beginning was that David did UNC's score, Matt did the time, and I did the visitors' score. The purpose of the wooden scoreboard was to provide a running tally of the score for the coaches' game film, and it was an idea Guthridge had brought with him from Kansas State in 1967.

There were only a few tricks to the job: First, we had to take our chairs out and put the scoreboard away in the last minute of the half and at the end of the game to clear the way for the players to run off the floor. (Conversely, we put the scoreboard out at the start of each half immediately after Dean Smith walked from the locker room to the bench.) Second, we knew to push the scoreboard to the right and out of the way if a player or players came flying at us. I was slightly concerned that one day some player would split his head on the scoreboard diving for a loose ball, but it never came close to happening—we had to push the scoreboard out of the way only a small handful of times in six years. Third, on the visitor's scoreboard, the sixes and the nines in the ones column were mixed up. So if you weren't paying attention, you could have a "9" showing instead of a "6" and vice versa. Fourth, while we certainly were allowed to cheer for Carolina during the games, it was sort of an unstated expectation that we should maintain a certain level of decorum (that is, not do anything the team managers we were sitting next to wouldn't do).

That was it. I was nervous at the beginning of that first game, but then the Blues scored a basket, I pulled back two wooden cards in the ones digit (very important not to pull back the tens digit—it had happened), and recorded two points for the visitors. I looked over at my family sitting on the other side of the court, and they clapped for me. By the end of the day, I had a good feel for the rhythm of working the wooden scoreboard—every so often, I had to push all the ones digits back over the board to show zero again. And I had seen a good preseason game in Blue Heaven from the closest possible range.

Couldn't beat that.

Well, actually, you could, but it took a lot more drama to do it. Carolina's first home game in 1982–83 was against Tulane. Carolina had already lost two tough games to St. John's and Missouri to open the season, and the defending national champions looked very much like going an unprecedented 0–3 when Tulane came to town and played well. We put the scoreboard away with a minute to go and I made it over to sit next to my parents for the final seconds, none too happy. To that point, I had never seen Carolina lose in person, and didn't like the idea of starting now. Carolina got the ball back down two with about 10 seconds to play, but Michael Jordan was called for an offensive foul for pushing off the defender with four seconds to play. Tulane's players started celebrating, and a timeout was called. On the inbounds play, the Tulane passer panicked and threw a bad pass in the general direction of Matt Doherty. Jordan tracked the ball down, turned, and as the crowd readied itself in anticipation, launched a high-arcing jump shot from what today would be three-point range. Swish!

Pandemonium, especially after the officials signaled that the basket counted. It was a miracle shot, and a heck of an introduction to turning the scoreboard. I actually remained in the stands through the three overtimes and didn't go back to the scoreboard (the last time I ever did that), and watched as Carolina finally pulled it out. The first of many postgame walks across the intramural fields with my parents and the Moreaus back to the parking lot on Raleigh Road turned out to be a happy one.

"I was sitting in the bleachers, and when Tulane had the ball with four seconds left, people were leaving. I started yelling to them that it wasn't over yet. They looked at me like I was crazy. On the in-bounds play two Tulane players ran into each other and the ball fell to MJ. A 25-ft jump shot later, I was vindicated."   —Mike Lloyd, 46, alumnus and tour guide in Henderson, NC

About eight weeks later, Carolina was on a roll when Virginia came to town on a Wednesday night. I was now a member of Boy Scouts Troop 39, which met in the University Methodist Church. The troop had three central activities: a monthly camping trip, paper recycling one week out of every six, and Wednesday night meetings. We were supposed to attend 75% of the activities to be considered in good standing, so I had missed the Carolina home game against Maryland a couple of weeks before. That had turned out to be the game in which Michael Jordan and Sam Perkins blocked Chuckie Driesell's lay-up attempt to win the game. For some reason, I didn't feel so bad about missing that, but I wasn't going to miss the Virginia game, so I skipped the Scout meeting.

Carolina and Virginia were ranked No. 1 and No. 2 nationally at the time. I watched in fascination and awe as Ralph Sampson and the rest of the Cavaliers ran by me out onto the court for pregame warm-ups, and began a habit of closely examining the opposing team's players during warm-ups, just to get a sense of who they were, how big they really were, whether they were making shots, and so forth. The teams went back into the lockers, the John Yesulaitus Carolina band played its famous 50-second version of the national anthem, and then "Here Comes Carolina" as Carolina's players took the court, followed by the assistant coaches. Finally, the familiar scene of a determined-looking Dean Smith striding onto the court, dropping his cigarette butt on the last bit of concrete, looking dead center ahead, and then stepping on his own cigarette without looking down as he moved onto the hardwood.

Intensity was high in the first half, but Virginia looked the better team. At halftime, David Simpson, also excited to be at such a big game, came down to say hi and added that Carolina's chances didn't look so good. It got a lot worse in the second half as Virginia executed its offense with precision and kept Jordan under wraps. After a Virginia basket and foul with about 10 minutes to go, I angrily slammed down the wooden cards to record the basket with such force that a manager turned his head and David Folds told me to calm down. I was so agitated that when Virginia led 56–42, I forgot about the 6s and 9s being mixed up and showed the score as 59–42, a mistake not corrected until Virginia scored again. That was the biggest mistake I can recall making in six years on the scoreboard job.

But some big baskets by Jim Braddock and Perkins turned it around, and got Carolina back into it. When Braddock nailed a crucial three with just over two minutes to play, the Cavalier lead was just three points. Virginia went to its delay, and Carolina was lucky to be whistled for a foul just as it looked like the Cavaliers were going to come up with a lay-up. Sampson missed his free throw, and with under a minute to play Braddock launched another three-pointer which would have tied the game. The shot didn't go in, but Jordan tapped it in beautifully. Then, all of the sudden Jordan stripped Carlisle of the ball in the backcourt and went in for the dunk. From where we were sitting, it looked like he took off too soon, too far away, and as Jordan hung in midair I worried that he would miss. He didn't. The videotape shows me (and David and Matt) jumping in exultation, along with almost 10,000 others. Timeout, and we put the scoreboard away. I didn't get a good look at Virginia's last play live—it was extremely crowded at court level that night—but I heard the crowd and saw the Tar Heels celebrating after Jordan came up with a game-clinching rebound. A game for the ages, and yet another night to bolster one's faith in the Tar Heels.

It was also the high-water mark of the 1982–83 season. Carolina dropped games to Maryland and State in February, and then lost again to State in the ACC Tournament semifinal as Jordan got in foul trouble. I missed watching that game, save for the overtime, to have a trombone lesson with Bruce; strangely, I don't recall being much agitated about what I was missing (as I surely would be today).

Still, another trip to the Final Four—and a rematch with surprising N.C. State—seemed likely when Carolina matched up with Georgia in the regional final. I had missed the first round game, against James Madison again, for a Scout trip (the Scouts always put the March camping trip the first weekend of the NCAAs, reasoning that this was more realistic than going the weekends of either the ACC Tourney or the later rounds). One of the scout leaders, David Jones, a junior high science teacher, had pulled the legs of a few of us by pretending to be listening on a portable radio to Woody calling the last two minutes of the game. He gave a dramatic recounting of what Woody was supposedly saying, acting all fired up, and went on to tell us Carolina had lost to James Madison after Braddock missed a shot. I was unhappy for about 10 seconds, and then David started laughing and laughing and admitted he had been putting us on. Someone had the real radio report and conveyed the fact that Carolina had in fact won. It was a good joke, and certainly had me taken.

After North Carolina took care of Ohio State in the Sweet 16, Sam Perkins made the famous mistake of asking reporters what conference Georgia was in. It was an honest question, and an entirely comprehensible one for a New York kid in those days before hour-long nightly highlight shows had become a national institution. But it was bulletin board material just the same, and Georgia ran Carolina out of the game. I watched the game at Paul's house that Sunday afternoon, as the Pritchetts were having another party for folks from church, and watched disappointedly as Carolina couldn't get back into it at the end.

"They can't win it all every year," said Mom, as the clock ran out. I knew she was right, but it was still a downer. Even so, the sense of anticipation about this tournament and this team was almost nothing compared to 1982, and there wasn't the pure hunger of 1981. I don't even recall thinking very much that winning back-to-back titles was a serious possibility. And maybe it didn't hurt quite so much because Virginia was already out, too. In any case, I was able to swallow the loss reasonably easily and then watched with equanimity and appreciation as Jim Valvano took State all the way to the title. Carolina had suffered a mild upset in 1983, but there was every reason to think Carolina would be playing the last weekend in March in 1984.

1983–84

In September 1983, *The Chapel Hill Newspaper* reported a story that made a lot of the natives excited and proud: Dean Smith had decided to offer a scholarship to Chapel Hill High School's six-foot scoring dynamo, Ranzino Smith, who would be playing for Carolina starting in 1984–85.

There had been a buzz about Ranzino since his eighth grade year, which got passed on to me through Treeby, who knew "Z" as a classmate at Phillips Junior High and then CHHS, as well as through George. George had played on a rec league basketball team with Ranzino coached by Z's dad, Marion Smith. (George recalls that Ranzino was very, very good at the foul line.) As a seventh grader, Ranzino had broken a hip playing football and missed playing basketball, but in eighth grade he came out blazing as the best player on the *ninth grade* Phillips team. Under coach Tony Yount, Phillips played an all-out pressing game and blew away almost everyone they played. As a ninth grader, Ranzino was averaging close to 30 points a game, even though his minutes were limited because most games were blowouts. And he was dunking in games. As a fifth grader in 1981 I went with my siblings to the last game of Ranzino's Phillips career against archrival Culbreth. The gym was packed, and everyone wanted to see Ranzino get another dunk. He finally got a chance, but missed it, although the ball bounced high off the back rim and fell through as Ranzino wore a sheepish grin downcourt. By that point, everyone thought, this is going to be a great high school player—and maybe even Carolina will recruit him.

Indeed, I heard that very question posed to Bill Guthridge one summer day during a church softball game, probably in 1982, after Ranzino had scored 15 points a game off the bench as a sophomore for the state runner-up Chapel Hill Tigers. Guthridge tried to downplay expectations by saying, "Well, I don't know if there's much use in today's college game for a six-foot shooting guard" and leaving it at that. I overheard this and was a little disappointed, but there was still a lot of hope and expectation that Ranzino would end up a Tar Heel. As a junior, Smith exploded, scoring around 30 points a game, and he had established himself as the best returning high schooler in North Carolina going into the 1983–84 season. And so while Dean Smith cautioned from the beginning (as reported in the stories about Ranzino's signing) that he wasn't sure how much the Chapel Hill native would be able to contribute, he gave Ranzino a chance to fulfill his dream. A kid from Ridgefield Apartments (the town's major public housing complex and almost entirely African-American) was going to play for Carolina. That was exciting to me and especially to my brother and sister's cohorts who went to high school with Ranzino.

*

It's a little astonishing to recollect how few games North Carolina basketball teams actually played in Chapel Hill in the last few years of Carmichael Auditorium—fewer then 10 a year, in most cases. By the time mid-January 1984 rolled around, the natives had gotten to see the Tar Heels at home only twice, in blowouts of non-conference opposition. In the meantime, the Tar Heels, with new freshman point guard Kenny Smith, had gone on the road and put a shellacking on just about everyone. The highlight by far, of course, was an early January win at Maryland, punctuated by Michael Jordan's windmill dunk at the buzzer, which was certainly the talk of Culbreth Junior High the next morning. In the first ACC home game against Virginia, the Cavaliers made a gallant, late run to make it close. Carolina was much sharper during the next home game in totally dismantling an excellent Wake Forest team that had enjoyed so much success in Chapel Hill, beating the Sweet-16-bound Deacons by 37 points in one of the most impressive regular season performances of Dean Smith's long coaching tenure.

On Super Bowl weekend, Carmichael hosted back-to-back games against Georgia Tech and LSU. The improving Jackets gave Carolina all it wanted on Saturday afternoon, but Brad Daugherty hit some foul line jumpers and the Tar Heels pulled away in the last 10 minutes. Kenny Smith was quoted in the paper as saying he was glad to have a game the next day, it was more fun than practicing.

And indeed, most of the LSU game was a lot of fun. Jordan had two incredible tap-in slams at the basket right in front of us, and Phil Ford, on injury hiatus from the NBA, told reporters that Jordan could step into the league right away. But the play that most people remember from that game spoiled not only the weekend but arguably the entire winter. With Carolina starting to pull away from the hot-shooting Tigers midway through the second half, Smith jetted free on a fast break and went up for a trademark dunk. John Tudor of LSU grabbed Smith from behind, and Smith came down hard—and stayed there. One of the awesome things about Carmichael Auditorium was how hushed the crowd could get, 10,000 people attentive yet silent when Sam Perkins or another Tar Heel stepped to the foul line. This time, Carmichael was silent for much longer, until Smith finally got up and was taken to the locker room with what turned out to be a broken wrist.

Remarkably, however, Carolina kept winning, as Steve Hale took over at point guard. Carolina had only one loss, at Arkansas by a single point, going into the home finale against Duke, and were odds-on favorites to become the first ACC team in a decade to go through the regular season unbeaten. At last, I got a chance to see a senior day game against Duke—and as I watched Sam Perkins, Matt Doherty, and Cecil Exum go to mid-court to be honored for their last game, I got emotional at the thought of Perkins leaving and had to turn away, glumly. The thought then hit me that this could well be Michael Jordan's last home game, too. He might go pro. That was too much to think about at that moment. Like Scarlett O'Hara, I told myself I would think about that tomorrow.

Exum hit an early short jumper and Carolina got an early lead, and Kenny Smith made his return, heavy cast and all. But by the end of the first half, it was clear Duke wasn't going to easily go along with the expected storyline. That Duke team matched up quite well against the Tar Heels, and Johnny Dawkins was capable of scoring on anybody. In the second half, concern grew to near-panic after Duke took the lead in the last minute. We put the scoreboard away, and I ran up to the concourse exit to watch the end of the game next to an usher. Danny Meagher missed a free throw, and Carolina had the ball, down two, with about eight seconds to play. Anyone in the gym had to think the ball would be going to Perkins or Jordan. Instead, the Blue Devils surprisingly let Matt Doherty dribble upcourt relatively unimpeded, and he pulled up for a 15-foot jumper, exactly the shot Doherty had often been criticized for being reluctant to take every time it presented itself. The ball rattled in at the buzzer, and another Carmichael miracle had come to pass—although the emotion was more relief than joy or shock. Doherty had gotten Carolina off the hook in a game that Duke, over the first 39 and a half minutes, probably deserved to win.

I ran back down to tend to the scoreboard for overtime. Jordan missed a baseline jumper badly at the end of the first overtime, but in the second extra period Carolina pulled away and Smith even got to pull Doherty and Perkins for final farewells on the bench. It wasn't 1978 and Phil Ford, but it was still quite an afternoon, the culmination of probably the greatest regular season of any Dean Smith team.

Unfortunately, it was also the last real high point. David Moreau and I skipped a day of school to go with our dads to Greensboro to see the first day of the ACC Tournament. Carolina had a ho-hum win over Clemson, then Duke beat Georgia Tech in a thrilling contest in the final seconds, abetted by a 50–50 block/charge call. That was bad news for Carolina—Tech was good but they weren't going to beat this Carolina team. Duke might be a different story, though.

Those worries proved well-founded as Carolina lost a second-half lead and then the game after coming back from a first-half deficit. I again missed most of the game with a trombone lesson, but saw Matt Doherty throw the last-gasp errant inbounds pass with two seconds to play that took away a possible shot to tie. Seeing Sam Perkins the next day in line at the K&W restaurant wearing a smile cheered me up a little, though I couldn't help but think that I'd rather be watching him on television that Sunday afternoon.

In the NCAA Tournament Carolina bounced back to beat Temple, while Boy Scout Troop 39 was on its customary March camping trip. The Sweet 16 opponent was Indiana, on a Thursday night. George was in Rhode Island, at his freshman year of college at Brown University, and was supposed to fly back the next day for spring break. Mom talked about how we would get to watch the game together on Saturday.

Meanwhile, Bob Knight talked to his ace defender Dan Dakich about how to guard Michael Jordan, and to Steve Alford about the importance of shooting the lights out against Carolina. Carolina fell behind in the first half as Jordan got two fouls and a seat on the bench. Smith, sticking with a strategy he had used all year, wanted to keep the somewhat foul-prone Jordan available to play an aggressive second half. Carolina made a run and actually played quite well at times in the second half, but Indiana kept its poise and eventually pulled away again in the final minutes. It was a narrow, crushing defeat.

Mom, Dad, and I watched the TV in despair as the final seconds ticked away and the cameras showed Smith and the Tar Heels leaving the court. Mom said, "Even Dean looks upset about this one." And Matt Doherty told reporters in the locker soon afterward about how he felt "cheated" to have his career end this way. Poor George, he had to stay up until 11:30 to watch the game on tape in Providence—and then find out Carolina had lost.

"Without a doubt, my worst memory is the NCAA loss to Indiana in 1984. It was the best team I had ever seen. The memories of Matt Doherty crying brought me to tears. I had to miss school the next day because I was so upset."   —Sheronda Harris, 30, social worker in Greensboro

It was painful to not win the tournament, to have to sit and watch Virginia beat a mentally spent Indiana team to go to the Final Four and then see Georgetown win a rather lackluster NCAA final over Houston. But perhaps the saddest part of the loss was simply not getting to see that team play again. There's nothing like the finality of that last loss in college sports (especially now that consolation games have been discarded). Sometimes I admire with jealousy the European club football system, where a major club can be involved in as many as four major competitions in a single "season," and where a loss in a given competition doesn't mean that the season is over and you never get to see that group of players play together again. In college basketball, once it's over, it's over. You build all season long to a certain peak of expectation, and bam, the balloon pops and suddenly expectation turns to mourning and post-mortems.

Some years the post-mortems go on longer than others. 1984 was one of those years.

*

If there was anything most people in Chapel Hill wanted in 1984 more than another national title for Dean Smith, it was a new senator from the North State to replace Jesse Helms. By that time, I was well aware of Helms' national reputation, and that he had said Chapel Hill was a zoo and that a fence should be put around it. On the other hand, he had met with our group of fifth graders from Glenwood in 1981 and stood for a picture with us when we took a spring day trip to Washington. And I was as mystified as most North Carolinians probably were by Jim Hunt's television commercials trying to link Helms to right-wing death squads in El Salvador (Hunt probably overestimated the median voter's knowledge of world affairs on that one). But pretty much everyone I came into contact with was not a big fan of Jesse.

In fact, my dad worked in 1984 as an unpaid advisor on national security and foreign policy issues to the Hunt campaign. Dad had developed a professional relationship with the Governor, who came to Chapel Hill High School in the spring of 1984 to speak at the high school's "Humanities Festival," which my sister Treeby helped organize. One afternoon after that, a bunch of people from the Hunt campaign came and met with Dad in our living room. I don't know what went on there, but I was impressed. A right-wing newsletter published in rural Orange County later wrote an article about Dad's working for the campaign, which wasn't that big a deal, except that it set the stage for one of George's best pranks of all time. George called Dad from college one night affecting a thick Southern accent and pretending to be a Helms staffer giving him a hard time. Dad fell for it and began stammering out a reply until George could no longer hold his laughter.

The Hunt-Helms race was a routine topic of conversation throughout the latter half of 1984. I vividly remember a church retreat I went to with my parents in the early fall of 1984. It was the kind of weekend where people sit around and talk about their life stories and try to get to know one another better. I had a good time, but a couple of things stick out in particular. One is that there was a Trivial Pursuit game played in teams, and I got paired up with Bill Guthridge. We went for sports every time there was an opportunity (then history), but didn't do very well. The second is that at some point all the men there engaged in a shooting-the-bull session about the upcoming elections. One person after another (Guthridge included) expressed a desire to see Hunt beat Helms. There wasn't much doubt about it, the majority of Chapel Hill locals I knew were invested in that election. Hunt represented education, progress, and liberalism; we thought Helms represented backwardness and thinly veiled racism.

> "In 1977, I was working for Luther Hodges, Jr., in his bid to replace Jesse Helms in the U.S. Senate. When Luther declared, we organized a statewide announcement tour, including a stop at the Governor's Inn. One of Luther's friends was Dean Smith, who has never hidden his political leanings or his disgust with the conservative views of Helms. Smith attended Hodges' announcement at the Governor's Inn and I—and many others—flocked to shake his hand or get his autograph. In fact, to some extent, Smith's presence overshadowed Luther's announcement. Hodges didn't seem to mind, but Smith, typically for him, was clearly uncomfortable stealing the limelight; he kept reminding people to pay attention to what Hodges was saying."
>
> —Paul Bernish, public relations consultant, Cincinnati, Ohio

About a month before the election, I persuaded my mom that we needed to drive to Raleigh one afternoon after school to go see vice-presidential candidate Geraldine Ferraro speak near N.C. State. We went, and by chance got to see Ferraro from about five feet away, which thrilled Mom. During her speech, Ferraro invoked not Dean Smith's liberalism, but shrewdly, Jim Valvano's miracle-working comeback skills displayed during State's national title run in 1983 as the model for what would happen in November. In the way that good politicians can, she made me for 15 seconds almost believe it. We went home exhilarated.

Going into election night, anticipation was high: the polls showed a dead heat in the Senate race. We thought there was a good chance for Hunt, and we had tentative plans that if it looked like a Hunt victory, the three of us (Mom, Dad, and I—Treeby had now also gone off to college) would drive over to campaign headquarters in Raleigh.

Well, we soon found out we weren't going anywhere. Hunt was projected relatively early as the loser. Helms was going to be re-elected. Chapel Hill values, Chapel Hill ideology, had been rejected by the body populace of North Carolina. It was tough to swallow. Dr. Moreau came over from next door and commiserated with my Dad for a good hour. I went out and shot baskets. At some point the gap between the candidates started narrowing, and Dad asked me to load up my beloved computer game "President Elect" on the Apple II, a game which simulated presidential elections that I had been playing pretty much nonstop weekends and after homework since early October. Dad wanted to know how many total voters the game projected for the state of North Carolina, to see if there were enough votes left to be counted so that Hunt might possibly close the gap. Hunt's tally climbed to 48%, but no higher. Helms had won. And that was perhaps the one time growing up in Chapel Hill I felt outside of basketball a collective pathos, a shared sadness, equivalent to how the town reacted to NCAA tournament losses by the Tar Heels.

1984–85

Fall 1984 also saw the brief flickering and then extinguishment of my scholastic basketball career. By ninth grade I was about 5-10 and one of the taller people in school, and my game had gotten better on the playground. On a good day I could certainly score in the toughest games Culbreth had to offer at lunch. And I was still playing lots of one-on-one against David Moreau, the projected starting shooting guard for Culbreth. Still, I was woefully out of shape, didn't plan on trying out, and only did so at the last minute, when Paul Pritchett said he was going out (he hadn't made the team before either). It was a good experience, but I couldn't make the mile time, and when we finally scrimmaged after 90 minutes of running around and drills, I would be too tired to stroke my 15-foot jumper. A week of basketball camp prior to then to prepare me—and a lot more jogging—would have helped. As it was, Paul and I got cut.

Shortly after those tryouts, Bill Guthridge paid a visit to our Troop 39 Boy Scout meeting. Guthridge showed a highlight film narrated by Woody about the 1984 season, then talked about some general principles of Carolina hoops and how that year's team was shaping up. Guthridge said that personal character and some of the values the Boy Scouts wanted to promote were really important in deciding who Carolina wanted to recruit, and that some of his best moments as a coach came in seeing the dedication of players working out on their own or jogging in the offseason beyond what the coaches expected. He also told us that Brad Daugherty, Steve Hale, and Kenny Smith were the three best players on the team, that Jordan would have played forward if he had returned as a senior, and that Ranzino Smith was doing a good job in practice but probably would not play a lot at the beginning.

1984–85 was supposed to be the last season for Carmichael Auditorium. It was also suspected to be the last season for Carolina's 18-year run of finishing first or second in the ACC regular season race. Nonetheless, Carolina rolled out to a 12–1 start, the loss coming to Missouri in a Hawaiian tournament. By far the highlight was a 75–74 win over a good Maryland team in Carmichael. To this point, I still hadn't seen Carolina lose a game in person, but it certainly seemed likely when Carolina trailed by three in the final minute. But Maryland missed free throws, and Dave Popson floated in the go-ahead basket from 17 feet to give Carolina the lead with about six seconds to play. Then Curtis Hunter stole the inbounds pass and made two free throws to ice it. Incredible game—and as it turned out, the last true miracle win in Carmichael.

My undefeated record as a live spectator didn't last much longer, however. Days after a scintillating win over a good State team at home, in which Ranzino Smith came off the bench for his customary two minutes at the end of the first half and converted a three-point play, Duke came into town and waxed Carolina up and down the court, led by Johnny Dawkins. Midway through the second half, long before he liked to use his timeouts, Dean Smith called one, and shortly thereafter he called another. No dice that Saturday afternoon, and it wasn't close at the end. I met my parents after the game, feeling numb and saying little, though I think deep down I already knew that I had grown up a little on account of what I had just seen.

I was considerably glummer eight days later, when Georgia Tech—another high-quality ACC team—came in and again beat Carolina soundly in Carmichael. On my birthday, no less. The ultimate superstition was gone. Carolina could lose a game I attended, and they could do so on my birthday. It's astonishing to think that I could have gotten to age 15 and thought any different. But while I probably knew it in theory, I hadn't seen a concrete demonstration of that fact until those back-to-back home losses to Duke and Tech.

Carolina rebounded from the losses and had a pretty sound February, the highlights being two excellent wins at Maryland and Duke. Steve Hale grabbed 11 rebounds in the Maryland win, which really impressed me. Brad Daugherty and Warren Martin had big games against Duke in a win that kept the top-two streak going and gave Carolina a share of the regular season title. In between, the Tar Heels played what was supposed to be the last game in Carmichael, an 84–50 victory over Clemson. Only, I wasn't there: Instead, I spent the weekend in Raleigh performing with the junior high all-district band, which I had successfully auditioned for a few weeks earlier. To me, it was a no-brainer. I had practiced hard for the audition and was proud, maybe even a little vain, about being the only person from the Culbreth band to make it that year. So David Moreau filled in for me on the scoreboard and I settled for reading news accounts.

A couple of weeks later, the minor disappointment of missing the supposed last Carmichael game was more than compensated by the chance to travel with my parents to Atlanta to see the ACC Tournament. It was interesting to get to see the inside of the pre-game university-sponsored functions with the boosters and the faculty and administration types and the buffets. Clear evidence that the game played by young men, disproportionately African-American and of varying economic backgrounds, was also entertainment of the highest form for North Carolina's elite. Then, as now, you could overhear 48-year-old white men in coats and ties and with half of an extra ring around the middle talking about the merits of playing Curtis Hunter or going big with Dave

Brad Daugherty takes a short jumper against Stanford in a December 1985 game.

Popson or Joe Wolf at small forward. Jim Martin, the new Republican governor, was at one of the events. More reassuringly, so was Pearl Seymour, who gave approval to the piano rendition of the Tar Heel songs I played to relieve the boredom of adult-only gatherings inside a large hotel suite. My seventh-grade English teacher, Lynn Carr, who was the wife of an assistant UNC football coach and a big Carolina fan, was there too, and before the Wake Forest quarterfinal game she told me that she felt really nervous and had a bad intuition.

She was onto something, as Carolina really had to pull a rabbit out of the hat to get to over-time against seventh seeded Wake Forest. Dean Smith got called for a technical in that game, and it was something for me to hear seven-eighths of the arena roaring in approval as the call was an-nounced. ABC (Anyone But Carolina) was the rule of the day. It was also interesting to see the soli-darity the very well-heeled Tar Heel fans in attendance showed in braving the torrents of ridicule. At one point, when underage junior Brad Daugherty was called for a foul or a travel, a middle-aged female fan yelled, "Give him a break, ref, he's only 19!" Carolina did get a couple of breaks, includ-ing a technical called on a Wake player, to take it to overtime, then pulled away to win easily. The next day was the rubber match against an excellent N.C. State team with Nate McMillan and several holdovers from the 1983 championship team, a club that would reach the final eight of the nationals. It was a tense back-and-forth game, played at maximum intensity. Carolina got the lead late and hung on to beat State by six.

The final against Georgia Tech started in terrific fashion, as Carolina played great defense at the beginning and ran out to a double-digit lead. But Tech slowly crept back into the game and got the majority of the crowd on its side. Like the State game, this one went down to the final minutes. Carolina turned the ball over with the scored tied at 50 and a minute to play, and the Yellow Jackets used a crucial offensive rebound off a free throw to build a three-point lead. The Jackets avoided any mistakes to let Carolina back into it, the buzzer sounded, and Georgia Tech's players and fans swarmed the court. Carolina had lost in the ACC Tournament for the third straight year, the longest such drought in my lifetime. I was sad, because I thought it would have been a perfect cap for a team that had really overachieved all year. But somehow, walking close to my parents in the crowd filing out of the Omni, I said to myself, "This is O.K., this is alright." If anyone else was going to win, much better Tech than Duke or State. Carolina would be due to win the tournament next year—and would have a much stronger team too. (A few weeks earlier, when the school bus conversation on the way to Culbreth turned, as it often did, to basketball, I had announced with great conviction that Carolina would be No.1 in the country in 1986. No one contradicted me.) And there was still the NCAA Tournament in 1985.

Carolina lost Steve Hale for the season on a Kenny Smith-type foul from behind in beating Middle Tennessee State in the first round. That was the year the NCAA field expanded to 64 teams, and hence the first time Carolina had played in the round of 64. No one took the game too seriously—the next day at school, only about half the folks had even watched it. It was expected Carolina would win easily, and they did. But without Hale, the prospect of playing Notre Dame in the second round on Notre Dame's home court seemed a lot tougher. It was a nail-biter, but with the Irish working for the last shot and the game tied, Irish point guard David Rivers lost the ball to Curtis Hunter, who pitched ahead to Kenny Smith for the go-ahead dunk. Smith then stole the long in-bounds pass. It was a terrific victory, and I ran outside that sunny March day in euphoria. Greg Gonzalez, another neighborhood kid who lived nearby, was outside shooting baskets and had missed the end of the game, so I walked over and recounted the whole thing to him in great detail. Carolina was in the Sweet 16 again.

Carolina was slated to play Auburn in Birmingham on a Friday night. This worked out well, as George this year would be back on spring break from Brown in time to see that one with me. Jonathan Broun was back in town from his spring break, too. It was another close, well-played game in a hostile arena. With Hale out and senior Buzz Peterson in something of shooting slump, Ranzino Smith got more playing time in this game. It had been an up-and-down freshman year for Z: While Smith had scored some big baskets at different points of the season and become a crowd favorite, he also had shot only 34% from the floor (largely because of an undiagnosed vision problem which would be corrected the following summer), and had been accused by one or two commentators of having visited the cookie jar too often.

As fate had it, however, Ranzino was the Tar Heel Auburn fouled with about 10 seconds to play and Carolina clinging to a two-point lead. One-and-one. I was watching upstairs with George in his room on this one, pacing nervously, at the same time excited and supremely anxious that the local hero was going to have a chance to ice the game. First shot, good. Second shot, good. Auburn came down and missed, Carolina rebounded, and Kenny Smith got another dunk at the buzzer to seal a 62–56 win. Absolute jubilation. Carolina had another stirring win, Ranzino was one of the heroes, and Carolina was on the brink of another Final Four. And then as the game cut out, the first commercial to come on was the new "Air Jordan" Nike commercial with Michael Jordan leaping through midair for a dunk, which we had never seen before.

The following day, Jonathan Broun came over, and as we were watching the other regional finals said, "I really don't think I want to play Memphis in the Final Four." A second later, Jonathan corrected himself and said, "No, no, I mean I would love to play Memphis in the Final Four!" Jonathan's slip revealed that the great win over Auburn had obscured what a tough obstacle Carolina faced in a senior-led Villanova squad. The core of that team had been freshmen in 1982, when Carolina easily outclassed the Wildcats in the regionals in Raleigh to reach the Final Four, and they had made a pledge that they would get to the Final Four before leaving school. Carolina would be the ideal payback victim. Even so, Carolina took a halftime lead and Ranzino made a couple of nice jumpers. But in the second half, Carolina was absolutely stifled offensively, no one could hit from outside, and Villanova pulled away to win by double digits. It was a very ugly way for the season to end, not playing well and not even being in the game at the end. No one would have thought at the start of the 1984–85 season that Carolina would find itself 20 minutes from a Final Four, but coming that close didn't make it easier to swallow on another losing, season-ending Sunday. But within a week or two, I felt proud about the season as a whole. And in 1986, there might be no stopping the Tar Heels.

*

So the season was over. That didn't mean that the games didn't continue, however. By 1985, I had become a serious devotee of "ACC-Tion," which was a very well-conceived and well-executed card and dice basketball game featuring the ACC teams and players. I had the 1982, 1983, 1984 and 1985 editions. You could coach Carolina against any ACC opponent, making all the substitutions, choosing offensive and defensive strategy, deciding whether a player would shoot or not, whether to go into the delay game. Each player had a card showing his attributes and the player's photo, and there were team cards for offense and defense intended to make the dice rolls produce statistically accurate outcomes as to which player would get the most shots and how many turnovers there would be. There was even a system to simulate home court advantage and momentum swings in the game. I don't think the many computer and video games that have followed ACC-Tion have done much better—most do far worse—in providing a statistically accurate simulation and allowing the player to make coaching decisions.

No one else in my family and no one I knew was remotely interested in playing the game with me, so I would play solitaire, coaching both teams as fairly as possible, and at least once replaying an entire ACC season (all 14 games for all eight schools, plus the tournament). When I ran out of the box score and time-keeping sheets provided with the game, I would give the last one to Dad who would have his office secretary run off another 50. Each game took about 30–45 minutes to play, and a reasonable estimate is that between ages 12 and 18, I spent between 500 and 1,000 hours playing that game. After 1985, the game was discontinued, and in frustration I actually made cards up myself for the 1985–86 teams and players based on their season statistics. Friday nights at midnight circa 1985 were likely to see me contentedly playing ACC-Tion. And yes, I was pleased when I coached Carolina to victory and annoyed when they lost, especially to inferior opposition. (More often than not, you were going to blow Clemson out, but it was possible in the game, as in real life, to go down to Littlejohn and lose a tight one.)

So I had a rich imaginary relationship with Carolina basketball and the most recent teams, as well as a real-life one, in 1985. The real-life component came to the fore that summer, when I attended Carolina Basketball School for the first time that June. I was in the rising sophomore group that played at Durham Academy's gym. UNC assistant Roy Williams was in charge of our group. He was great, really impressive. Williams would stop the entire camp to point out a kid who had set seven screens on one possession to say, "Here's a kid who's not the most talented player, but is going to make a high school team because he works so hard." Williams showed us shooting drills that I still use to this day and said 15 minutes of that full-movement drill was better than an hour of just shooting standing still. On "hump day," the Wednesday of camp, Williams moved us from push-ups into a game of "Simon Says." It was impossible to avoid the feeling of wanting to do the right thing and impress Roy and the other coaches.

I was at best an average player in that group. I didn't have too hard a time keeping up, and the fact that most of the really talented rising 10th graders were pushed on to the highest group meant I didn't have to worry about things like being dunked on. I still wore glasses that summer, and those glasses, along with my longer-than-average hair, immediately earned me the nickname "Rambis," after the bespectacled Lakers forward. Everybody called me Rambis, including Roy Williams, who took about five minutes one day to work with me on my free throw stroke. The team I was on was pretty good and won our mini-league, and one of the highlights of my career was driving past somebody for a lay-up in the final and hearing Roy Williams yell, "Rambis drives and scores!" Later that day, as we were moving out of Granville, I saw Bill Guthridge, who asked me if I had a good time and wanted to know if my team had won its league. I was happy to be able to reply "Yes" to both questions.

So that first year at Carolina Basketball School was an unqualified success, especially since I had avoided getting any "tours"—the punishment of extended running, leg lifts and pushups that befell campers who missed curfew, didn't make their beds, were late to go anywhere, or got a technical foul in a game. Outdoor clinics were held every afternoon at Granville Towers with the likes of York Larese, Al Wood, and Michael Jordan. In 1985, Jordan had just finished his rookie year

Steve Bucknall looks on as Ranzino Smith attempts a free throw against Wake Forest during the 1985–86 season.

with the Bulls and the Air Jordans had just come out. Michael picked out a nine-year-old camper who was wearing little Air Jordans to help demonstrate defensive drills. It was a fleeting moment, but great.

I spent one week at basketball camp in 1985, but four weeks at music camp at Appalachian State. That difference appropriately reflected my relative commitment to playing trombone vis-a-vis playing basketball. Ironically, however, insofar as I had an identity that year at camp it largely came from carrying a basketball around the ASU campus. I made an effort to shoot outside daily (there were a couple of campers there to shoot the breeze about UNC with) and go to the ASU gym on weekends. One weekend in the middle of the camp, I went up to the ASU student center on an early Saturday morning to hang out, escape trombone, and watch the TV broadcast of the Live Aid concerts from England and then Philadelphia. (There had been rumors of a Beatles "reunion.") In the student lounge, I bumped into a familiar face—Lynwood Robinson, the Appalachian State point guard who had transferred from Carolina early in the 1982–83 season. Lynwood was a little surprised, but certainly not shocked, that I knew who he was, and I showed him the UNC shorts I was wearing. This was really the first chance I ever had for an extended conversation with a former Carolina player, and we hung out there for a good couple of hours, talking and watching the concert. (Lynwood was into Sade.) I can't recall much of the specifics, other than how nice he was and how much he emphasized that he still loved Chapel Hill. Robinson was getting ready for his senior year in Boone. Finally, we split ways and on a high from that, I shot baskets and then wandered back to the dorm, in time to see Bob Dylan play at the tail end of the Live Aid thing. Strangely, it was my most memorable day at trombone camp and the one day in the month I didn't pick up the horn at all.

1985–86

That summer at Boone saw me start to grow out of my junior high social shell and feel a little more confident in interacting with my peers, a little less likely to just retreat into my own head. I was anxious to make a break with Culbreth days. A trip to McPherson Hospital in Durham for my eye check-up in August helped considerably, as I acquired contact lenses and put away a pair of glasses for the first time in memory. David Moreau's older sister, Page, gave the two of us a ride to the first day of Chapel Hill High School, and I was excited.

I don't think it's too much of an exaggeration to say that in Chapel Hill, junior high school had the social structure you see in most American high schools, whereas Chapel Hill High itself was more like a small college. At CHHS, there wasn't a unitary social structure, dominated by athletes or artists or rock bands or anyone else. There were a lot of different spheres, but not one that commanded the awe of everyone else in school. When football players wore their jerseys to school on game days, nobody as far as I could tell cared. Chapel Hill High won a state basketball championship my junior year, but probably no more than half the school was interested enough to go to see the Tigers play. Sports were still cool and respected, but so were a lot of other things. Some friends like David Moreau continued to play sports (soccer and then football), others like Tom Williams involved themselves in student government, others did drama or any number of other activities.

Music really didn't have a great deal of cachet (except for rock bands), but at least there wasn't a marching band, so it wasn't simply an appendage to football. And so I got to Chapel Hill High and set out to organize my time around playing trombone. There was playing in band, sitting in with the undermanned jazz band for their concerts, playing in the Piedmont Youth Orchestra at Hill Hall on Saturday mornings, playing in the pit orchestra for school musicals, weekly lessons, auditions for all-district and all-state competitions. It was a pretty good organizing principle for high school.

The one moment I seriously questioned that principle was around 3:15 on a late September afternoon, when a P.A. announcement said that anyone interested in playing junior varsity basketball should report to Tiger Gym by 3:30. Of course part of me was interested. I was in somewhat more respectable physical condition, and I would have had a better chance of making the J.V. than I had had of making the team back at Culbreth. The bulk of the Culbreth team intended to focus on other sports in high school and didn't have plans to try out, and the best players in our class from out of Phillips would be joining the varsity. So there just might be room for a warm body on the J.V. team. I stopped in my tracks for a moment and pondered the alternatives. I could walk into that gym, and who knew what would happen. Or I could carry out the music plan and not look back. What I probably couldn't do was both. Roy Williams had said to be a serious player and to raise yourself up a level, you had to play four hours a day against the best players you could find. I hadn't done that, and it wasn't feasible that I would start doing it now. Being even on a J.V. team would mean giving up a lot of things, probably ending trombone lessons too. Being a basketball player was not my comparative advantage in terms of either talent or of establishing a social identity in high school. After a few seconds of genuine indecision, I decided to keep walking and go on home. I didn't often regret that moment, although sometimes even now, flush off a hot shooting day in pickup games, I look back and wince a little.

*

So in the fall of 1985 I immersed myself in music. Mike Dessen, a bona fide trombone prodigy from Chapel Hill who was good friends with George and Treeby and had taught me during ninth grade, had graduated and gone to Eastman School of Music. Consequently, there was a first chair slot open in not only the CHHS band, which wasn't a very big deal, but in the Piedmont Youth Orchestra as well, which was a somewhat bigger deal. The orchestra was conducted by UNC Music Professor Don Oehler, who was very nice and sometimes would drop references to Carolina basketball in rehearsal in his occasional non sequiturs. The main piece we worked on that fall was Schubert's 9th Symphony, a grand, ennobling work with a spectacular trombone part, including a fortissimo segment where the trombone takes the melodic lead at the very climax of the last movement. It was the biggest part I had yet had to play as a trombonist, and I studied and practiced intently. And when I wasn't doing that, I was likely listening to a recording of the piece.

That immersion was probably a good thing, considering what else was going on in the family. My brother and sister were off at school, and my parents where shuttling back and forth between Chapel Hill and Louisiana to visit and care for my grandfather, who was in the process of dying. I flew to Louisiana to visit my grandparents in late October. I had a good visit with my grandfather, who was still mentally sharp and was glad for the visit. A few days later, he died. My dad and the elder David Moreau came and retrieved me from a Boy Scout camping trip with the news. After the funeral, it was decided that my grandmother Frances, the Dean Smith fan, would come back with us to Chapel Hill. And so she did, and stayed with us for a while until we found her an apartment in the nearby Glen Lennox complex.

The youth orchestra concert in which we were to play the Schubert piece was scheduled a few weeks after the funeral, on a Sunday near the end of November. The concert was to take place at 6 p.m., and North Carolina was scheduled to open its basketball season against UCLA at 7 p.m. in what was originally supposed to be the first game played in the new arena. My thoughts were totally on the concert all day long, not dwelling on the fact that I wouldn't able to do the scoreboard against UCLA. Fortunately, my trombone chops were good that day and the concert went exceedingly well. My parents and grandmother, along with my cousin Laura Andress, were there. It was great. But the night was still young yet. Dad and I took a quick car ride from Hill Hall to near Carmichael. We got there in the middle of the second half, with Carolina already up about 18 points on UCLA. The blowout got worse after we arrived, punctuated by a rare eight-point play involving a made basket, an intentional foul, a technical foul, and then a basket on the ensuring possession. Brad Daugherty was 13–13 and made five free throws for 31 points, and Jeff Lebo had a great freshman debut. It was an awesome performance, and Carmichael was at its very best. The Tar Heels ended up winning 107–70, a staggering victory.

We went home, and my grandmother Frances had stayed up. Just before going to bed she told me with a big smile how much she liked the concert, and while extending her hands out from her chest a couple of feet said her heart was "this big." (And in fact, Frances came to just about every musical performance I was involved in over the next three years.) I smiled and walked upstairs, crawled into bed and lay awake, eyes opened in the darkened room. How could you top a day like that?

*

I certainly didn't have many better days than that in high school, but Carolina showed throughout the first half of the season that the UCLA game was hardly a fluke. Carolina had a team to drool over, and stormed through the December pre-ACC slate unbeaten, winning most of the games by very wide margins.

The final game at Carmichael was set for Saturday, January 4, in the ACC opener against N.C. State. George was home from school and would be going to the game. A few days before the game, we happened to be walking through University Mall, when George spotted Marion Smith, Ranzino's father, who recognized him. We stood and talked for a few minutes with Mr. Smith, who told us he was excited for Carmichael to be on fire "one more time." Meanwhile, Jim Valvano added to the pregame hype by promising that he had plans to make history, win or lose. As Valvano walked right by me and the scoreboard onto the court at tap-time, I still wondered what he had in mind.

Carmichael indeed was incredibly loud, pretty much throughout the game. Brad Daugherty and Chris Washburn matched each other shot for shot as State stayed close for most of the afternoon, before Carolina pulled away to win by 11. When the buzzer sounded, Valvano grabbed the game ball and laid it in for what he later claimed was the "last shot in Carmichael." None of the Carolina coaches had thought of that! And that was it. Not much fanfare, no "official last game in Carmichael" hoopla (such respects had been paid in the Clemson game at the end of 1985). When I walked out of the back door at Carmichael that afternoon, I was mainly just happy about the win. I wasn't thinking about how much I would come to miss the peculiar smell of the crowded Carmichael concourse, the student bleachers right on top of the bench, the sound the horn made, the little tower that showed how many fouls a player had, the familiar overhead scoreboard, or just how loud that place could get, even on a relatively quiet night. The scoreboard would be going to the new gym, so my job was secure, and the new gym promised to be great. I knew something precious was being left behind, but unconsciously assumed that that preciousness could be transported to the new building as easily as a rack of basketballs.

A few days before the Duke game, my parents attended the dinner that officially christened the Student Activities Center. And to no one's surprise, the building was named after Dean Smith. When my parents came home, Mom made a snide remark about the food served at the dinner, but also a totally sincere remark about how humble and gracious Smith had been in accepting the building title. Smith said he could permit the building to bear his name only because the name served as a link to all the players who had built the tradition. With what Smith had accomplished, most schools would have been anxious to not only name the building after him but to put a statue of the coach out in front of the building too. And maybe that will indeed happen someday—but not, surely, as long as Smith, who would be embarrassed by such a display, is alive. (There is a bust of the coach inside the building, however.)

I actually had never been in the building or even gone by to take a good look at it until the day of the Duke game. Dad drove me over to Smith Center at about 10:30 a.m. We walked in through the service entrance, and had a good look around. Coming out from the tunnel where the television trucks are located, into the back concourse, and through the black curtains, the view as we stepped into the arena was awe-inspiring at first. What a big place! Look how blue! Look how bright and shiny! I can't remember if at that moment I remembered the Bible's skepticism toward human architectural feats, but I'm sure the thought occurred to me not long after that first day. And the plaintive statement from Smith that the new arena, though nice to have, reflected society's misplaced priorities was fresh in the mind. Still, I looked around, took a deep breath, and accepted it.

We went to lunch, picked up George, who was still on vacation, then came back for the game, which would have been a prime attraction if it had been played on the hardcourt behind Teague Dorm. Carolina and Duke were No. 1 and No. 3 in the polls, both undefeated in the conference. The arena filled up and a buzz was in the air, increasing to a peak as tip-off approached. We pulled the scoreboard up to the end of the Carolina bench, sat down, and then I turned to Neal Harrell, a fellow scoreboard turner, and said, "This is awesome." The game started, and Duke had the lead for most of the first half, until Mike Krzyzewski got a technical foul, which allowed Carolina to gain momentum and take the lead. In the second half, Steve Hale put on a remarkable exhibition of basketball, burning Duke three times for backdoor cut lay-ups, sinking left-handed short jumpers, and generally showing he was the savviest player on the court. Carolina pulled away, and only a flurry of Duke baskets in the last minute cut the margin to six, 92–86.

That would have made for a memorable weekend in itself, but it wasn't over yet: Carolina flew to Milwaukee Saturday night to play a Sunday TV game against Marquette. Clearly tired, the Tar Heels found themselves in deep trouble, down nine with just four minutes to go. But Jeff Lebo came up with a crucial steal in the backcourt and lay-up to help Carolina come back, and Kenny

Smith hit two free throws in the final seconds to win the game, 66–64. Carolina had outscored Marquette 13–2 over the last four minutes. The day after debuting the building named after him, Dean Smith had pulled another rabbit out of the hat for a vintage come-from-behind, "how did they win that?" victory. The Tar Heels were still undefeated. And to this day I believe that if the NCAA Tournament had started the last weekend of January in 1986, Carolina would have finished the season undefeated, too.

*

One of the best parts of my three years of high school was homeroom. In contrast to Culbreth, where all of us at the end of the alphabet sat mostly silently for 10 minutes a day for three years, homeroom at CHHS was a relatively jovial affair. That was partly because homeroom came after first period and was hence experienced as sort of a coffee break in the day. But in our case, it was also because the Ws, Xs, Ys, and Zs got assigned to Tony Yount for three years. Mr. Yount had been the very successful basketball coach at Phillips for many years, but had moved to the high school to teach government and run the yearbook. He had a reputation for being an outspoken liberal to the point of obnoxiousness. Across the hall was Mike Hickman, a UNC grad who had a reputation for being an outspoken conservative to the point of obnoxiousness (and beyond). Good-spirited verbal jousts across the hall between Hickman and Yount not infrequently punctuated home-room. Other times, we talked about politics, from school to national. But between Tom Williams, Deon Williams, Ron Wiegerink, Alan Windham, Tony Yount (who had an analysis for everything) and me, we also had a critical mass such that on any given morning a conversation about the Tar Heels could easily break out.

Given that crowd, there was no sidestepping the issue the February morning after the wheels started coming off the 1986 season. Carolina had lost away to Virginia earlier, but that game was quickly written off when the Tar Heels started a new win streak, highlighted by a thrilling victory at Georgia Tech in which Mark Price missed a potential game-tying free throw in the final seconds of overtime. That was a fantastic victory, and David Moreau and I whooped it up in the backyard while shooting baskets afterwards.

After Carolina had a couple more easy wins, there was an eight-day layoff before playing Maryland at home on a Thursday night. Carolina wasn't particularly sharp most of the night and simply could not defend Len Bias, but still held a close lead.

But apart from the action on the court, I sensed that something else troubling was happening too: The crowd now expected Carolina to win, expected Carolina to win handily. Whereas the Smith Center crowd had been loud and passionate during the first three games against Duke, Georgia Tech, and then Notre Dame, all bona fide big games, now there was almost an air of enti-tlement in the crowd, a slight complacency. The fans were just a bit too sure that the familiar script would play itself out yet again. And perhaps that complacency carried over onto the court when Kenny Smith missed a one and one with the Tar Heels nursing a two-point lead and under 10 sec-onds to play. I was sitting right under the basket when he missed, and watched in horror as the

Terps got the ball up to Jeff Baxter. Somehow, I knew he would make the 20-footer at the buzzer to tie the game. He did, and the building was shocked. Carolina seemed to lose its way in falling behind in overtime, and then lost Steve Hale to a lung injury after the senior dove for a loose ball near mid-court, an injury that would disrupt the rest of the regular season. The final ignominy was when Maryland got a basket when a Terrapin inbounds passer threw the ball off the back of a Tar Heel player, collected the ball, and scored.

It was a stunning defeat—even though Maryland was a legit Top 25 team and had maybe the best player in the country in Bias. I had a difficult time processing what had just happened, and the sight of 20,000 people leaving a building grousing didn't pick up the spirits much. Then the Heels took loss No. 3 a few days later in Raleigh to N.C. State, another tough game. The Tar Heels did manage to pull out the senior night game with Hale back in the lineup against Virginia, but it was an ugly win. Then Carolina went to Duke for the season finale, played well, and lost largely due to a raft of missed free throws.

And so Carolina entered the ACC Tournament having lost three of four games, after a 25–1 start, and just a couple of weeks after *The News and Observer* had run an article discussing whether the 1986 team was the best Carolina team ever. Winning the tournament would put things back on track and prove Carolina really was the best team in the league. The Friday morning of the tournament, Alan Windham came into homeroom and said Carolina needed to kick some butt this weekend, in a very serious tone. That afternoon, as I waited for a ride home from a pit orchestra rehearsal, I told my friend Tamar Bland, who played the trumpet and followed the ACC closely, how much I was looking forward to the weekend. If Carolina made it to the final, I told her, I was probably going to get to go to the game in Greensboro.

That didn't happen. Instead, Carolina suffered a Friday night nightmare in losing again to Maryland. Steve Hale and Warren Martin returned from injuries, but Joe Wolf got hurt in the first half. After Maryland took the lead with a huge run in the second half, Dean Smith put players like Madden, Ranzino, and even Steve Bucknall into the game in a desperate effort to catch up. But things just got worse. Carolina went down in a ball of flames.

There was some slight optimism after Carolina beat Utah in Utah in the first round of the NCAA Tournament, and quite a bit more after a good performance against UAB in the second round. The Sweet 16 game would be against Louisville. The day of the game, folks at school were excited over the announcement that the high school phenom J.R. Reid had committed to Carolina. That was considered major news.

And I felt good about Carolina's chances of beating Louisville. Indeed, Carolina played very well during the game. I watched alone in my parents' bedroom and started jumping off the wall when Joe Wolf hit a big jumper with about five minutes left that tied the game, after Carolina had trailed by 10. The Tar Heels were playing well and with a lot of heart too, and a narrative of a heroic victory was already being spun in my head and heart. But it all went south the last several minutes of the game, and Carolina just couldn't hit any more big shots. After the fouling was all over, the Cardinals had won the game by 15 points—I remained very annoyed when subsequent accounts of the game made it seem like Louisville had won easily. It was a Final Four-type game between what were probably, over the course of the year, two of the best five teams in the country. Dean Smith said after the game that this had been a truly great Carolina team and that he was disappointed for it. It was very hard to swallow, to go from 25–1 to not winning either of the ACC titles and not making the Final Four.

In a lot of ways, I took 1986 harder than 1984, because the disappointment wasn't just one game, it was a whole series of events stretched over a month. If 1984 was like Goliath getting knocked off by one really lucky and really accurate slingshot, 1986 was like seeing Goliath slip, try to get up, and then completely fall over on the rocks shifting beneath his feet.

But life went on, and in fact my own life was starting to get better in a lot of ways. By the second semester of 1986 I had turned from someone with a lot of social insecurities and an introspective, occasionally dour outlook (a dourness that made a sharp contrast with my unshakeable optimism when it came to the Tar Heels), into someone who was actually pretty happy, day to day, moment to moment, with who I was and what I was doing. I continued doing a little bit of sports writing my sophomore year. That included a couple of stories filed for *The News and Observer* as a stringer about the girls' soccer team and the football team at CHHS, and a couple of stories for the student newspaper. Dan Broun, a senior when I was a sophomore, was co-editor, and he assigned me to do a story about Ranzino Smith. So I talked to Tony Yount and Ken Miller, the high school basketball coach, and then figured, why not, and called Z in his dorm room at Granville Towers. (I think I probably knew that "journalists" weren't supposed to do that, but instead arrange interviews through the sports information office, but this was *The Proconian*, how serious could it be? A beat writer would have been fried alive for that sort of breach of protocol, but I got away with it.) In a stroke of luck, Ranzino picked up the phone the first time I called and gave a nice interview for about 10 minutes, saying his goals at Carolina were to graduate and win a championship. The story eventually ran with the headline "Ranzino: From Tiger Gym to the SAC." (The piece ran during the very short period before the new arena became known as simply the Dean Dome.)

In the summer of 1986, my plan was to repeat the drill of a year earlier, going back to Carolina Basketball School for a week and then to Boone for music camp for a month. This time at basketball camp, I was much more clearly in over my head, even though I was probably in better shape than a year earlier. I was grouped with all the high school players now, a decent percentage of whom were Division I prospects. Our sessions were held in the Smith Center, and Ken Miller, the CHHS coach, was in charge of group. It was definitely quite an exciting thing to run on to that court each morning, do some laps, and then do lay-up drills. I started the camp with a reasonable amount of confidence, and on the first day won our mini-group's free throw shooting contest. That meant that just before lunch, I competed with five other campers to see who would win the daily contest. We were all given one practice free throw, and I made mine. But when it came time for the real contest, I missed my first shot and it wasn't particularly close. Still, I didn't feel too bad until former UNC player Randy Wiel came up to me and said, "Hey! Were you trying to make that?" I said, "Yes, I was." Wiel taught the defensive drills for the camp and was probably the most in-your-face teacher we had there—he got your attention in a hurry. Wiel asked me if I had been nervous and I said that I guessed so. He said, haven't you had to shoot in front of other people for your high school team? No, I replied, actually I didn't play high school the previous year. Wiel said O.K.—but get control of yourself, you can do better.

Later that afternoon outside Granville, as I came in from shooting on the outside courts, Wiel spotted me and called me over. He asked if I remembered what he told me, and I said, "Yes—and I won't miss another free throw." Wiel said, no, no, that's not the point, the point is to remain cool and calm so you can do your best. I nodded and went on my way (whereas if I had been totally self-confident and secure that I really belonged at the camp, it could have been an opportunity to sit and really talk with Wiel for a while).

Anyway, the next day came, and again I won our mini-group's free throw contest. This time there were no practice shots, and I went up to the foul line and bricked the first shot. A clearly disappointed Wiel rolled his head and looked away. Even worse, my miss meant my team had to get on the bus back for lunch last, meaning our tired legs had to stand another 15 minutes. So now my teammates were mad at me. And they made sure not to let me win the mini-foul shooting contest again the last three days.

That was a humbling experience, as was getting dunked on in front of the entire camp, which also happened to me that week. And our team did poorly, below .500 and finishing third out of four in the mini-tournament (a fact I admitted glumly to Bill Guthridge, who again asked at the end of the week how my team had done).

There were some good moments, though. At one point I got to play against Chapel Hill High's 6-8 senior center Matt Schroeder, who had about five inches on me, and I won a compliment from Ken Miller for pressuring Schroeder when he caught the ball on the perimeter. For some inexplicable reason, Schroeder let me take and make a little five-foot jumper over him in that game, too.

> "While at Carolina, I got to play against a team that included Brad Daugherty, Kenny Smith, Curtis Hunter, and Buzz Peterson on the blacktop at Granville Towers. I had to guard Kenny Smith, and at that time I realized that these guys play at a level that is so far above the average person that it is unimaginable."   —Arlen Pegg, 37, accountant in Appleton, Wisconsin

At another point, Dean Smith himself came in, wearing golf pants and a pink golf shirt, and observed one of our scrimmages for about 10 minutes. He yelled out to me that I had set a good pick, and later yelled "Take him!" after I got stuck in the corner and no receiver was open. (I didn't have the guts to go all the way to the hoop, but I took two dribbles and found an open man.) At the time, it didn't seem like such a big deal, yet those brief words of instruction still ring clear as a bell in my mind 15 years later. Indeed, a common thread among those respondents to the North Carolina Basketball Fan Survey who also attended the camp is that a positive compliment from Smith himself for something as simple as a pick or a hustle play stands out as their most lasting memory, too. It would be presumptuous and inaccurate to say that playing at Carolina Basketball School's highest level really allowed one to experience what it would be like to play for Carolina or for Smith everyday in practice. But it did provide a whiff, one I'm grateful to have experienced.

But that sort of reflection on the camp experience only came later. During the week itself, the basketball was in part overshadowed by the stunning news that Len Bias of Maryland had died from a drug overdose. A bunch of campers had gathered in Granville that Tuesday to watch the NBA draft, in which Brad Daugherty was chosen No. 1 by the Cleveland Cavaliers. By lunch the next day, the Bias story had broken, first by word of mouth and then in the afternoon edition of *The Chapel Hill Newspaper.* Inside Granville, I saw a couple of Carolina players walking around visibly upset. I called my friend Tamar, the hoops junkie, from a pay phone and we talked about it for a while. The campers then went to the Smith Center for the afternoon clinic. Dean Smith was there and gave a talk, as did James Worthy. It had to be an awkward moment for them. No one made any explicit mention of Bias's death, but Phil Ford gave an impassioned speech about staying away, away, away from drugs and alcohol. Ford got the point across well, and in light of subsequent events, I continue to remember the speech poignantly.

I don't remember having any particular analysis or interpretation of Bias's death, other than being really, really sad. I liked Bias as a player. And in subsequent months I followed with interest as Dean Smith piped up from time to time on behalf of Lefty Driesell, who was eventually ousted from his job. It's a conceit of Carolina fans to think that what happened in College Park that summer couldn't possibly have happened in Chapel Hill, and I think that was my initial, unspoken assumption. But I suspect that Dean Smith knew better, and may well have thought, "There but for fortune...."

*

Those five days in June 1986 marked the highest level of basketball I ever reached on a sustained basis. It was a useful episode, to get to compete against my peers at a pretty high level, and realize that I couldn't cut it. Despite all the hours of jump shooting in the backyard, I wasn't in the top half, and probably not even the top three-quarters, of a camp in which maybe the top one-tenth went on to play Division I basketball, and which had only one camper in my age group that would be good enough to some day play for Carolina (Hubert Davis, who went during a different week). The philosopher John Rawls speaks of the value of appreciating the life paths other people have chosen that you yourself could not and did not. To this day, my appreciation of high-level basketball players rests largely on the experience of having had a glimpse of what it took to be really, really good, the discipline and conditioning and psychological wherewithal it took, and knowing that I couldn't do it.

Eventually, I would come to the same realization about the trombone, but in the summer of 1986, I had much greater success in the practice room than I had had on the hardwood. I was still slightly embarrassed about a poor audition I had played a year before for Cannon Music Camp, and I had in mind that I wanted to get one of the top three trombone slots in the Camp so as to qualify for the camp orchestra and a gig with the North Carolina Symphony. The day before leaving for Boone, I went to the Fourth of July fireworks display in Kenan Stadium with my friend Erin Kimrey and elicited a promise from her that if I somehow got first chair in the orchestra, she would come see the concert with the Symphony. (Erin played flute, had been to Cannon a couple of years before, and knew what it was all about.) Lo and behold, I went to Boone, immediately hit the practice room, played the audition in a relaxed frame of mind, and had as good an audition as I could have possibly played. A day later, the results were announced and it turned out I had indeed gotten first chair in the orchestra, having leapfrogged four people who were ahead of me the previous year. I was stunned for a couple of days, so stunned I didn't play very well in rehearsals.

But eventually I gathered my wits and had a really good camp. And I wasn't a loner that year, either, but made quite a few friends and basically was happy day in and day out. One of the camp counselors, a trombonist named Caren Davis, said she'd never seen such a change in a person from one year to the next. Erin did indeed come to the finale concert, and although I couldn't hit all the high Ds and Es in our piece, the guy from the North Carolina Symphony could, so there were no worries. It was a great summer, and the first one I had ever experienced in which, day in and day out, there were positive interactions with just about everybody and pats on the back of various kinds. I was considered cool, my abilities were respected, and if it had lasted much longer, I probably would have become completely and irreversibly full of myself! Yet, if my summer playing basketball showed how far the talent gap was between what I could actually do and my childhood dreams, that summer playing trombone was as close as I came in high school to replicating what it must feel like to be an elite basketball player whom everybody likes and wants to please.

1986–87

That good feeling carried over back to life in Chapel Hill at the end of the summer and helped take me into the next phase of growing up. After months of hanging out, Tamar the trumpeter and I started going out that fall, and it's fair to say that friendship defined my junior year of high school. Tamar was the only 16-year-old I knew who read books for fun, books with ideas in them. She had a strong social justice conscience and a very deep love for music, both playing and listening. And she was a basketball fan to boot—even if she was a hybrid Duke/Carolina fan, the Duke allegiance coming from her father's position on the Duke faculty. I didn't care. It wasn't always the easiest of years, but it was one I remain grateful for. Somewhere amidst all the ups and downs involved, my emotions and understanding of other people began, painstakingly, to catch up with the rest of me in the growing up department.

In fact, 1986–87 became the first school year that I did not experience and do not remember primarily in terms of how Carolina did during the basketball season. Going out with Tamar was not the only reason for this. My dad was away for the entire fall: He had been sent by new UNC President C.D. Spangler to Harvard for an advanced management program at the business school there. That left my mom and me alone in the house, with Mom also spending a great deal of time with grandmother Frances. As the anniversary of my grandfather's death approached, Frances sank into a funk, and her depression led her to get physically ill as well for several weeks in November. In the middle of all that, our dog, Franny, got hit by a car and had a broken leg. There was a lot going on that fall.

Of course, I cared very much how well Carolina did once the basketball season started. Yet a lot of the things I remember about 1986–87 are a little different than the previous years. I remember the skeptical smirk Tamar had the morning after I tried to rationalize Carolina's upset loss to UCLA in early December. I remember the game against Illinois in December, in which freshman J.R. Reid had an incredible second half dunk, mainly because my grandmother went to the game, her first and only game in the Smith Center. Leesie Guthridge drove Frances, my mom, and me home after the game. Frances was elated at having gone to the game, and we knew then she was out of her funk. I remember driving home on a Sunday afternoon with Tamar from the All-District band concert in Raleigh we both played in, seeing some 10-year-old kids playing outside on Long Leaf Drive in Chapel Hill, and stopping to ask them who had won the Notre Dame–Carolina game we had missed because of the concert (Notre Dame had), an episode Tamar thought was amusing.

Those are all pretty happy memories. Basketball-wise, the '87 Tar Heels were truly a fantastic team. Apart from UCLA, Carolina annihilated most of their opponents in the first half of the season, and continued to do so in ACC play. In a Saturday night game against a pretty good Georgia Tech team, the Heels played without Kenny Smith, yet had perhaps the closest thing to a perfect game I've ever seen from a Carolina team in winning 92–55. The Sunday morning after that one, we saw Dean Smith at the Chapel Hill Country Club dining room, where we sometimes went after church. As usual, Smith asked my dad how Frances was doing, but then Dad congratulated Smith on the Tech game and Smith thanked him with a wholehearted smile and a twinkle in his eye. He liked what he had seen as much as the rest of us had. The very next game Kenny Smith returned to score 41 points as Carolina rallied to beat second-place Clemson on the road. Carolina went on to finish 14–0 in the conference, 27–2 overall in the regular season.

The first weekend in March in 1987 presented a pleasant, yet very real, quandary for me. I had three options that weekend: I could audition for the All-State honors band in Greensboro, a privilege I had earned by getting third chair trombone in the district. Making that band was not something many folks from CHHS got to do, and it had been a goal of mine. The second choice was to play in a basketball tournament with the Chapel Hill Rec League all-star team, which I had been named to after scoring about 18 or 20 a game for a losing team in the high school age league. The third choice was to go with my dad to Landover, Maryland to see the ACC Tournament.

As was often the case with these things, I hashed out the dilemma with my trombone teacher Bruce Reinoso. The basketball all-star team was quickly (though with some regret) ruled out. That left the choice: audition or ACC tournament. In ethical terms, this seemed to me like a clear-cut case where you had to decide whether life was about your own accomplishments or about watching someone else's. To put it in terms of Kantian ethics, it seemed as though my duty was to forget about the Tar Heels and go to the audition (the outcome of which would be very uncertain). Yet, my inclination was that I wanted to go to the tournament. I loved that team, and I wanted to be there in person to see them win the tournament, after seeing them come so close in 1985. How to decide, then? I might have adopted a prudential self-interest argument, reasoning that if I went to the audition and didn't make it, which was quite likely, I would feel bad about both the audition and what I had missed and so would have the worst possible outcome. But that wasn't an argument Bruce would buy—the risk of the audition was precisely the price of making life about one's own accomplishments.

Instead, Bruce offered me a different way to look at it: Going to the tournament could be a special time with my dad, and that would be valuable in itself. In my self-centeredness, I hadn't thought about the relational consequences of the choice until Bruce put it that way. I just assumed that my parents were truly indifferent to my choices when they would tell me, "It's up to you." It hadn't occurred to me that my dad, who hadn't been around in the fall, would like to have a whole weekend with me, and in Washington, DC, to boot—or that I would like it too, apart from the basketball.

After Bruce offered that way of thinking about it, I decided to stop learning the assigned piece for the audition. Instead, I missed a day of school to go up with Dad to the tournament. Carolina beat Maryland easily on Friday in the noon game. Dad and I stayed for all three of the other quarterfinals. Paul and Mebane Pritchett were there, too, and we sat next to them for those games. The highlights were seeing sixth seed N.C. State upset Duke, and then Wake Forest rallying in the second half behind Muggsy Bogues to beat second seed Clemson. I walked into the concourse after that game and saw a grown man in Clemson orange crying unabashedly. It was the best team Clemson had had since 1980, and the Tigers looked favorites to at least make only the second tournament final in the school's history. (Clemson has never won the ACC tournament.) Instead, they lost in the first round. I felt bad for the fan. The ACC Tournament can be a cruel spectacle.

Dad and I got there early the next day for the semifinal against Virginia. While sitting in the Carolina section at the Capital Centre, I sort of struck up a conversation with Bill Cobey for about 20 minutes before the game. Cobey had been the athletic director at UNC before becoming a Republican congressman from the North Carolina 4th District. But Cobey had been beaten by Democrat David Price in November 1986, a fact I wasn't unhappy about. Nonetheless, Cobey and I had a fairly in-depth theological conversation that day before the game. He really wanted to know what I thought about the Bible and what theological books I had read, and he related his own views. He came across as an incredibly sincere religious conservative, and I was impressed. All of which made me feel slightly foolish a couple of hours later when I jumped up and down and hugged Dad spontaneously when Scott Williams flipped in a hook shot at the buzzer to force a second overtime. I sort of worried that maybe Cobey, sitting right behind us, observed this and thought I cared more about basketball than the Bible. (At that moment, I undoubtedly did.)

But that anxiety was short-lived. Carolina went on to win, and I bounded out into the concourse after the game whooping and hollering. Then I sat with Paul Pritchett and watched Wake and State play to double overtime as well. Unfortunately, Wake didn't win, but certainly beating State would be a piece of cake, I thought, especially after dodging the bullet Virginia had thrown at the Tar Heels. And, I added on the way back to the hotel, I don't think Kenny Smith is going to miss any more foul shots like he had against Virginia. Carolina just couldn't have that. The narrative firmly planted in my head was of Kenny Smith going out a national champion in his senior year, just like Jimmy Black had five years earlier.

The next morning, Sunday, Dad and I ventured out to the National Mall in Washington, and then walked over to the brand new Vietnam Veterans Memorial. It was a beautiful, earliest wisp-of-spring morning. People placed flowers under names on the wall as a few hard-done-by veterans milled around the area, anxious for a quarter, a dollar, anything. I think I produced a coin or two, but it wasn't enough to keep me from feeling a little cognitive dissonance as well as some guilt about the fact that I cared more about basketball than about where those guys had slept the night before.

But those difficult thoughts slipped from the mind as we went back to the hotel, and then went out to the arena. We got there about an hour early and saw J.R. Reid and Scott Williams joking around and practicing shots from mid-court before the game. Several Carolina fans had signs made up saying, "17–0!" It looked certain to be a sweet day for anyone who loved Carolina blue.

But it wasn't. Carolina played a lead-footed first half and allowed State to take a 32–25 lead, as the likes of Chucky Brown and Mike Giomi put up strong games for the Pack. Carolina played harder, sharper and for the most part better in the second half, but State, a legitimately talented team that hadn't yet put it together, was playing with confidence too. Carolina trailed by a point but had the ball with just over 10 seconds to go. Carolina could not get the ball in to Kenny Smith, but instead in-bounded to Wolf, who came forward and took an uncomfortable looking 18-footer that missed badly. There was a mad scramble for the ball, and coming up with it was none other than Ranzino Smith. Ranzino had an open look at the basket and for a second a storybook ending to end all storybook endings looked possible. But Z's shot, a little hurried, missed everything and the State players had a mob scene on the court. Dean Smith said after the game that Kelsey Weems' denial of Kenny Smith on the inbounds play made the difference—Kenny would have found a way to get to the basket or make a play.

It was an empty, empty feeling walking away from that gym. The kind of feeling that causes the facial muscles to automatically form a frown. Dean Smith, in an uncharacteristic expression of his own disappointment, was filmed placing his hand in the lens of a TV camera. We filed out into the parking lot, had to sit in the car awhile before traffic cleared, then made the drive home. I felt a little better when we stopped at some fast-food place, saw some other Carolina fans making the same sad trip, and shared the news that Carolina would be playing Penn in the first round of the NCAAs on Thursday. The announcement of the next opponent provided a frame of reference to look forward to besides what had just happened, and it helped a little.

Homeroom was glum the next morning. Tony Yount said he had talked to Ranzino and that Z wished he had set his feet, wished he had known there was time to set his feet, before shooting. It was now five years and counting without an ACC Tournament championship, titles that had come like clockwork in the late 70s and early 80s.

Optimism returned within a week. After deciding to play defense in the second half, Carolina crushed Ivy champs Penn in the first round in Charlotte. Unfortunately, senior Curtis Hunter was injured in garbage time and lost for the year, a disappointing end to Hunter's career. Word then came out that Joe Wolf might miss the second round game against Michigan with an ankle injury, and I became seriously terrified. This great team was in danger of having it all end, and so soon! But when game time came, Wolf played and played well, and Carolina put on an impressive offensive exhibition in blowing away the Wolverines.

So Carolina was back in the Sweet 16. And to double the good news, Chapel Hill High had won the Eastern regional and advanced to the 4-A state basketball championship game, to be played the following Saturday in the Smith Center. I was the sports editor that year of *The Proconian*, the student newspaper, and we had run a picture of this tall German exchange student named Henrik Rodl in the basketball preview issue. I had spotted Henrik the very first day of school and like everyone else asked, "Who is that guy?" To my later regret, I never went up and said hello to him those first few days of school, even though he always had a smile on his face and seemed approachable. I did find out that he played basketball and was going to be on the team at CHHS. After the first couple of days of practice, I asked my friend Ron Wiegerink, a backup forward on the varsity, how good this guy was. Ron said with a big smile, "He's really good." With Rodl playing small forward (leading the team in points, rebounds, and assists) and future Division I guard Major Geer leading the way, Chapel Hill High cruised through the season with only one loss. When the March issue came out, we ran a picture of the Dean Dome on the back with a caption "In the Tigers' future?" And now it had come true. I was an incredibly lazy sports editor— Demetrius Alston, another student in journalism class, wrote all the basketball stories. All I contributed was in helping interview Ken Miller and in putting together a story about the season as a whole when it was over. But to have a potential state champion to write about—that was pretty neat by any standard, regardless of what was going on with the Tar Heels. I even got issued a pass to sit in one of the boxes at the Smith Center being used by the media during the finals.

But the Tar Heels were still by far the top basketball priority, and morale was back at a peak level when Carolina dispatched Notre Dame in the Sweet 16 to avenge their earlier loss. The two huge dunks near the end by J.R. Reid, who had scored 31 points, were talked about all day long at school on Friday. That Saturday morning, I went to orchestra rehearsal as usual at Hill Hall, then stopped by to see my grandmother in Glen Lennox. It was a clear, windy day with a nice Carolina blue sky. I sat there talking with Frances, eating one of the ice cream sundaes she always had stored away. The words "Final Four" kept bouncing through my head. I had a contented, relaxed feeling, and thought to myself, you should really enjoy this whole day, this is special.

And perhaps it was, but again for the wrong reason. Syracuse was a much better team than anyone in Chapel Hill knew. Jeff Lebo was ill and ineffective during the game. Meanwhile, freshman Derrick Coleman took out his jealousy of J.R. Reid's media hype by dominating the glass. Carolina played hard and had a good look from Kenny Smith to tie the game in the last minute, but Smith's shot from the corner, though dead-on, hit the back iron, and Carolina never got another chance. The Tar Heels had lost again, another upset in March.

> "I watched the 1987 Elite Eight with Syracuse with my dad. I cried hard after it was over. After it ended, I can still hear Jim Nantz in the studio say how a great UNC senior class would never go to a Final Four. That was like driving a stake right through my heart. And my dad looked at his crying son and said, 'Whoa, you really wanted those guys to win'."
>
> —Dan Crotchett, 23, student in Greenville, SC

I was absolutely crushed. I remember calling over to Tamar's house a few minutes after the game to see about meeting up at the Chapel Hill High game in a couple of hours, and barely being able to speak as I talked to her father, who told me he understood how bad I must feel. I pulled myself together and drove to the big temple of light blue, whose regular tenants had just experienced such a major disappointment. And to my surprise, the many CHHS students and parents who were there were all in good spirits, able to put the Carolina game out of mind, excited about the game at hand, and a smile returned to my face. Chapel Hill High beat West Charlotte to win the state title, as Rodl was brilliant running the four corners in the fourth quarter.

> "At a charity game in 1987, in which Joe Wolf and Kenny Smith played, there was a little boy who looked to be about five years old standing at half court on the sidelines, wearing a #30 jersey that hung down to his ankles, admiring the Jet as he ran up and down with the team. Finally, Kenny noticed the boy, and as he ran past, 'high-fived' him. As soon as Kenny's hand left the boy's, the kid—with his hand still in the air—started jumping up and down, and he jumped up and down all the way across the half-court line. I remember Kenny looking back and seeing this kid and breaking into a big grin. I remember thinking that the kid would probably never wash his hand again, and how much the high-five must have meant to him."
>
> —"Terri Tarheel" (Internet handle for a 45-year-old female paralegal), Jacksonville, NC

I was really happy for the team and for the school and didn't feel so awful about the day, all told, when it was over. But the next morning, the disappointment of the Syracuse loss hit me again with full force when I looked at the morning papers.

*

But life went on. By the spring of junior year in high school, the idea of "college" and "getting into college" suddenly loomed very, very large, no longer just a background thought that you might invoke in order to force yourself to do homework during lunch. I had had very clear messages from a pretty early age that my parents did not want me or my siblings to go to UNC. They wanted all of us to get out of Chapel Hill and see something else, and I think they specifically wanted to be sure George and I got away from UNC sports. And so they had worried when I messed up in a couple of classes as a sophomore and had a somewhat erratic performance in chemistry as a junior. I worried a whole lot less about it until maybe the tail end of the applications process.

In 1987, I again spent the summer where my trombone would take me, which in this case was to Governor's School West in Winston-Salem, where I played in the orchestra. Tom Williams was there too, in social studies, and Kunda Biswas, a trombonist who had sat next to me in band for four years, was there in science. It was good to have friends from Chapel Hill there, but the real benefit was meeting bright kids from all over North Carolina, which I hadn't really done before. The way the school worked was that we would go to a philosophy-type class in the morning which involved a cross-section of students from all specialties, then spend the rest of the day in our focus area. Most everyone was friendly, and most folks who cared about such things were Carolina fans, with a minority of State fans and no open Duke fans that I can remember. There were some decent quality pickup basketball games, and a good group of us arranged to borrow a TV to see the UNC–UCLA alumni game played that summer, which was fun. What I most enjoyed, however, was being exposed to a bunch of interesting ideas—both the folks running the orchestra and the director of the school got a kick out of trying to provoke students. I didn't improve as much on the trombone as in previous summers, but it was still six weeks well spent.

1987–88

After corresponding faithfully all summer, Tamar and I split up at the start of the new school year. We still saw a lot of each other through music, however, and with a little time our friendship survived and thrived.

That helped make for a rather different senior year, and one which served as a pretty good bridge to college. Chapel Hill High in those days was known for letting seniors get away with creative schedules, and I took advantage. I didn't take band first semester senior year, but instead took a Latin course at Carolina three days a week with Professor Sara Mack. I would make the short drive from the high school to the UNC campus during lunch period, and then when I returned to

CHHS, got credit in a high school Latin class for studying and occasionally helping the students in Latin IV, which I had already taken.

Adding to the sense that we were practically in college already was the practice several folks I knew had of going to Davis Library on UNC's campus to "study" on weeknights. I started doing it too, which helped me make some new friends like Karen Price, Aeon Schmoock and Kari Barnes. People who had the same classes could talk about the Ibsen play, or collaborate on math homework, and so on. But most of all we could just talk and enjoy being away from our parents' grasp. We looked for all intents and purposes indistinguishable from Carolina students, and by now most folks lived pretty independent lives, with a car of some description (I drove the family heirloom, a 1971 red VW), perhaps a job, but in any case a lot of places to go and things to do as soon as the bell rang at 3:15.

Another perk of senior year was getting to take Fred Kiger's AP American History class. Fred Kiger was and perhaps still is the single most popular person in the town of Chapel Hill not to have been a scholarship athlete. Mr. Kiger had two careers going: the first as a junior high and then a high school history teacher, the second in sports television and radio production. Kiger had been a statistician for the basketball team as an undergraduate at UNC in the 1970s, and went on to work in a variety of capacities for television and radio producers of UNC and ACC basketball. In 1987, in fact, he was the color man to Woody Durham's play-by-play on the UNC football broadcasts, and he took a leave of absence from school in the winter of 1988 to help cover the Olympics for ABC. When he was around, Kiger befriended more or less everyone he came into contact with. Kiger's classroom was covered with an eclectic variety of historical, especially Civil War, memorabilia, mixed in with sports mementoes and a poster of the movie character Freddie Kreuger. And class was usually as laid back as the environment: AP History consisted less of lecture than guided conversation about what we were reading about in the textbook. Every so often, review sessions would be mixed in with games of "trash ball." Just about as often, Kiger would spend a few minutes in class shooting the breeze about what was going on with Carolina and the different players and ex-players. One day, this went on for about 25 or 30 minutes before Fred asked us, "O.K., how are we going to move from this back into American history?" I was proud of myself for pointing out that John Kuester was now coaching at George Washington University, which set us back on track.

*

But more serious things were going on that fall, beyond the usual senior fare of college application worries and the like. October brought the unspeakable news that sophomore center Scott Williams' parents had died in a murder-suicide after an argument in California. Williams, on the advice of his brother, stayed with the team and was taken literally into the care of the Carolina basketball program, in an example of the Smith ethos at its best. The rest of the season one could look at Williams and only guess at what was going on inside his head and heart.

That fall also brought a couple of brushes with the realities of university politics which helped relieve me of naiveté about Chapel Hill and the institution around which it is built. The first case at hand was that of Dick Crum, the North Carolina football coach who had followed five strong seasons with four pretty average teams, and perhaps equally important had not won over a lot of impartial observers with his personality. Impatience boiled over after an upset loss to Wake Forest and then a close home defeat to Clemson, when a win would have put UNC in position to win a league title. One night in the week following that game, I heard my dad, now promoted to university provost, talking to the chancellor about what was going to be done about it. By the time it got to that stage, the ultimate outcome was no longer in doubt: It was a matter of when and how Crum would be pushed out, not if. Boosters had already lined up to arrange a buy-out. The story was all but out of the bag when the 5–5 Tar Heels took the field against Duke in the season finale, then played a listless, depressing game that Duke won easily. It was difficult to watch a once-successful coach go out like that, with an uninspired performance and with little sympathy from anyone (save for Crum loyalist John Kilgo, who gave Crum a very nice valedictory on the coach's last TV show after the Duke game).

Yet just two hours after that Duke game, it was a distant memory: The big news instead was how a North Carolina team without suspended J.R. Reid and Steve Bucknall had beaten No. 1 Syracuse in the Hall of Fame Tipoff Classic, with Ranzino Smith winning event MVP honors. Dean Smith had pulled one out of the hat again. The contrast between Carolina football and Carolina basketball was never starker than it was on that November day.

The other piece of university politics struck even closer to home. In August, Christopher Fordham had announced his retirement as Chancellor of UNC, and Provost and former Dean of Arts and Sciences Sam Williamson became the leading in-house candidate to succeed him. The fact that Dad had been sent by C.D. Spangler to the advanced management program at Harvard Business School the previous year solidified the perception that he would be the university system president's preferred choice as well. But it was far, far from a "done deal," and Dad knew it. So early on that fall, he had a conversation with me telling me that he was going to go for it, but he wasn't too sure what would happen and we would live with it either way. The chancellor search was well down the list of things I thought about that school year, but it formed a sort of background drama. I thought it was pretty likely that it would work out for my dad, but I didn't dwell on it and talked with other people about it only rarely.

*

Against that backdrop, the 1987–88 season as a whole seemed pretty unremarkable, other than the ongoing story of Scott Williams. Unlike the previous two seasons, no one seriously thought this team could cut down the nets at the end of March. Yet given the talent and experience lost, it was a remarkably good year. Carolina won the ACC regular season outright with an 11–3 record. The losses included a shock defeat to Wake in Greensboro and a last-second loss to Duke at home when Robert Brickey blocked Jeff Lebo's jumper at the buzzer.

The most memorable game for me was an overtime victory over N.C. State at home. Carolina won in a very well-played game after State had used some late hot shooting from Rodney Monroe to wipe out a Tar Heel lead and force an extra session. My friends Karen Price and Kari Barnes were at the game, sitting next to Dean Smith's parents in the loge directly above the corner where the scoreboard rested. Karen had those seats because her father was the U.S. Congressman from the 4th District, and the chief of staff of David Price's North Carolina office was Joan Ewing—Dean Smith's sister. Kari was there not just as Karen's best friend but because she was a State fan. At the end of the game, Kari sat there glumly in her N.C. State t-shirt, but Dean Smith's mother Vesta leaned over and told her, "You played a really good game."

Temple played an even better game when they came to town a few weeks later on a Sunday afternoon. The Owls blew North Carolina off the court in the second half. When the game was over, Carolina's players ran back into the dressing room silently, the coaches walked back into the tunnel with a frown, and then the sportswriters came, looking absolutely shocked. I dwelled there for a couple of extra minutes, soaking it all in, even though it was a loss. Why? Because it was my last game turning the scoreboard after six years. I was going to miss the Clemson finale (and Ranzino Smith's last game) because of an All-District band weekend. I was reluctant to put the scoreboard up when the clock ran under a minute, and the usher had to come prod us with about 45 seconds to go to get moving. There was still a slight chance Carolina might get sent back to the Smith Center to play NCAA first and second round games (the no-home-court rule had not yet been implemented), but I knew this was probably it.

One interesting new wrinkle to the season was a friendship with my pre-calculus tutor Mark McCombs, who taught math at UNC. Mark was an excellent teacher and a huge, huge Carolina basketball fan who later became a regular tutor for the basketball team. My need for help in pre-calculus was a direct result of my lack of motivation and propensity to spend much of second period passing notes to friends while our teacher Bud Stuart solved equations on the board. Mark would come over on Sunday afternoons and we'd usually talk about Carolina for about 10 minutes, do math problems for about an hour, then shoot baskets for a while (Mark was a worthy one-on-one opponent). Of course, the formula varied a little bit—when Mark came over about an hour after Duke beat Carolina in the season finale, we both vented about the game and some of the calls. That actually probably made it a little easier to concentrate on the math part that day.

The first weekend of March 1988 presented the same dilemma I had faced in 1987. The ACC Tournament, an audition for the all-state honors band, and the rec league all-star team tournament all fell on the same weekend. But as it worked out, the audition was at a high school outside Greensboro, not very far from the Greensboro Coliseum and the tournament. We got there midway through the first of half of Carolina's win over Maryland.

Mom had been very kind to let me share her ticket with my friends the first two days, but an ACC Final was worthy of her attention, and so Mom, Dad, and I drove to Greensboro Sunday morning fully expecting to finally see Carolina win an ACC title in person and avoid a third loss to Duke. I had gotten a phone call Saturday night saying I had made the honors band in the audition—surely that was a good omen that this would be a perfect weekend. It looked good for Carolina at halftime and early in the second half. Duke was tired, and Carolina had a working single-digit lead. Coach K tried to shake things up by substituting five players with about 15 minutes to go.

The move worked. After that substitution, momentum changed. For a long stretch beginning at about the 10- or 11-minute mark, Carolina simply could not get a basket against Duke's half-court defense. The nadir came with about seven minutes to play, when Steve Bucknall received a pass wide open underneath the basket, then dribbled the ball off his own foot and out of bounds. Duke entered the final minute with the upper hand, with the ball and ahead by a basket. In a brilliant defensive play, J.R. Reid poked the ball from behind out of Danny Ferry's hands. Carolina had a fast break chance with freshman King Rice leading the way. But a Duke defender got back to make Rice lay it up at an awkward angle. The shot missed, and Duke recovered. Bill Guthridge jumped up from the Carolina bench absolutely irate that there had been no foul called on Rice's shot, yelling at the officials. Duke hit its free throws and won the game.

The same, involuntary frown as a year before came back over me. Except this year it was worse. The 1987 State loss was something of a fluke and was immediately recognized as such by everyone. No State fan was very likely to rub it in too hard after that win. This was a different story—a grudge match between two archrivals whose individual players were said not to like each other so much. And the Duke fans were very, very quick to start talking about their "triple crown" as the crowd filed out after the game. That was tough to swallow. It was also hard to believe that Carolina hadn't won the ACC Tournament in six years—or that Ranzino Smith, the local hero, would graduate without a title.

Duke also got the spoils of victory, namely the No. 2 seed in the East with first-round games in Chapel Hill. Carolina was sent West to play North Texas State. The Thursday the tournament started, both Fred Kiger and I missed school to be at the Smith Center. Kiger was working for CBS on the production, and I would be wiping sweat on the floor, a role I had assumed once or twice over the years during Carolina games when someone hadn't shown up. One of the afternoon games was a great near-upset involving N.C.A&T and Syracuse. A&T led most of the game, and their fans were raucous—the place at points during the game was as loud as any Carolina game that season. But the Orangemen pulled ahead late to win going away. Derrick Coleman, who had come over and simply taken the sweat towel out of my hands without asking like the other players did, started taunting one of the Aggies at the foul line, which told me all I needed to know about Derrick Coleman.

Then the Blue Devils hit the court that night. It was a much fuller house, though not any louder, as Duke handled Boston University easily. There was one highlight, however. At one point, after a player had dived on the court, I had to run out to the hash mark during a stoppage. After I wiped the sweat up, I heard Danny Ferry say, "Excuse me sir, can I use your towel?" I pretended not to hear him and ran back to the sideline, not turning to see the look on his face. What can I say—instinct took over. Two days later, Rhode Island upset Syracuse in a thriller, and I bolted to Raleigh for a trombone lesson, not bothering to stick around for Duke's easy win in the second round.

Meanwhile, Carolina had dispatched North Texas State. But serious worries lay ahead: Loyola Marymount, the run-and-gunners. No one knew what to expect against the Lions. The Friday night before the game, I sat on the couch quietly, looking out the window, knowing that Dean Smith was working on some way to handle the shot-every-five-seconds style of LMU. I wondered if it would work, nervous that Smith's coaching reputation was on the line in some measure. A loss to LMU would not be easily forgotten by anyone.

I needn't have worried so much. Carolina blew out to a 65–40 halftime lead and eventually won 123–97. Ranzino Smith had 27 points as well as his first and only dunk as a collegian. For about a week, I had the VCR set at the spot where he went in for the stuff. Carolina then flew out to Seattle for a rematch with Michigan in the Sweet 16. Playing against the same core players who would win the national title a year later, Carolina pulled out a victory, as J.R. Reid had a tremendous game, including a tap-in of a missed free throw with about a minute to go. The game was played late on Friday night, and afterwards, as was the habit after big wins, I went outside to shoot hoops, and was joined by David Moreau and the crew of people watching over at his place. John Payne was especially psyched, saying that was a "serious win." We played three on three for about an hour, riding the high that only a hard-fought NCAA victory can produce.

Unlike a year before, I felt little anticipation before the regional final against top seed Arizona, only a largely unsuccessful attempt to think that just maybe Carolina could spring the big upset. There was a youth orchestra concert at Hill Hall to play, which ended conveniently just before tip-off. Carolina had a two-point lead in a close, defensive-minded first half but had missed a chance to be up by more before halftime. The second half was a nightmare, as the combined forces of Steve Kerr, Sean Elliot and Tom Tolbert put together a run that Carolina simply couldn't match. Arizona ended up winning by 17. It was hard to watch. A crestfallen Ranzino Smith was interviewed with a towel over his head after the game, saying that he would never experience what it's like to play in a Final Four or win a championship. Steve Bucknall said that it would be up to the guys returning on the team to figure out what it took to break through to the next level.

*

It's fair to say that by 1988, I had reached a point where the basis for being happy day in and day out, the basis for my self-esteem, was not very dependent on whether Carolina won or lost—so long as there wasn't a prolonged losing streak to deal with. The proportion of time I spent thinking about Carolina basketball was starting to decrease. And the time I spent thinking about politics increased rapidly. By my senior year, I thought of myself as a social justice activist/writer in the making. I joined Tamar, her friend Beca Carter, and a few others in the "Human Rights and World Issues Club" at school, which met once a week at lunch to write Amnesty International letters of appeal for prisoners or to hear a speaker. Betsy Dawson, my Latin teacher, was the adviser and organizer.

One day an activist named Patrick O'Neill came to talk to us. Patrick had recently completed a jail sentence for a protest against nuclear weapons at an arms plant. He gave a very memorable talk

Warren Martin guards the basket as Thad Williamson, James Clark, and Neal Harrell operate the manual scoreboard during the 1985–86 season.

illustrating the amount of resources going to military purposes as opposed to human needs and told us that working for "peace" should be our "sixth course" if we were taking five courses. I didn't see Patrick again for a while, but I didn't forget him either—or fail to notice that he made a living in part by writing sports articles for *The Chapel Hill Newspaper*.

The 1988 presidential election provided another focus of attention. I was the only one in the crowd of young white liberals at CHHS I knew who supported Jesse Jackson—so much so that I handed out Jesse literature at school. There had been a presidential candidate "forum" on education issues held at the Smith Center in the fall of 1987, and Jackson impressed me the most. Most of the other folks I knew who were politically conscious, like Karen Price, favored Michael Dukakis as the Democratic candidate, on grounds that he had a better chance of winning in November. In the process of trying to defend my attachment to Jackson, I made myself well-versed in the different issues, what I thought, and how Jackson's views fit my own closer than the others. I was at a moment where any new piece of information, or any new angle at all would be fresh stimulation and force me to think things through again. My biases were pretty fixed, but my exact views were not. It was a stimulating time from that point of view, the process of becoming a political junkie.

But that didn't mean I stopped being a basketball junkie. A few weeks after the season ended, Dad invited me to come with him to a part of Carolina basketball I hadn't seen before—the season-ending banquet, held in the Smith Center. It was going to be Ranzino Smith's goodbye. After the various awards were given out, including outstanding senior to Smith, Ranzino took the microphone to give his valedictory speech. It went well, until near the end it became clear Z was reluctant to end it, didn't quite know how to wrap it up and say good-bye. Finally, he did.

Afterwards, Dad told me that what Ranzino had just had to do was one of the toughest things anyone has to do, to say goodbye to a time in their life that was special to them, that meant everything, at a moment when the future was uncertain, and that Smith had done well. But neither of us knew at that moment that before very long all the Williamsons would soon be in Ranzino's shoes.

Shortly afterward, the word came that the chancellor search committee would not include Dad's name among the two sent to University President C.D. Spangler for consideration. Instead, two outside candidates were forwarded. If Dad had been included in the list, the ultimate outcome would have been inevitable. But it didn't happen. The news was the top headline in *The Chapel Hill Newspaper*, where Dad was quoted, in his one parting shot, saying he was "disappointed for myself and for the University." The day we learned the outcome, the Moreaus, the Simpsons, and other family friends all came over. It was almost as if it were a funeral. I wasn't happy, but I wasn't deeply upset, either, until a private moment with Dad that afternoon, in which he told me that he hadn't told my grandmother Frances yet, and how hard that was going to be.

Frances was a big part of the story of how someone from the paper mill town of Springhill, Louisiana could end up with a doctorate from Harvard and in a top academic position at a major university. To take one example, when my father was in high school, there wasn't a chapter of the National Honor Society at Springhill High School—so Frances started one, mainly so Dad could be in it. That kind of assertiveness carried over into her other commitments as well: while no radical activist, she had been an early advocate of sex education and integrated schools in Louisiana, and was unbending in her devotion to the Presbyterian Church and the American Bible Society. She had an ethic of leadership, and a value system in which education was at the pinnacle, both of which had carried over into my dad.

And so at that moment, it hit me that even at age 52, Dad still cared about the pride his mother would feel if he were named the chancellor—and that he was worried that the slight to her pride might be worse than the slight to his own.

So it was a tough few days. But we were fortunate to have so many close friends there for us offering support, including kind words from Fordham, Spangler, and William Friday, which meant a lot at the time. And my grandmother proved she still had a pretty thick skin. I personally didn't feel any resentment toward UNC or anything like that, even though my understanding of what had happened was that there had been a political power play. But most fortunate of all, another door opened for my parents to walk through, a door that made just as much sense in terms of their own narrative history and life callings as the UNC job, perhaps even more. Dad interviewed for and was offered the job as President at Sewanee, the University of the South, an Episcopal-funded liberal arts college and theology school in Tennessee. My uncle, Thad Andress, and four of my cousins had gone to school there, and my parents had taken an "education for ministry" class based on material developed at Sewanee. The job was a chance to blend academic administration and the exercise of leadership with a faith mission. It was a good fit, and within a couple of weeks Dad was announced as the new vice-chancellor and president at Sewanee.

It's very difficult for me to imagine what would have happened if the UNC committee had gone the other way. Certainly, my parents have not spent a great deal of time looking back. At Sewanee, my parents had their share of headaches, but they were spared the media scrutiny that comes with the Chapel Hill job: They worked hard but had time to rest and be themselves. There was a lot of money to raise, and theologians to wrestle with, but there wasn't a medical school, or a business school, or a multi-million dollar athletic department to worry about. Sewanee turned out to be a blessing in my parents' lives.

As for me, the fact that my parents moved away from Chapel Hill the year I graduated from high school was a blessing in just this sense: I left Chapel Hill before I got sick of it, before the mostly positive impressions in my mind about the town could be cluttered. If every time I went home, Dad had been running around Chapel Hill managing crises while *The News and Observer* wrote articles about him and various groups on campus criticized him, maybe I would have come to feel differently about the place.

In fact, a short time before my parents made their plans, I had finalized my own: I would be following my brother's footsteps to go to Brown University in Providence, Rhode Island. My trombone tape and the application claim that I would major in the underutilized field of Latin (a ruse Mom thought of) apparently offset the imperfections in the transcript, and after checking out the school one more time I was happy to go north.

Apart from the usual end-of-high school stuff and graduation—in the Smith Center—there were two more really notable events before I left Chapel Hill. The first was giving a sermon on "Youth Sunday" in late May at the Church of the Holy Family. Every year one or more seniors from the youth group would give the sermon—both George and Treeby had done it, and I always assumed I would, too. I was the only one my year who wanted to—David Simpson and Drew Partin didn't want to, neither did John or Melissa Payne. (Paul Pritchett and his family had moved to Atlanta before our senior year.) We all had shown up pretty faithfully every Sunday at 6 p.m. throughout junior high and high school, even though we had a lot of different leaders and not a great deal of consistency in what we did, other than eating. Laura Simpson, Jenny Partin, and Megan Guthridge were almost always there too. (One time, the leaders had us pretend we were members of other people's families, and I got handed the role of playing "Bill Guthridge" at home. Megan said I had it all wrong. I had better luck playing David Simpson's dad, as I recall.)

David Simpson and I had come up through the ranks the whole way at Holy Family, from pre-kindergarten through everything the church had to offer, and now this was the last step. In the sermon I said that it was a blessing to grow up in the church—but that I also thought the church was irrelevant to too many of my peers at school. But more lasting probably than the message was just the sense of looking out into the congregation, seeing my parents, the Simpsons, the Fultons, the Guthridges, and all the other families I had grown up with in Holy Family, and recognizing that I had a stake in all these people, and that they had a stake in me—and in David, Drew, John, and Melissa. And that sense wasn't just a feel-good warm fuzzy pronouncement of community either. It was a recognition of the fact that over many years the church and its members had shared in the task of teaching, nurturing, sometimes scolding us—and above all, conveyed to us that we belonged to the church, and that they cared about us.

The second notable event was a summer internship I started the week after high school ended, in David Price's constituent office in Raleigh. Three days a week, I drove over there to work about five or six hours, under the supervision of Joan Ewing, a truly wonderful person who made me feel appreciated out of all proportion to what I actually contributed to the enterprise. Capping the summer was the Democratic Convention in Atlanta—I went and worked as a volunteer security guard, checking credentials and seeing at close range just about every prominent liberal politician in the country. Karen Price was there of course and we caroused around late after the convention was over. I felt sure the Democrats would win this time—as sure as I had felt about Carolina making the Final Four and winning the whole thing again in 1987. Despite what had happened in November 1984, I hadn't fully absorbed the lesson that in politics, frustration outruns fulfillment just as much as it does in basketball.

But by 1988, I could honestly say that given a choice between a Democratic president and Carolina winning the NCAA title in 1989, I would have taken the Democrat, without thinking twice. Which is simply another way of stating that at the end of the long process of character formation I had gone through growing up in Chapel Hill, basketball was still very important to me— but other things were even more important. My parents and the surrounding institutions didn't allow me to think that life could be lived vicariously through other people's accomplishments, or that the only meaningful accomplishments were those you could reach playing a sport.

And with regard to Carolina basketball, I had come to understand that what made it special, that what made it worthy of our attention and loyalty, was precisely that it seemed to express the town's own best values, its own best picture of itself, the right way of doing things in the world. I also understood that Carolina basketball was not the work of gods or of far-off Hollywood producers, but very human products of very human people, some of whom my family knew. I knew that Chapel Hill didn't live up to its own best image of itself in all respects, that the genuinely progressive sensibilities of the town rested upon inequalities of class and race which high school ended up reproducing rather than mitigating, and that sometimes people in Chapel Hill became complacent about real human problems both inside and outside the town's borders, just as the Smith Center crowd sometimes got complacent at games. By that time, I probably, if pressed hard enough, even would have conceded that Carolina basketball itself didn't always live up to its own best ideals, either. But awareness of flaws in one's community and best institutions need not detract from love and appreciation of them any more than awareness of flaws in one's own self or closest kin means you love yourself or your family any less.

In Book VIII of *The Politics*, Aristotle's book about the constitutions of city-states, the philosopher writes that "it is not right that any of the citizens should think that he belongs just to himself." Rather, it should be recognized that the city-state has a stake in the citizens, and the citizens a stake in the city-state. By 1988, an irreversibly large part of my identity—who I was—was wrapped up in Chapel Hill. But after leaving town, I couldn't readily participate in its activities, in its politics, in its civic life in any regular way. I could, however, continue to participate in Carolina basketball by following the team, and know that in cheering for the team I was also cheering for the community I grew up in, and all the people in Chapel Hill—peers and elders alike—who, knowingly or not, had made contributions to my life and come to have a "share" in it.

2

College and All That, 1988–1994

During college, Carolina basketball was pretty far down the list of my priorities—behind class work, trombone activities, various forms of political activism, writing a column on political issues for a student newspaper, and perhaps right on par with intramural sports. Which is ironic, because just about anyone who knew me well at Brown knew I was a huge Carolina basketball fan and that my mood was directly affected by how well Carolina did. My roommate freshman year wasn't into sports and didn't understand it at all, which was fine. But an African-American math major from New York City named Malik Sievers totally understood, and even better he had a TV, so we became fast friends. I watched Carolina finally win the ACC Tournament in 1989 in Malik's room, and got a lot of strange looks when I started yelling up and down the halls like it was Teague Dorm when Danny Ferry missed his desperation shot and Carolina won 77–74. I also watched Carolina lose the heartbreaker to Glen Rice and Michigan in the Sweet 16 in Malik's room, along with my friend Dan Shuster. Dan was from Bloomington, Indiana, and his feelings about the Hoosiers were pretty close to how I felt about the Tar Heels. Indiana lost that night too, and he was profoundly grateful when I told him that he should feel good about Indiana's season, that they had over-achieved in winning the Big Ten. The two of us went out to walk the streets and share our melancholy.

A key challenge throughout my four years in Providence was to find someone who had cable television and would be willing to let me watch the ESPN Carolina games at their place. Trying to see the locally broadcast games via satellite was out of the question at that point—I was content to call up a 1–900 sports service for those scores. (I could read in detail about the games I didn't see in *Carolina Blue,* the weekly newspaper that I was delighted to get every week.) For 1989, I had a stroke of good luck in befriending a Maryland fan named Steve Berman, who was a senior, lived off-campus, and had cable. One day in a section meeting for a history class, I started scribbling down the names of Carolina's returning players and projecting how much playing time they would get, as I often did when a little bored during class. Steve looked over my shoulder at my notes, noticed I had written down "Lebo, Reid, Bucknall" etc. in my notes, and struck up a conversation after class. Steve was glad to have anyone who cared about ACC hoops as a friend, and I ended up watching several games at his house.

Steve called me one night that spring to tell me that J.R. Reid was going pro, and I knew then that 1989–90 would be a difficult season. Carolina had an 8–6 start that tested the faith of its fans. However, Carolina put together the first truly cathartic win in the five years of the Smith Center, a 79–60 spanking over Duke marked by George Lynch's 30-foot three point bank shot at the first half buzzer to give the Tar Heels a 45–21 lead. Carolina went on to beat State away in the next game, but it was rough sledding the rest of the year. Going into the last week of the regular season, Carolina was just 6–6 in the conference and in real danger of missing the NCAAs. I nervously called a score service and was delighted to learn that Carolina had somehow beaten an excellent Georgia Tech team by two. Then Carolina beat Duke in Cameron in the regular-season finale—I watched happily on a common room TV with several high school friends of Duke player Greg Koubek. They didn't have much to say when it was over.

A few days later, though, I received a terrible phone call. My friend Dan Shuster from Bloomington, Indiana, who I had seen less of but still considered a close friend, had been found dead in his bathtub after committing suicide. It was a shock, and for the next few days I was in a surreal daze. I met Dan's parents and family after they came to campus, and helped plan and carry out a memorial service on campus. From Dan's apartment, I retrieved one of his prized posses- sions, an audiotape of an Indiana-Michigan game in Assembly Hall in the mid-80s. Dan had been a faculty brat much like myself, and loved going to games in Assembly about as intensely as I loved going to Carmichael. And in the last few conversations we had, Dan would always mention how hopeful he was that Indiana native Eric Montross would become a Hoosier, and how that would signal in a golden era for IU basketball. But Dan had had an incredibly painful life, from early childhood all the way through college, and though we were both religion majors, when he looked into the abyss, he saw something different than I did. Dan was a very gentle and thoughtful per- son, but he wasn't sure that existence was in the end all for the good. I knew that was his philo- sophical temperament, but I didn't know it would find such violent expression.

When something like that happens, you fall back on whatever resources are at hand. And one of the resources at hand for me was the fact that basketball season was still going on. Two days af- ter Dan was found, I took a break from the grieving to watch Carolina lose in overtime to Virginia in the first round of the ACC Tournament. That was one loss of which it truly could be said that I didn't feel worse after the game than before it started—I was happy at least for the two hours while the game was being played. Life went on into the next week. Eric Montross came out and an- nounced for Carolina, and spring break came. I headed by train to New Haven, where my brother was in graduate school at Yale. Carolina had No.1 Oklahoma in the second round NCAA game as a No. 8 seed, trying to make a tenth straight Sweet 16. George and I watched the game on a lounge TV in the graduate student dorm. We were incredibly into the game, so much so that the game be- gan attracting a small crowd of folks wanting to know what was going on. Prayer would not be too strong a word to describe my thoughts in the last minute. When Rick Fox hit his shot at the buzzer to win it, we were jumping up and down hysterically and hugging each other. It was an incredible win for a team that had taken more losses—and more flak—than any Carolina team in at least two decades. And at that particular moment, it was for me a shot of life-affirming elixir.

*

By my junior year, I spent most of my waking hours thinking about and being involved in politics of one kind or another. I entered college with a moral conviction that everyone deserved to have a job, health care, good education, decent housing, and a decent neighborhood environment, and an interest in what sort of policies could achieve those goals. But as time went on, I began to take a more critical view not just of problems of poverty and inequality, but of capitalism as a system. Those evolving views found expression in a weekly column I wrote for a student newspaper, and it found expression in activist activities. During the fall of 1990, library workers at Brown went on strike to keep their Blue Cross/Blue Shield health insurance, and I was a spokesman for the group of students who took the lead in supporting the union's case. That was also the year of the military buildup in the Gulf, and remembering Patrick O'Neill's injunction that peace should be a sixth course, I organized a weekly multi-faith prayer for peace involving Christian, Jewish, and Muslim students.

In terms of leftist students at Brown though, I was probably something of a moderate. I didn't see that defeated factional positions taken in 1917 in Russia had any relevance for the United States, and was too interested in practical alternatives to accept blanket ideological statements. But I still felt angry at American society, angry about the role the American government had played in the various Latin American countries I studied as a double major in history, angry about its bloated military budget, angry about its tolerance of inequality. Yet how angry could I be at a country that had certainly provided me with a great childhood and a lot of opportunities? A sharp cognitive disconnect between my political ideology and the comfortable, mostly happy, upper-middle-class milieu of my family in Chapel Hill began to emerge. This was ironic, because my moral values were shaped entirely by Chapel Hill liberalism. And I never thought that the people and families I knew in Chapel Hill were "the problem"—the folks I knew were all doing honorable work, in education or in a profession or in public service of some kind. For several years I had a hard time reconciling everything I had come to know and believe about American society and my mostly positive appraisal of Chapel Hill, and, for lack of a better term, my parents' world.

I'm pretty sure, however, that my alienation from mainstream American culture would have been a lot more thorough had it not been for my love for Carolina basketball, which never wavered. Unlike soccer-loving leftist intellectuals in Europe, I couldn't claim that support for Carolina represented a form of solidarity with the working class neighborhoods of Manchester or Birmingham or London. I could claim that it represented solidarity with the most progressive elements of the South, however, by pointing to Dean Smith's involvement in civil rights in Chapel Hill and other liberal causes. And in February of 1991, during the Gulf War, when my alienation from the mainstream media and the bulk of national public opinion was at a peak, I drew a little comfort from the fact that North Carolina, unlike many college basketball teams, did not immediately stitch an American flag onto their uniforms when the Gulf War started.

This fact did not go unnoticed—a letter-writer to *The Chapel Hill News* complained that when Dean Smith was asked during a radio call-in show why the flag wasn't on the uniforms, Smith had replied, "Well, why not wear the flag for the homeless and other worthy causes?" The flag finally did go on the uniforms, but I was among what were probably the few Carolina fans who appreciated Smith's initial stance.

And when Carolina did start wearing flags, I didn't think for a second of turning the TV off. In truth, I cared about beating Duke, winning the ACC Tournament, and finally getting back to a Final Four a lot more than about whether the flag was on the uniforms or not. When Carolina did all those things in March of 1991, I certainly wasn't thinking about the war while the games were being played—indeed, I was very, very relieved to have something to think about, a source of meaning, outside of politics. Being involved with both the library strike and to a lesser degree some of the antiwar protests at Brown had been a bruising experience, stressful and at times rough on the ego, mostly because of the internal politics of campus organizing. I was thrilled to get away down to Chapel Hill that March to stay with my sister, now in graduate school at Duke, and see Carolina beat Temple to make the Final Four. I met up with Tom Williams, now a Morehead Scholar at UNC, after the game, went with him to Franklin Street, and soaked in a very different kind of mass gathering in the streets than the ones I had participated in with regard to the war a few weeks earlier in both Providence and Washington. Both kinds of mass gatherings produce their own highs, their own rushes of adrenaline. But on the whole I was happier to partake in a community celebration than in an expression of social conflict.

So much so that I decided to come back to Chapel Hill that summer and attend summer school at Carolina. In Chapel Hill, I stayed in Granville Towers, took a class on the history of religion in the South, and did an internship in the afternoons with the Financial Democracy Campaign, a Durham group which was fighting to make sure that some of the assets seized by the federal government during the savings and loan bailout went to community-based and low-income groups instead of being handed over on the cheap to large financial institutions.

Most nights, I would play basketball on the Granville court. One Friday night, rising sophomore Pat Sullivan and a friend of his from New Jersey were out there and agreed to play another guy and me in a two-on-two game. The court was a little wet, so I ran behind a puddle to get my jumper off over Pat. But I had no hope of guarding him—he shot mostly jumpers, but just to be sure I knew my place he took it in and dunked it one time. It was all really fun, and then we sat around for a couple of hours talking about the season and his high school career and Coach Smith, while taking wild HORSE-style shots from on top of the wall, beside the swimming pool, and so forth. I was impressed with what a nice guy Pat Sullivan was—it was a definite highlight of the summer.

Another highlight was playing in the Granville three-on-three tournament before an audience that included former Carolina player Kevin Madden. Our team—me, my summer roommate, and his sister's boyfriend—were playing a team that featured a 6-8 guy from Carolina's JV squad. Our only hope was to shoot the first available shot, and early on I got hot and hit a couple in a row, including about a 20-footer off one pass, which elicited a verbal reaction from Madden. I was pleased but maintained my game-face cloak of masculine toughness, not smiling. On the next play, the ball came inbounds to me about 10 feet away on the right, and I caught the ball and took a turnaround in one motion. The next thing I knew the basketball was in the adjacent swimming pool, the victim of a massive blocked shot by the 6-8 guy. And that brought a much larger reaction from Madden and the crowd than my little jumper had. All I could do to save face was to go ahead and smile. We lost the game in short order afterwards.

*

I graduated from Brown in 1992 and moved to Washington, DC that summer, in hopes of finding a research or writing job with a progressive political bent. I lucked out big time, thanks to a friend from college who I had known from activist work who was working at the Institute for Policy Studies, a progressive thinktank that was at the very top of my wish list when I moved into town. I applied for a job and ended up getting a paid internship that turned into a full-time job, working for a political economist named Gar Alperovitz on "The Good Society Project." The primary aim of the project was to explore and specify what sort of political and economic institutions progressives should aspire to build so as to bring to life the values of liberty, equality, community, democracy, and ecological sustainability. At the core of this vision lay not a giant state but locally based, democratically governed firms. A secondary aim of the project was to ask how the society might get "from here to there" by building on democratically based economic institutions like worker-owned firms and community land trusts. A third aim was to generate specific policy proposals to help support those kinds of institutions (some of which candidate Bill Clinton had expressed an interest in).

This was great opportunity for me at a time I was somewhat adrift politically and intellectually. I had lost faith in the Democratic Party and was not interested in working for a Congressman or something of that nature—indeed, I had written a couple of blistering articles criticizing Mr. Clinton on the basis of his Arkansas record, saying he had a track record of duplicity. On the other hand, I didn't want to be a sideline critic, a pure academic who has given up making an impact on the world. And I wasn't interested in going overseas to do political work in places like South Africa—I wanted to help change American society. The Good Society job allowed me to focus on long-term, hopeful visions of what the future might conceivably look like, without denying the real problems of the present or falling into the belief held by some radicals that everyday Washington politics and policymaking are essentially irrelevant.

And, unexpectedly, working on the project helped reconcile the tension between my positive assessment of Chapel Hill and my rather harsh assessment of American society. One of the core ideas of the project was that a desirable political-economic system would be one that ensured that geographic communities of substantial size be securely anchored by stable, rooted capital—such as might be provided by a large-scale public institution. Towns and cities with big public universities, state capitals, even county seats tend to have more efficient governments, better outcomes for children, higher quality of life, and to be affected less by economic downturns. At the heart of our critique of the existing political-economic system was the observation that cities not sufficiently anchored by public institutions could be victimized if the private firms providing jobs left town or failed, and that local-level democracy suffers when local politics consists mostly of trying to lure and keep mobile private firms. So what we urged was a policy not so much of building universities in every town but of encouraging more localized and democratic ownership of private capital, to lessen the dependence of communities on the investment decisions of private companies.

Seen in that light, the fact that Chapel Hill was such a nice place to grow up could be seen not as an anomaly but as indicative of how every community might benefit if there were a stable source of good jobs in town, year in and year out, whether the market was up or down, like the university provided. That thought allowed me to regain and indeed deepen my appreciation for the town. Instead of worrying so much about the bourgeois comforts of my family's social milieu and whether they could be justified on ethical grounds, I began to be more appreciative of how rare it was to have a community in which so many families have long-term roots and a real sense of neighborliness. And I came to recognize that the root reason why there could be such stability was the presence of the university. This didn't mean my critical thoughts went away completely. But it was nice to be able to think of my hometown as in at least a partial sense a model for what a good society might look like.

*

There were two additional nice things about moving to Washington, besides the job. The first was that my sister decided to move to D.C. to take a job in the State of North Carolina's Washington office, and she in fact lived just two blocks from me on Connecticut Avenue. Treeby's future husband, Robert (Robbie) Brown, also was in town. He was a big Carolina fan, as was his family, and pretty much always willing to talk about the Tar Heels.

> "In 1993, I remember it was so great after the game just walking up and down Franklin Street in the rain, everybody was just in a great mood and everybody was shaking each other's hands and total strangers were hugging out of happiness. It was Carolina heaven."
> —Craig Stanley, 37, Oak Harbor, Washington

The second nice thing was simply being back within the range of the ACC regional network, which permitted more detailed attention to the Tar Heels than was really possible in Providence. 1992–93 was a magical season, not only because of the final result. The famous comeback to beat Florida State happened on my birthday. When Carolina made the Final Four, Robbie and I drove down to North Carolina to stay with the Simpsons, and I watched the national semifinal on the big screen in Carmichael. The Moreaus, Simpsons, and other Chapel Hill folk were all there, all as happy as I was. I met Tom Kerby up on Franklin Street afterwards and bumped into a lot of high school friends, including Tom Williams, in town from New York, on Franklin Street. Robbie and I headed back to D.C. and work on Sunday, and watched the final against Michigan with Treeby. With about two minutes to play, George called to ask, "Who invented this damn game anyway?" By about 11:15 p.m., the phone was ringing off the hook.

*

A few weeks later on a sunny weekday afternoon, I walked up to Bill Guthridge from behind, tapped him on the back, and said, "Nice to see you here." The location was the Rose Garden at the White House, where the Carolina basketball team and the Texas Tech women's team were being honored by President Clinton as national champions. My cousin, Collier Andress, had worked for Clinton strategist James Carville during the campaign and now had a job in the White House, and she very thoughtfully arranged for me to be invited to the ceremony. Guthridge asked me what I was up to and how I thought the new president was doing with his program. I told him how much I had enjoyed watching the team and added that it would have been a special team even if they hadn't won the whole thing. "But I bet you're glad they did," Guthridge said knowingly. Touche! A few minutes later I took a seat behind Senator Helms and the ceremony took place. Dean Smith, after being very complimentary toward the new president and wishing him well on his hundred days, had to run back to reclaim the microphone from Clinton because he had forgotten to have George Lynch give Clinton his Carolina "1" jersey as a keepsake. Smith strode forward very naturally, but when he got to the microphone it sort of hit him what he had done. He asked "Can you believe the nerve of me?" to interrupt the president? Clinton threw his head back and laughed, as did everyone else.

1993–94 wasn't as charmed a season of course, despite 28 wins and an ACC Tournament Championship. But though I had my suspicions on that count, I didn't know it for a fact the day I bought a ticket through a newspaper scalper to the East Regional 2nd round in Landover, Maryland for $100. I hadn't seen a game in person that year, and didn't want this to be the first team I hadn't seen live since 1977. So I borrowed Treeby's car and drove to the doubleheader, not unhappy to be sitting in the back row. I bumped into Mark McCombs, the math tutor, in the concourse and he told me he was planning to make it to Charlotte for the Final Four.

But Carolina got taken to the woodshed over the first 25 minutes by a senior-led, perimeter-shooting Boston College team. When Derrick Phelps got hammered from behind and knocked out of the game by Donya Abrams, I exchanged harsh words with the man in the luxury box just above me who was yelling at Dean Smith to get off the court and stop whining. There were a lot of Carolina fans there, but the majority of neutral locals were passionately anti-Carolina, and there was a somewhat hostile atmosphere in the arena.

Carolina then made a great comeback with Jeff McInnis playing point guard to tie the game before losing by three. It was a pretty horrible moment, and I was so disconcerted that I made three wrong turns on the highway on the way home. Dad called and said he was sorry, and that he felt bad because "this was probably Dean and Bill's only chance to win it back-to-back." My girl-friend, Adria Scharf, who had been an intern with me at the Institute and was now back for her senior year at Swarthmore College outside of Philadelphia, couldn't believe and didn't fully understand at first the ramifications of Carolina losing this game. We went to New York the next weekend and visited Tom Williams in an effort to avoid college basketball. The only real silver lining to the month was Dean Smith's television commentary at the Final Four. Amidst his ample praise for a Duke team that made it to the final game, Smith managed to point out that Carolina had been "lucky" to beat the Blue Devils twice during the regular season. Beating Duke has never provided paler consolation.

What a difference a year makes. On April 5, 1993 I was at my highest point emotionally. The very next season, I came as close as I ever have (and ever will) to getting an ulcer as a result of following Carolina Hoops. And almost simultaneously, life "hit me with a ton of bricks" that almost permanently knocked me out. It's funny how I can vividly remember the feelings I described in the previous answer, but as I write this answer out I feel basically nothing out of the ordinary. Chalk one up for that familiar psychological concept: Repression. I left the bar I was watching the Boston College game in with extreme pains in my abdomen, pains that didn't leave me for a couple of days. I remember thinking as I was leaving that "this just isn't THAT important, Steve, that you should feel physically sick following a game." I started to realize that day that I was sorely in need of some perspective. All I can say is, be careful what you wish for.

But in this case, it wasn't just one game that ate away at my insides that year. That BC game pretty much summed up the entire 1994 season. It's like your first crush growing up. You have these incredible feelings raging inside of you, as if you've just seen the most beautiful creation in all of history...and it's all yours. You feel as if your life is a dream, and you have a permanent ticket to ride. But something just isn't right. You can't put your finger on it, but little by little things just don't go your way. This beautiful creature is missing something on the inside, something that is preventing a connection. She smiles at you occasionally, and she is almost always friendly, but she keeps her distance. And gradually things just spiral downward from there, and she slips away despite your best efforts to prevent it. Sometimes I really wish I could just wipe 1994 off the calendar, as if it never existed.

Moreover, the incredible tragedy that occurred on the basketball court that year was nothing compared to the incredible personal tragedy that I suffered. Remember I said that I felt like I needed some perspective? That perspective came on April 1,1994...the day before the Final Four.

I got home from work and had a message on my machine to call one of my fraternity brothers. This guy had never called me, and I wondered why he seemed so urgent to talk to me. So I called him, and I was informed rather matter-of-factly that two of my best friends throughout my entire college career had been in a collision that morning. One of them, my former roommate, was in a coma at UNC Hospitals, and the other one was dead.

I could write an entire novel on the profound effects that this event has had on my life. I'm merely mentioning it here in the context of my worst memory related to UNC basketball. The guy who died was a close friend, and we watched every single game together that year in 1994. We had some of the best times that I have ever had together that year, and we suffered mightily together that season as well. It was almost a lifetime rolled into one tumultuous basketball season, and it all came to a sudden and tragic end. Then, suddenly I was left holding all the pieces, having to figure out how to put "humpty dumpty" back together again.

—Steve Andrews, 30, tennis coach, Fayetteville, NC

3

Covering the Team, 1995–2000

The first two chapters have provided a fairly detailed account of my first 20 years as a Carolina fan, and how my understanding of and attitude toward Carolina basketball evolved over that time. In 1995, by a stroke of good fortune that matched the good fortune involved in getting the scoreboard job, I had the opportunity to cross the line from being a highly engaged fan to being a part-time journalist and columnist covering Carolina basketball. Admittedly, the line between the two was neither clear-cut nor one I ever fully crossed, and I operated at truly the lowest rungs of the media. What led to the experience being different from just a story of a big fan getting to go hang out in the locker room and meet his heroes was that my time covering the team coincided with a period of incredible transition in North Carolina basketball, punctuated primarily by the retirement of Dean Smith.

During that period of time, on two separate occasions—in early 1997 and throughout much of the 1999–2000 season—competitive challenges on the court created a near-crisis atmosphere among media and fans concerning North Carolina basketball, leading some to believe that the Carolina blue sky was about to fall. Both challenges tested the courage of fans and sympathetic media. But the second challenge, surrounding the 2000 season, hit home particularly hard for me, for two reasons: First, much of the media maelstrom centered around what I regarded as patently unfair and even ignorant criticism of the one Carolina basketball figure whom I had known more or less continuously from a young age and for whom I'd always held high appreciation—Bill Guthridge. Second, my interaction with Carolina fans during the 1999 and especially the 2000 seasons forcibly impressed upon me the fact that not all who considered themselves fans of Carolina basketball saw the enterprise through anything like the same lenses I wore. The experience of writing and publicly articulating my thoughts and feelings about what was happening, even for rather small outlets that could not begin to compete with the pronouncements of the corporate sports media, made me think more systematically about what was important about Carolina basketball. And the experience of being much closer to the team and its players (although not nearly as close as the full-time journalists—I was never an 'insider') deepened my understanding of what Carolina basketball is all about.

The following chapter thus reports in some detail—far greater detail than in the previous chapters—on the five seasons from 1995–96 to 1999–2000. The closer focus on those seasons will provide the opportunity to convey some of my experiences as a journalist, and it will provide an interpretation of some of the major events involved in the transition from the end of the Dean Smith era through the Bill Guthridge era to the start of Matt Doherty's coaching regime. More than this, however, this chapter will also convey some of the reasons why I am concerned about the interaction between players and coaches on one side, and fans and media on the other, in this era of heightened fan interest and Internet journalism. In particular, it will bring into sharp focus the specific issue that largely motivates the writing of this book: My concern that a situation might soon emerge where the hype and media attention surrounding Carolina basketball consumes the thing itself, and where the basest instincts of American sports fans might someday overturn the patient, principled work of Dean Smith, who, with the assistance of Bill Guthridge and many others, painstakingly built a basketball program that was not reducible to wins and losses.

When some fans started lambasting Bill Guthridge during the difficult moments of the 2000 season, the Carolina head coach took the high road by shrugging his shoulders and going about the business of coaching, and other observers simply saw it as what happens to all coaches when things don't go as well as expected. But to me, the idea of Guthridge being so disrespected by people who thought you could just sweep away all his good work and bring in someone "better" was as painful and as infuriating as a multinational corporation's decision to close down a steel plant to relocate to some other locale with a slightly higher projected return would be to a steelworker who had given 20 years to that plant. That nightmare didn't come to close to happening, of course. But the very idea that anyone calling himself a Carolina fan would want it to happen made me alternately nauseous and fighting mad at points during the 2000 season. That idea, which I found so alien to my understanding of what Carolina basketball both is and is supposed to be, also inspired many of the reflections that inform this book. In thinking through what it means to be a Carolina fan, I believe there is much to be learned from reconsidering the broader lessons of the 1999–2000 season and indeed the end of the Smith/Guthridge era as a whole, significant parts of which I was fortunate to witness at relatively close range. This chapter thus provides both an extension of the "fan memoir" presented in the first two chapters and a closer look at those events.

*

Adria, my girlfriend, spent the summer of 1994 in Washington, D.C. after graduation, but then went back to her hometown of Seattle to start a graduate program in sociology. Intensely lonely after her departure and in need of a diversion from work pressures, I did two things. First, I joined the local YMCA, which had some excellent pick-up basketball games. Second, I bought an external modem to stick on the 286 DOS-based PC I was using at home, and opened an email account. My initial intentions were to be able to email Adria and to be a part of the Bob Dylan discussion group on Usenet, where people regularly made arrangements to swap bootleg tapes.

Only a few months later, when the 1994–95 basketball season started, did I venture on to a college basketball discussion group, *rec.sport.b.co.* When I got there, I was pretty shocked by what I found—an incredible amount of vitriol and disinformation directed at North Carolina basketball, ranging from accusations of academic fraud to tawdry rumors to plain mean-spirited attacks. Of course, a lot of other schools got cracked on as well. In the days before school-specific, web-based message boards became highly developed, this Usenet group represented something of a Wild West free-for-all.

I suppose I could have laughed at it all and walked away. Eventually, I did just that to the Usenet forum and to electronic bulletin boards in general. But my initial inclination was to engage and try to confront error. So I soon started posting messages on the board, occasionally picking fights with Duke fans and others. Sometimes I learned something from the exchange or was forced to think about a point in a new way, and sometimes I got "flamed." But I enjoyed writing in my comments and didn't mind at all being associated as a Carolina diehard. During the 1994–95 season, too, I started taking notes during games showing the sequence of baskets for both teams, and I would post this "synopsis" on the Usenet group. Every so often, I printed out a few and sent them to my brother, who was in Germany doing research for the year.

Having the Internet available pretty much ensured that it was possible to think about Carolina basketball year-round, if one wanted to. By the summer of 1995, if I wasn't thinking about whatever I had to think about at work, or about politics more generally, or if I wasn't making a Bob Dylan bootleg to send someone in New York or Texas or Australia, odds were high I would be thinking about how Carolina would be able to cope with Rasheed Wallace and Jerry Stackhouse going to the NBA after their sophomore seasons.

So it was something of a no-brainer for me to take a couple of minutes and volunteer to write an article when a new publication called *Inside Carolina* put out a pitch on the Usenet group looking for fans to write preseason previews of their favorite ACC school. In fact, I had already spent hours and hours on a fun little project, writing a "North Carolina Basketball Frequently Asked Questions" file, totaling about 50 pages, which was posted on the Internet. That document listed a lot of Carolina's accomplishments, gave a subjective listing of Carolina's top 10 wins since 1975 over each ACC opponent, discussed Carolina's worst losses and best wins, and talked about who might one day replace Dean Smith. I posted the document in late October 1995, and it elicited a mostly positive response. Even the Carolina-haters enjoyed my re-telling of Carolina's worst losses and mostly had only minor bones to pick with the rest. That document, plus my note, got the attention of *Inside Carolina* magazine publisher David Eckoff, who invited me to write an article previewing the 1995–96 Tar Heels.

Delighted, I penned a short column projecting a fair amount of gloom and doom unless Serge Zwikker and Ed Geth stepped up to become solid contributors. (Hey, I didn't realize just how good Antawn Jamison would be!) Eckoff liked it enough to invite me to cover a November pre-season exhibition game in Chapel Hill. I came down with Robbie Brown (now my brother-in-law) for the weekend to stay with the Simpsons, and met up with Tom Kerby to go to the Sunday afternoon exhibition game. My assignment was to cover the game and also come up with a story on what it meant for everybody—fans, players, and coaches—to be back in Carmichael Auditorium. So I walked around the gym and picked out several folks to talk to, including an usher I remembered from my scoreboard days, most of whom were happy to wax romantic about the old days. But in the Carolina locker room, the players made it pretty clear they were happy they played in the Smith Center. I was impressed by how approachable and comfortable the Carolina players were talking to anyone, complete stranger or not. And I was really impressed by young Shammond Williams stating in a clear, determined voice that despite what everyone thought, this was going to be a great Carolina team.

On the way out of the locker, I spotted Bill Guthridge and he came over to say hello, wanting to know what I was doing there. It meant a lot to me that he seemed not only amused but also genuinely pleased to see me show up in that context. I asked him a couple of questions about what it was like for him to be back in Carmichael. Then he said, "When will we get to see you again?" That invitation was more than enough to make me think it would be worth my while to be a part-time sportswriter for a while and take advantage of whatever *Inside Carolina* had to offer.

*

The main thing the magazine had to offer was a wide-open forum, pretty much open to anyone who could put three sentences together and had a passionate interest in things Carolina. There were four big reasons why there was an opening for another publication about UNC sports. First, the established *Carolina Blue*, which I still read at the time, was widely regarded as being merely a mouthpiece for the Carolina Athletic Department view of the world. Second, and closely related, neither *Carolina Blue* nor anything else represented the perspective of a younger generation of fans. Third, interest in recruiting was skyrocketing, and any new publication that promised any new information about recruits was bound to attract interest. *Carolina Blue* didn't cover the recruiting process, reporting on prospects only after they had signed. *Inside Carolina*, on the other hand, already had a very aggressive recruiting reporter with a gift for gab and for talking to high school players, Zeke Martins, who had his own 1-900 number. Fourth, and perhaps most important, the Internet was just starting to emerge as a viable forum for sports reporting, and the territory was wide open for a new publication to stake out space and attract attention on the World Wide Web.

I could never really relate to the recruiting rationale for a publication like *IC* (more on why later), but I could relate to the other three reasons. Once or twice while shooting the breeze, Robbie, George and I had said something to the effect of "what if there were a politically conscious version of *Carolina Blue* that spoke to us directly," and sort of chuckled. *IC* wasn't that, but it was about as you close as you could expect, and it actually existed. Eckoff, a UNC Business School graduate, had started the publication while working a job at IBM in the Research Triangle. David strongly believed in publishing a range of views with minimal editorial oversight and not censoring writers, on the view that readers should be able to make up their own minds about contested issues. That commitment was what made it possible for me to write there and write about a lot of things that didn't directly touch on games—and it was ultimately what caused me to depart the magazine. But for a long time, the opportunity to say pretty much anything I wanted to say about any issue pertaining in any way to college basketball or the University of North Carolina was incentive enough to keep me on board.

*

The other attraction, of course, was the chance to interact firsthand with the team and the coaches at games, ask questions, get the story straight from the horse's mouth, and also get some sense of the players' personalities and demeanors. In his book about Michael Jordan and the NBA of the late 1990s, author David Halberstam laments that NBA locker rooms are no longer a site for genuine exchanges between players and journalists, and instead that what takes place is a ritualized exchange of information in which both parties understand they are exploiting one another. Halberstam adds that he misses the old days of the 1970s NBA, when he wrote his superb book about the Portland Trailblazers, *The Breaks of the Game*, a time when reporters could spend long hours hanging out with players in coffee shops and airports. The relationship between Carolina players and the media today falls midway between those extremes, at least as I saw it. For the most part, it is the same faces interviewing the same players game after game, and a sense of familiarity definitely develops. This was true even for a relative interloper like me, who showed up every now and then and usually didn't make any effort to introduce himself. When I started covering the team, my mindset was that I was there to cover the team, not to become their friends.

But as time wore on, I grew to genuinely like certain players after repeated interviews—particularly the core players on the 1997 and 1998 teams. Many Carolina players are naturally friendly people, and all have been well trained to treat people with respect, which is how journalists are almost always treated by players, whether they deserve it or not. In interview situations, it's pretty much up to the players to draw the boundaries on what they are and are not willing to talk about in regard to either basketball or their own lives. While different players draw the line different places, a substantial number are willing to be quite forthcoming with their thoughts and feelings on any number of topics. At the same time, however, there is a very, very sharp break between who is on the "inside" of the family—the players and coaches—and those on the outside, however supportive or friendly. And with the possible exception of the radio commentators who cover the team full-time from an unabashedly partisan perspective, there is no doubt that the media is considered by the team to be outsiders.

Which is completely understandable. It is natural that college-age students hailing from a mix of backgrounds and going through the demands of being a big-time college basketball player should suspect they have little in common with the mostly middle-aged, overwhelmingly white, and not particularly athletic corps of reporters who approach them with questions before practice sessions and after games. A common view among players is that almost all of the reporters never played the game at a high level: what do they know?

Such feelings are especially likely to emerge during hard times. During the 2000 season, forward Jason Capel responded to criticism of point guard Ed Cota's defense by telling the Associated Press, "For people who never played basketball, who can't guard a trash can, to say he can't guard anybody is a bogus thing to say. The guy is out there playing 38 or 39 minutes, it's tough. That (criticism) should come from somebody who has actually guarded somebody." Brendan Haywood, the object of his share of criticism and then some during his UNC career, stated his intent during his senior year to eventually go into broadcasting and analysis, because there should be more former players who really know what's going on in the media. Roy Williams, the longtime Carolina assistant and Kansas head coach, supposedly once told a media assembly that his assistant coaches had more basketball knowledge in their little fingers than all the writers in the room.

Such comments struck a nerve with me once I began covering and commenting on the team. I knew for sure that I didn't know a great deal of the X's and O's of basketball—even after looking at Dean Smith's book on the subject countless times. What I always remembered from that book were basic principles of what Smith believed in doing on offense and defense, which I figured counted for something, but even now my eyes glaze over when I look for very long at play diagrams of the kind found in books on basketball coaching. What I did know and appreciate, however, was that the game isn't as easy to play as it looks, and that playing well is physically and mentally demanding—especially at a level where any lapse is usually swiftly punished. So I approached interviewing the players with a baseline of great respect for what these guys were able to do, not just physically, but mentally. And not being very much older than them, I tried to look at things from a player's point of view as much as possible.

I don't know that I was very successful in doing that. Indeed, the tendency of writers is to identify more with the coaches than those who play the game, and to see the players collectively as "kids," some of whom are "good kids" and some of whom are not so good, but all of whom are not so different than the group of players that was here five years ago or will be here five years hence. That tendency is probably a natural result of writers finding it easier to identify with people closer to them in age and life experience, as well as a result of being around for a long time and seeing players come and go. And it is also a result of the simple fact that, for the most part, what the majority of readers want to know about is the output produced by those kids on the court. Most readers don't care about how what happens on the court fits into the context of what's going on in a player's life. If a Max Owens or an Ed Cota has a subpar game, we only know that fact about what they did that day, not about how well they did on a test, or how they helped a friend, or how they went out of their way to be nice to a stranger. To be sure, feature stories on players' personalities and life stories do get published and can be a great source for humanizing the players. But during the heat of the season, players are valued by most fans and most writers mainly for their numbers in the box score as well as the numbers on the scoreboard—and the players know it.

*

Another reason, far less exalted, why I was mainly interested in the player's perspective when I started covering the team was that I was convinced that the main variable in whether Carolina won or lost was the development of the players as individuals and as a team, and how well they carried out the coaches' game plan on a given day. What was going on with the coaching input, what Dean Smith and his staff were doing, was in my mind a constant, a given. They knew what they were doing, without question. The fundamental question was whether the players could carry it out.

That question loomed particularly large in 1995–96 as I started writing for *Inside Carolina*—but I also knew that the answer the players provided on the court would reflect back on Coach Smith, inevitably. Up through 1995, Dean Smith had had a remarkable 29-year run of unbroken success, in which all the disappointments, even the toughest ones, were only relative. Every other school in the ACC had been on the yo-yo over that time period, sometimes up and sometimes down (including Duke, which had seen an 11-year run of NCAA tournament appearances snapped with a 13–18 season in 1995). But it looked quite likely that the 1996 UNC team might be the one to finally fail to win 20 games, finish in the top three in the ACC, and make the NCAA Tournament.

After a stirring win against Kentucky to make another Final Four in 1995, Carolina experienced what at that point was an unprecedented personnel blow, as Rasheed Wallace and Jerry Stackhouse each went pro after their sophomore years. That meant that a promising incoming class of Antawn Jamison, Vince Carter, and Ademola Okulaja would be relied upon for immediate help, a very unusual situation for a Smith team. The norm at North Carolina had usually been for great players to have at least a year as an understudy. On rare occasions, a freshman would start immediately, but even in those cases Smith could also call upon veterans at the same position. But in 1995–96, at least two freshmen were certain to start, and there was little in the way of a safety net. If Jamison, Carter, and Okulaja didn't turn out to be very good, Carolina certainly wouldn't be, either.

The personnel overhaul also led Smith to make a key tactical decision with long-term consequences. For the second consecutive year, Smith would instruct his team to play primarily a sagging man-to-man defense mixed in with zone, instead of using aggressive, trapping schemes intended to take a team out of its offensive rhythm. In 1995, Smith made this move primarily because of a lack of depth outside the top five players. In 1996, the move made sense for a lot of reasons: Carolina wanted to be sure its two remaining veterans, Jeff McInnis and Dante Calabria, were on the court as much as possible without fatigue or foul trouble. In Serge Zwikker, Carolina had a 7-3 center who could not be asked to do anything defensively on the perimeter. Also, the trapping schemes could be difficult for new players to pick up and execute, and this team couldn't afford to pick up many confidence-killing losses early on. Even so, to change defensive philosophy for two straight seasons made it even more difficult in subsequent years to switch back to the old style of play based on pressuring the other team into turnovers and bad shot selection.

But at the time, all Smith and anyone else interested in Carolina basketball cared about was seeing if this depleted team could live up to past standards. The team motto for the year, in fact, was "Still Carolina." And if Smith could pull off a decent season in 1996, the two following years would probably be very good ones. Most important, as far as I was concerned, Smith could finish his career without any blemishes on the streak of unbroken good seasons. For years, voices had popped up here and there saying that Smith was slipping, that the game had passed him by, that maybe he couldn't relate as well to young players. Others questioned recruiting decisions. By 1996, it was evident that Smith might coach at most another five years—but it didn't seem at all assured that the Smith era would end on a high note, as opposed to a fading out. Most college basketball coaches have their careers end by being fired, and even very successful coaches who enjoy long tenures at the same school often see significant slippages in their final years (as was the case with John Thompson at Georgetown, Bob Knight at Indiana, and Denny Crum at Louisville). Rather than witness that sort of scenario, most Carolina fans, myself included, wanted Smith either to never quit, or to be sure to go out on top.

So a lot was riding on the 1996 season, and as it started I tried to prepare myself and also others for the likelihood that Carolina would be scratching and clawing all season long to get an NCAA tournament berth, and that they might fall short. But to almost everyone's amazement, the 1996 team got off to a terrific start, losing just two games, both close, to Villanova and Texas before conference play started. The first tough conference test would come in early January at Maryland. Since College Park was just a subway ride away from downtown Washington, I got the assignment to cover the game for *IC*. Excited about this, I got to the gym very early, in time to hear the assortment of catcalls directed by Maryland fans at the Carolina players warming up ("Four years of hell, Vince Carter, you're going to have four years of hell") and in time to say hello to Bill Guthridge and say "good luck." Both teams played well the entire game, which went into overtime. After several momentum swings in overtime alone, Carolina had the ball for the last possession with the score tied. The entire Cole Field House crowd rose to its feet as Jeff McInnis dribbled the ball and eventually shot and missed. There was a wild scramble for the ball, but Dante Calabria got to it first. While lying on the ground, he threw the ball behind him in the general direction of the goal—right to Antawn Jamison, who put the ball in at the buzzer for his 31st point.

It was an incredible end to an incredible game, and for the one and only time I didn't do much to hide my reaction on press row, leaping up to follow the Tar Heels off the court and get ready to ask them all about how they had pulled it off. In a winning locker room, even if a win was expected, there's a feeling of jovial masculinity in the air, and everyone is everyone else's friend. Players are talking to each other, poking each other, telling each other about someone they might have seen in the crowd, talking to assistant coaches, and of course, talking to reporters and TV men. In this instance, I wanted to hear how Okulaja, Carter, and Jamison felt about getting their first win in classic Dean Smith "how did they do that?" style and to ask McInnis about the running dialogue he had over the course of the game with some vociferous Maryland fans. They all told me, but what I remember more than the specifics of what they said was the look of satisfaction and pride on their faces and the easy smiles. Winning clearly had its benefits.

*

The stereotype of athletes talking to reporters after the games is that athletes use the same stock phrases over and over and in predictable fashion. That stereotype is not without basis—although I came to think this was mainly a reflection of the predictable nature of the questions directed toward them. And in the case of Carolina players, there was a long-standing view that Dean Smith kept a muzzle on his players. That may have been true at some point. But it wasn't particularly true by the time I started interviewing players, and encountered straight shooters such as McInnis, Calabria, and Okulaja. Even Antawn Jamison and Shammond Williams, who could be counted on to be studiously polite and to say the expected thing, spoke with genuine emotion, not as programmed robots. You never knew when a Jamison, in explaining a bad stretch of play, might unload a zinger such as "We just went brain dead for a few minutes out there."

This point is worth making simply by way of challenging the "dumb jock" view of big-time college athletes, or the related view that athletes at the big-time schools are spoiled, one-dimensional people wrapped up in their own self-importance, and not really interesting as subjects in their own right. True, not every Carolina player in the recent past has been a Renaissance man-type scholar athlete with a wide range of other talents and interests beyond the basketball court—although some have been, or have come close. But if you weren't expecting to find 12 Bill Bradleys in the locker room, what you found instead was a collection of very interesting people with compelling narratives of their own, all of which happened to include basketball.

It was also interesting to me to recognize firsthand the obvious fact that the players approach the games and the season primarily as events in their own lives, not in terms of the narratives sportswriters and fans routinely impose on those events. Like fans, after a big win or tough loss, players are likely to think about what this means for the conference standings and so forth—but unlike fans, they also have to start thinking about how they personally are going to process and learn from the game just played and then prepare for the next one, and at the same time meet all their other demands. And whereas fans and writers habitually use the long shadow of the past as a baseline for evaluating new events, players generally do not. Instead of recalling what happened against such and such opponent five or 10 years ago, the frame of reference players bring to the events of a season is their own personal experience, from what happened to them in high school to what the coaches had told them in practice to the comments they heard from classmates on the day of a big game.

True, occasionally Carolina got a player who had grown up a big Tar Heel fan, but they were usually walk-ons, like Charlie McNairy. Someone like Ademola Okulaja didn't know anything about what had happened in the 1970s or 80s or early 90s—he just showed up in Chapel Hill on a tip from his German club teammate Henrik Rodl, who had advised simply that the experience would be worth it. The players on each individual team, year in and year out, play for themselves and for their teammates. And while the concept of "Carolina," as in the team motto "Still Carolina," could be used as a tool to get players to have pride in each other and buy into what the coaches wanted them to do, that concept became real to players only in the concrete form of their own lived experiences and interactions with the coaches and their teammates. Or to put it more clearly, the players were not simply widget-making drones in a factory that produced this consumer product called "Carolina basketball." Rather, they were active participants, active creators in producing a shared team narrative, a narrative that blended their own lives with the rules and teachings and guidance offered by the coaches.

The dominant content of that narrative, of course, was first, how well the team succeeded in playing winning basketball and second, the consequences that flow from what happens on the court. But what was particularly obvious to me, at least in looking at the 1995–96 team, was that success was not at all guaranteed, and that all the banners and uniforms didn't mean that Dean Smith couldn't have an NIT team or even a losing record. And it wasn't immediately obvious that the cast of characters assembled in Chapel Hill was going to be good enough either to have a decent season in 1996 or to form the core of the Top 10 team North Carolina fans expected to see four years out of five. Shammond Williams was a definitive case in point: his recruitment to North Carolina had been called a "joke" by one prominent recruiting expert, and in his appearances as a freshman in 1995, he quickly gained a reputation as good shooter but erratic ballhandler. Shammond was a good student, a natural leader, and had other interests, including a long-term career ambition to come home and be mayor of his hometown in South Carolina. This was not someone who needed pro basketball to have an interesting life—he could easily have chosen simply to use his basketball scholarship to get his education and go on. Instead, Shammond Williams worked incredibly hard on his game, year-round and often all night, for four years, absolutely determined to prove doubters wrong. By the end, Williams was among the most effective perimeter players North Carolina has ever had, and he has gone on to become an established NBA player.

But it didn't happen automatically, and it didn't happen because it was pre-ordained that Carolina was going to continue to have winning seasons forever. It came by virtue of Williams' own effort, combined with the quality of the guidance that he received from the coaches. For me, the process of seeing that kind of evolution unfold—with the awareness that this just might not work out, Shammond Williams just might not be good enough, and the team just might turn out not to be good enough—became the most interesting and satisfying part of following the team closely.

In professional sports, fans and sportswriters are accustomed to treating players and coaches alike as inputs into a product. If the product is not acceptable over a given length of time, one of the inputs must be flawed and changes should be made. It is an entirely understandable and certainly economical model for evaluating pro sports teams.

But that model is seriously flawed as a way of looking at college teams and college players in general, and perhaps especially at North Carolina. Why? First, because it is both ethically and analytically wrong to see the players as simply or even primarily commodities, not ends in themselves with their own narratives. Indeed, the personal and character development of the players is supposed to be the reason we have intercollegiate sports. Whether character development was really the highest purpose in Chapel Hill or anywhere else is an open question, but at least Carolina's coaches did take seriously the idea that they wanted their players to leave school with more wisdom, better judgment, and greater self-discipline than when they arrived.

Second, even if we accept the economistic analogy, the most important "inputs" into the process of creating winning basketball—the players—change dramatically over time in many cases. Serge Zwikker and Shammond Williams couldn't do the things on the basketball court as rookies that they ended up doing as juniors and seniors. Brendan Haywood developed footwork and low-post moves he didn't have as a freshman. Or, in a rather different case, Vince Carter's mental approach to the game and ability to stay locked in mentally and harness his extraordinary physical talents evolved dramatically from his freshman to his junior year. That the players change and grow so much in a pretty short period of time seemed to me to be the essence of college basketball, and a major source of the drama underlying the games and seasons.

That commitment to seeing college basketball mainly in terms of an educational or growth process is probably the main reason I never became too zealous about recruiting, other than following it in a general way. To me, the idea that you could get the best high school players, just plug them into a lineup, and then automatically have a better product was a misleading way of thinking about how good teams are developed and sustained. The real question was not how good they were in high school, but how much they would be capable of developing in college under a Smith system in which players were expected to take a large share of responsibility for their own growth and development.

And the answer to that question depended on not just how high a player could jump, but what kind of person the player in question was, how coachable he was, whether he would be likely to be in it merely for himself or could have a team-oriented approach, and how he might mesh with the players already in school. That's the kind of information you can't get from watching games at an all-star camp. And it's not the kind of judgment I trusted recruiting reporters to make—I had a lot more faith in the judgment of Smith and Guthridge.

To be sure, this sort of complacency about recruiting is a luxury that came with being a Carolina fan. With Carolina, you knew that even if the Tar Heels "missed" on someone they wanted or made a mistake or two along the way, there were many other good players out there who would be interested. At struggling schools (and indeed, early in Smith's career), in contrast, getting or not getting a prospect can mean a coach's job—if Jerry Stackhouse had made a different decision as a 17-year-old, Les Robinson might still be coaching at N.C. State. My mindset was that Carolina had always gotten in enough talented prospects to be competitive at the highest level, and the program's popularity did not seem to be declining in any way. Why start worrying now about the decisions of some 17-year-old player? The real story lies in how the ones who do come develop when they get there. Or to put it another way, how fun would the actual games and the season be if you could somehow win a national championship and go undefeated each year simply by virtue of the recruiting process?

*

But recruiting information from any source undoubtedly attracted the attention of readers, which helped keep a small publication like *Inside Carolina* alive. There are two additional ways a small publication might earn attention over time. The first is by providing quality reporting and analysis—that was the part I and several of the other writers were interested in. The second is by stirring up controversy of various sorts. One way *Inside Carolina* did that was through a column called "Fly on the Wall," an anonymous column that provided observations and barbs pertaining to North Carolina sports. No target, not even Dean Smith, was safe from the column, although usually the most bitter and sarcastic comments were aimed at other schools. Not surprisingly, people within the North Carolina Athletic Department hated the column. Yet it became perhaps the most popular feature of the magazine and what *IC* relied upon to generate what Eckoff called a "buzz." I didn't think there was anything particularly wrong with the column at first, as usually there was an obvious humorous intent, but as the tone of the column changed over time to become increasingly mean-spirited, my opinion of the Fly soured.

Small publications—and indeed, much larger ones—can also stir up controversy and attract attention by providing speculation and gossip about what might be going on with the players on the current team. With the advent and growth of the Internet, it was by 1996 possible to circulate (or invent) rumors faster than ever before, and some of these became a source for speculation. Rumors claiming that a current player is in trouble with the law, is in trouble grade-wise in school, or is thinking about transferring are the most common fare. Most of these rumors are not taken seriously by anyone at any level of the media (even the bottom of the barrel, which *Inside Carolina* represented), but some do indeed become topics that make it into print.

A good example came in the latter part of the 1995–96 season. After the good start, North Carolina struggled in the second half of the season, losing six of the last nine league games, most of them nail-biters that the Tar Heels could well have won. Dean Smith had done a great job in the preseason getting the team ready to get off to a good start, but by February Carolina seemed to have already peaked while others were getting better. As the losses mounted, some wondered why the much-ballyhooed freshman Vince Carter wasn't making more of a contribution. Carter had been considered the most talented of the three freshmen, but while Antawn Jamison was having an all-conference rookie year, Carter's minutes had gone down over the course of the season. Ademola Okulaja, a more experienced player with excellent defensive skills and court savvy, replaced Carter as the starting small forward, and Shammond Williams got most of the minutes as the third guard, reducing Carter to all but a spot role. By mid-February, rumors began to circulate that Carter was unhappy and was going to transfer, and it was reported that Carter's high school coach had flown to Chapel Hill to see what the matter was. Given how close Carter already was to Jamison off the court, I thought the rumor implausible on the face of it, but who really knew? Already, some Carolina fans had gone into a near panic at the prospect of "losing" Carter. When I traveled to Chapel Hill in late February to cover the last home game of the season, a shock loss to Florida State, the postgame locker room found Vince Carter surrounded by reporters obliquely asking him how he was doing, fishing for hints of discontent. I was incredibly impressed to see the young, already media-savvy freshman hold his own, stay composed, and say firmly that he was a Tar Heel and that there was no problem.

What the truth of that situation was, I don't exactly know, nor does it matter at this point. It is likely that Carter was indeed disappointed in his playing time as a freshman, that he may have called home and expressed unhappiness, and perhaps the thought of leaving school crossed his mind. All of which are perfectly normal emotions for any college basketball player, and indeed, for any college freshman, period. But those normal ups and downs of college life were matters of public interest if the student concerned was a North Carolina basketball player. And members of the media, especially the lower-tier media, had every incentive to exploit that interest by publishing speculation or, at the least, asking a player directly to comment on a rumor. The latter course is good journalistic practice, and I think the reporters who asked Carter those difficult questions in February 1996 did the right thing by giving the player a chance to clear the air. Even so, the very existence of the rumors put Carter in a difficult and unenviable position for any 19-year-old.

It is precisely for these reasons that Dean Smith and his successors wanted to protect the privacy of his players and the privacy of his team and not turn the conflicts and ups and downs his teams experienced into a soap opera for public consumption. But an enormous number of fans and media consumers would be intensely interested in learning the details of the players' lives and how they interact with one another, or who doesn't like whom, or who Dean Smith told off in practice last week, or who's in the doghouse. That desire gives incentives to journalists to push for inside information whenever the opportunity presents itself. What constitutes a legitimate story to pursue and what sort of story about a player's personal life should be left alone entirely is a matter of journalistic judgment. Even so, the incentive existed for a small publication or an Internet site to distinguish itself from the competition by discussing rumors or "insider" information that daily newspapers would not touch, and that worried me.

Even more troubling was the emergence of various electronic bulletin boards devoted to Carolina sports. Like some other small publications that covered the ACC, *Inside Carolina* sometimes cited unnamed sources ("we hear that...") in its accounts—but it actually was pretty conscientious about avoiding deeply inappropriate stories or outrageous claims that could not be substantiated. But the electronic boards lacked even minimal standards—indeed, speculation and gossip were their very lifeblood. Not only that, but the revenue-generating capacity of message boards further increased the incentives of a small publication to stimulate controversy—what better way to stimulate a lot of discussion on the message board and increase revenue than printing a provocative article ripping on a player or a coach? As time went on, that worried me too.

*

A much bigger worry in 1996, though, was the question of whether the Jamison-Carter-Okulaja group was going to be able to put it together on the court. By early in the 1996–97 season, there were strong reasons for doubt. Expectations for this team were high, as freshmen Ed Cota and

MATT DOHERTY ON THE INTERNET

Q. What's the biggest change in the climate surrounding the players since when you played?

A. I think the biggest change is the Internet, and that's not all been good. Just because people's opinions are aired upon the Internet, players read the Internet, and one minute they could feel great about themselves and the next minute they could feel bad about themselves. The Internet can cause inner turmoil. We have to understand that that's just water cooler talk. But now that it's in print on the Internet, it almost looks like it's coming from a newspaper. The Internet gives people's opinions credibility, and that more than not negatively impacts the team.

Q. What can you do about it?

A. Not a whole lot. You can encourage the kids not to read it. You know, I don't mind some web pages, it's the message boards, it's the chat rooms that get dangerous, because that is just faceless commentary that can hurt some people's feelings.

Q. Do you think in a few years after it gets old, people will realize it's just garbage and there's no reason to look at it?

A. Well, people still read the *Enquirer*. When you walk by the grocery stand and see that Elvis is alive, you still read it.

Vasco Evtimov and junior transfer Makhtar Ndiaye replaced the departed Calabria and McInnis, and everyone else was a year older. But Carolina started the year on the wrong foot with a loss to a quick, talented and deep Arizona team in the Tip-Off Classic in Springfield, MA. Smith had hoped to return in 1996–97 to the trapping style of defense that had been his teams' trademark, but the performance against the Wildcats persuaded him to drop those plans.

Now living in New York as a graduate student at Union Theological Seminary, I covered that game from press row. During the postgame press conference, I asked Smith whether he was disappointed that the game had been reminiscent of some of the losses at the end of 1996, when Carolina fell way behind and simply couldn't respond. Smith frowned and said no, he was thinking about this year. When I walked into the unhappy Carolina locker room, Bill Guthridge stood at the door and gave me a pat on the back as I said, "Well, long way to go," which turned out to be quite an understatement.

Since Union was on break for all of Thanksgiving week, I was able to fly down to Chapel Hill for Page Moreau's wedding and for Carolina's next two games, against Richmond and Pitt. The Richmond game was a struggle, and the Carolina brain trust looked very, very worried with about 10 minutes to play. Then Cota hit a long three-pointer to help spark a game-winning rally. Smith admitted after the game that the win was a huge, huge relief for him and his staff, and that he had been shaken by what he had seen against Arizona. "I have a vision for them, seeing them do this, and I don't see it done," Smith told reporters, adding that he would have to be patient with this team. A few nights later, Carolina again struggled, this time against Pittsburgh, but pulled away in the final 10 minutes for a comfortable win as Antawn Jamison scored 36 points.

Carolina went on to rack up six more wins against inferior opponents in various locales before traveling to Princeton to meet the Tigers on a sunny December Sunday in New Jersey. This was a special game to be at, as Carolina rarely got to play in such a small, intimate gym, or against an opponent that played such decidedly old-school basketball. North Carolina got off to a good start early as Okulaja had a steal and a dunk, but at the game's first timeout, Smith was extremely animated in talking to his club—Carolina had already been burnt on a backdoor cut. Carolina built a double-digit second half lead, but the Tigers rallied to cut the lead to three with just over a minute to play. Cota, playing in front of his parents as a collegian for the first time, answered with a bucket and then hit the free throws to ice it. After the game, Smith looked genuinely pleased to be in Princeton and to have gotten the win. He noted that he had stayed up very late watching video of the Tigers to prepare for the game, and that playing this kind of opponent would be good for the team. But, the coach warned, the team was going off to Europe over Christmas, and wouldn't have much time to prepare to visit Tim Duncan and Wake Forest when they got back. Smith said all this with a big smile, as if he were savoring the moment, knowing that rough seas probably lay ahead.

The Tar Heels returned from their European trip, traveled to Winston-Salem, and promptly got their butts kicked by Wake Forest on a Saturday night. In the big scheme of things, the loss was excusable, since Duncan and the Deacons had been projected as the best team in the school's history and a national title contender. And it looked like Dean Smith's vision was not so far off when the Tar Heels ran out to a 20-point lead over a good Maryland team in the following game in Chapel Hill. Watching at the beach with my parents while on break from school, I was excited. Carolina seemed to have found an offensive flow missing to date. I thought the Smith Center should have been going nuts in response to such a performance—but the crowd seemed relatively quiet. Then Maryland began chipping away, and suddenly Carolina couldn't score, couldn't get a basket to stop the bleeding. The Terps came all the way back and ended up winning going away in a shocking turn of events, as the Smith Center crowd started filing out early.

Things didn't get better for the Tar Heels a few nights later in Charlottesville, as Carolina fell behind by over a dozen points at halftime. A game second half effort wasn't enough, and after the game there was a players-only team meeting. Reporters noted that yelling and screaming could be heard from outside the Carolina locker room. It was hard to know whether that was a good thing or a bad thing at that point. But at 0–3 in the ACC, there was little doubt that Carolina was undergoing a serious crisis of confidence.

I drove eight hours across eastern Tennessee and western North Carolina from Sewanee to Chapel Hill to cover the next two games against N.C. State and Georgia Tech. On break from seminary, I had been in a foul mood, largely because of the Tar Heels' struggles, so much so that my mom asked me if I was all right. I said I was—and added that I considered the journey to Chapel Hill almost like a faith mission. I shared the fan's superstition that somehow my actions could make a difference, that showing good faith by coming all that way to see a struggling team play might work out in some cosmic sense. And on the other hand, if this was really the moment that Carolina was going to have a really bad season, I probably wanted to be there to see that, too.

When I got to Chapel Hill, I found that not everyone still had faith that Carolina was going to be O.K. Down at Jeff's Campus Confectionary on Franklin Street, everyone had a theory for what was going wrong—including the guy who opined that Mount Zion Academy with Tracy McGrady and Max Owens could beat the Tar Heels. There was a letter in *The Chapel Hill Newspaper* saying that Dean Smith should resign. Later that week, *The News and Observer* ran a long article blaming Carolina's problems on recruiting decisions (a similar article also appeared in *Inside Carolina*). *Goheels.com*, a new website operated by Jim Heavner, the local media magnate, had run a column questioning sophomore Vince Carter's work ethic and heart.

Against that backdrop, it was truly moving to sit on press row and watch Carolina take the court against N.C. State to a very loud, prolonged standing ovation from a packed Smith Center. Chastened by public criticism in a variety of media outlets, local and national, the crowd was there ready to do its part. But midway through the second half, UNC went on a long offensive drought that allowed State to build a lead. With just over two minutes to go, I began to compose in my head the article I'd have to write saying that Carolina had fallen to an unprecedented 0–4 in the ACC. State had a 56–47 lead and the ball, and was taking it up after a missed Carolina shot when Jamison knocked the ball loose and Shammond Williams recovered it for a lay-up. After a stop, Williams hit a three to cut the lead to 56–52, and after a steal, a Jamison basket cut the lead to two with under a minute to go. State missed a free throw, and Williams was fouled with a chance to tie, but could only make one of two. But State missed yet another free throw, Jamison scored to give Carolina the lead, and then Carter stole the inbounds pass and made two free throws. State failed to score and Carolina had pulled off an incredible miracle comeback, winning 59–56.

After the game, the crowd rushed on to the court, and Carolina's players made no effort to hide their joy. I stood in the tunnel watching the participants walk off the court and into the locker area, and was amazed to see Carolina's players running and jumping through the tunnel, followed by Dean Smith, Bill Guthridge, and Dave Hanners, each of whom was walking very calmly with no obvious outward emotion, as if they were still a little troubled by what they had seen. It was an interesting contrast. However, Phil Ford, the other assistant, was pumping his fist and smiling. Moments later, outside the media room, an elderly N.C. State booster congratulated Smith but then muttered very loudly, "That was just typical."

In Smith's press conference, I had one of the first questions and asked Smith if the team had been under too much pressure for this game. In a memorable reply, Smith said yes, the team was under a lot of pressure—and that maybe we should all remember that "There are a lot of people in China who don't care whether we win or not." It was his way of trying to keep things in a little bit of perspective—and also of saying that while Carolina had just come very close to falling to perhaps its biggest low since Smith's very early years as a coach, it wouldn't be the end of the world if that happened, despite what most people in Chapel Hill thought.

But if Smith would have liked the media and the public to look outside the fishbowl of Carolina basketball every once in a while and not take the whole thing so seriously, it was also obvious that he was indeed taking the situation very seriously. In the extraordinarily emotional Carolina locker room, Shammond Williams fought back tears as he talked about his missed free throw in the last minute and what it meant to win the game. Vince Carter said he didn't care if people called him the worst player to ever play for Carolina, he was going to come out and try to improve. Ademola Okulaja said that the letters to the editor attacking Smith angered him. Antawn Jamison said that it had been hard being around campus the previous few days, but now Carolina was back. And all of the players talked about how Smith and the coaches had told them after the Virginia game to forget about 0–3 and 9–4, that the slate had been wiped clean, and that Carolina was starting off a new season at 0–0. That may seem like a rather corny psychological technique, but the Tar Heel players bought into it. It turned out that while most everyone else in Chapel Hill was freaking out about Carolina's poor start in January, Dean Smith was busy coaching.

After that remarkable night, Carolina beat Georgia Tech with much greater ease in the following game, and Smith told the media how happy he was to be "talking about a good North Carolina win," the obvious implication being that the State victory, comeback and all, didn't fall into that category. But Carolina wasn't yet out of the woods. Tough losses on the road to Florida State and Duke sandwiched around a stirring win over a highly rated Clemson team left North Carolina at 3–5 in the league, 12–6 overall, and decidedly on the bubble in terms of making the NCAA Tournament. In a midseason column for *IC*, I wrote that having shown they could beat a top 15 team in the Clemson game, maybe Carolina could go 5–3 or 6–2 the second go round, as long as they didn't get into a mental framework of "Oh, no, what will happen if we lose this one?"

Then something unexpected happened. The team clicked. Carolina had a home game against Middle Tennessee State after the Duke loss, and the team played nearly a perfect game in front of an appreciative crowd, all the way down to the play of the reserves in the last minute, as freshman reserve Terrence Newby soared in for a dunk. The team looked like it was having fun. Carolina then paid back Florida State and Virginia for the earlier defeats in surprisingly easy fashion at home. Suddenly, Carolina was having no trouble scoring points. What had changed? Ed Cota, the 20-year-old Brooklyn freshman, had found a comfort zone as well as a very special chemistry with Antawn Jamison. Whereas Carolina fans had long been used to seeing somewhat plodding big men who had to throw a variety of fakes to get their shot off inside, Jamison's pure quickness enabled him to just catch and shoot, and if it was inside of six feet, the ball was usually going in. Serge Zwikker had become so adept at hitting the baseline shot that Carolina started running plays to get him open. And Ademola Okulaja continued to provide the glue for the team and to hit shots when called upon.

But probably the most dramatic individual improvements came from Vince Carter and Shammond Williams. As late as January, Jamison had said of his teammate, "Vince is a great player, but sometime he just loses his head out there." After moving to 5–5 in the league, North Carolina played a very tense game in Reynolds Coliseum against N.C. State, the kind of game where both teams played with more effort than execution. A late State turnover gave Carolina a chance to win it, and Ed Cota delivered a little floater from the left to put Carolina ahead by one with five seconds left. That's a dangerous amount of time, as any good college team can take it coast to coast in that amount of time for a lay-up or at worst an open, makeable jumper. No time-out was called, and State pushed it up and got it into the hands of Danny Strong, a good shooter, to take the last shot. But Carolina had hustled back smartly, and two Tar Heels ran at Strong as he took the shot. The one who got a piece of it on the way up to seal the victory was the previously maligned Vince Carter.

A few days later in Atlanta, Carolina played very sluggishly and trailed Georgia Tech by 16 points with only nine minutes to play. Suddenly Shammond Williams hit two three-pointers, and Okulaja hit one too. Carolina got right back into the game and, down two, moved the ball on a fast break to Williams for a three-pointer, who gave Carolina an improbable lead with a minute to play. Carolina went on to win. Williams, who had sometimes looked like the weak link earlier in the season, now had the full confidence of his team and his coach not only as a shooter but as a ballhandler and an emotional leader.

The final piece of the puzzle fell into place a few days later when Carolina got its rematch against Wake Forest. The first half of the game was, simply, The Night That Vince Carter Put It All Together. Carter nailed three consecutive three-point shots en route to 20 first half points, as Carolina jumped out to a shockingly large halftime lead. Early in the second half, Carter took it to the basket and dunked over Tim Duncan, drawing a foul—a dramatic play and a dramatic state-ment. Wake made a run late, but Carolina held on to win. Suddenly, there was no more doubt about whether Carolina was a good team or would be in the NCAAs. Carolina had turned into a borderline great team, a Top 10 team with legitimate postseason aspirations. All in a few short weeks! Dean Smith's vision was starting to emerge.

To see this unfold was for me immensely gratifying. In all my years of following Carolina bas-ketball, I had become more emotionally invested in this team than in any other. That was partly a result of being around the players at different points in the season and having some sense of who they were. It was partly because some of the public criticism and doubting of Smith, although mild in retrospect, had angered me, just as it had angered Ademola Okulaja, as smacking of ingratitude.

And it was partly because I was now writing fairly detailed columns after each game. The col-umns consisted of observations (and quotes if I had covered the game in person) about how the game fit into the season as a whole, as well as my amateur's eye prescriptions for what Carolina needed to do to get better. I began getting feedback from readers of the *Inside Carolina* website on a regular basis. Apparently, there was a market for what I was doing, although I think that at that point probably no more than 2000 or 2500 people read any single article I wrote for the site.

But mostly, my investment in the team rested on a childlike faith that no matter how grim the situation, Carolina basketball was going to continue to be successful, continue to maintain its consistency. That was my hope all season, but I wasn't at all sure rationally that it would happen. Even now, looking back, I remain struck by how easily the 1996–97 season might have gone into the tank at any number of moments.

Instead, the Tar Heels translated each narrow escape into increased confidence, and by late February an *expectation* that they would play well and win each time out. Which is exactly what happened over the remaining regular season schedule against Maryland, Clemson, and Duke. I covered the payback win against Maryland at College Park, a day where Carolina executed brilliantly on offense all afternoon long and refused to let a good Terrapin team get back into it. Just after the game, I saw Bill Guthridge, who said, "That was better than in December, wasn't it?" I also stood near Dean Smith just outside the Carolina locker as the coach was handed a Diet Coke and a copy of the stats sheets before going to meet the media. Smith looked tired and spent at that moment, and though I didn't say anything at the time, I asked myself, "I wonder how long he can do this?" Carolina's players were a happy bunch, but the aura was one more of satisfaction at a job well done than that of euphoria at a great escape. The open self-doubt of a month before was gone.

Winning had become a habit, to repeat an old coaches' saw. But with each new win, the bar was raised a little higher: Carolina was now a favorite to win the ACC Tournament and go deep into the NCAA Tournament. Could they do it? In the ACC Tournament, the Tar Heels answered the first question with an emphatic "yes." After a close but ultimately comfortable win against Virginia, Carolina played Tim Duncan and Wake Forest for the third time in the semifinal. The Tar Heels were unfortunate not to have a lead at halftime and enough things had gone wrong to cause worries. But then Carolina came out and played perhaps the best half of the season to win going away, taking the season's euphoria to yet another level. The Tar Heels then beat State for the third time in the final as Shammond Williams, tournament MVP, hit three consecutive three-pointers midway through the second half. Incredibly, the North Carolina Tar Heels, who had over the latter part of 1996 and the first half of 1997 had gone 6–11 against ACC opponents, were now league champions, indisputably its best team, and a No. 1 seed in the East with first-round games to be played in Winston-Salem. Smith as usual gave all credit to the players. Bill Guthridge was interviewed on the radio after the game and said, "This is the kind of game you can look back on in a few years and say, that was pretty special what we accomplished that day."

*

It was also pretty special six days later when North Carolina pulled away in the second half to defeat Colorado and give Smith the all-time Division I record for coaching wins and advance to the Sweet 16, a win that ranks high on Carolina fans' list of all-time great moments. I watched that game in Seattle (visiting Adria) with Tom Williams, who now lived out there. Adria and I were staying at the home of Neil Jacobson, a clinical psychologist with a doctorate from UNC, and his wife Virginia Rutter, a doctoral student at the University of Washington. In his late 40s, Neil was a very thoughtful, impressive person with a zest for life and a magnetic personality. And he was a serious Carolina basketball junkie—on top of an extremely impressive professional career as a nationally recognized researcher on marital therapy and domestic abuse. When Adria and I first watched a Carolina game with Neil during the 1994-95 season, we hit it off with both shared basketball and political interests. After that, it was a given that we would go over there when in town—Neil liked to have little "Tar Heel parties" with people he could share his satellite dish with. One time, we brought Tom Williams over, and he became a regular too. During the first round game against Fairfield, Neil and Virginia were in Hawaii, and Neil couldn't see the game, so he called up every 10 minutes during the second half and had me give the play-by-play over the phone.

Adria and I stayed through the next weekend as well, as Carolina advanced to regional play in Syracuse. Tom, Neil, and I watched nervously as Carolina struggled every which way but finally beat California to advance to play Louisville in the regional final. Dean Smith looked absolutely exhausted in his postgame press conference and admitted, "I'm a night person, but this one got to me." The next afternoon, a refreshed Smith regaled reporters in a wide-ranging press conference, covering everything from recruiting changes since the 1970s to why Clifford Rozier transferred to Louisville in 1991. Smith looked happy, glad to be in that position with his team, completely in his element. Virginia, Neil, Adria and I watched the media session via satellite, and Adria made a comment about how rare it was to see someone of such obvious character and integrity speaking in the public sphere.

Twenty-four hours later, North Carolina ran out to a big halftime lead against Louisville. But the Cardinals made a good comeback to cut the lead to three, and memories of the Maryland nightmare of 10 weeks before began to surface. Dean Smith told his players during a timeout with eight minutes to go that they'd had a good run and maybe it was over, which fired up Ademola Okulaja and the rest of the team. A few minutes later, Carolina was up by 20 again, the bench was jumping up and down, and Carolina fans were cheering appreciatively. When less than a minute remained, Smith reached over and shook Bill Guthridge's hand for the 787th time to celebrate Smith's 879th career win, both men smiling broadly. The 1997 team had come all the way back from the edge of the precipice to the highest plateau in college basketball, playing beautiful basketball in the process. As Smith put it at one point during the run, not even the fondest Carolina fan could have imagined everything that had happened in the second half of the season. In a world in which faith in what you are doing and perseverance through difficult times are not always visibly rewarded, Carolina's players and coaches had demonstrated to fans, observers, and themselves that with a little patience, visions—like the vision Smith had for his '97 team—can be realized.

The lasting lesson seemed to be that if that team could turn it around, no situation was too desperate, at least where Carolina basketball was concerned. That notion may seem crazy now, and it certainly seemed crazy in early January 1997. If luck had not been kind to the Tar Heels at a couple of key junctures, the virtues Carolina's coaching staff demonstrated in continuing to teach the team and the virtues the players showed in staying together, staying on the same page, and believing in what their coaches had to say might not have been rewarded so handsomely. And if there hadn't been talent to begin with, if that Carolina team hadn't always had the seeds of a beautiful flower within it, it might not have ended so happily, either. Many coaches work hard, many players play hard, but most don't get anywhere near the Final Four. Most of the time, the Book of Ecclesiastes seems to be right—all human works are vanity, it all comes to naught. But by a combination of talent, virtue, and luck, the endeavors of the 1997 Tar Heels came to fruition. An Aristotelian belief in the benefits of exercising human virtue had trumped the Augustinian emphasis on the limitation of human works, at least for one extremely uplifting and gratifying moment.

In the end, as it turned out, Ecclesiastes and Augustine were right—Carolina got beat in the Final Four by Arizona, as the Wildcats revealed some flaws that had been concealed for weeks. The 16-game win streak had ended, and Carolina went home disappointed, as so often before. But one bad game wasn't enough, not by a long shot, to erase the glow of what 66-year-old Dean Smith had done with the 1997 Tar Heels—or what the players had done for themselves.

*

For the October 1997 issue of *IC*, I wrote an article called "The Last Class" talking about how the incoming freshman class of Brendan Haywood and Max Owens looked slated to be the final players Dean Smith would coach for a full four years. Smith had four more years on his contract, he would be 70 in 2001, and that would probably be that.

As it turned out, the thought was in the right place—I was just off by three and a half years. One Wednesday night in early October, I came home after a very full day out and about at Union Theological Seminary to receive a couple of phone messages saying, "turn on ESPN." Word that Smith was going to announce his retirement had come out. I later found out that Smith's friend Pearl Seymour had known for a couple of days what was going to happen, and that Bill Guthridge had been making extra preparations for weeks knowing it was pretty likely that he was going to have more than assistant coach responsibilities before long. But at that moment, nothing but a flood of emotions and memories. I spit something out for the website that night, and wrote another piece after waking up involuntarily at 5:30 a.m. the next day. The press conference came in the afternoon, which Adria, in from Seattle, watched with me for about 15 minutes before I had to scamper off to class. I could handle Smith walking away from coaching, or so I thought, but I couldn't handle Smith walking away from the public spotlight as easily. For a while after his retirement, Smith got lots of attention of course, but eventually it would fade out, and there'd be no more press conferences extolling the Smith way of doing things, no more long stream-of-consciousness comments which it took a Talmudic scholar of Carolina basketball to fully interpret. Smith still had his health, and still had a lot to contribute. But someone whose very presence in the public consciousness had what I considered to be an ennobling effect on the entire culture—especially the culture of North Carolina—had stepped down, and it was impossible to think he wouldn't be sorely missed.

The subject of who would replace Dean Smith had occupied countless hours of speculation among North Carolina fans for years. I never had a firm opinion on how exactly it would turn out, but I had always had a clear preference for what I thought would be the best thing to happen: Bill Guthridge should get to be the head coach. I didn't expect that would happen, though.

As late as the winter of 1997, when I was staying in Chapel Hill with the Simpsons, who are close friends with the Guthridges, Dr. Simpson had clipped an article from the Charlotte paper about Guthridge. Dr. Simpson seemed proud to show me the article, which contained Guthridge's advice on how to be happy as a No. 2 person. Only a few months before that, before the Tip-Off Classic against Arizona, I had been chatting with Guthridge about the team's trip to the Basketball Hall of Fame in Springfield, MA, and joking to him that "one day we'll have to get you in there."

"I already am," Guthridge said with a mischievous smile.

"You are?" I asked, thinking for a second that I had somewhere along the line missed something really big.

"Yep, in a picture next to Dean." At the time, that was more than good enough for Guthridge.

Some people later spoke as if Guthridge's contentment with being Smith's right hand man, as opposed to a head coach elsewhere, meant there was something wrong with him. What it in fact reflected, I thought from day one, was that Guthridge had made a decision that he loved Chapel Hill and Smith's program too much to leave, and that he valued being an important part of North Carolina basketball more than he valued individual advancement. To me, it was a remarkable story about the value of being happy where you are and of choosing stability over the rat race, loyalty over personal ambition (and also of being supported by one's family in those choices). And by 1997, the Carolina basketball program was truly Guthridge's life work, just as it was Smith's life work, albeit in a different role. Guthridge had invested almost all of his professional life in helping build and maintain Carolina basketball, and for years he had watched out for the best interests of the program like a hawk. Indeed, his competence and capacity to handle many of the details of the program had literally added years onto Smith's coaching career.

With that as a backdrop, one thing was for sure: Bill Guthridge wasn't going either to take the job or to stay on as head coach merely for the purposes of ego gratification. He was going to take the job because it was the best thing for North Carolina basketball, and stay coach as long as he thought it was the best thing for North Carolina basketball.

*

Bearing all that in mind, I wrote in a piece shortly after the coaching transition that Carolina fans should understand that Bill Guthridge could not possibly owe them anything in excess of what he owed to himself, which was to steward as well as he could the program he'd devoted almost his whole life to and indeed helped embody. That said, I also fully expected Carolina to continue to be very successful on the court under Guthridge, and that while Smith would be missed, Carolina would retain its identity, play the same kind of basketball as in the past, and maintain its consistency (although I wasn't sure the "streaks" of NCAA appearances, 20-win seasons, etc. would necessarily continue forever). And I wrote that Guthridge's head coaching career probably would be judged most on whether the team could continue to win the close games.

The 1997–98 season confirmed those expectations. Guthridge recognized he had a veteran team with four players who had been regulars in the trenches together for three years, plus Ed Cota

The North Carolina bench during the final minutes of a win over Seton Hall at the Great Alaska Shootout, November 1997.

and the Senegalese center Makhtar Ndiaye, and he appeared to give more on-court freedom to Carolina's players offensively, so long as they continued to play together. Defensively, Carolina stayed for the most part with the sagging man-to-man defense, which also worked well, and although Carolina wasn't looking to trap and create turnovers very often, they were able to fast break quite a bit off of rebounds.

By early November, when I traveled to Chapel Hill to see two exhibition games, Carolina already had the makings of a very entertaining team that ran the court hard, passed the ball well, and played with a lot of flair. Guthridge looked comfortable in the head coach's hot seat in dealing with the media, and the crew of beat reporters seemed to appreciate that he spoke more directly than Smith had. After the second exhibition game, one newspaper writer joked that he would report that Guthridge had caused an international incident after the new head coach had ripped the traveling team from Venezuela for a lack of hustle and not running back on defense—Guthridge had said pretty bluntly that his team would have been better off spending the afternoon practicing.

What made 1997–98 special was a combination of three of the hardest-working and mentally determined players North Carolina has ever had—Antawn Jamison (referred to by Guthridge as a "warrior" at every opportunity), Ademola Okulaja, and Shammond Williams—along with a shooting guard of boundless talent, Vince Carter, and a remarkable distributor of the basketball in Ed Cota.

The wild card was "sixth" starter Makhtar Ndiaye. Ndiaye had been accepted as a transfer from Michigan by Smith as a stopgap after the early departure of Rasheed Wallace. Well-liked by his teammates, Makhtar was temperamental—on and off the court. During the 1996–97 season, Ndiaye had cursed a beat reporter for a major newspaper, and he had been testy with the media on other occasions (including with this reporter). But at other times he would flash a wide smile and be positively charming. The only other player to see significant consistent minutes was the freshman center Brendan Haywood.

After a couple of easy wins at home, Carolina flew to Alaska at the end of November to participate in the Great Alaska Shootout. The previous summer, I had made plans to cover the tournament for *IC*, and also arranged for Adria to cover the tournament as a photographer on the baseline. Carolina played UCLA in the opener and was absolutely awesome. Carolina won the game by over 40 points, actually exceeding that remarkable romp in Carmichael over the Bruins at the start of the 1985–86 season. Ed Cota seemed to anticipate every cut Vince Carter or Antawn Jamison would make before they made it, and consistently put the ball on the money time after time. Offensively, at least, the team already looked better than at the end of the 1997 season. The result was what soccer commentators would call a "comprehensive" victory. After both that game and an equally lopsided win in the semifinal over Seton Hall, Guthridge told the media this was the players' accomplishment, and that we would best use our time by talking to the players about it.

The players certainly had plenty of stories to tell. Antawn Jamison had almost been injured on a team dogsled ride earlier in the week when he fell out of the sled. Since he wasn't hurt, everyone else thought it was funny, but Jamison said he didn't plan on going on any more dogsled rides. Ademola Okulaja reported that the highlight of his trip was winning a huge teddy bear from a carnival contest. Makhtar Ndiaye said he had called home to Senegal to tell his parents about all the snow in Alaska, and that they couldn't believe it. The young freshman Brendan Haywood admitted that he had been picked on and hit the most during a team snowball fight. This was a team having a good time.

There was also a nice sense of community among the Carolina fans who made the trip to Anchorage—Adria and I went and visited Leesie and Megan Guthridge in the stands, sitting amongst various players' parents. And it was amazing to see how many local Alaskans had a Carolina interest. The Alaska Shootout was a big deal in Anchorage, a sellout every year, and a little difficult to get tickets to. The fact that Carolina was there made it a happening. So half an hour before the tournament final against Purdue, with his father's permission, I interviewed a nine-year-old kid whose face was painted Carolina blue. He had traveled to Anchorage from another part of Alaska with his father to see the game. He said Vince Carter was his favorite player, and picked the Tar Heels to win by 50.

Antawn Jamison works for position on the low block.

Vince Carter blocks out on the defensive end.

It didn't quite work out that way, as Carolina fell behind in the first half against a good Purdue team. But the Tar Heels rallied to get right back into it. Shammond Williams, who had voiced some dissatisfaction with the number of shots he was getting and appeared to miss Smith the most of all the players, had the green light at the end of this one, and buried two long three-pointers with a hand in his face in the final minutes to put Carolina ahead to stay.

Carolina had won the tournament, and also the first close game for their new coach. It was a happy scene all around backstage after it was over. Somehow, redshirt freshman Orlando Melendez wound up getting to hold the tournament trophy, a large golden bowl, and the perpetually cheery Melendez let me take a close look at Carolina's latest hardware. I was reluctant to leave the scene, and with some time to kill before our flight back to Seattle, Adria humored me while I went onto the court about 45 minutes after the game to shoot hoops with some local teenagers. I hit a couple of jumpers from the spot where Shammond had hit his, we scrounged up a souvenir Carolina hat someone had left behind in their seat, and headed to the airport in the best of spirits.

It had been a terrific weekend of snow, ice, and basketball. But though I was thrilled that Adria had enjoyed taking the pictures, meeting Bill Guthridge, and even interviewing a few players, there was a lot more going on with us than just that. Only weeks before it had looked like we were going to become just another statistic in the file labeled "Long-Distance Relationships That Didn't

Work Out." It had been four and a half years together, and it was about time that some decisions about what we were doing got made. Aware of all this, Virginia Rutter and Neil Jacobson had us stay at their house to provide a comfortable space for us during the week before the tournament. Neil, the marital therapist, largely played it coy and stayed out of it—until he asked us if we would be willing to be guinea pigs for a practice therapy session with a visiting marital counselor for his graduate seminar on marital therapy techniques. I was—and still am—somewhat skeptical about America's therapeutic culture and dedication to individualistic self-help. But amazingly, that session did wonders for us. And more important, Neil told us that the unanimous consensus among the students in his class was, "Neil, Neil, don't let them break up."

So both Adria and I were on a high when we went to Alaska. But when we got back to Seattle, I certainly had no idea what would happen. Adria's father, Peter, who had been probably the No.1 fan of our relationship, was going to drive me to the airport, and at the last second Adria decided she better come along and put off getting back to schoolwork.

We walked into the Seattle-Tacoma airport together, and discussed the options, none of which seemed very satisfactory. Until Adria said, "Well, we could get engaged." Adria had set aside dozens and dozens of proposals that I had made with varying degrees of seriousness over the years. But suddenly, she had turned the tables and was dead serious. A couple of minutes later, we called home to Sewanee and told my parents what happened, then Adria went out and told her dad, who high-fived her.

We then had to part ways. Dead tired still from the overnight plane back from Anchorage, I crawled onto the redeye back to New York, amazed at what had just happened, and sincerely praying to God that this was the right thing. I'm sure there would at least have been some buzz between us after that great trip to Alaska if Carolina had lost, but depending on how it happened, I might have been in a funk or the chemistry might have been different. I'm not sure whether, if the Alaska tournament had turned out differently, what happened an evening later in the Seattle airport would have been different as well. My wife and I are both glad we didn't have to find out.

"In 1993, while I was stationed in San Diego, Dean Smith called me at work to tell me 'Chris (my girlfriend) is ready to wear your wings.' He stated he didn't know exactly what it meant, but knew it was important to both of us. This was my future wife's way of letting me know she was ready to marry me. Coach Smith called me with what little time he had between an ESPN interview and catching a flight out of RDU. He didn't even understand what it was all about, but took his valuable time to do something for someone he didn't know from Adam, that would change our lives forever."
                                                              —Chris Schuyler, 47, military officer in Dumfries, VA

*

One of the things I most appreciated about Union Seminary was the month-long January vacation, which made it possible for me to cover the team fairly closely at least for part of the season. I spent the better part of the break in 1998 driving around the South to see the Tar Heels play road games against Georgia, Clemson, and Maryland, as well as two home games in Chapel Hill.

The games at Georgia and Clemson were particularly fun—Adria again served as a photographer at both. The Tar Heels were not at their best in Athens against Georgia, who was shooting the ball well and had a really good game from their talented rookie, Jumaine Jones. Carolina was down by about seven with just two minutes to play—and yet managed to tie the game up, with Okulaja hitting the game-tying free throws in the final minute. Okulaja then hit a three to start overtime and give Carolina its first lead in a while, but it took a Vince Carter lay-up on a well-designed, well-executed play with two seconds to go to give Carolina a two-point win. A look at the faces of Carolina's coaching staff after the game showed that to win such a tight game in Smith-like fashion meant a lot. But almost before I could finish congratulating Guthridge after the game, he was congratulating me on the engagement announcement.

I don't think one can fully understand the abuse that North Carolina basketball gets, the mean-spirited reaction the Tar Heels often inspire in opponents' fans, until one has been to a game down in Clemson. Especially in his last seasons, when a well-publicized antagonism developed between Rick Barnes and Dean Smith, Smith made it clear that his sole goal in visiting Clemson was to win and get out of town as soon as possible. And on January 2, 1998, I could see why. The venom displayed by Clemson students seated behind the baskets went beyond the heckling present in Cole Field House or University Hall, and included the occasional taunt with racial overtones directed at individuals such as Antawn Jamison and Makhtar Ndiaye. Whether the players could hear them or not, I don't know, but it's hard to believe they weren't aware of the train of verbal abuse. Indeed, at the end of this game, a couple of players at the end of the Tar Heel bench talked back a little to the crowd. The word "hate" could be fairly used to describe the climate in Littlejohn that day.

Clemson had a good basketball team, too, so it was a lot to contend with as Carolina sought to go 2–0 in the ACC (having already beaten Florida State away). It was a close game when Coaches Guthridge, Ford, Hanners, and Pat Sullivan traded notes outside the Carolina locker in the first minute or two of halftime before going in and talking to the team. Whatever was said on this occasion hit the spot, as Carolina grabbed the lead in the second half, and—despite a couple of mistakes in the last minute—went on to win the game. It was a great victory in the most hostile of environments, and you never saw a more genuine smile than the one Bill Guthridge wore when the game was over.

*

Carolina continued to impress in home routs of Georgia Tech and Virginia, playing particularly well against the Yellow Jackets. Bobby Cremins and even his best player, Matt Harpring, expressed some awe of Carolina in postgame comments. When the Carolina team bus rolled into the back en-

Shammond Williams soars for a dunk against Clemson, 1998.

trance of Cole Field House at Maryland the following week, it was carrying the No. 1 team in the country. In an exceptional game against the Terrapins, Carolina lost a narrow lead due to a couple of mental mistakes with seven or eight minutes to play. It remained tight down the stretch, and the Tar Heels had by far the best looks to win in regulation, but Vince Carter and Shammond Williams each missed open jumpers on Carolina's final possession. Maryland made the plays in overtime, and Carolina fell to their first loss of the season after 18 wins. The Maryland fans stormed the court in a wild scene, so wild that the first thing I said to Guthridge after the game was, "Did you make it out of there okay?" He had, but he looked a little stunned, as I just stood there a few feet away trying to imagine what kind of feelings he might be having. Carolina wasn't invincible after all. But there was no panic or over-dramatized disappointment in the Tar Heel locker room after the game. Carolina's players knew they were still very, very good.

Indeed, Carolina had no problems bouncing back from the Maryland loss, and they quickly started a new win streak, including a blowout of Biblical proportions against Florida State. The next big test was against Duke, in Chapel Hill. After Duke had gone 2–14 in the ACC in 1995 without him, Mike Krzyzewski returned from back injury and burnout with a renewed focus—and soon, better personnel than ever. When Duke brought in a recruiting class that included Elton Brand, Chris Burgess, William Avery, and Shane Battier, it became obvious that Duke was not going to be 2–14 again anytime soon. So I wrote in the summer of 1997, months before Dean stepped down, that Carolina better hope they get the best of the Blue Devils in 1998, before Antawn Jamison left and before Brand et al started putting it all together.

The hype before the Carolina–Duke game reached unbelievable levels that year, although the only story I saw that was genuinely interesting was one about Dean Smith's plans to watch the game on television. Carolina responded to the pressure and the emotion of the situation with a brilliant performance—sparked in the first half by, of all people, Makhtar Ndiaye, who hit a couple of jump shots. Once the Tar Heels got going, Duke had no one who could stop Antawn Jamison, and the Tar Heels ran out to a 24-point lead. But then Duke, a potent three-point shooting team, made a run of its own to cut the lead all the way down to four with just a few minutes to play, greatly assisted by a technical foul called when Ndiaye slammed the basketball on the ground. Guthridge briefly chewed out his senior after yanking him. For a couple of moments, there was some doubt— maybe this Tar Heel team was capable of another collapse on the scale of Maryland in 1997.

No. Carolina essentially blew out Duke again in the final minutes of the game, starting with a tough shot by Vince Carter. Duke started missing again, Carolina gave the ball to Ed Cota, and Cota distributed the ball magnificently. The icing on the cake was when Cota tried to lob the ball to Carter off the backboard for a playground dunk. The pass was perfect—but Carter missed the dunk. Not to worry, the crowd was thrilled by the attempt, and the ball came down into the hands of Shammond Williams, who made an open three. That play seemed to typify the sense that Guthridge trusted his players to make good decisions, and was willing to tolerate a little showtime as long as it was a good basketball play. When the game ended, Carolina had won by 23, and the partying commenced. A few days later, I learned firsthand from Vince Carter that he slept in late the next morning (a Friday), as did a lot of other Carolina students, no doubt.

In short, Carolina was having a great season. Antawn Jamison and Vince Carter were up for All-American and national player of the year honors, Guthridge was being discussed as a coach of the year candidate. Those three flew up together to New York during Carolina's off week for a media luncheon for national player of the year nominees. I asked Bill Guthridge if he ever wondered

what would have happened if Carter, Jamison, and Okulaja hadn't shown up right at Carolina's most dire moment of need, the summer of 1995 after Stackhouse and Wallace went pro. Guthridge paused for a moment and said, "No."

But the climate of unambiguously good feeling didn't last wholly intact forever (it never does). Carolina again showed it was vulnerable by losing at home to N.C. State. State got the lead early on some hot shooting by C.C. Harrison, Carolina's players got caught talking to the referees too long and not getting back once or twice, and then when Carolina tried to come back, the Wolfpack made 25 consecutive free throws. In the subdued Carolina locker room, I saw 11-year-old Albert Jamison, with the same distinctive eyebrows as his big brother, hanging out next to the lockers. Antawn Jamison and Vince Carter later reported that little Albert's message that day was, "That's all right, you all are still going to win the ACC and go to the Final Four!"

Ademola Okulaja

That was the mindset as Carolina traveled to Greensboro for the ACC Tournament, after a disappointing loss at Duke in which Carolina had played brilliantly for 30 minutes but lost its lead when Ndiaye fouled out. The loss cost Carolina a piece of the regular season title, and now the Tar Heels would need to win the tournament to get the No.1 seed in the East. Carolina did just that, paying back all three of its regular season losses by beating N.C. State, Maryland in an overtime thriller, and then Duke. The final was still close at halftime, and I walked around outside in the New York drizzle, with that nervous feeling when you know that what happens in the next hour, although totally out of your control, is going to have real-life lasting consequences.

What happened was that Carolina whipped Duke in the second half, pulling away to a double-digit win, punctuated by two emphatic dunks by Antawn Jamison. Carolina would be a No. 1 seed in the East, and would be sent to Hartford—a couple of hours away from Union Seminary and New York City, but in relative terms, my backyard.

I didn't have tickets, and the press credential for *Inside Carolina* was going to be used by another writer. But David Eckoff, resourceful as always, came up with the phone number for the Navy box office. Unlike many schools, Navy, Carolina's first round opponent, wasn't expected to "travel well" and thus put their ticket allotment up for sale to the general public. So I expected to go to Hartford to sit in the Navy section. But the Thursday morning of the tournament, at Penn Station, I saw two guys wearing Carolina stuff, obviously getting ready to make the same trip I was on Amtrak. So I went over and said hello, and immediately we got into a long conversation. One of the guys was a lawyer from Fayetteville who, as it turned out, knew old friend Jonathan Broun, who had started his legal career as a public defender in Fayetteville. I showed him a copy of *Inside Carolina*, and we started talking about this and that pertaining to the Tar Heels. On the train the lawyer revealed that he had an extra ticket in the front row of the Carolina section that he would sell to me for face value plus a subscription to *IC*. No problem there. Before long, having disposed of the Navy ticket, I was inside the Hartford Civic Center, sitting in the first row behind the Carolina bench. Even though I was missing a Church History lecture to be in Hartford, I felt like someone upstairs was looking out for me that day.

After a slow start, Carolina beat Navy easily that day, winning 88–52. Saturday was bound to be tougher—Carolina would be playing UNC–Charlotte for the first time ever. I connected with the lawyer again on the morning train, and he again sold me a first-row ticket. We hung out at a McDonald's before the game and exchanged some smack with some Charlotte fans. The 49ers were a good team, what Bill Guthridge later called "the best 8 seed I've ever seen," and had been on a two-month roll since recovering from early-season injuries. They had an excellent point guard, Sean Colson, an excellent big man in DeMarco Johnson, and as soon became apparent, a good freshman three-point shooter named Diego Guevara. Both teams played well, but the 49ers were a little better in the first half. Carolina had a strong second half, but couldn't put the 49ers away. UNC-C kept making clutch shots and played a very physical game inside, bumping and holding Jamison at every opportunity. Down the stretch, Carolina did most everything right, including make free throws, but Guevara hit a three-pointer with a few seconds left to tie the game.

In a smart but audacious play, Jamison released down the court and Carter threw a successful length-of-the-court baseball pass to Jamison, who went up for a shot. The shot was partially blocked by Johnson and fell short. It should have been overtime then and there—but the referee had blown an inadvertent whistle, probably thinking Johnson would foul Jamison. Because of the whistle time had not run out, and Charlotte would have the ball with a couple of seconds to play and a chance to win.

Bill Guthridge showed his disbelief at the call, but I was amazed at how composed he was given the circumstances. Carolina had had a great year, but everyone knew that to go out in the second round would be a disappointment of the first magnitude, and would put an end to Guthridge's honeymoon as a coach—even though Charlotte was a good team, a Top 20-quality team. Carolina had played hard against a truly inspired opponent. They might not have deserved to win yet, but they at least deserved not to lose. And now they might, because of a referee's errant whistle. But no one on the Carolina sideline flew off the handle—or forgot to think about how to defend Charlotte's last undeserved shot.

Charlotte ran an inbounds play and got a halfcourt shot off which missed. The Tar Heels (and the referee) were off the hook. In overtime, Shammond Williams hit a three-pointer right off the bat, Carolina took command of the game, a key Charlotte player fouled out, and the Heels were on their way to the Sweet 16 in Greensboro. I stayed for the second game and watched Shammond Williams, who had scored 32 points, walk into the stands for a lengthy hug with his family. There was no better indicator of how much the win meant to Carolina's players.

*

I had to juggle two contrasting goals in the final two weeks of March 1998: Finishing my master's thesis on the decline of Mainline Protestant Churches in the United States since 1960, and seeing firsthand what was going to become of this 1998 team. What made it possible for me to even think about doing both was the graduate student's best friend, spring break. I had tickets for Greensboro already, so after four days of nonstop thesis writing, I came on down the morning of the regional semifinal, to stay with Bob and Becky Brown, my brother-in-law's parents, in Greensboro. Bob Brown had been an undergraduate at Carolina in the 50s and was about as true Carolina blue as you could get.

In front of what amounted to a home crowd, Carolina got the job done against Michigan State, looking sharp from the beginning to take a nice halftime lead. The Spartans threatened early in the second half, but Carolina pulled away again to win comfortably. After the game, I sort of participated but mainly watched as the sharks descended upon the losing school's fans: Carolina fans wanted to get prime lower-level seats off of the disappointed Michigan State fans, and big piles of green paper suddenly appeared and changed hands.

Bob Brown went to the Michigan State game, but he was too nervous to come watch the regional final against Connecticut two days later, so Becky took his place. There was a festive air in the crowd even before the game started, especially as word came in that Utah was demolishing defending champion Arizona—an announcement that caused Vince Carter to turn his head and his raise his eyebrows a little while doing his pregame stretches. I spent some time visiting with the Simpsons and Leesie and Megan Guthridge, and then with Tom Kerby, who somehow had fantastic seats down low. For Carolina to win this game would mean so much to my core Chapel Hill connections. And to make a Final Four would be the boldest possible statement that the tradition of Carolina basketball could and would continue after Smith's retirement.

My only worry was that Carolina was too much of a favorite, and that there might be too much pressure on the players and the coaches. Connecticut was a great team, the Big East champions, and indeed the exact same group of players would go on to win the national championship a year later. Even a 360-degree dunk by Vince Carter wasn't enough to make the Huskies go away in the first half. In the second half, Connecticut did a good job of containing Jamison and getting a hand in the face of Shammond Williams. Richard Hamilton, the future All-American, had an open shot from the wing to give Connecticut a lead and a big momentum boost with just about four minutes to go. That ball hung in the air long enough for the consequences of the shot to race through my brain. But when it came down, it was off the rim. Shammond Williams rebounded and immediately looked to push, throwing a long, three-quarter-court chest pass to Vince Carter, who caught the ball and in one motion passed to the trailing Antawn Jamison for an emphatic dunk. It was a spectacular play, and after that, the Tar Heels never looked back.

A few minutes later, North Carolina was celebrating another regional championship—and with a little extra mustard, too. Williams started playing drums with the pep band. Makhtar Ndiaye picked up a trombone and started blowing into it, and then climbed atop the scorer's table. Makhtar was in a good mood, and even went so far after the game to say that the players wanted to win the game to cheer up the victims of the several tornadoes that had touched down in the Piedmont that weekend. Tears flowed from coaches and players in the locker room. Nobody wanted to leave the arena—it was a Carolina love fest.

And with good reason. The standard for the 1998 team was always going to be postseason success, which meant minimally a Final Four. But to accomplish that goal when everyone expects it, and as the team everyone wants to beat, is very, very difficult. Many of the greatest Carolina teams under Dean Smith, 1976, 1984, 1987, 1989, had failed to do it. Given Carolina's run of four Final Fours in seven years prior to 1998, I wasn't sure all the fans understood that. Carolina had beaten the Big East Champion and the Big Ten Champion in decisive manner, along with a Top 20 caliber club in Charlotte, by far the most difficult road to the Final Four successfully navigated by a Carolina team since 1977. That Carolina was favored in each individual game belied the reality that statistically speaking, the odds were pretty high Carolina would lose somewhere along the way. Even if you thought Carolina should beat Charlotte 80% of the time and Michigan State and Connecticut 70% of the time, the odds of beating all three back to back would have been less than 40%.

But Shammond Williams wasn't worrying about such statistical constructions after the game when he made it clear that the narrative he had in mind could end only with a national title, soon replacing his celebratory smile with a stern game face. With Arizona, Kansas, and Duke all out of the tournament, North Carolina looked like the best team still standing. And Carolina's core players had all already experienced a Final Four, experienced the taste of losing, and, hopefully, knew a bit more about what it would take to win such a game. And so the familiar dynamic kicked in: Winning the regional provided only temporary satiation of the appetites of players and fans alike—the larger effect was to increase the hunger to win the whole thing.

*

Unfortunately, that hunger was not going to be satisfied in 1998. Utah jumped on Carolina early by shooting three-pointers, placing tall, physical players on Antawn Jamison, and getting right in Shammond Williams' face on the perimeter. Carolina had several chances in the latter part of the first half to keep it a really close game, but Jamison, clearly rattled, missed some big free throws, and Carolina trailed by 13 at halftime. Then Makhtar Ndiaye fouled out with over 15 minutes to play. Still down double digits with eight minutes to go, the Tar Heels began to play unmistakably better, and closed the lead to just two points with two minutes remaining on a Cota jumper. Guthridge decided to spring a full-court press on Utah to force the issue, but Utah guard Andre Miller broke the press, then faked out Antawn Jamison for a lay-up. Carter missed a one and one on the other end, and several free throws later, Carolina had lost in the national semifinal again.

Jamison kissed the floor at the end of the game, but he and everyone else in Carolina blue were heartbroken. Interest in Carolina basketball had actually increased since Smith's retirement, but that final loss was like seeing the air go out of a balloon. Jamison, it was thought, almost certainly would go pro, and quite possibly Carter would leave too, while Shammond Williams would graduate. It was the last chance for this group of players. Shammond had shot 2-12, Jamison 7-19, the team as a whole a season-low 39%. Carolina fans were so deflated by the loss that only a small handful turned out to greet the team on their return home.

I was bummed, but didn't have time to luxuriate in unhappiness—my master's thesis was due in three days. Even so, I took a couple of hours and banged out post-Utah and end-of-the-season columns, figuring I was playing a pastoral role. I saw the job of being a columnist as not unlike giving a sermon—afflict the comfortable (point out the mistakes after a win) and comfort the afflicted (insist the sky was still Carolina blue after losses). So after bad losses, I wanted to express the full pain of the loss and yet insist that it wasn't all that bad—even though that was tough to do at the end of a season.

After getting the columns out there, the only way I could cope was to throw my head into the rest of my life, everything else that was going on. Fortunately, there was a lot going on for me at that particular moment. The Monday before the Final Four, I had given a (real) sermon at Union Seminary on peace and disarmament, and on the day of the game I gave a talk to a local group about economic justice issues. My first book, an annotated bibliography of proposals to alter American society, had just come out. The master's thesis was due in a few days. Adria was about to visit from Seattle. And after turning in the thesis, we were going to visit Cambridge, MA to look at graduate school options for a doctorate in political theory. I had a lot of other things to think about.

But all that could only blunt the pain, not eliminate it. This was a loss that Carolina fans took hard, especially younger fans. But for all the fans' disappointment, the people who felt the most pain and who would have the hardest time escaping it would be those who lived through it firsthand—the participants. In fact, I began to wonder how exactly people who had hung around as long as Smith and Guthridge had were able to absorb all those disappointing losses, all the long rides home, all the possibilities for second-guessing themselves (and being second-guessed publicly), and still maintain their psychic health.

Obviously, in the immediate aftermath of losses, family members and confidantes, the closest friends, must have had important roles in helping the vanquished cope. But what about after the initial shock wore off—how could one avoid being plagued by doubt and retain the ability to get on with it?

Perhaps one way is to develop selective memory—remember the wins more than the losses. But's that not a real option for coaches who intend to learn from the past. Having spent time seeing Guthridge, especially, in action, both inside the gym and far away from it, I began to suspect a more plausible answer. Guthridge was naturally pleasant to just about everyone he met, and had the capacity to take genuine pleasure in a wide range of people. Over the decades, he and Smith each had built incredibly rich networks of friends and associates. Coaches in general tend to have strong social networks, by the very nature of the business; but because of the kind of people Smith and Guthridge were, theirs were exceptionally strong. Guthridge had often played the role of the disciplinarian within the Carolina program, of coming down on players. But based on my observations, his dealings with people outside of the program seemed to consist of a string of positive interactions. He talked to many, many people every day, perhaps more than he wanted to at times. But being in that web of mostly positive interactions with people whose respect you have is a good recipe for being a pretty happy person.

There is also the capacity for putting losses in a larger perspective that you would expect veteran coaches to have. No single loss, no matter how disappointing, was going to undo everything Smith and Guthridge had built up or change who they were. Long before they reached the mid-1990s, their self-esteem, both personal and for the most part professional, had been detached from the outcome of individual games. Smith or Guthridge might say after a loss or a poorly played win that they had not done a very good job coaching during the game or in preparation, but it was obvious that they did not mean to say they didn't think they could coach in general.

Finally, there's the realization that time heals all wounds. Probably no Tar Heel was more disappointed the night of the Utah game than Shammond Williams. Williams had shot 1–13 against Arizona in the national semifinal as a junior, and everyone knew it. Coming in to the Utah game, he was a plausible candidate for Final Four MVP if he shot well and Carolina won the national title. If defenses focused on Jamison and Carter, he was going to get good looks. Instead, Williams stumbled through another nightmare of a game. And Williams was a senior. His personal develop-

BILL GUTHRIDGE ON DEALING WITH DISAPPOINTMENT

Q. How do coaches keep a sense of balance in dealing with all the disappointments and setbacks that are involved in the job?

A: One key with Dean Smith was he never got too high after a win or too low after a loss. I got a little higher and a little lower than he did. But that's one of the keys.... I do think it gets easier to handle as you get older.

Q. Was the experience any harder as a head coach compared to being an assistant?

A: I don't think so. When I was an assistant coach, I wanted to win just as badly.

ment as a player was perhaps the single biggest variable in making Carolina not just a good but a great team in the last part of 1997 and in 1998, and he had put his desire for a national title on the table as openly as Jimmy Black had in 1982.

About a year after the Utah game, I had a chance to interview Williams during an NBA summer league in Boston, where Williams was getting what amounted to a tryout for the Seattle Supersonics. I asked him how often he thought about the Arizona and Utah games. Williams replied that he didn't think too much about those games and was focused on the future, but allowed, "I wish that there were a few things I could have done to help us out more, but it just didn't happen that way. Maybe it happened for a reason, maybe it didn't."

Maybe it happened for a reason, maybe it didn't. That's a fair way to describe the experience of any big loss or disappointment. And though the loss to Utah was disappointing, it was hard to feel *that* sorry for the people with hurt feelings. Carolina fans had been spoiled rotten. The departing players left with an impressive array of accomplishments. Bill Guthridge had been named national coach of the year in what was, until the end, almost a dream first season, and the second-guessing to which he was subjected after the Utah game (whether he should have ditched his rotating starting lineup, whether he should have played the bench more all year) was pretty mild and little different from what any coach who loses in a championship game environment could expect.

*

After Vince Carter and Antawn Jamison announced their decisions to go pro, it became obvious that Guthridge's job was about to get a lot, lot harder. Carolina's top two recruits—Jason Capel and Kris Lang—were both top-quality high school players, and Capel in particular was highly coveted because of his court intelligence and overall skills. But neither player was nearly as talented as Jamison or Carter, and both would now be called upon to become major contributors as freshmen. Additional new blood came in the form of Ronald Curry, a blue chip quarterback in football who also had become a high-school All-American in basketball. Some thought Curry would become one of the greatest athletes ever to grace Chapel Hill. Also returning would be sophomore Vasco Evtimov, a Bulgarian native who held French citizenship, after a year serving in the French military. Evtimov had been a multi-dimensional, highly demanded high school player in Long Island, but was unable to get off the bench very often for the 1997 team.

Unfortunately, Evtimov was suspended for half the season for playing as an amateur in a French professional league during his year away, an extremely frustrating experience for all concerned. That absence ensured that Carolina would start two freshmen—Capel and Lang—plus a sophomore center with little experience, Brendan Haywood, alongside returning starters Ed Cota and Ademola Okulaja. Carolina was going to have less offensive explosiveness than the previous two seasons out of the shooting guard and power forward slots, and Haywood playing a lot meant that the team would be more halfcourt-oriented and unable to press much. But Carolina would still have a master distributor of the ball in Cota as well as a great defensive player and tremendous overall leader in Okulaja.

That combination proved unexpectedly potent through the first half of the season, as Carolina ran out to a 17–4 record and a spot in the national Top 10, with all but one of the losses being very close. The wins were highlighted by a major upset victory over No. 2 Stanford in the preseason NIT tournament in New York, as well as a couple of impressive road victories over rivals North Carolina State and Wake Forest. By the end of January, a team many analysts would have picked to struggle had all but earned an NCAA bid, and doing well in the NCAA tournament seemed a real possibility.

It seemed obvious to me that this great start in the wake of losing Jamison and Carter was evidence of a fantastic coaching job by Bill Guthridge—and indeed, I still think what Guthridge did with the 1999 team represents his most impressive accomplishment as a head coach. But despite the fine start to the season, there was some grumbling building up on the periphery of the people who followed Carolina basketball.

Some of the grumbling was by people who were frustrated by Carolina's continued use of a relatively passive defensive scheme. As in the previous four seasons, Carolina played mostly a sagging man-to-man defense that didn't try very much to overplay the passing lanes and didn't often try to trap the other teams' ballhandlers with two players to create turnovers. The defense instead was designed to take away easy shots inside and to always have good position for defensive rebounds. The principle of giving help on drives to the basket meant that sometimes three-point shooters would be open long enough to get a shot off, though hopefully not without some harassment. In statistical terms, the defensive scheme proved very effective—Carolina held the opposition to just 39% shooting in 1999, and only 33% on three-point shots. And other teams, discouraged from getting the ball inside, shot seven fewer free throws a game than the Tar Heels. But Carolina created few turnovers, and watching this style of defense could be frustrating for a spectator, since the result of any given possession seemed to be more the result of what the other team was doing rather than what Carolina was doing. If the other team got hot and hit the difficult shots that were available, it looked to observers like there wasn't much Carolina could do about it.

I could understand that frustration with how Carolina was playing—but I also understood why Guthridge thought this was the best strategy for the team he had. The Tar Heels were not particularly quick at any position, didn't have a point guard who could pressure the ball very well, and had a big, ambling center who would be more effective blocking shots as a help defender rather than chasing anyone on the perimeter. Nor did Carolina have the quality depth needed to make the trapping strategy work well. And the Tar Heels were, except for two players, very inexperienced. My view was that this was simply something Carolina fans would have to live with and accept—with the hope that in the near future, North Carolina could indeed return to the more familiar, more aggressive, and more entertaining style of play. (And indeed, Guthridge and the coaching staff signaled their intention to return to pressure defense in 2000 shortly after the end of the 1999 season.)

But a second layer of criticism slowly began to emerge that I found deeply disturbing: personal criticism directed at Guthridge and his style. Guthridge, at age 61, tended to sit during the games, carefully observing what was going on while plotting his next move, not often getting too perturbed or too excited about any particular possession. He picked his spots carefully with the referees, unlike Duke's Mike Krzyzewski, who would often spend parts of timeouts barking at the officials. In short, Guthridge didn't act like he was the star of the show or that anyone had come to watch him.

Some Carolina fans grumbled that this personal style meant Guthridge wasn't intense enough. When Carolina began struggling a bit in the second half of the season, they claimed that Carolina wasn't playing well because the coach wasn't into it enough.

Those criticisms seemed to me to be extremely ill-considered, for several reasons. First, what coaches are paid to do is communicate, not gesticulate. There are different styles of communication, and what is more important than any particular style is that a coach be himself. And based on how well Carolina had played with such a young team all year long, and the knack Carolina still had for winning the close ones, I didn't see any problem at all on that front. The players to a man told reporters that what Guthridge was teaching them was no different than what Smith had taught: As Ademola Okulaja later put it, "From Coach Smith to Coach Guthridge, that really wasn't a change." Practices were organized with the same level of detail. No one had taken down the detailed performance chart for each player in the locker room.

And history had shown there was no correlation—none—between sideline histrionics and championship basketball. Yes, some championships had been won by demonstrative sideline coaches like Bob Knight. But many others had been won by less demonstrative coaches. John Wooden, the UCLA coach who won 10 NCAA titles in 12 years, firmly believed that coaches should sit down while the ball was in play, and practiced what he preached. Wooden would have agreed with UNC women's soccer coach Anson Dorrance's statement that "If you have to yell at them from the sidelines, you haven't coached them."

Second, I thought that most, if not all, of the perception that Carolina wasn't as aggressive as they used to be could be attributed to the sagging defensive tactics, as well as to the fact that the

1999 team simply wasn't as talented or flamboyant as its predecessors and had some obvious personnel limitations.

And third, I knew for a fact how intense Bill Guthridge was, how hard he worked, how much he wanted to win, and how much his players respected him. As an assistant, Guthridge was known as a stickler for detail, the coach who would visit classrooms to make sure players were actually there and who would demand that everyone be on time everywhere. And while Guthridge didn't have the intimidating presence Smith had, he could convey a sense of the importance of having your act together, having your "ducks in row" (as another Midwesterner, Dixie Wier, used to put it to our fifth grade class) and holding yourself accountable to a high standard. Exceptionally well-organized, he believed in running a tight ship, and expected everyone else to do the same. In fact, what Guthridge projected and in turn expected was what some philosophers would call a "manliness"— a quality of self-confidence and deep self-respect which comes from the practice, the habit, of having your act together, doing your homework, being organized, and taking care of the details.

This didn't meant that sometimes Guthridge would not come down hard on players in ways more typical of coaches. In fact I saw him bark at players unhappily in huddles more than Smith had in his last two years. But those exchanges were not the predominant mode of communication. Some could look at that fact and say, gee, he should yell at the players more like those other coaches do. But it seemed equally and in fact more plausible to say that the rarer use of that tool made it all the more effective when it was really important to get the players' attention.

And although Guthridge was indeed extremely nice to the people he met as a coach, and very diplomatic and generous when discussing other programs and future opponents, those qualities disguised the fact that Guthridge had very sharp, definite opinions about players, issues, and people that reflected his own high standards, opinions which informed his actions and decision making. But, just as Dean Smith had, most of those judgments he kept to himself, in the sense that he didn't talk about them in public.

*

The night before Carolina traveled to play Duke in January 1999, I had a couple of hours to kill, so I drove out to East Chapel Hill High School, in part to see the new school for the first time, but mainly to take a look at East's star junior forward, Chris Hobbs. Just before tip-off, Bill Guthridge walked in and invited me to sit with him. In a day and age where dozens of recruiting experts gush poetically about any high school player who can run, jump and shoot, Guthridge insisted on relying on his own judgment. Even as a head coach, he took on much of the work of scouting high school players. Hobbs was obviously on the radar screen, and after having seen him play in his two previous seasons, Guthridge wanted to see what the prospect looked like as a junior. So we sat together, watched the game, and talked about various things. Guthridge looked around at the mostly empty gym and talked about what a shame it is that Chapel Hill doesn't do a better job of supporting its high school teams. We also talked about *Inside Carolina* a little bit and he told me pretty bluntly that he thought the magazine had done some unethical things. I didn't press for specifics—at the time I too was getting more and more irritated at the increasingly negative tone of the publication. And on a related point, I agreed with Guthridge when he said, "The fans should enjoy the team they have now," rather than finding reasons to complain.

A few minutes later, Quin Snyder, the Duke assistant, entered the gym and came over and said hello with a big smile. When Snyder went out to the concession stand and returned to his seat with a hot dog, Guthridge good-naturedly poked at him a little bit, saying, "Is that your dinner?" Guthridge then told me that Snyder was a really good guy and would soon be a good head coach. Naturally enough, we started talking a little bit about the Duke game the following night, and I offered the optimistic thought that the players in their pre-practice interviews that day looked pretty focused, ready for the challenge. Guthridge nodded but said, "I don't know if we're good enough." Duke was just as good as feared, if not better, and had lost only one game, on a buzzer-beater to Cincinnati in Alaska. No one in the ACC had come close to the Devils so far.

And as it turned out the next night in Cameron, Carolina wasn't quite good enough. But they were darn close. The Tar Heels played a good first half, with Ademola Okulaja playing particularly well, converting two three-point plays inside late in the first half. Carolina trailed by only four at halftime. In the second half, North Carolina took a small lead and stayed right with the Devils until Ed Cota had to leave the game with about eight minutes to go, after a minor injury. Carolina then made a couple of critical turnovers, allowing Duke to push ahead for good.

All in all, it was a valiant effort by Carolina, and if a couple of calls had gone the Tar Heels' way in the last few minutes, the game might have gone all the way to the wire. Guthridge was calm and composed in the press conference and praised his team's play. But as he left the media podium to go back to the Carolina locker room, we made eye contact, and I could see the disappointment in his face. There were no moral victories at Carolina, and it didn't matter that Carolina was the underdog. Guthridge still wanted to win, wanted his players to win, even though he knew the odds were not in Carolina's favor on this occasion.

Plato divided the human soul into three parts: An appetitive part concerned with bodily pleasures and possessiveness, a spirited part that produced passion and courage, and a reasoning part. The well-ordered soul, Plato thought, was one in which the rational part ruled over both the spirited and the appetitive parts. In the world of college basketball, however, many announcers (such as ESPN's Dick Vitale) and fans talk constantly about passion and emotiveness, as if those qualities were the highest ends for a coach or a player. And for participants in some sports, such as linemen in football, passion and courage may indeed be the most important traits.

But basketball is not that sort of sport. Basketball is a sport that demands good decision-making and good judgment at every position. Passion and intensity are important, but as tools to help the body achieve the goals the mind sets for it. If the goals the mind sets are wrong or in error, passion and intensity alone won't get the job done. Sprinting as hard as you can back down court won't often make up for an unwise pass that gives the other team an uncontested lay-up. Crashing the offensive boards as hard as possible won't offset persistent bad shot selection, in the long run.

To be sure, playing at maximum intensity all the time does help win basketball games. More-over, it is very difficult to do. Even trained athletes will sometimes have lapses of concentration or face resistance from their bodies in making the extra effort all the time, to run down court quickly or challenge a shooter. But even rarer than a player or team that can play with maximum intensity is a player or team that can read the movement of the players on the court, making consistently good judgments in determining what is and isn't available, what sort of play is or isn't likely to work, and what sort of play a team needs at a given moment. What made Carolina basketball so consistently successful during the Smith-Guthridge era was precisely a quality of being able to make better decisions than the opposition, of being "smarter" in basketball terms—while also playing hard. Carolina aimed to play smart, play hard, and play together at all times. Often, of course, Carolina simply had talent and size superior to the opposition. But in games against oppo-nents with comparable physical tools, it was generally the playing smart and playing together side of the equation where the Tar Heels were more likely to have a consistent advantage (especially since almost every opponent came out fired up to play the Tar Heels).

In different ways, both Dean Smith and Bill Guthridge had coaching styles that reflected that emphasis. For both men, what Plato would call the rational part of the soul was clearly in charge—neither was going to get swept away by base desires or a need for ego gratification, and neither was likely to let his anger or spiritedness overwhelm his judgment. Sometimes that might happen, but not very often.

But that didn't mean that either man lacked a passion for the game, for winning or for seeing the players hustle. Far from it! Those motivations could be taken as a given. Bill Guthridge put in all the hours he did into the job in all its aspects—essentially seven days a week during the season, with no morning, afternoon, or night wasted—precisely because he had a passion for excellence and for seeing Carolina succeed. He wanted to win, as much as or more than any other coach in Division I. And for his coaching style, the best way to do that was to keep his emotions in check while the game was going on and focus on the task at hand, to keep the rational part of the soul firmly in charge and not get into a see-saw of emotional ups and downs.

It thus drove me crazy when some critics of Guthridge focused on his bench demeanor or sup-posed lack of intensity. That sort of criticism seemed to me to reflect a fundamental misunder-standing of both who this coach was and what the task of coaching is in general.

Though I often disagreed, I had much less of a problem with criticisms that focused on some specific decision or judgment Guthridge had made—so long as the critic tried to at least think through why the coach had made his decision. Coaches make decisions all the time before and during games, not all of which lead to positive results, and certainly Bill Guthridge, like all other coaches, made mistakes along the way. But the fact that a given decision leads to an undesired re-sult does not automatically mean the decision was not thought through carefully or was without basis, or even that the coach should not do the exact same thing again during the next analogous situation.

A lot of sportswriters don't acknowledge that basic truth before launching into criticisms of game tactics. And in terms of pure basketball knowledge, almost no writers about college basketball (myself included) are equipped with the technical understanding of the game to say definitively that one play or tactic was absolutely foolhardy or ill-advised. At best, most writers can report what the coach tried to do, and then report what happened. Evaluating whether a given decision, even if it leads to a bad outcome, was mistaken in itself in any particular case seems to me a far more dubious enterprise for sportswriters. Almost always, the coach had a plausible reason for making the judgment he did.

The best that can be done is to observe over a substantial period of time whether a coach's decisions tend to produce the desired results or not, especially in very close games where a tactical decision is more likely to alter the outcome. Through the 1999 season, Guthridge had a record of 58–14 overall, including a mark of 13–6 in games decided by six points or less or in overtime. And that last figure didn't include either of the 1998 wins over Duke or the win against Stanford in November 1998. No one pretended that Smith was not missed. But given that record, I found it hard to see how the performance of his successor represented a very significant drop-off in terms of making smart decisions to win close games.

*

The Duke loss on January 27, 1999 was Carolina's fifth of the year, and it came while Jason Capel was out fighting mononucleosis. An injury to Cota caused the point guard to miss a home win over Georgia Tech, and to play only limited minutes in a loss to Clemson. Carolina then lost two games, to Maryland and the rematch to Duke, as heavy underdogs. The Duke loss became the focus of some discontent, although the idea that Carolina should have beaten Duke in Okulaja's senior game represented more wishful thinking than rational analysis—the Blue Devils had gone 15-0 in the ACC prior to that game, no one had come particularly close to beating Duke, and they were overwhelming favorites to win a national championship. The home finale was actually close until nearly midway through the second half, when Duke went on a run that the Tar Heels could not answer. Despite the circumstances, Carolina fans were not used to losing by double-digits at home, and some began to react badly.

Even so, I thought Carolina had had a good season, relative to both preseason expectations and to what any other school recovering from such a massive personnel loss had been able to achieve. Carolina was 22–8, 10–6 in the ACC, and a Top 12 team nationally. I still felt that way about the season a week later, when Carolina again got whipped by Duke in the ACC Tournament Final. That loss came less than 24 hours after a stirring win over a Maryland team with Steve Francis that had put Carolina away convincingly in both regular season meetings. Max Owens and Jason Capel shot the lights out for the Tar Heels, who built a 23 point lead in the second half, then held off a furious Maryland rally with the assistance of a couple of nice plays by sophomore reserve Brian Bersticker. That win was easily Carolina's best performance of the year—and it showed that

Carolina, even in an "off year," could put one over on Gary Williams and a superior Maryland team at tournament time.

What changed perceptions of the 1999 season was what happened four short nights after the Duke loss, 3,000 miles away in Seattle. Carolina was sent west as a No. 3 seed to play Weber State, which featured a 6–5, slashing guard named Harold Arceneaux. Capel, Carolina's best mid-sized defender, was hurt again and available only for spot duty, meaning Arceneaux would have a clear match-up advantage against either the weaker Max Owens or the slower Ademola Okulaja. Arceneaux took full advantage to score 36 points, using a variety of drives, moves, and jumpers. And his teammates helped the cause—Weber State sank 14 of 26 shots from the three-point line as a team. Carolina looked a step slow in defending the perimeter early on, and once Weber State got confidence and showed they were not going to be blown out, they started hitting tougher shots too. Meanwhile, Carolina got literally no production out of 7-footer Brendan Haywood. Guthridge turned to Vasco Evtimov, who was starting to come on strong at the end of the season, and the Bulgarian sophomore delivered a double-double off the bench. Carolina trailed by 10 with four minutes to play, but made a furious comeback and had a chance to tie with less than a minute to play. But Evtimov could sink only one of two foul shots with 15 seconds remaining, leaving Carolina a point behind. After two Weber St. free throws, Max Owens turned the ball over with less than 10 seconds to go. Even then it wasn't over, as Cota stole an inbounds pass and scored to cut the lead to one, but after another Wildcat foul shot, Arceneaux intercepted the Tar Heels' last-ditch in-bounds pass. Carolina had lost in the biggest upset of the tournament.

That loss was a bitter pill to swallow. I felt horrible for the players, especially Okulaja, and I felt bad for Guthridge and the coaching staff. And I felt bad to some extent for North Carolina fans, who now had to watch the entire tournament and Duke's expected coronation knowing Carolina had lost. A loss to "Weber State" would be an invitation to teasing from other teams' fans, who delighted in seeing Carolina suffer. ACC fans had been raised on the conceit that smaller schools in obscure corners of the country could not have good or even great players, too—indeed I remembered how my friend Karen Price teased Kari Barnes, the N.C. State fan, after the Pack lost to Murray State in 1988, a similarly "unknown" opponent.

But then, how bad could you feel for Carolina fans? The tournament had expanded to 64 teams in 1985, and Carolina had won in the first round 14 straight years. No other school had done that. If you projected Carolina to be a winner in 90% or even 95% of those games based on being a stronger team, the law of averages was still eventually going to catch up to you. One of those cylinder chambers would have a bullet in it some day. That bullet came in the form of Harold Arceneaux plus a Tar Heel team that was a little flat defensively, despite the heroic efforts of Okulaja, Evtimov, and Cota.

As it turned out, in their next game, Weber State shot just 7–22 from the three-point line, and yet still took Florida to overtime. They were a legitimate team that shot the lights out from the perimeter against Carolina. The distance between a "smaller" school and a big school on an off day (with a key injured player) was smaller than most people assumed. Even so, I knew Carolina fans were going to be really hurt by this loss, so I stayed up late to write an immediate postmortem in which I noted that nights like the Weber State loss were a risk you had to take if you wanted to be a college basketball fan.

Some Carolina fans interpreted this event more or less the same way I did. Others started lashing out. One of the biggest targets was the sophomore Haywood. With no points and just one rebound in 20-plus minutes against a smaller opponent, Haywood's performance was bound to figure in any analysis of the loss. But some fans, using Internet message boards and other media, attacked Haywood personally, said he was a useless player, and so forth. Tough stuff for a 19-year-old—and a good explanation for why within a year Haywood was talking openly about how some self-proclaimed Carolina fans were not true fans at all.

The other obvious target was Guthridge, and some message board types started complaining, saying he was too old, that Roy Williams would be better, and so forth. I thought that sentiment represented the worst of Carolina fans, and a profound lack of gratitude and respect, for all the reasons noted above. To me, to disrespect Bill Guthridge was to disrespect Carolina basketball, just as surely as disrespecting Dean Smith would have been.

So I was pretty upset when the harping on Guthridge made it into *Inside Carolina* front and center with an article by another writer saying Guthridge should quit, printed just after the Weber State game. I thought the substance of the article was obnoxious, but perhaps was even more troubled by the baseline assumptions of some writers and fans who seemed to care only about games won, not the ethical dimensions of Carolina basketball and not the human beings who put in all the hard work that made the wins, the vicarious pleasure consumed by thousands of fans, possible. I began to think very seriously of quitting the magazine, and for a time in the spring of 1999 thought I would, before being persuaded to stay and work with two new editors. It was a tough dilemma—on the one hand, I still appreciated having a forum and the access to the team that *IC* permitted me. On the other hand, I was increasingly embarrassed to be associated with the magazine in any way and didn't want to be part of something that could actually harm Carolina basketball. In the end, I agreed to come back for another year, deciding that getting my own point of view out was the most important thing, even if I no longer had much respect for the forum I was using.

The media maelstrom after the Weber State loss was considerable. But even at that stage, the complaining about the coaching staff was pretty limited to the Internet fringe—the major media outlets did not yet join in. For the average basketball journalist, 58 wins in two years spoke for itself, despite the Weber State loss. But from the point of view of the standard print media, the Weber State loss did mean that Guthridge would face a measure of doubt going into his third season that hadn't really existed before.

*

A lot of people expected Carolina to have a better team and a better season in 1999–2000. The coaching staff made a commitment that they wanted to go back to a pressure defense style, which Guthridge said was a "more fun" way of playing. To do that would require depth at every position.

And Carolina looked like they would have just that: As of June 1999, the projected roster had at least two quality players at every position, counting incoming recruits Joseph Forte and Jason Parker.

But by the time basketball practice started, a substantial portion of that depth was no longer there. The first loss was of forward Vasco Evtimov. Perhaps frustrated by his ordeal with the NCAAs the previous season, Evtimov apparently just wanted to play basketball without the red tape. So Evtimov accepted an offer from a Greek professional team, and passed up his last two years in college. The news was disconcerting, because I still regarded Evtimov as a player with excellent potential. And, he was a natural hustler with a big heart, a floor burn guy—and with Okulaja gone, I wasn't sure Carolina had that on the roster.

Then Carolina found out that Jason Parker, a power forward recruited out of Charlotte, would not be eligible and would be enrolling in a military academy. On October 2nd, projected backup point guard Ronald Curry, a key component in Carolina's plans to apply pressure on defense, ruptured his Achilles tendon playing quarterback against Georgia Tech. He would miss all of basketball season.

Then, returning starter Kris Lang became ill with fever-like symptoms for weeks in the fall, causing him to lose his fitness. When Lang started feeling better and tried to get the fitness back, he over-trained and came down with shin splints. Lang would play in pain all season long. Finally, reserve center Brian Bersticker, a good shooter who had come on strong at the end of 1999 and looked like a player who could be effective in an up-tempo game, developed foot problems, culminating in a broken foot in the fifth game of the year. He would be out for the season.

The attrition wasn't limited to the players. Assistant coach Phil Ford, a recovering alcoholic who had stayed clean for a decade, was arrested for drunk driving in late September. It soon came out that he had had a previous relapse two years earlier, shortly before Smith's retirement. Ford entered a rehabilitation clinic in October, before rejoining the team as an assistant coach in mid-November. Ford's problems were painful to witness, even for those outside the program. And for those inside, in addition to the emotional stress of seeing a close friend experience both private anguish and public humiliation, the Ford situation absorbed time and energy—and, at the same time, placed new demands on the remaining coaching staff while he was away.

The final piece of the preseason nightmare was a Halloween night fight in which Ed Cota and Terrence Newby were implicated in injuries caused to several UNC students. Apparently, some friends of Cota's had gotten into a fight with a group of UNC students, and Cota and Newby were present at the scene. Cota and Newby claimed they were trying to break it up, but the injured students accused them of kicking and punching the victims. While the local police launched an investigation, Cota and Newby were suspended from the basketball team for about 10 days. And so Guthridge was presented with yet another source of stress and demands on his energy—and with the task of trying to install a new pressure defensive system with his top two point guards unavailable for a crucial stretch of practice. And the fight undercut both players' status as senior leaders— younger players such as Jason Capel were angry that their teammates had been involved, however tangentially, in something that could threaten the team's season. The Cota-Newby Halloween fight issue in fact was not fully resolved until after the end of the season.

By any standard, all that was a lot for one team to absorb. And while this team was expected to be good, it was not yet a veteran team. It was a team dominated by players who had one year of substantial experience (Owens, Haywood, Capel, and Lang), but who had not yet had to play leadership roles. Ademola Okulaja had made the 1999 team a lot better than it would have been otherwise, but he was gone, along with his savvy, leadership skills and knowledge of what it took to win. This new group of players would have to learn what that took themselves.

Yet despite all those considerations, expectations were still sky high when the season started. Carolina had just had a terrible football season in which the coach had narrowly averted being fired, and Carolina's fans were anxious for some good news, as well as to wipe away that Weber State game. (Dean Smith always had said he was happy when Carolina football played well, because it diverted attention and scrutiny away from basketball in the early going.)

So it was good news when Carolina did get off to a good start by winning the Maui Invitational in Hawaii, beating Southern California, Georgetown and Purdue—three quality teams. Carolina started a small lineup with Cota, Haywood, Owens, Joseph Forte, and Capel (playing power forward), with Lang available only for limited minutes off the bench, and it worked well. The biggest revelation, however, was the play of the freshman Forte, who came out firing from the opener and totaled 62 points in three games. It was clear already that Forte was not just an impact player, but someone who could become one of the best guards Carolina had ever had. Carolina fans started to get excited.

But that excitement was tempered by losses to highly-ranked Michigan State and Cincinnati in December. Capel struggled playing power forward against those big, bruising teams, and the Tar Heels were badly beaten on the backboards. Haywood struggled against Michigan State, in particular, and again began to hear criticism from the fans. Carolina had played respectably well and lost to what were probably the best two teams in the country. Even with a depleted front line, I thought the losses showed that Carolina could be competitive against the very best, but just weren't good enough to beat them yet. Maybe they would be by the end of the year.

But the last two games before Christmas caused everyone to re-evaluate the situation. Carolina lost a close game to Indiana in New Jersey, due to a combination of poor shooting by Forte and Capel and some defensive breakdowns in the last 10 minutes. That disappointment was compounded by a miserable night against Louisville on the road two days later. Louisville cut through Carolina's attempts at pressure, created turnovers, and ran out to a 15-point halftime advantage en route to a 17-point win. Suddenly, the skeptics were out in full force.

Up until that point, Guthridge had persisted with the plans to apply defensive pressure and play a lot of players. Deep reserves Orlando Melendez, Terrence Newby and Michael Brooker were all still seeing minutes off the bench, and Carolina was trying to force the issue defensively. After the Louisville game, Guthridge decided that wasn't going to work in 1999–2000, and that Carolina would revert to a contain-type defense. That decision, in turn, meant that the starters would be expected to play longer minutes. And with Lang now healthy enough to start, he would go back into the lineup. Max Owens would go to the bench—Joseph Forte had beaten him out for the shooting guard spot. Meanwhile, Guthridge was starting to work in football player Julius Peppers, who had joined the team in early December, for more minutes.

In the long run, all those coaching decisions paid off. But the immediate dividends weren't so clear when Carolina fell into a four-game slide in January. Carolina had lost at Wake Forest by surrendering a second-half lead, precisely the kind of game where an Okulaja was missed. Carolina seemed to lack leadership to respond to runs. Then a home loss to UCLA typified the problems with a more passive defensive style—the Bruins shot the ball very well, Carolina's new defense didn't seem to be that effective yet, and Lang and Haywood were repeatedly beaten to the ball for offensive rebounds by Dan Gadzuric and Jerome Moiso. Those lapses aside, Carolina played hard and rallied from deficits twice—but the Heels could not get over the hump in the final minutes, and they missed two game-tying shots in the final seconds for a very disappointing loss. Then the Tar Heels traveled to Virginia and played a very good offensive game, but again could not get the defensive stops it needed in the latter part of the game and ended up losing by two points to a much-improved Cavalier team.

As the losses mounted, the critics got louder. One Internet columnist wrote that Carolina's players were either "uncoached, or uncoachable." My view was quite different: The players were coachable, and they were being coached, but they weren't quite good enough, they hadn't quite figured out how to pull out close games, their habits weren't yet built up enough on the defensive end, and they hadn't yet mastered how to play for a full game with no lapses in intensity and no mental mistakes. Kris Lang would turn his head too late on defense, or Capel would force a bad pass inside, or Haywood would get beaten to a spot, or Forte, the talented freshman, would commit an out-of-control charge on a fast break. In short, they were coachable, and they were being coached, but they weren't finished products yet.

To me, the entire scenario had January 1997 written all over it: Carolina had a new core group of players who hadn't yet built up the habit of winning. The difference was, the 2000 group of players had a lot more adversity off the court to deal with, and not quite as much talent on it. I didn't know whether 2000 would turn out as well as 1997 in the end—but also thought it was crazy to rule that out. Carolina was still being coached and taught the same way in practice as they had been for years, they had a head coach who'd been through and seen just about everything in 30 years on the sideline and wasn't about to give up. There was a chance they could turn it around—the key variable would be how the players grew both individually and as a unit.

My insistence on hopefulness was a distinctly minority position in late January 2000, however. I started getting a lot of emails from people who couldn't believe I was still saying this team might turn out O.K. yet, which bothered me a little bit. What bothered me a lot was when *Inside Carolina*'s web site ran a long piece attacking Guthridge and the job he had done as a head coach—written by a recruiting analyst who regularly talked to high school prospects Carolina was considering. I obviously disagreed with the piece. But I also thought it was wrong for the magazine to permit someone who was part of the recruiting scene to also rip on a head coach's ability to coach basketball (as opposed to simply commenting on a coach's recruiting efforts). What if a prospect interviewed about UNC by a writer clicked on the Internet and found a piece written by that same person saying that Carolina was not being well-coached and that players who went there might be wasting their talent?

I'm not sure whether or not that constitutes a breach of journalistic ethics. I was, however, sure that this sort of thing could be damaging to the program. I thought it inappropriate for a magazine that covered North Carolina basketball and existed solely because of the great love so many people have for the program to be actively damaging Carolina basketball. I didn't agree with the publisher's view that *Inside Carolina* was not concerned with promoting UNC but covering it. To me it wasn't so much that *IC* was not promoting UNC, but that it seemed to be actively trying to tear it down. It looked to me that if Carolina continued to have a tough season, that *IC* was going to host an anti-Guthridge campaign. I didn't want to be a part of that in any way. I couldn't stop that from happening, but I could avoid having my name and my work appear alongside it.

So prior to a planned trip to Chapel Hill to cover home games against Florida State and Maryland in late January, I began looking into the possibility of quitting *IC* and joining another website, *uncbasketball.com*, which had a different attitude towards the program: namely, it believed you could be honest and be positive at the same time. The site was very professionally run, and the editor, Ben Sherman, had demonstrated a capacity for discretion as to what he would and would not print. Michelle Donohue Hillison, fellow graduate of Holy Family kindergarten, was the assistant editor and ran the section on the women's team. The only downside was that joining *uncbasketball.com* would probably mean the end of my media access, and before making a final decision, I wanted to cover the games I had planned to go to, talk with editor J.B. Cissell at *IC* and discuss the situation, and then decide.

The Florida State game was supposed to be a good chance for Carolina to get back on the winning track, and it probably would have been, had Ed Cota not fallen sick the day prior to the game. Without Cota available, suddenly Carolina was in for a dogfight against a quick FSU team. Point guard was the one spot on the court where UNC would have been able to count on a big advantage against the Seminoles, but now Guthridge had to go with senior Newby, who was somewhat mistake-prone, or unproven freshman Jonathan Holmes. Making matters worse, Forte got his fourth foul early in the second half on a charge, and Carolina's offense stalled for a long stretch with him out of the game. Holmes came on and played a spirited game and got the bulk of the second-half minutes at the point, but FSU took advantage of his small size and inexperience by putting 6-8 Ron Hale on the freshman, which helped force two crucial turnovers in the final minutes of the game. Forte tied the game with just over a minute to go, but then got beat in the paint by Hale for FSU's go-ahead basket. Carolina ended up losing by five.

I saw a Carolina team that had played its heart out, but wasn't quick enough to get to FSU's swingmen Hale and Anderson—and couldn't come up with the defensive stop when it was needed most. Jonathan Holmes, the almost-hero of the game, sat in the locker room, crushed. Joseph

Forte insisted that everybody was still hanging together. And Jason Capel answered a reporter who questioned the team's intensity by saying, no, that's not it, "guys are playing hard out there." But not well enough. Meanwhile, veteran sportswriter Caulton Tudor asked Guthridge if the recent bad streak had made him reevaluate his own coaching future. Guthridge interjected and said no, he hadn't thought about that and was worrying about the team. "We've been through times like this before," said Guthridge. "You just have to overcome them." One win, Guthridge added, and the team would be back on track.

Even so, it seemed clear to me that Guthridge was very unhappy, really not himself that day. Down in the dumps myself, after the game and the write-up I drove over to the Simpsons to spend some time commiserating with David and Suzanne. Suzanne was really upset about how Guthridge and the team were being treated in the media, and was especially sad about the FSU loss, because she knew the Guthridges had family members who had flown in from Kansas for the game. The losses were taking a toll, and Suzanne ventured the thought that if it continued like this, maybe Guthridge would step down at the end of the year. "I would hate to see it end like this," she said, "he's such a good guy." Suzanne also told me not to stop writing about the team, not to bail out. That mutual therapy session cheered me up a little. The Simpsons were going to remain unquestionably loyal to their friends the Guthridges. So were a lot of people not as close to the situation, like Dan Broun, now living in Durham, who with his wife Becky wrote a letter of encouragement and support to the coaching staff right after the Florida State loss. My core circle of Chapel Hill people were determined to stand by who and what they believed in—not simply as a matter of supporting "my team, right or wrong," but because of their positive appraisal of and genuine concern for the human beings involved.

More important, Guthridge and his staff were determined not to let the season go into free fall, and to get that one win that would put things back on track. That task got a little easier with some intervention from the elements, as several inches of ice and snow blanketed the Triangle the day before the Maryland game. The storm caused officials to postpone the game a day to Thursday night (my birthday, the 27th). However, by Thursday, conditions were still bad and few out-of-towners were expected for the game. So university officials opened the gates to all students with an ID, and said they were free to inhabit the lower level seats of the Dean Dome so long as an actual ticket holder for a given seat didn't show up.

The result was magnificent—a veritable social revolution inside the Smith Center. The students—young, passionate, and not yet very rich—inhabited the seats usually held by the middle-aged, jaded, and comfortable. Forty-five minutes before the game, the students began testing their strength with "Tar!" ... "Heel!" chants back and forth between spectator sections. The noise was important and impressive. But just as important and impressive was the climate of unconditional love for the team the students created, the same immediate bond between student body and team that existed in Duke's Cameron Indoor Stadium and that once had existed in Carmichael. It was nothing short of a Carolina basketball revival.

"Carolina beating Maryland at home during last year's snow storm was very emotional. I was a few rows away from the court. It was exciting to see the crowd be so into it and be such a factor. Watching the expressions of joy and excitement on the faces of the UNC players and feeling so relieved and happy for the team moved me to tears."

—Sharon Hodge, 39, doctoral student in Durham

Carolina jumped out to an early lead against Maryland, a Top 20 team, the players looking sharp and on their toes, appreciative of the way the fans roared with approval for every good play. Even so, Carolina was down at halftime, thanks to a run of three-point shooting from the Terrapins. In the second half, however, Carolina immediately made a move to tie the game, and then Max Owens stepped off the bench to hit a three from the corner to put Carolina ahead. The Tar Heels looked sharp—Ed Cota at his best, anticipating where Haywood or Lang or Julius Peppers were going to go and getting the ball there, while Jason Capel hit shots and cleaned up the defensive backboard. With five minutes to go it was still a two-point game, but Carolina then ran off seven unanswered points to take command and eventually the game. With just a couple of minutes left, I reflected on press row on what I was seeing. Tears started to form as I thought about how the passionate crowd reflected the true spirit of Carolina basketball, the same love and passion that I had grown up with in Carmichael, and the hand of fortune that seemed to be at work in delivering that revival of spirit at the time a Carolina team needed it most. I didn't know if I was ever going to cover another Carolina game on press row, since I was still planning to quit *IC* after the game. But, I thought, if this is the last game I cover, I can live with it; I can live with the high and glow of this game for a long, long time.

Bill Guthridge was very much his old self after the game, smiling again, and even joking when I said I was glad that they had won on my birthday, "We won it for you, Thad." The players, too, were clearly buoyed by the win: Ed Cota talked about how he expected to win this game, and how he still had confidence in his teammates, while Jason Capel announced there was no way Carolina was going to lose its next game at Georgia Tech. All the players talked about what it meant to have the students so close and the spirit and support they had offered. "Our best fans," noted Haywood, "usually have to sit up in row double-Z." It was nice to have them down close.

Carolina indeed used the Maryland win to begin a stretch of much better basketball. Carolina won four of the next five games, the loss being an overtime classic to another great Duke team, with the Tar Heels rallying from 19 down to tie the game. (I wrote my first column for *uncbasketball.com* after that one, having finalized the *IC* decision.) The team moved to 16–9 overall with five games remaining. It looked like Carolina would safely make the NCAA Tournament with 19 or 20 wins. But the Tar Heels still needed to get a couple more victories to earn their ticket to the big dance.

Unfortunately, Carolina's good stretch of play did not carry over past an eight-day February layoff. Carolina had often not done well after such layoffs in the past, and in February 2000, Carolina stumbled early against Virginia's pressure defense, falling behind by 13 points at halftime. The Tar Heels had fewer turnovers in the second half, but were still too anxious offensively, and just when it seemed as though Carolina's defense had figured out how to shut down Virginia, the Wahoos brought in shooting specialist Keith Friel, who knocked down three three-pointers in quick succession to knock out Carolina's hopes.

It was a disappointing loss, and one that took away Carolina's margin for error. In the last four games of the regular season, the Tar Heels lost at Maryland and Duke, as expected, and then eked out crucial wins at Florida State and at home to Georgia Tech in overtime. Carolina played well at crunch time against FSU and Tech, but the inability to put either team away earlier was worrisome. The Maryland game was decided by a big run by the Terrapins just before halftime. Most embarrassing was the Duke game—Cota was injured early on and had to leave the game for several minutes. While he was gone, Duke went on a 21–8 run to take a 15-point halftime lead. In the second half, Carolina failed to clamp down on Duke's outside shooters, and even though the Tar Heels played dramatically better on offense—Cota ended up with 13 assists—the result was another dispiriting double-digit loss.

So Carolina entered the ACC Tournament with a lot of question marks. Clearly the Tar Heels were a very good offensive team, shooting an excellent percentage from the field—but Carolina also made some dreadful turnovers. Carolina also had good overall defensive statistics—but seemed unable to guard teams with quick, mid-sized perimeter players who could shoot three's, and was still prone to lapses at inopportune times. And Carolina could stay with a really good team such as Maryland for 38 minutes in a hostile environment—but not 40, which is what it took to win. So it wasn't as though Carolina was just a lousy team, even before March 2000. But they were a team that had lost a few more games than I or most had expected (12 in the regular season, compared to my own preseason projection of seven to nine losses). And it was a team a lot of Carolina fans and many in the media had already given up on. Carolina was a team of "underachievers" that lacked team spirit and sufficient intensity—that was the common media line on the Tar Heels. Based on the emails I was getting, not too many of my own readers believed me when I claimed there was still time to improve, and that this team was not far away from being pretty darn good. I still didn't know if it would happen, but thought it might.

That insistent hope made me as disappointed as anyone when North Carolina was defeated by Wake Forest in the first round of the ACC Tournament. It was a tough, defensive game in which neither team shot well. Carolina got good looks from the likes of Forte with three or four minutes to go that might have swung the advantage in the Tar Heels' favor decisively, had the shots gone in. Wake then took advantage of slow defensive rotation to get a big lay-up from Robert O'Kelley to go in front. Carolina couldn't catch up, and went home losers to the delight of the Charlotte crowd. Most analysts, like Dick Vitale, claimed Carolina lacked heart and pride. I didn't see that at all in this game. I saw a team that had played very intense basketball, that had played pretty good defense and had done a fine job on the boards, but that just hadn't shot very well. Joseph Forte, a 46% shooter, was 3–14 from the field and 1–4 from the line, and Max Owens was 0–3 off the bench. Better shooting would have made it a comfortable win. In pure basketball terms, I thought it was the best performance by Carolina since before the Virginia loss. Wake was a good team, a team that played Duke tough in the ACC semifinal and went on to win the NIT. Carolina wasn't that far from being a good team, either.

That was one part of the story. The other, bigger part of the story was that, with that loss, Carolina's season had hit a new rock bottom emotionally, for players, coaches, and fans alike. I wrote a little homily for Carolina fans after the game encouraging everyone to forget about basketball for a couple of days, but inside I was churning all weekend, frightened that Carolina would get left out of the tournament for the first time since 1974. With one of the toughest schedules in the nation, a 9–7 ACC record, and quality wins over Purdue, Maryland, Miami, and UNLV, Carolina would be all right, I thought. But there was a definite element of doubt, increasing a little bit as each new upset in the conference tournaments came in. Meanwhile, Bill Guthridge put his team through the toughest practices of the season, trying to work the Wake loss out of the team's system and build up that missing sense of cohesiveness and team confidence that might yet put Carolina over the top. But judgment rested in the NCAA Committee's hands.

When Sunday night finally came and Carolina was announced as a No. 8 seed in the South regional, the clouds from the Wake game seemed to lift, albeit slowly. Carolina had a new lease on life. Bill Guthridge gave the media some very upbeat quotes and said his team looked forward to competing in the tournament.

My main concern at that point was that Carolina win one game in the tournament, some little taste of success to build on for the next season. But not many people thought even that was very likely—Carolina had been written off by the national media and almost all of the local media as a dead horse for 2000. If while on the bubble they had played a little tight at times, now they had nothing left to lose. And that attitude began to emerge during the week in player statements to the media. Carolina's players were fired up to be in the tournament. By the day before the Missouri game, I had become genuinely optimistic, and told both my brother and brother-in-law that I would be really, really disappointed if Carolina didn't come out and play with a lot of enthusiasm against Missouri.

Carolina did exactly that against the Mizzou—the Tar Heels took the floor with an obvious spring in their step, a confidence in who they were and what they were doing. Something had changed—Carolina had the same constituent parts as before, but there was now a sense of a whole that Carolina had shown some of while winning five of six in midseason, only a lot stronger now. What had changed? A lot of theories were suggested, most of which had a little truth in them: Carolina had rallied together in the face of criticism and pooled their individual frustrations into a common hunger to win; Carolina didn't have any pressure anymore; they were playing better defense; Guthridge had figured out how to put a charge into this team; they were doing a better job on the "little things," like fighting through screens; they now accepted their roles better. But the most persuasive single explanation was probably that offered by Ed Cota: the players were finally now doing correctly the things that the coaches had been asking them to do all along, from the first day of practice, especially on the defensive end. The habit-building work of an entire season undertaken by the coaches had combined with a mental breakthrough on the part of the players to produce a team that suddenly was pretty good.

Good enough to beat Missouri, handily, with Brendan Haywood shaking off his Weber State nightmare of a year earlier with a career-high 28 points. Carolina had its one win and a little pride back. But one win wasn't going to be nearly enough to even start to salvage the season. Only beating Stanford and going to the Sweet 16, and getting the 20th win of the season could do that. Stanford was No. 1 again, and significantly better than the team Carolina had beaten the previous season. I thought to myself that Stanford's lineup was different enough now that Carolina probably would not be able to duplicate what it had done tactically in that game. On the other hand, I also knew that Carolina's players and coaches would be thinking and expecting only one thing when they hit the floor Sunday afternoon against the Cardinal: win.

To my amazement, Guthridge and his staff conjured up a game plan that led to an almost exact duplication of the way that November 1998 win over Stanford unfolded: Ed Cota controlling the tempo, Carolina avoiding turnovers and preventing Stanford fast breaks, and good inside-out defense, with Haywood neutralizing the Collins brothers and Mark Madsen in the paint. Stanford led by seven points late in the first half, but six points from Julius Peppers late in the half gave Carolina a one-point lead and a large share of momentum in front of a pro-Carolina crowd in Birmingham at halftime. In the second half, the game remained tight, and at one point it looked as though Stanford might break on top for good, but the Cardinal couldn't hit the backbreaking shot. With the score tied at 47, Guthridge's December decision that Carolina was going to rely on Joseph Forte, despite some of his freshman qualities, for backcourt scoring paid maximum dividends as the rookie hit back-to-back three-pointers to give the Tar Heels a six-point lead. After that, Stanford rushed their shots and seemed to lose their composure. Carolina hit its free throws to close the game out. The Tar Heels had done it!

When the final buzzer sounded, I don't think I was the only Carolina fan across the country to simply burst out crying with tears of joy. Certainly in the Carolina locker room, the coaches and players had the same reaction. After Forte had hit his shots to give Carolina the lead, I already began to well up as I thought about what this game would mean to the team, what it would mean to Guthridge, what it would say to all those who had ripped into the coaches or given up on the team, how it would show that Carolina was indeed still Carolina, and how happy the Simpsons and Megan and Leesie Guthridge, and the Brouns in Chapel Hill would be. I was at the beach in South Carolina with my parents watching the game, who were into it just as much as I was and had the same reaction I did. Mom cried, too, and hugged me when the game ended. Dad simply said, "I'm so happy for Bill it's unbelievable."

All season long, I had wanted more Carolina fans to understand better the hard work the players and coaches put in, that nothing about Carolina's standards or expectations had changed, and that instead of criticizing the coaches at every opportunity, good fans should be appreciative of their efforts in the midst of more than their share of adversity. But I also knew that no analytical argument I made after the fact could possibly substitute for a great victory on the court in proving that point—and that what Carolina's players and coaches wanted most was not some writer saying they had tried hard, but to experience trying hard and succeeding. The Stanford win was that great victory, the on-court success that said far more than a thousand columns ever could.

"Carolina basketball can be humbling and gratifying. Only the true fans understand that the players are ultimately responsible. We all knew who the true fans were last year when they jumped on the bandwagon during the tourney. Only us true fans have been supportive through the hard times."   —Donny Overton, 28, accountant in Rocky Mount, NC

All true—but Carolina's players wanted more. Yes, 20 wins and a Sweet 16 appearance were the marks of a decent Carolina season. But why stop there? Upsets in the South region meant that at least one quite unexpected team—North Carolina, Tennessee, Tulsa, or Miami—would end up in the Final Four. And suddenly, it appeared that Carolina had as good a chance as anyone to be that team. Was the Missouri–Stanford week just the work of a team that had revved itself up into an emotional fever pitch, or the mark of sustained, lasting improvement?

Carolina helped answer that question with another stirring win, this time over Tennessee, rallying from seven points down in the last five minutes to win 74–69. Carolina had a frustrating second half, and Haywood fouled out with eight minutes to play. But back-to-back lay-ups by Cota put Carolina ahead, and the Tar Heels put the clamps on defensively to clinch the win.

In the regional final against Tulsa, Forte netted 28 points, as Carolina spurted to a 10-point advantage in the second half, then held off a furious Hurricane rally to win 59–55. Carolina again controlled tempo and avoided committing too many turnovers or getting beat to loose balls by the quicker Tulsa team. And now Carolina, just two weeks removed from the NCAA bubble and media and fans announcing that the sky was not only falling, but had in fact fallen, was in the Final Four, cutting down nets and taking team pictures on the court. Bill Guthridge was smiling again.

*

The night after the win against Tulsa, the Guthridge family gathered in Kansas for a memorial service for Guthridge's 96-year-old mother, who had died the previous week after a long illness. In press conferences and interviews that week, Guthridge was pretty open about his feelings about his mother, and he even used the occasion of playing Tulsa to relate some memories of his Kansas childhood. That storyline, combined with Carolina's on-court turnaround, made Guthridge a sympathetic and admired figure in most major media outlets during the week going into the Final

PHIL FORD ON THE 2000 SEASON

Q. In 2000 when the team and Coach Guthridge were being criticized, what was that like for you, as someone on the inside?

A. Well, as someone on the inside, I could understand both sides. The fans, they support us and they're great, but sometimes fans don't see the whole picture, they aren't with us every day in practice. I think to be a coach at a highly recognizable school, you have to have a pretty tough skin. That's part of your job. I don't think you're ever going to please everyone. I mean, gosh, Coach Smith was even criticized. I mean, how do you criticize Coach Smith? And you know, Coach Guthridge hung in there and he taught me a lot that year as far as my coaching career goes, about handling a basketball team and handling adversity with a team. I think when things are going well, everybody's winning, everybody's happy, I'm not saying it's easy to be a coach, but it's a lot easier than when you're going through some tough times. But the way he handled that team, didn't let them give up, and let them know that the staff was still behind them, that no matter what you're hearing on the outside, as a unit, we're behind you and we know you can do it, don't give up—and look how things turned out. I mean, that was just amazing to me.

Four. But that sudden change of heart simply reflected the sports media's overwhelming tendency to judge every coach and player by their most recent results.

Carolina lost to Florida in the national semifinal after rallying from a big early deficit to lead by as many as six points. While the loss was close enough to inspire the usual "what if?" game (as in, "What if Ed Cota didn't get into foul trouble?"), the defeat did little to dampen the glow created by the Final Four run. The consensus among Carolina fans was that the Tar Heels had actually played better against Florida than they had in the national semifinals in 1997 and 1998. If Carolina could get quality point guard play to offset Ed Cota's departure, it looked as though Bill Guthridge's tough year in 2000 would be rewarded not just with the Final Four appearance but with the chance to coach a team of seasoned veterans that had already been through the wars, a team that could have a more typical "Carolina" year in 2001 and perhaps return to the Final Four. It was a prospect I was looking forward to.

Instead, Guthridge retired in June 2000, citing exhaustion. It was an understandable decision. In basketball terms, Guthridge had certainly achieved his goal of "keeping Carolina at the same level" as under the Smith era: In fact, Carolina's accomplishments on the court under Guthridge (80–28 record, two Final Fours, one ACC Tournament title) matched nearly exactly what Dean Smith had done in his final three years as coach (77–24 record, two Final Fours, one ACC Tournament title). On the court, the biggest single difference between 1995–1997 and 1998–2000 had, in truth, less to do with Carolina than with the fact that the Duke teams Guthridge had to contend

Q. How did the criticism of Coach Guthridge in 2000 make you feel?

A. I was hugely disappointed. In fact, it wasn't fair. I mean, I recruited those guys, you can blame me if they're not doing the job.... But I think that those three years were a tremendous transition. It couldn't have worked any better.

—Dean Smith

with were much, much better than the ones Smith had faced at the end of his career. And like Smith before him, Guthridge was leaving his successor with a very talented team that would have an excellent chance at early success. More important than those considerations, I was happy that Guthridge was going out on his own terms—and that the happy story of the man's 33 years of coaching in Chapel Hill had the happy ending it deserved.

*

Even so, I still remained a little disturbed by the events of the 2000 season. Five years of covering the team and four years of writing an Internet column 25–30 times a season had put me into contact with a wide range of Carolina fans (and a few Carolina haters). Those interactions forced me to confront the fact that not everyone had the same assumptions about Carolina basketball that I held, and that there was a diversity of attitudes among fans toward the game and the participants in it. At most schools, generating fan interest—attracting a greater quantity of fans—is far and away the most pressing concern for coaches and administrators. Sufficient quantity of fans was certainly not a problem for UNC, however. What was becoming a problem, I worried, was the *quality* of fans Carolina had. And I became persuaded that the type of fans Carolina had, what sorts of attitudes they had, might in time have a tangible effect on the program itself, and on how future administrations might react the next time a Carolina team had a difficult season.

The rest of this book, then, takes up two distinct but interrelated tasks: First, posing the general question of whether, in the broadest possible context, being a serious Carolina basketball fan is in fact a good thing, and whether there are better and worse ways to be a fan. (As the next chapter shows, I think that there are.) Second, using two complementary sources of original data, I undertake an empirical assessment of who North Carolina basketball fans are, what they believe in and value, and how being a Carolina basketball fan fits into their lives. To those questions we now turn, starting with a discussion of the moral and ethical issues involved in being a Carolina basketball fan.

4

Critical Reflections on Being a Carolina Fan

Part One of this book provided a description of both the socialization of one Chapel Hill–bred Carolina basketball fan and the experiences and reflections of one part-time North Carolina basketball journalist. The narrative of Part One also reflects one specific notion of what being a Carolina fan is, or should be, about—a notion that is not universally shared.

We now shift gears rather dramatically. The aim of Part Two of the book is to turn attention away from my personal experience and toward the experiences of North Carolina basketball fans in general. Chapters Five, Six, and Eight all directly report on the experiences of a wide range of Tar Heel fans. But that empirical look at Carolina fans is prefaced in this chapter by a more theoretical discussion of the pluses and minuses associated with being an intense UNC fan. Being a North Carolina basketball fan suggests both positive and negative things, many of which have emerged already, either implicitly or explicitly. It's now time to put my cards on the table, and give a more direct account of both what seems to be healthy about Carolina fans and what seems to be worrisome about them, before diving into evidence about how fans actually think and behave in subsequent chapters.

Chapter Four thus begins with a more explicit statement of some of the positive things I have come to associate with North Carolina basketball and with being a North Carolina basketball fan. I then turn to some of the less pleasant and less praiseworthy aspects of being a contemporary North Carolina fan—the underside of modern fandom. Those less pleasant aspects in turn can be grouped into two broad categories: Unpleasant aspects that result from a distortion or corruption in some sense, of the norms and standards of fanhood itself (as I have come to understand it), and criticisms that can be made of North Carolina fans of all stripes (some of which are also applicable to sports fans in general).

POSITIVE EFFECTS OF BEING SOCIALIZED AS A NORTH CAROLINA FAN

Community

For people who grew up in Chapel Hill during the Dean Smith era, college basketball was inescapable. The Tar Heels formed a common bond and a common rallying point for local residents. For Carolina to win represented a victory for Chapel Hill, and an opportunity to celebrate the place of Chapel Hill. This form of community identification of a town with its team has already been fleshed out in some detail—but my experience is unique only in the specifics. Many other Chapel Hill natives born anywhere between 1940 and the present feel the same way.

Carolina basketball also serves as a common bond for the students of the University of North Carolina. Visit Granville Towers 90 minutes before a game, and you will see streams and streams of students walking together to the Smith Center. It is a primary topic of conversation all year long, the fuel of countless mealtime conversations and late-night bull sessions. Many Carolina undergraduates define their four years there with reference to the basketball team's great triumphs and heartbreaking disappointments. Of course, some students at Carolina think that basketball is too dominant in campus culture, and not getting caught up in the whole thing becomes a means by which some students (particularly those of an artistic or political bent) distinguish themselves from the larger student culture.

The ties Carolina basketball creates among residents of Chapel Hill and on the UNC Campus itself represent two forms of community. A third form of community feeling generated by North Carolina basketball is the identification with the team felt by North Carolina residents outside the Chapel Hill area who call themselves Tar Heel fans. Carolina basketball is not experienced as part of the lifeblood of the local community in this case, but it is seen as something one can be proud of. Indeed, UNC basketball probably represents the primary way by which the state's flagship public university allows residents from throughout the state to make a claim on the university as belonging to them, in some sense. And in communities where there are divided sports loyalties, committing oneself as a North Carolina fan and not an N.C. State or Wake Forest or (less likely) a Duke fan is a major statement about who you are, and one that will likely influence whom you choose as friends.

A fourth form of community feeling generated by North Carolina basketball is the identification with the team felt by transplanted Chapel Hillians as well as UNC alumni. Seeing the Tar Heels play on TV 3,000 miles away becomes a way to express identification with one's school and/ or hometown. And it might be the occasion for gatherings with other Tar Heel fans and alumni in one's local area. This phenomenon, of course, is widespread and not at all unique to North Carolina basketball: Visit any sports bar in any major city for a college game and you will see gatherings of alumni from major sports-playing schools.

A fifth form of community generated by North Carolina basketball is relatively recent: the Internet. The most well-known and most easily criticized Internet "communities" are the message boards on various North Carolina and ACC-related web sites. Over time, different contributors to the message boards develop reputations and identities. However, this form of community is intrinsically limited by the fact that few contributors post under their real names, instead using aliases. A rather different form of Internet community is the email list-serve. The largest North Carolina basketball-related list-serve (so far as I am aware), operated by Andrew Markham, dates back to 1995 and has over one hundred members, and about 75 regular contributors. (North Carolina head coach Matt Doherty was in fact a member of the list-serve—albeit a "lurker"—for a short time when he was an assistant coach at Kansas.) Members of the list share reactions and commentary on games with each other, discuss recruiting, tell jokes and pull each other's legs. From time to time, the sense of camaraderie and shared affection members of the list have for one another spill over into real life.

A stirring example of this came in June 1999, when my friend Neil Jacobson, the Seattle-based marital counselor noted in Chapter Three and a frequent contributor to the "Heel-Hoops" list-serve for three years, died unexpectedly of a heart attack at age 50. My announcement of the news to the list-serve was greeted with genuine shock. Over a hundred members of the list-serve provided virtual signatures underneath a long letter penned by list-serve member Andrew Robinson of New Orleans, and sent to Neil's widow, Virginia Rutter. In contrast, Virginia received only a short and perfunctory note from the University of Washington's president after Neil's death. The type of community present on the North Carolina basketball list-serve rivals that reported by scholars who have found that, in some circumstances, Internet-based communities can produce quite compelling social ties, even among people who have never met or have met only briefly.

That Carolina basketball (and many other sports allegiances) is capable of producing feelings of tangible community in all these ways is an interesting sociological fact. Social scientists such as Robert Putnam of Harvard University have amassed a wealth of data demonstrating the decline of numerous kinds of community ties, from formal organizational membership to informal social gatherings, over the past 30 years in the United States. Examining the causes and effects of this decline and of broader changes in community life in the United States is now a major cottage industry within academia, occupying the attention of economists, sociologists, political scientists and ethicists. Strong community ties have been linked to an array of positive outcomes, from health and psychological well-being to economic productivity.

So to the extent that Carolina basketball is an occasion for developing social ties of various kinds, however informal, most scholars would acknowledge that it is a good thing. What is particularly impressive is that basketball (like many sports) has the capacity to generate social ties across generational, racial, gender, occupational, political and geographic boundaries. Members of the Heel-Hoops list-serve, for instance, range in age from college-aged to the retired, and in political persuasion from rock-ribbed Republicans to Ralph Nader voters. Whereas a number of sports teams worldwide actually reinforce religious or ethnic prejudices and are linked with xenophobic forms of community, Carolina basketball (and ACC basketball more generally) has had by and large the opposite effect. This becomes particularly clear if we ponder the role college sports have played in generating and sustaining new norms regarding race and racial equality in the American South over the past generation.

Even so, the answer to the further question of whether being a fanatic for Carolina basketball in fact has positive consequences for community ties is not obvious. We might think instead that excessive devotion to sports crowds out other forms of community attachments. We will return to that question shortly.

Loyalty

One word that gets talked about a lot with respect to North Carolina basketball is "loyalty." The most common use of the word pertains to the relationship between Dean Smith and his coaches and players. Smith is known for standing by his players and helping them in life decisions long after they have left Chapel Hill, even in the case of players who transferred away from UNC. Likewise, Carolina players have consistently spoken well of Smith and the program he built. Some journalists and observers have, for lack of a more appealing metaphor, likened the strong mutual personal bonds within the UNC program to those present in Mafia circles, with Dean Smith as the "godfather."

But how do North Carolina fans relate to that vaunted "loyalty"? Clearly, Dean Smith appreciated having many "loyal" North Carolina fans, but he didn't expect those fans to be able to call upon him for a job reference or life advice as a former letterman would. Moreover, there is this question: What does it mean for a fan to be loyal? One might mean that one should be loyal to "North Carolina basketball," in the sense of wanting what was best for North Carolina basketball. For some fans, what is best for North Carolina basketball in turn implies a range of considerations, and for others it simply means how many basketball games Carolina can win.

Alternatively, one might mean that a loyal fan is someone who should be supportive, almost unconditionally, of the human beings actually inside the program, be they coaches like Dean Smith, Bill Guthridge and Matt Doherty, or the players on scholarship at a given time. Loyalty of this kind means being supportive even when the team is losing or not living up to expectations.

A third concept of loyalty is based not simply on what is best for North Carolina basketball, and not on personal support toward the people inside the program, but on loyalty toward the ideals North Carolina basketball is thought to represent. A person inside the program who is thought to violate those ideals thus can be the legitimate target of criticism in the name of loyalty to a set of ideals. This conception of loyalty with respect to North Carolina basketball came to the fore in March 1998, after Makhtar Ndiaye, frustrated by the Final Four loss to Utah, made accusations of racial taunting against a Utah player, accusations that later had to be retracted. Many North Carolina fans were embarrassed by the incident and Ndiaye became (and to some extent remains) an object of scorn among Carolina fans. (On the other hand, Ndiaye is still very much part of the North Carolina basketball family—he was named a co-captain of the 1998 team at the team's postseason banquet, despite the Utah incident, and was even listed by former teammate Brian Bersticker as Bersticker's all-time favorite Carolina player in the 2000–2001 media guide.)

PHIL FORD: THE FANS SUPPORTED ME

Q. Last year when you had to go the clinic for rehab, did you get a lot of support from the fans?

A. It was unreal. There was some criticism involved there, but there was a lot of support not only from the fans here at Carolina, but the coaching staff and the university community in general. I also got support from Coach Odom, from Coach Krzyzewski, from Coach Shyatt—the support I received was just unbelievable. Sometimes you know, you go on the road, and the fans and the kids had a good time with it, but you know, that's part of my life. That's a disease that I have. I'm very glad for the fact that I have the support that I do have.

The thing about it is, my life is in a fish bowl, and there's nothing wrong with that. It was my mistake, I lived up to my mistake, I know I wasn't taking responsibility for my disease, and that's the main thing with an addiction disease, whether it's eating, drinking, or anything, just taking responsibility for that disease, and I wasn't doing that. And now I try to do it, every day one day at time, and the best thing I can do to make amends to people I may have upset or offended is to stay sober the rest of my life.

In contrast, fewer fans had a similar negative reaction to Phil Ford's drunk driving arrest (and the revelation of a prior offense) in the fall of 1999. Despite the potentially lethal nature of Ford's actions, they were interpreted by most fans through relatively compassionate lenses. Ford was, as Dean Smith put it, someone who had a disease that needed to be treated. Some Carolina fans thought that Ford should have been dismissed, but there was no great uproar and little surprise when it was announced that Ford would remain on the staff. Some Carolina fans even thought that retaining Ford was powerful, moving evidence of the degree of loyalty that members of the North Carolina basketball family have for one another.

Loyalty to the program, loyalty to the people inside it, loyalty to a set of ideals: I grew up believing in all three forms of fan loyalty. And as long as Dean Smith remained the coach, there seemed little need to separate out those three conceptions of loyalty. Dean Smith was Carolina basketball, and he was someone who stood for the right things. I differed from some fans, however, by insisting that the same equation held for Bill Guthridge, that as someone who had invested his life's energy and talents into Carolina basketball and who always would have the best interests of the program at heart, Guthridge deserved the same loyalty and recognition. Many Carolina fans agreed with me, but some began to argue that if Carolina could win more games with a new coach, there should be a new coach.

On the other hand, some Carolina fans (usually not the same people as those who criticized Guthridge) expressed real disappointment when it was reported early in the 2000–2001 season that Matt Doherty used profanity at times in coaching his players, a departure from the decades-long practice of Smith and Guthridge, who eschewed such language. The fact that Smith did not curse was a mark of pride for some Carolina fans. Now Carolina had a coach who did curse. Which form of loyalty would win out—personal loyalty to the new coach and his way of doing things, or loyalty to an idea? That question is one that may re-surface in years to come.

In fact, while some Carolina fans (especially older ones) have been dismayed by Doherty's language, few to date have grumbled very much or very loudly in public. (A handful, no doubt, rejoiced.) Much more grumbling was heard about an earlier decision made by Doherty: to bring his own staff of assistant coaches from Notre Dame to Chapel Hill and give notice to Guthridge's assistants, Dave Hanners, Pat Sullivan and Phil Ford. Some Carolina fans thought that this action violated North Carolina's long tradition of loyalty.

Doherty countered, sensibly, that not bringing in the coaches that had helped him be successful in South Bend would have been disloyal on his part. But the concern of some Carolina fans for the fate of a school's assistant coaches in a business that is often quite harsh and unforgiving reflected something significant about those fans: They valued the loyalty shown by members of the Smith program toward one another, saw it as admirable, *even though they themselves could not directly participate in it.* Indeed, some fans saw that loyalty as valuable and unique precisely because American society, with its relentless cycle of business takeovers and its habit of discarding places and people, so often seems to devalue long-standing loyalties and relationships.

This is not to say that "loyalty" is a morally supreme value that can trump all other considerations. Moreover, as we have just observed, different conceptions of loyalty can conflict with one another. But long-lasting relationships in which human beings feel compelled to stand by one another, even through difficult times, are in general a good thing. Carolina fans are justified in both admiring that quality in the basketball program established by Dean Smith, and in trying to emulate that sense of loyalty in their own families and organizations.

Learning to Deal With Disappointment

As the foregoing narrative indicates, if I learned one thing early on as a Carolina fan, it was that North Carolina wasn't always going to win. And more important, I was taught that losing need not be an occasion for recrimination against the participants or anyone else. Even so, it took a long time, and a lot of pain, before I could learn to harness my emotions in the aftermath of losses. I don't know if it's a good thing that I was socialized in classic WASP male style to internalize one's grief—maybe it would have been better if I had cried tears every time I was crying on the inside. But I do know that learning you weren't always going to get your own way, even with respect to the things you really cared about the most was probably a good lesson. If nothing else, learning to accept defeat was a good preparation for a life involved in political questions (particularly as a left-winger in the United States!).

Inability to process defeats in a healthy way has been identified by sociologists of sport as a major negative characteristic of some sports fans in the United States. Psychologist Daniel Wann of Murray State University has developed a model of how "highly identified" spectators respond to their favorite team's losing: Whereas fans with "low identification" experience no loss in "social identity" after defeat (although they are happy to "bask in reflected glory" along with highly identified fans should the team win), highly identified fans experience a literal blow to their personal identity, and do not have the option of detaching that personal identity from that of the team (i.e. "cutting off reflected failure"). In Wann's model, such fans are likely to lash out as a coping strategy in the immediate aftermath of a loss, directing their anger most logically at the victorious team's fans or participants. However, if such targets are not available, "The irate fan, unable to lash out at the cause of his distress, acts aggressively towards his spouse in an attempt to reinstate his lost esteem." Wann's findings show the potentially serious consequences of not learning how to deal with disappointment. And, as discussed further below, they also demonstrate the crucial importance of being able to separate out one's own identity from that of the team in order to help process defeat.

Character: Doing Things the Right Way

I grew up thinking that North Carolina basketball was an exemplar of how to achieve something significant in the world while doing it the right way. As discussed in the following section, part of the reason I thought that had to do with the social and political values Dean Smith represented within the state of North Carolina. But the importance of self-discipline to achieve anything significant also rang through loud and clear, a message that got reinforced through some of my periodic interactions with Carolina players or with Bill Guthridge, and most of all through the quoted words of Dean Smith. (To this day, I often find myself repeating Smith's dictum that being late is a selfish act, because it says that you think your time is more important than someone else's.) Of course, there were many other actors in my life who played a much more important role in communicating that same message to me, starting with my parents. But having the people whom you considered your heroes also be role models certainly reinforced the message.

As will be seen in subsequent chapters, a large percentage of hard-core North Carolina basketball fans associate Carolina basketball with traditional values regarding character development, the importance of hard work, discipline, and taking pride in what one is doing. Included in that number are many Carolina fans who do not share Dean Smith's politics, but nonetheless respect his commitment to those values. During an era in which few public institutions, educational or otherwise, seem particularly interested in moral education and the cultivation of character, Smith and his program seemed to many Carolina fans to be a welcome exception to the general trend.

> "We don't want to have a holier-than-thou type attitude, and we don't want the fans to have that, either. But we have tried to do things the right way."
> —Bill Guthridge

Liberal Social Values

Dean Smith is more liberal than any North Carolinian who has ever been elected governor or a United States senator. He opposed the war in Vietnam, supported civil rights activity, set about almost as soon as he became head coach to integrate his all-white basketball team (a goal not achieved until his seventh season), supported a nuclear freeze and opposed the death penalty. He also questioned the influence of advertisers (especially beer advertisers) on college basketball, let it be known that society had more pressing needs than pumping more money into college sports, and said that American society placed too much emphasis on being No. 1. In some parts of the country, those opinions would not be particularly controversial, although it would be unusual in any case for a basketball coach to be associated with them in a public way. But in the context of North Carolina, some of Smith's views had a positively countercultural quality.

It would be a stretch to say that Smith's views impacted to a great extent my own views, or those of other Carolina fans who admired his liberal outlook, in any detailed way. Until Smith's recent memoirs, I had never heard him give any sort of detailed explanation of the reasoning behind most of his views. Smith did not regularly tell the media that he believed in a loving God, not a vengeful one, or publicly complain about the death penalty. But Smith's well-known politics did increase my own affection and admiration for the program, as it did for a significant minority of Tar Heel fans.

Not all of the social values associated with Carolina basketball can be translated into a clear cut, left-right political spectrum, however. Fans of a variety of political persuasions were impressed by the generosity of spirit that came to be associated with Carolina's coaches, by the stories of personal kindness on the part of Smith, Guthridge, Phil Ford and other people associated with Carolina basketball. Smith couldn't make the world be like he wanted it, but he could affect the things within his control. There was a lesson in that, too.

Never Giving Up

Still another lesson that being a North Carolina fan inculcated was that one never need lose hope in a game. If Carolina was down 10 with four minutes to play, Carolina might not necessarily win the game, but there were good grounds for thinking it wasn't over yet. Carolina's capacity to win games in the late going rested upon hours of practice going over late-game special situations, and it rested upon Smith's own tactical acumen, but above all it represented a relentless competitiveness and belief that obstacles could be overcome. Carolina fans are extremely proud of the many comeback victories enjoyed by the Tar Heels. Some have taken it to heart and applied the metaphor of a Carolina come-from-behind victory to contexts beyond basketball and sports. Carolina basketball seemed to teach that there is a reasonable ground for hopefulness even in dire circumstances.

"We always seem to pull a rabbit out of the hat...I'm a very senior officer, and I apply the can-do, winning attitude each and every day in my military career. I can only hope that some day the military could have as much pride as UNC basketball has."

—James Hamilton, 37, naval officer in Virginia Beach, VA

A dramatic example of a fan who has applied that lesson to his own life is Steven Sullivan, a fan in Columbia, South Carolina, and a recipient of two kidney transplants. Sullivan became a Carolina fan as a young child, and on occasion as a kid traveled to Chapel Hill to see games with his father. A talented golfer, Sullivan began experiencing health problems and rapid weight loss during the 1980s. Doctors informed Sullivan that he was experiencing kidney failure.

After the diagnosis, Sullivan was placed on a regimen of dialysis three times a day. A series of complications weakened Sullivan's legs, and he eventually lost the ability to walk. While on dialysis, Sullivan recalls, the days meshed together to the point where it became impossible to distinguish one day from the next.

Sullivan wore a North Carolina outfit during his hospital stays in recovery, watched every Tar Heel game, surrounded himself and his wheelchair with Tar Heel paraphernalia, and boldly set the seemingly impossible goal for himself of one day returning to Chapel Hill to see the Heels play in person as he had as a kid. Sullivan says the values associated with North Carolina basketball resonated with him at a very early age when he watched Phil Ford and his Tar Heel teammates on TV: "I've always liked their style. I've always been a person to never give up."

During his bout with kidney failure, Sullivan had concrete evidence that Carolina basketball was more than just about what happened on the court. After learning of Sullivan's condition, Dean Smith began sending Sullivan letters about twice a year. Sullivan says the letters simply wished him well and encouraged him to stay positive. Sullivan kept the letters, along with other UNC-related material, nearby during his frequent hospital stays. "I'd show the letters to my doctors, and it kept my spirit up," recalls Sullivan. "Every time I was doing bad, I'd say I'm going, I'm going, I'm going to make it back to Chapel Hill."

Sullivan finally received a kidney transplant from his brother in 1989—along with the prognosis that he had at most five years to live. Sullivan continued to live with his mother in Columbia, and a month after the transplant began using a walker to re-learn how to walk. Amazingly, within six months Sullivan was not only walking but playing competitive golf again.

In July 1999, 10 years after Sullivan was given five years to live, he received a second kidney transplant, this time from his wife, Wanda. While in recovery from complications from this second transplant operation, Sullivan frequently watched Tar Heel games in the hospital while holding his newborn daughter. In January 2001, Sullivan finally fulfilled his dream of returning to Chapel Hill—he saw Carolina defeat Wake Forest in the Smith Center, 70–69. Reflecting on his experience, Sullivan says his connection with Carolina ". . .gave me hope. I probably wouldn't have met my wife or had the chance of having a child without it."

Basketball games in general may make a poor metaphor for life. But the ethos and spirit displayed in them can on occasion carry over into other, more serious arenas. Just ask Steven Sullivan.

Knowing Your Place as a Fan/Enjoying Wins More Than Losses

A final lesson I took to heart early from North Carolina basketball is that when all was said and done, I was only a fan. Not a participant, but a spectator. That being the case, how could I as a rational person make my self-esteem, what I thought about myself, rest on the accomplishments of other people, or more specifically, on the outcome of a game over which I had no control? Yes, it is appropriate and instructive to appreciate and enjoy the talents and accomplishments of others. It is in the nature of human beings that we enjoy other people performing in various activities, striving to do their best. But something goes amiss when consumption of other people's accomplishments crowds out full engagement with one's own endeavors. Growing up in Chapel Hill, I was fortunate to hear that message loud and clear from people like Bruce Reinoso, my trombone teacher, as well as from my parents and their friends. (In my specific case, it probably also helped that I knew firsthand that Bill Guthridge would probably be more impressed by someone like me doing well in school than by my knowledge of Tar Heel trivia.)

As noted above, sociologists of sport like to use the term "bask in reflected glory" to describe the positive feeling sports fans enjoy when their favorite team wins a game or a championship. Yet there is a natural propensity for sports fans to want to go beyond basking in someone else's glory, and to feel like they are actually participants in the accomplishment. What complicates the issue is that in college basketball, fans present at a home game sometimes can indeed be active participants and help influence what occurs on the court, albeit indirectly. However, that contribution is inherently a collective effort, not reducible very often to the actions of any one person. Furthermore, only a very small percentage of the people who see any given (televised) game see it in person. And only the superstitious among television viewers or radio listeners believe that anything they do during the game could possibly have any effect (however small) on what happens on the court. (Of course, one or two Carolina fans have been known to be a little superstitious!)

My own conclusion with regard to Carolina basketball is that my ability to take pride in the accomplishments of the players and coaches would increase to the degree that I put as much effort and persistence into my own pursuits as they did into theirs. I couldn't share in their accomplishments, but I could share their ethos to some degree. Most important, fully recognizing that what the Carolina basketball players do is essentially their accomplishment, not my own, made it less likely I would feel cheated if they didn't win or didn't play well. One could point to days in one's own life where one wasn't as productive as one hoped to be, or didn't make quite the extra effort. And separating out one's accomplishments from those of the team would make it possible to appreciate the wins and high moments for what they are—gifts given to the fans that are earned by the hard work of the players, not entitlements. Gifts, not entitlements, not something that fans deserved.

Of course, it's hard for highly committed fans to live up to that ideal of recognizing the distinction between one's self and one's team. When it doesn't happen, as Wann and co-author Nyla Branscombe have found, highly committed fans are susceptible to depression and rage following a loss. Probably most fans can avoid the rage that the sociologists describe, but firsthand experience leads me to think that depression or feeling down in the aftermath of a loss can be harder to shake. Even fans who rationally know better feel pain, sometimes profound pain, at losses. The psychological trick is to try to get more pleasure out of wins than pain out of losses. Maximizing pleasure from wins implies maximizing identification with the team on the occasion of wins. Minimizing pain implies reminding oneself sharply that one's self-esteem shouldn't rest on the outcome of a game (particularly one played by someone else).

As we have seen, sociologists who study hard-core sports fans have found that highly identified fans have a hard time "cutting off reflective failure" when their team loses, that is, separating themselves from the loss. But while this may be true as a generalization, there is no reason why this *necessarily* must be the case—especially if more sports fans were to become more self-conscious about how they handle defeat.

I would suggest that it is possible for one and the same person to have two seemingly opposed ideas at the same time: a profound longing to identify with a team, with the accomplishments of others, and a cool rational understanding that this is not really so. And with some practice, it's possible to condition oneself to emphasize identification in the aftermath of wins and separation in the aftermath of losses. This is why you don't often hear winners of big games saying, "It's only a game." The inherent tension in this process of alternating between wanting to identify with the team and recognizing one's own, very limited place as a fan and observer is not easy to negotiate, though common sense, experience, as well as the data collected for this book suggest that it does get easier with age.

Perhaps the best practical test of appropriate fanhood is what I call the "Carolina Basketball Can't Ruin My Day Test." The test is simple—witnessing Carolina lose a basketball game, even by 26 to Duke in the ACC Tournament in a dreadful performance—should not ruin one's day. Carolina's losing might make for a less happy day, and might even spoil one's mood for a while. But it shouldn't stop one from going jogging, taking time to reach out to someone at church, working on a project, enjoying time with family, or any other constituent part of a given individual's day. I know firsthand that this is a hard test to pass for Carolina fans. It doesn't apply to Carolina's actual players and coaches. I also hesitate to apply the test to the small minority of spectators who see a given game in person, especially those who have made significant effort or borne significant cost to be at a game. But I don't think it's too high a bar for the fan who simply watches a game on TV or listens to it on the radio, be it alone or with friends. Feeling bad about a game someone else played shouldn't cause someone to waste a day of his or her life—even if a couple of hours of hurt and low activity is inevitable.

NEGATIVE ASPECTS OF BEING A NORTH CAROLINA FAN

The foregoing discussion largely emphasizes the positive aspects of being a North Carolina basketball fan: the sense of community it provides, the opportunity to identify oneself with concepts of loyalty, good character, and positive social values, and the emphasis on never giving up. I have also suggested that keeping the games and the role of fans in perspective is a constituent part of being a healthy fan.

It's time now to turn to the less pleasant aspects of fanhood in the modern era. The discussion will first focus on four tendencies present among at least some Carolina fans that appear to be a corruption or a distortion of the positive ethic of fanhood articulated above. That discussion will be followed by an examination of possible external critiques of North Carolina fanhood (however construed).

Winning Is the Most Important Thing

The first potential corruption of the positive ethic of fanhood described above is the belief that winning games and championships is the *most* important part of North Carolina basketball.

All North Carolina fans are interested in seeing their team play good basketball and win games. But many Carolina fans believe that what makes Carolina distinctive is an insistence that not only following the letter of the NCAA rules but also ensuring an education for players and setting a good example are priorities which are not to be skirted for the sake of winning. These Carolina fans are proud of the fact that the Tar Heels do not exclusively recruit academically marginal players, that almost all the players graduate, that Dean Smith for many years tried not to over-recruit, that Smith refused to promise the moon to potential recruits, and on and on. (A very small percentage of Carolina fans have even criticized Smith for putting too *much* emphasis on winning by using the Four Corners tactics.) For this sort of Carolina fan, seeing UNC go on probation or force out a coach with long-term ties to the program would be far more painful than seeing North Carolina have a losing season. For that to happen would put Carolina fans in the same class as Kentucky fans or other schools' fans, from whom Carolina fans take pride in distinguishing themselves. And so these Carolina supporters get irritated and disturbed when they hear other self-proclaimed Carolina fans ripping into players and coaches when the Tar Heels lose.

Or at least, these fans *say* that winning really is not the most important thing. As will be discussed further below, whether the long-time values associated with UNC basketball would be able to withstand the pressures generated by losing remains an unanswered question. For now, however, it is enough to observe that unless we deny that college sports have any educational function at all, or unless we think those who play and lose are simply wasting their time, winning cannot be made the supreme goal of college athletics: what is most important from an educational point of view is all that is involved in the *process* of striving to win, only a small fraction of which is witnessed by fans.

Entitlement

A closely related corruption of the positive fan ethic is the view that being a North Carolina fan makes one entitled to witness winning basketball every winter. The problem with this sensibility requires some teasing out: Again, virtually every Carolina basketball fan *does* expect to see reasonably good basketball played each winter. But that does not mean that each Carolina fan has been issued an "IOU" for 25 wins by the players, the coaches, or the athletic director at UNC. For most Carolina fans, being able to see winning basketball and bask in reflected glory a couple of dozen times a year is a free gift.

But this is not necessarily true for all fans. A small minority of fans are substantial donors to UNC athletics. Naturally, these donors have more influence over the Athletic Department than the average fan. And as in the case at other schools, there is an enormous temptation for persons giving $5,000 or $10,000 a year or even much more to a school to expect to see a good team on the court. But once that mindset steps in, a critical question emerges: Do the donors think they actually hold a receipt payable in games won? If they do, then their donation to the university athletic program is not a gift at all, but an economic transaction.

To put it another way, to the extent that donors see wins on the court as reaping the returns from an investment, they must admit that they are not benefactors but rather customers (or at most, corporate stockholders), no different in kind than patrons of a professional sports team. Some big donors at UNC and elsewhere undoubtedly do think of themselves that way. But others do not, or at least would feel uncomfortable being described in those terms. The only way those donors can avoid that description, however, is to openly disavow the notion that a gift makes one entitled to a certain outcome on the court or a certain kind of season.

Seeing Players and Coaches as Commodities

Fans who place primary emphasis on winning and feel entitled to see a good team are likely to come to view players and especially coaches as commodities, not ends in themselves. It needs to be acknowledged that this view of players and coaches is in fact the norm in professional sports, as well as in major college sports. If a coach doesn't win enough games, get rid of him. If a player doesn't live up to expectations, waive him, trade him, cut him. Get someone else in there!

There is something very wrong about seeing college athletes as commodities—at least if one still believes that "amateur" athletics in the United States have a purpose distinct from professional athletics. College players do not get paid, and they have other responsibilities and commitments outside of their sport—like going to school. At some schools, of course, the notion of "earning your scholarship" is taken rather literally, and players who do not pan out to be good enough get booted off the team. That has not happened at Carolina. But such players as Ed Geth and Michael Brooker were not infrequently described by some fans as a "waste of a scholarship," because they did not make very prominent on-court contributions during games. For those fans, it didn't matter whether Ed Geth or Michael Brooker had a good experience in college, or learned to develop interests outside of basketball, or whether they had a good influence on teammates or on other students and community members, or whether they went on to have successful careers and become assets to the communities in which they live.

Viewing players' worth solely in terms of their statistical output means not viewing players as well-rounded people who are ends in themselves. At many big-time schools, the coaches, fans and players make no pretense that scholarship athletes are there to do anything other than play basketball. Carolina fans have long claimed that at UNC, things are done differently, which is why some Carolina fans are highly allergic to *ad hominem* criticism of players that makes claims not just about what a player did or didn't do on the court, but about the worth of that player as a human being.

> I know everyone wants to win, and that's extremely important, but you're dealing with kids, young kids. The more I got into my coaching career, I tended to see that more. You don't look at them as kids, you see a guy 6–8, 250 pounds, you don't think of that guy as a 17-, 18-year-old kid, you know what I'm saying? 17 or 18 years old.... I've got a 9- and 10-year-old right now, and 17 and 18 doesn't seem too old! I think sometimes we get wrapped up in the wins and the losses instead of the effort that the young guys are putting in.　　　　　　　　　　　—Phil Ford

For fans not to view the players as commodities, as interchangeable pieces of meat, would be quite a countercultural position to take within the climate of present-day college athletics. To claim that coaches, too, should not be seen as commodities, cuts even deeper against the established grain.

By the time I started following Carolina basketball in the mid-1970s, Dean Smith, as well as Bill Guthridge, already had the equivalent of tenure as professors of basketball at UNC. The metaphor of "tenure" is deliberately invoked here to suggest that during the Smith-Guthridge era, at least, the coaches were seen as respected educators and teachers, not just basketball instructors. (Smith and Guthridge could certainly fit in and more than hold their own in conversations with any member of the UNC faculty—and most UNC faculty members knew that!) To have tenure at a university means that the community recognizes that one's presence as a teacher is valuable in itself, whether or not one does as good a job teaching this year as last or is as productive publishing articles and books as one hoped.

Smith certainly had just that sort of recognition and respect from the university community in Chapel Hill, as did Guthridge, although they of course were not given their tenure with no strings at all. If for some reason Smith had stopped working hard as a head coach, it would have been noticed (although no one who knew Smith thought there was any chance that would ever happen). But Smith's position was so secure that very few people on the UNC campus would have begun thinking of him as disposable if Carolina happened to have a couple of bad years while he was still the coach (even though there would have been significant grumbling among Carolina's spoiled fans).

When Smith retired and Guthridge became the head coach, I believed that Guthridge, too, had long before earned his own "tenure," his own right to be regarded as more than a disposable employee, and I felt that however it went for him as a head coach, he should be able to go out on his own terms. That presumption was certainly held by Smith, the athletic director, and most other people close to the program. And it was shared by many fans—but not all. When Carolina lost a total of 24 games in the 1998–99 and 1999–2000 seasons, some Tar Heel fans acted like a few more losses than expected outweighed the 30 years of service Guthridge had provided to the program, and the fact that Guthridge's work over the years had contributed to hundreds and hundreds of wins, dozens and dozens of players graduated, and the buildup of an enormous well of goodwill around the Carolina program. Fans clamoring for a new coach in the (misguided) belief that someone else would automatically do better made the implicit value claim that winning as much as possible here and now was more important than loyalty or any other consideration, and that a new basketball coach should be seen more like a temporary employee than a tenured professor, even if he had been around three decades.

The Guthridge situation was unique for a lot of reasons—and in the end, of course, the coach did go out on his own terms at his own time while leaving an excellent base for his successor to build upon. It should also be noted that despite the clamor from some Carolina fans prior to the Final Four run of 2000, UNC Athletic Director Dick Baddour (who has dismissed coaches in other sports) stood squarely behind Guthridge. So the Guthridge story ended well. But the question remains, if some Carolina fans are willing to display ingratitude toward someone who helped build a level of success that is too easily taken for granted, how would they treat a completely new coach with far less experience and a much shorter track record?

Or to put it directly, how will Carolina fans treat Matt Doherty when disappointments and frustrations occur in the future ? As someone who can be replaced at will, like last week's newspapers? Or as someone who deserves respect? Using again the tenure analogy, it would be reasonable to say that Matt Doherty has not yet earned the "tenure" of a Smith or a Guthridge, and is not automatically entitled to the same level of deep, deep respect earned by his predecessors over three decades. But it is also reasonable to say he is entitled to, like a young assistant tenure-track professor, a five-to-six year period in which to prove himself *and* a working presumption that he will indeed succeed as a coach.

In today's college sports, five to six years is a very long time. And the University of North Carolina has already shown that, where there exists sufficient pressure from boosters to make a change, it is willing to cut short coaches who don't meet expectations on the field. Unless Doherty is an absolutely overwhelming success on the court each and every season, some Carolina fans here and there are likely to start complaining and speaking of Doherty as potentially disposable. In contrast, it would be very surprising if in years to come contributors to Internet message boards began saying that a young history professor at UNC had a few flaws and that UNC should dump him in favor of this other, supposedly brighter, professor at Cal–Berkeley or some other institution.

The predisposition to see coaches as disposable is disturbing for several reasons. First, it shatters the idea that North Carolina basketball operates according to norms closer to those of the university of which it is part than those of the rest of the business world, where loyalty and tenure are almost forgotten concepts. But the idea that Carolina basketball is different somehow from the rest of the world is one of the main things that makes the program attractive to many fans! Second, treating people simply as commodities is disrespectful in and of it itself—whether the context be Carolina basketball or any other endeavor involving people's livelihoods. Third, the tendency to see coaches as disposable is itself a recipe for instability in the program. A carousel of coaching changes such as that experienced by UCLA after John Wooden's retirement would almost certainly wreck the ideals associated with the program and lead to inconsistent results on the court.

On the other hand, coaches do have to be held accountable, and even at the Division III level the won/loss record is a relevant fact in evaluating a coach's performance (although it need not—indeed, should not—be the only relevant fact). The question is whether coaches are in fact seen as not just field generals but stewards of an educational process, and correspondingly, whether they are held accountable according to a process close to that used by academic institutions for evaluating other teaching positions. That process is designed to be deliberate, to encompass a range of considerations, and to resist short-term pressures, as opposed to the much shorter time frame dictated by fans and boosters who want results now, and believe coaches are only as good as their last game or last season. Most of the college basketball world now operates under the latter system of accountability. If the segment of Tar Heel fans inclined to see coaches as disposable get their way, so, in time, will North Carolina.

The Temptation to Judge From a Distance/Arm-Chair Coaching

A common assumption among many sports fans is that they can judge from afar how well a coach is doing. Fans' impressions of coaches are formed both by what happens on the court and by how coaches are represented in the media in its various forms. And most fans know at least some of the basics behind the fundamentals and strategies of the sport, enough to form an opinion about what decisions a coach should make, who should be playing, and so forth.

For the most part, that ability to debate a coach's decisions is simply part of the fun of being a fan. Indeed, if the policy decisions of lawmakers were debated by the public with as much zeal as North Carolina and other college basketball fans debate substitution patterns, we would have both a more knowledgeable public and a more accountable government.

There is nothing wrong, then, with fans forming their own opinions about the substitutions, strategies and tactics of their favorite basketball team. What becomes problematic, however, is when coaches make decisions that are different from those a fan might make, and that fan goes on to conclude that the coach must not be very smart. As noted previously, few journalists—let alone fans—have the technical acumen to definitively state that any given tactical or personnel decision was wrong in some absolute sense. One can only point out what was tried and whether it worked this time or not, and over a long period of time observe whether a coach's decisions tend to be generally successful or unsuccessful.

> You know, the scrutiny here is probably more than any other program except for Notre Dame football, and I got to witness that. There's a saying that one of the best things about the job is there's a lot of interest and one of the bad things about the job is there's a lot of interest. Any time I make a move, whether I go zone, or substitute, if we lose the game, we're going to be scrutinized.
>
> —Matt Doherty

For fans who are deeply engaged in North Carolina basketball or some other team, it may not always be easy to admit that the people inside the program who see the players every day and who study tactics on a professional basis are more qualified to make good judgments about how to coach a basketball team than the fan is, in the same degree that their dentist is more qualified to work on their teeth than they are. And it may be difficult for highly committed Carolina fans to acknowledge that their information about what is really happening inside the program, and the full range of challenges of all types a coach has to deal with (many of the toughest of which never get discussed in the media or even the rumor mill), is, in the end, limited at best. But when a substantial segment of fans loses the ability to pull back in the wake of a frustrating loss and say, "Wait, the coach probably had a good reason to do what he did," a poisonous environment can emerge.

In the case of North Carolina, Internet posters and other critics of Bill Guthridge created what was for several weeks during the 2000 season a very unpleasant climate, in which some (by no means all) fans were too quick to, first, blame losses on the coach, and, second, translate disagreement with a coach's moves into blanket judgments about the coach's ability. But the attitude in question here neither began nor ended with Guthridge's three years as coach. In 1965, Dean Smith was hung in effigy outside Woolen Gym after a loss to Wake Forest. And sure enough, after a remarkable honeymoon over most of his first season, some fans began ripping Matt Doherty after North Carolina dropped five of its last 10 games to finish 26–7 in 2001.

Everyone interested in sports becomes an armchair coach at one time or another. And lots of people working 9-to-5 jobs of various types would love to be involved in sports as a coach. Those facts, in themselves, need not be problematic. What is problematic is forgetting the vast gap between being an armchair coach and being one in real life.

EXTERNAL CRITICISMS OF NORTH CAROLINA BASKETBALL FANS

Much of the preceding section may read as if one type of North Carolina fan is criticizing tendencies present among other North Carolina fans. And indeed, the preceding discussion is intended both to explain and clarify the problematic tendencies of some fans, as well as express clearly the author's assessment of those tendencies. But the discussion now turns to an even tougher set of issues. I pose five critical questions that can be asked of all stripes of North Carolina fans—questions that in fact may hit home the hardest when directed to those who most strongly adhere to the positive vision of fan loyalty described above and who reject the "winning is everything" view.

Doesn't "Virtue" Result Only From Winning?

The first and perhaps most fundamental of these questions is whether the various virtues commonly associated with Carolina basketball—loyalty, class, doing things the right way, stability—are in fact decorations that would disappear or quickly decay if the winning stopped. And if Carolina is winning all the time, someone else is losing most of the time! Carolina being at or near the top year after year in the ACC implies that most if not all of the other schools will rotate in and out of the bottom tiers of their league, with their fans and coaches experiencing relative failure. It is structurally impossible for every ACC school to be consistent winners and have stable coaching situations that stretch over decades. Someone must lose, someone must fail.

> If we weren't winning, we wouldn't have been coaching very long. As coaches, we tried to recruit the best type of people, and we tried to work very hard to make them better players, and to continue the success. Anyone can say they're going to win, but when you win year after year, you have something concrete to show for it. That showed the stability of the program and the opportunity players would have if they came.
>
> You work hard, you try to get the best players, and you try to win with class and sportsmanship. If you do that, you can be there a long time. If you don't, you're going to get fired.
>
> —Bill Guthridge

Given that fact, why should Carolina get to win all the time? What is the moral value in that? Carolina fans' first response would likely be, "We should win because we are the good guys!" To which other schools' fans or the outside observer might reply, "No, you only have the luxury of being good guys because you win all the time, you have all the TV appearances, you get the best recruits, you have the biggest budget. If you didn't have all those advantages and started losing, you'd act no better than the rest of us! (And besides, you're not as 'good' as you think you are, anyway!)"

Is a coherent rejoinder to this question available to North Carolina fans? One might argue that virtues themselves produce wins. But no one thinks that virtue can consistently trump talent. Every year, at every level of basketball, wonderful people, including on occasion people who directly pattern themselves after Dean Smith, have unsuccessful, disappointing seasons. Former Carolina point guard John Kuester, whom I've interviewed on two occasions, is a very impressive person, a very highly regarded assistant coach with the Philadelphia 76ers, and a true believer in the Smith legacy. And he had been a successful young head coach in the 1980s before encountering a nightmare, injury-racked season at George Washington University in 1989, finishing 1–27. Kuester was replaced by Mike Jarvis a year later. Virtue wins games? Really?

A more subtle reply might go along these lines: "Having a basketball program in which people are respected and treated well doesn't in itself win basketball games—being a great competitor is what wins basketball games, and we acknowledge that there is no special moral worth as to whether our guys win this particular game or championship as compared to your guys. But what having a classy program does is show that winning games is not necessarily inconsistent with doing things the right way and treating people well. We acknowledge that Dean Smith might not have been around much longer if he hadn't suddenly started winning a bunch of games in the mid-1960s, and that it was in some degree a matter of luck that the right players arrived at the right time to make that possible. We know that virtue and success don't always go hand in hand, but even so, we think that showing it is possible to get to the top and stay at the top while maintaining a strong moral ethos is a statement in itself."

Another possible reply would be to say: "Of course we know that success on that court, period, is the reason why North Carolina basketball has had such stability and enjoyed such popularity. But that doesn't mean that the positive example it sets is not real. All it suggests is that in American society, you have to win, win, win first, before you can be taken seriously about anything else. We recognize that Dean Smith wouldn't have been famous and wouldn't have had such attention paid to his good traits if he hadn't won 879 games, but that fact reflects society's misguided emphasis on winning, not anything about Dean Smith."

Both those possible replies seem to this author a fair response in the context of this hypothetical dialogue. But a much tougher test is the one that real life almost certainly will one day present North Carolina fans: If you have to choose between winning and your professed values, which would you dump? It would be surprising if some day in the near or perhaps distant future North Carolina fans (and UNC administrators) did not have to make that painful choice.

Beyond that dilemma lies another issue, which is almost never discussed in the context of competitive sports: Don't Carolina fans realize that all that winning over the years has inflicted psychic pain on fans of other schools? For years, Carolina fans have described the resentment they have felt from other schools as a mark of jealousy, but in my case, at least, it was perhaps not until the lowest moments of the 2000 season that I really felt what it was like to be on the "other side" in terms of losing games.

When Duke culminated a four-year era of relative dominance in the ACC with a national title in 2001 won by Mike Krzyzewski at his peak, some writers shrewdly pointed out that now Carolina fans finally knew what it was like to face Dean Smith. But the jealously of seeing a rival step into a period of relative ascendancy is a much subtler psychic pain than that of being on the bottom, year after year, while your biggest rivals gets all the best players, the media attention and glory, and also win the most games. That's the position N.C. State fans have been in for the past

DEAN SMITH ON CAROLINA FANS AND WINNING

Q. Do you think Carolina fans would trade a scandal for a national title?

A. I think early, yeah, real early. Carolina football in the late '40s, it wasn't all up and up.

Q. What about Carolina fans who say that they'd keep following the team if it started losing, so long as it kept its values?

A. They mean that, but I think you and I know different. It's still very important that we keep scoring.

10 years and which all the other ACC schools have been in at one time or another during the last 30 years. True, pain and disappointment in sports are often relative to expectations, and at most of those schools, most of the time, the expectations have been quite a bit lower than has been the case in Chapel Hill. Even so, the question remains: Can Carolina fans really fathom the pain that each thrilling Tar Heel victory over the years has produced in opponents? Probably not. But it's worth trying.

The Corporate Takeover of College Basketball

A second critical question to be asked is the degree to which North Carolina fans (and indeed college sports fans in general) are willing to stomach the commercialization which now surrounds the college game. A number of issues could be considered under this heading—for instance, whether the increasing corporate presence in college basketball (and high school basketball) is slowly corrupting the game itself. This section, however, focuses primarily on an issue of particular relevance to UNC: Whether and under what conditions a public university's basketball team should agree to help advertise a large corporation's products, particularly a corporation with a dubious labor history.

In 1997, UNC's Athletic Department signed a five-year, $7 million deal with Nike, the global shoe manufacturer, in which the shoe company would provide lavish outlays for equipment and uniforms for the university's teams, as well as additional perks (such as bonuses for coaches), in exchange for having North Carolina place the Nike trademark swoosh on its uniform. (As in the past, Dean Smith planned to give most of his sneaker bonus to charity as well as to assistant coaches and support staff.) At the time, Nike was a central target in an ongoing campaign by labor rights activists worldwide to expose and redress the existence of sweatshop working conditions in factories used as suppliers by subcontractors to major American-based corporations. Activists cited dozens of first-hand reports from locations like the Caribbean, Indonesia and China which described Nike shoes being made by poor, uneducated people working long working hours in brutally unhealthy working conditions, with no ability to form labor unions, and at wages often too low to secure even the mere necessities.

It was not surprising, then, that UNC's deal with Nike attracted significant protest from student activists in Chapel Hill, beginning in 1997. Marion Traub-Werner, an undergraduate who had researched the issue closely (and had even interned for another larger shoe manufacturer one summer in order to gain an industry perspective), and several other students met with Dean Smith in the fall of 1997, and then took the case to the public in several protests and rallies. The students' demand was rather modest: that the university join a consortium of schools pushing Nike into better behavior and better oversight of its subcontractors, and threaten to drop the deal with Nike if working conditions did not demonstrably begin to improve.

The administration's initial response, as articulated by Chancellor Michael Hooker, was to point out that globalization is a fact of life—and that some economists think that sweatshop conditions are a necessary and in fact desirable stage of economic development in some very poor nations. The students and other protestors countered that they did not want Nike to pull out of poor countries completely, but to stay in those countries while being more generous, paying above a market wage. In other words, unlike some earlier critics of sweatshops, the students now did not contest the legitimacy and even necessity of some low-wage industrial work. The question was, "how low?"

Nike's own analysis of production costs showed that the wages paid to factory workers made up no more than 4% of the retail cost of a pair of sneakers. Students argued that Nike could easily absorb an increase in its labor costs while maintaining profitability, and that consumers would likely be willing to pay an extra dollar or two for a sneaker they knew was made in relatively humane conditions. They also argued that history—including North Carolina's own violent labor history—showed that improvements in working conditions did not come through the operation of the market alone, but only through organized interventions into the market to change baseline employment rules.

UNC did in fact agree in 2000 to join the Workers Rights Consortium, an organization started by students at a number of major universities which uses independent investigators to monitor the behavior of clothing manufacturers overseas, in addition to its membership in the Fair Labor Association (another watchdog organization which has been heavily criticized by activists as overprotective of corporate interests). And the Nike issue became a great opportunity for public education about the realities of globalization—a class at UNC during the spring of 1998 was devoted to Nike's overseas business practices. But UNC has not acted in any way that would threaten the Nike deal itself, and in 2001 began talks with the company about a new deal. (A press release by the UNC Athletic Department stated, however, that UNC would express concern about Nike's labor standards during the negotiations.)

The financial incentive for UNC to stay in the Nike deal and sign future endorsement deals is obvious. Even at North Carolina, Athletic Department budgets strain to stay even. Fielding teams in 25 nonrevenue sports costs millions of dollars. So does building expansions to the football stadium and training facilities. North Carolina probably could have found a way to balance its Athletic Department budget without taking any Nike money, but it might have involved sacrifices of some kind: perhaps the sacrifice of long-term ambitions to be a football powerhouse, perhaps dropping a sport. Those were sacrifices that UNC was not prepared to make in the name of concerns over international labor rights. (On the other hand, to its great credit, UNC has to date refused to balance its athletics budget by selling corporate advertising space within the Smith Center or Kenan Stadium.) Alternatively, UNC could have argued that if nonrevenue sports are so important but cannot support themselves, then the public should be prepared to help pay for them. Unfortunately, the North Carolina state legislature would probably be even more unsympathetic than the UNC Athletic Department to an argument that it should send more money to Chapel Hill (and Raleigh, Greenville, and elsewhere) to pay for field hockey teams, when a private company is happy to foot the bill.

Even so, the troubling fact is that UNC athletics, including the basketball team, are funded in part out of the profits of a huge multinational corporation, profits built in part on paying workers very, very small amounts of money, far less than what a comparable American worker doing the same work would earn and far less than the value of the shoes produced by those workers. Carolina basketball, in short, is bankrolled in part from the profits earned by the winners in a global capitalist system.

That fact is disturbing to those who take seriously the values of liberalism and humanitarianism and social progress long associated with Carolina basketball. (It was disturbing enough to me in 1997 that I twice interviewed Marion Traub-Werner for *Inside Carolina* and even gave a five-minute speech supportive of the students' position during a rally outside South Building that November.) But is it really a new fact?

Probably not. Before Carolina basketball was bankrolled by Nike, it was bankrolled in part through the donations of businessmen in North Carolina, some of whom also had disturbing labor practices. More to the point, Carolina basketball and indeed the university in Chapel Hill in general has always been funded out of the social surplus of a state economy marked by strong anti-unionism, racist labor practices, and most dramatically, the use of migrant farm labor. Carolina undergraduates concerned about labor rights could drive a couple of hours in any direction from Chapel Hill and find human beings working in conditions almost as disturbing as those described by anti-Nike activists inspecting subcontractor factories in Asia. (And to its credit, Students for Economic Justice at UNC has in recent years launched campaigns on behalf of farm workers in North Carolina as well as housekeepers and other low-wage employees at UNC itself, in addition to its work on the sweatshop issue.)

However, the fact that the university is inextricably intertwined with the political economy of the state in which it resides does not mean, and has not meant historically, that it cannot play at least a mildly progressive role within that state. In the 1930s, researchers at UNC studied and documented rural poverty, the lives of tenant farmers trying to scratch out a living during the Depression, and helped call attention to their problems. In the 1940s, Chapel Hill produced leaders like Frank Porter Graham who advocated education and social progress and rejected the politics of race-baiting. In 1995, the university withstood controversy and threats from legislators to sponsor a summer institute focusing on the health impact of tobacco, and since 1998 has hosted the North Carolina Prevention Partners program, which aims to reduce smoking in the state.

The Nike deal indicates, however, that the relevant stage for the University of North Carolina is no longer simply the state of North Carolina, but the whole planet. Elements of the current global economic system in which Nike—and, by extension, UNC—are implicated are just as retrograde and backward as North Carolina's own political economy was 75 years ago. That North Carolina basketball uniforms now bear a swoosh is not in my view a cause for celebration, both because (as former President William Friday has emphasized) it represents a compromise of the university's independence and because it would seem to offer a de facto endorsement of Nike's labor practices.

But the presence of the swoosh need not be a cause for resignation, either. The fact is, the accumulated prestige and worldwide recognition of Carolina basketball means the program and the university as a whole have quite a bit of weight to throw around in conversations with Nike, weight that could help produce tangible improvements in working conditions thousands of miles away—if the Carolina athletic department and university have the courage to use it. What now stands as something of a blemish on Carolina basketball, and indeed on UNC's long record of supporting social progress, could be turned into an opportunity for the university to become a leader in shaping (however modestly) what labor practices will and will not be considered morally legitimate in the new global economy.

Already, as a result of public pressure, Nike has increased wages for many of its poorest workers, although many observers of the company continue to report on abysmal working conditions in many Nike plants, and although the company has rejected the idea of ensuring a livable wage for all its workers as "unrealistic." Clearly, there is still plenty of room to raise the bar higher, beyond what Nike has been willing to do so far. The university could help raise that bar by boldly and unmistakably insisting that Nike meet specific standards suggested by watchdog groups (such as permitting surprise monitoring visits at subcontractor factories), that the company continue to raise workers' wages, and that it eliminate workplace abuses such as mandatory overtime and fines for talking, as a precondition for allowing the university's student-athletes to be used as billboards for the company.

Such a bold stance would carry some risks for the Athletic Department's bottom line—and indeed, a decision to take that sort of stance could happen only as the result of a decision by a courageous chancellor willing to ride out some controversy. But taking risks is the price of making history. And the risk involved in this seems rather minor compared to the competing goal of using a great public institution's stature and accumulated goodwill to challenge and reshape the world around it, just as UNC has over the course of many decades done so much to reshape the state of North Carolina. UNC alone cannot change the basic dynamics underlying contemporary global capitalism, but it can do its part to make the system a little more humane. The moral value of nameless workers on the other side of the world being able to buy a little more food, rest a little more, and get injured less often on the job far outweighs the moral value of coaches getting some extra cash, athletes getting free uniforms and shoes, and a university athletic department being able to do everything it would like while also balancing the budget.

*

That, at least, is the argument I would make to the relevant administrators in South Building, and it is the argument that has been urged by UNC students and a number of supportive faculty members. It is not an argument, however, that I have heard many Carolina basketball fans make. Indeed, of the 606 responses to the North Carolina Fan Survey, only two people mentioned the Nike deal in discussing things they would change about Carolina basketball. And, in all probability, most Carolina basketball fans simply don't care very much about the Nike deal, or would simply endorse whatever they think is in the university's best interests. (This is not to say that fans do not care or are not aware of the increasing corporate influence in college basketball—but they are most likely to care when it affects them directly, such as when CBS lengthens the TV timeouts almost every year during the NCAA tournament.)

But just because the majority of fans at present don't care about a given issue does not mean it is not important or that there is not benefit in thinking about it, whatever one's conclusion. I don't for a minute think that the Nike deal erases all that is good about the University of North Carolina in general or its basketball program in particular. But I also don't think passionate appreciation for what is good about Carolina basketball is inconsistent with a willingness to hear and take seriously morally important criticisms of the university and its athletic program. And I don't think that appreciation for Carolina basketball or the university as a whole is inconsistent with the suggestion that on some issues, the university has not yet taken all the steps it could to extend its own historic legacy as a force for social progress in the state of North Carolina and beyond.*

Class Bias and North Carolina Basketball: Is UNC Basketball the Plaything of an Economic Elite?

The Nike discussion leads us to yet another critical question about North Carolina basketball: Doesn't Carolina basketball have an upper- and upper-middle-class accent, from the tenured faculty who go to the games and sit about 25 rows up in the Smith Center to the big donors who sit in the rows closer to the court?

The short answer is, "yes." Indeed, the upper-class bias of the Smith Center crowd has for years been the target of populist resentment among out-of-town Carolina fans, who in general have been as happy or happier than fans of opposing schools to attack the "wine-and-cheese" atmosphere in the Smith Center.

---

*It is heartening that UNC administrators indeed took the labor issue more seriously than ever before in negotiating a new, eight-year deal with Nike, which was announced just before this book went to press. The $28 million deal calls on Nike to reveal the location of the subcontractor plants manufacturing UNC athletic equipment and merchandise, and to ensure that those plants meet UNC's own labor code of conduct. This policy will also apply to non-Nike manufacturers of apparel used by UNC employees. While it is troubling that the sheer size of the deal will make the Athletic Department more dependent on Nike money than ever before, this is clearly an important, precedent-setting step in the right direction on the labor issue.

Most faculty members at any college, of course, are going to be middle- and upper-middle-class people with middle- and upper-middle-class values. But it is also true that a bourgeois air pervades the Smith Center in a way it never really has at other ACC venues such as Reynolds Coliseum, Cole Field House, University Hall—or even Carmichael Auditorium. In those arenas, students have had the best seats and set the tone for the whole building. In the Smith Center, in contrast, big donors who gave money to support the construction of the arena have most of the best seats. Not only do they have the best seats, they also have the right to pass on those seats to their children (provided their children pony up their dues to the Rams' Club). Feudal aristocracy died in most of the Western world by the nineteenth century, but its spirit remains alive and well in the lower level of the Smith Center on game nights.

Recent changes to put more students in risers on the lower level of the arena have modified that situation somewhat. But isn't there still something odd and troubling about a game being played by mostly African-American players, some from pretty humble economic circumstances, being witnessed and enjoyed by an overwhelmingly white, largely affluent audience?

Perhaps—but only to the extent that that white audience views the athletes as commodities, as pieces of meat. I'm not persuaded that the inequality evident in the Smith Center is in itself a good reason for criticizing Carolina basketball or its fans. Who shows up in the Smith Center is a reflection of background inequalities and an uneven distribution of privilege, and holding season tickets is an expression of class privilege. But if it weren't a basketball game, it would likely be the opera hall or some other venue whose clientele is likely to be quite class-specific.

And in fact, the distribution of who actually attends a basketball game is probably considerably more egalitarian than the distribution of those who go to the symphony. Pretty much anyone who wants to can get in the door of the Smith Center for at least a game or two a year for face value via public ticket sales, even if it's only an exhibition game. (Just don't expect to sit downstairs.)

The radical social theorist in me in fact rather appreciates the fact that the distribution of human bodies in those plush light blue seats on game nights, as well as the distribution of parking spaces and quick exits after the game, brings into the open social class relationships that are often concealed. Moreover, I find it ironic that the passion of the best-heeled Tar Heel fans is directed to an endeavor that at its roots celebrates egalitarianism: basketball, a game open to all comers, whether they hail from the broken-glass playgrounds of a decaying urban center or from a comfortable suburb.

In any case, the emphasis often given to the Smith Center crowd can obscure the fact that only a small percentage of Carolina fans actually go the games. Most sit at home and watch on TV, where the seats are often plusher than even the first row of the Dean Dome and tickets are cheaper (even if you go all out for the satellite dish). And those who sit at home and watch form a very broad cross-section of society. The fact that the University of North Carolina chose to eschew public funding and build its new basketball arena in a way that left a public institution in indefinite hock to private contributors is unfortunate. But that regrettable fact does not offset the role that both Carolina basketball and sports in general play as a form of glue holding together a fragile, fragmented society.

Does College Basketball Corrupt Education?

A fourth critical question is whether college basketball fans are participants in the corruption of higher education. Big-time college basketball, it is charged, brings athletes on campus who really shouldn't be in school. It directs attention away from the heart of a university's mission: research and teaching. It contributes to a campus culture that emphasizes alcohol and partying and de-emphasizes learning. And, in the process, the semi-professionalized system of college sports exploits the sweat of athletes by making millions of dollars of revenue, which, outside of their tuition receipts, the players never see a penny of. These issues pertain not to out-and-out cheating and open corruption of other kinds, which Carolina has avoided (to the great pride of its fans), but to structural features within college sports, features that North Carolina definitely exhibits.

A full discussion of these issues is beyond the scope of this book. All have recently received excellent treatment in detail by other authors: See James Shulman and William Bowen's *The Game of Life* for discussion of the educational issues, Murray Sperber's *Beer and Circus* for the campus culture issue, and Andrew Zimablist's *Unpaid Professionals* on the athlete exploitation issue.

The relevant question here is whether, even if one believed that these criticisms of college sports are accurate or largely accurate (and, as we shall see, some Carolina fans think they are), that should make one any less of a fan. Does a faulty system of college sports mean that the games themselves and the dozens of narratives that overlap with each contest are no longer meaningful? It is not obvious that the answer should be "yes." Other sports—especially soccer, the world's most popular game—have seen the most brazen forms of corruption at the club, national, and international levels, with little apparent effect on interest in sports or in the games. Brazilians know their system of club football is corrupt to the core, but that won't stop them from celebrating any less boisterously if their nation lifts the World Cup in 2002. The same could be said of Carolina fans.

The harder question is, would Carolina fans be willing to make sacrifices in the name of significant reform of college sports? Would they be able to stomach restrictions on scholarships or tighter eligibility rules which made it harder or impossible for North Carolina to get the best players? If the NCAA moved to a system in which only those who really wanted to be in school played college basketball and others went on to a developmental league out of high school, and the level of play seen in Carolina games was significantly reduced, would Carolina fans remain supportive? What if a maverick UNC chancellor wanted Carolina to "unilaterally disarm" through tough new standards or even an end to scholarships, or if the ACC as a whole moved toward that model? Would Carolina fans accept moving in a direction that essentially made it impossible for the Tar Heels ever to win another national title?

Undoubtedly, interest nationwide in Carolina basketball would shrink considerably if the Tar Heels somehow moved to a less professionalized, more Ivy Leaguish model in the future. (I don't think Matt Doherty or any other relevant person is planning on that happening.) But some hard-core Carolina fans would remain, conceivably even enough to fill up the Smith Center from time to time. The fact is, however, that the institution is already committed to big-time sports past the point of no return, and that UNC is not likely to play a major leadership role in pushing for more than token reforms in the structure of college sports and all its attendant hypocrisies.

Swallowing that reality is a price one pays for remaining a fan of North Carolina basketball or any other big-time school. Most of us have already learned how to check our critical consciousness at the door with regard to those questions once the game starts. Even so, one must wonder, if even fans of a school like North Carolina that openly professes it wants to do things "the right way" can muster no great enthusiasm for serious reform in college sports, who will?

Do Sports Undermine Community and Cause People to Live Vicariously?

The fifth and final major strand of critical questioning of Carolina basketball fans is whether they, and sports fans in general, are using their allegiance to their team as a pale substitute for finding happiness in their own lives, or as a substitute for making contributions to their community in direct ways. Sports fans may use being a fan to gain a sense of community identification not really present in their everyday life, but is that gain at the expense of real community?

The Reverend James Forbes, minister of the Riverside Church in New York, is an old friend of Dean Smith dating back to his time as visiting intern at Binkley Baptist Church in 1962. In a talk I attended at Riverside in December of 1996, he put the issue this way: "If I spend the evening watching a ballgame, watching the Yankees in the World Series, what have I really gained at the end of it, other than a slice of vicarious struggle?" I was impressed by that comment—but also left the forum early to go home and watch UNC play LSU on TV. (Forbes himself, a wonderful preacher and person, allows his church to be used as home base for one of the largest youth basketball programs in the country.)

Another writer who has explored this issue is Jamie Quirk, author of the book *"Not Now, Honey, I'm Watching the Game."* Quirk, a North Carolina native and former sportswriter who covered the 1982 North Carolina team as a beat writer, developed an analysis of what he calls "sportsaholism" based on his work as a therapist with couples in which the husbands were absolutely consumed by sports. The sports fans Quirk described would spend more than 30 hours a week watching games, crowding out quality time with spouses and children. Needless to say, that level of sports watching also crowds out a wide range of other activities, such as involvement in civic and community organizations.

Intrigued and troubled by Quirk's provocative analysis, in 1999 I began research examining the relationship between both sports participation and sports spectatorship and what social scientists call "social capital." Social capital refers to the webs of relationships that hold people together. Communities with strong social capital develop norms of reciprocity and social cooperation; communities with weak social capital produce socially isolated, atomized individuals who are less likely to trust one another and who are less capable of working together effectively. Common measures of social capital include the number of organizations to which one belongs, whether one believes other people are trustworthy, how much one participates in political activity, and how much time one spends socializing with other people.

To examine how interest in sports affects social capital, in 1999 I analyzed the same data set used by Harvard professor Robert Putnam for his much larger, comprehensive analysis of social capital trends in the United States, published in the book *Bowling Alone*. The marketing firm DDB Needham has since 1975 been collecting detailed data about the habits of a cross-section of thousands of Americans. That data includes detailed information about Americans' civic and political participation, as well as their overall social attitudes, along with detailed information about the degree to which Americans participate in sports, attend sporting events, watch sports on television, and consider themselves sports fans.

My analysis of this data revealed several basic relationships. After applying controls for race, income, gender, and other standard demographic variables, participation in sports activities of various kinds was shown to have a modest but positive linkage with community engagement, political participation, social trust and life satisfaction. This linkage is somewhat stronger for non-competitive athletic activities such as camping, hiking, and working out than for more competitive sports such as tennis, but the relationship is a positive one across almost all activities. Participation in sports is also shown in regression analyses to be a positive predictor of increased social capital, although for various methodological reasons I hesitate to make any strong claims that participation in sports *causes* an increase in social capital. In general, however, the evidence suggests that people who get outside or go the gym and play games are more likely to be involved in a range of community activities and have a positive outlook on life than those who do not.

The situation is more ambiguous with respect to sports spectatorship, however. Attending an athletic event over the course of the year has a quite strong positive correlation with community involvement and socializing with others. But watching games on TV has only a weak correlation with community engagement (although its correlation with socializing with others is pretty strong).* And there is no correlation whatsoever between saying "I am an avid sports fan" and stronger community engagement. (Likewise, watching ESPN highlights shows also has no correlation with increased community engagement.) While sports activity in general seems to be positively related to engagement in the community, interest in politics, and a positive outlook on life, attending games in person appears to have a stronger positive effect than watching the games on TV. To put it in vivid terms, people who attend more athletic events are less likely to tell researchers that "I'm what you'd call a couch potato," whereas people who watch more sports on TV, not surprisingly, are more likely to say that the "couch potato" description fits them.

Two important qualifiers should be added here: First, it may be the case that for some people being more involved in the community causes people to watch fewer sports on TV, rather than the

---

* "Community engagement" is measured here as the number of times one went to a club meeting, volunteered, attended a religious service, or worked on a community project within the past year. "Socializing" is measured as the number of times one played cards, attended a dinner party, or entertained guests at home in the past year.

other way around. What is important to note here is simply that more community involvement seems to go hand-in-hand with participation in sports, but less so with watching games on TV.

Second, being a sports fan does not generate only positive outcomes. Sports fans are also somewhat more likely than non-sports fans to engage in a fistfight, or to say that men are naturally superior to women. But these basic findings are relatively encouraging: It does not seem that sports spectatorship in general is a major negative cause of declining civic participation, political participation, and social trust. Indeed, there seems to be a positive relationship between caring about sports and caring about the community. And direct participation in sports (which is, not surprisingly, positively correlated to interest in spectator sports) is a healthy predictor of increased participation in other spheres of life.

But these findings leave aside two important questions: First, although being engaged in sports may be better for social capital than sitting around and doing nothing, perhaps it might be even better if leisure time spent following and participating in sports was spent in some other activity, instead. The DDB/Needham data allows us to make some provisional judgments on this question: Going to an athletic event actually has a positive correlation with community engagement on par with reading a book or magazine or socializing with friends and a bit stronger than other widespread activities such as gardening and walking. Watching a game on television, on the other hand, has a weaker link with community engagement than going to the game, reading, gardening, socializing or walking. But it is slightly more beneficial than renting a video, and far more beneficial than TV-watching in general (which is a strong negative predictor of community engagement). The basic picture is that going to a game is one of the more effective leisure activities in generating ties to community. But while watching a game on TV has a slight positive linkage with involvement in the community, many other leisure activities are substantially more likely to generate community ties.

Second, the data described here does not really capture the phenomenon of the hyper-committed sports fan described by Quirk. There is not a separate category in the survey data for fans who watch 30 hours or more of sports on TV a week, and there is not a category for fans who say that following a particular team is among the highest priorities in their life. In the absence of such data, it's hard to make firm judgments using more than anecdotal evidence on the relationship between being obsessed with one's favorite team and being a positive contributor to the community. People who love sports may have a zest for life that carries over into other spheres. (Indeed, recent research by Daniel Wann, who compared fans and non-fans of Murray State basketball, has shown that following a sports team provides a tangible boost to one's psychological health.) Alternatively, people obsessed with a sports team may be wasting their lives watching accomplishments of other people's making. Or perhaps both phenomena are present in different kinds of fans—or even, at different times, present in the very same individual. We will return to this question about the relationship between sports fanhood and community engagement in Chapter Eight while discussing results of the North Carolina Basketball Fan Survey.

*

This chapter has discussed on a theoretical level the pros and cons of being a North Carolina basketball fan. In the process, it has posited an ideal of what being a "good" fan entails, and it has discussed possible sources of corruption of that ideal. The chapter has also discussed some of the fundamental challenges to both the general idea that being a devoted fan of a big-time college sports team at the start of the 21st century is a worthwhile activity, and the more specific idea that a successful college sports team could somehow also be regarded as exhibiting important virtues that are not reducible to winning.

It is time now to turn from theoretical discussion of these issues to take a hard look at who highly committed Carolina fans are—what they value, the ways they follow the team, the reasons why they follow the team, how much importance they place on being a fan, how they handle the highs and lows involved in being a fan, and many related questions. We start this inquiry by tracing the experiences of 15 committed Carolina supporters as they follow the team over the course of a single season.

5

The Fan Diaries Project and the 2000–2001 Season

Chapter Four talked at a fairly abstract level about some of the pros and cons of being a hard-core UNC basketball fan. It's now time to roll up the sleeves and look concretely at what some actual people think. What are the habits, values and attitudes characteristic of Carolina basketball fans? What does the experience of being a fan involve? The first cut at answering these questions comes in the form of fan diaries kept by 15 individuals over the course of the 2000–01 season.

The diarists were recruited via an open invitation to participate in a research project issued on *uncbasketball.com* in October 2000. Each diarist was asked to keep track of specific information regarding how they experienced each game (in person, television, etc.), their own reactions to each game, how much time they spent reading and talking about each game and their own productivity and mood the days following the game. The diarists recorded this information and transmitted it to me via email as the season went along. It should be noted that the diarists participated in the project solely on a volunteer basis, and I had no means (or desire) to sanction participants who missed games or provided incomplete data; I simply relied on periodic prods of the participants and expressions of appreciation to keep the diarists engaged. Even so, while the diary entries are not a pristine, complete data set in the sense of having entries for every game for every participant—roughly 75% of the total possible entries were submitted—the diarists by and large were quite conscientious in providing the data. The data they volunteered collectively comprises an enormous amount of information about how Carolina basketball fans experience basketball season at the turn of the century.

The 15 diarists are in a variety of walks of life and stages of life. Four of the diarists lived in the Chapel Hill area during the 2000–01 season, four more lived in other parts of North Carolina, one lived in South Carolina, and the rest lived in a range of locations: Wisconsin, New York, Washington state, California, and Pennsylvania. The diarists include people in their 20s, 30s, 40s, and 50s.

Some are UNC alumni, and some are not. A variety of political orientations are present among the diarists. The diarists also reflect a variety of temperaments and attitudes regarding Carolina basketball.

I made no effort to censor or respond to the many opinions expressed in the diary entries about a range of issues pertaining to Carolina basketball; I simply encouraged the diarists to speak their minds and collected the data. Even so, there is good reason to think that the fan diarists may not be fully representative of the larger fan base, and the potential for what social scientists call "selection bias" should be acknowledged. First, the pool of people who could be diarists was limited to Carolina fans who own a computer and were aware of *uncbasketball.com*. Second, it is reasonable to hypothesize that the kind of fan who would be willing to make written notes about his or her own activities and participate in a research project over the course of the season—for free—might be individuals who are somewhat more thoughtful and reflective than the "average" Carolina basketball supporter. (They also might be somewhat more fanatical!) Third, it is possible that prior familiarity with the author's views on Carolina basketball attracted a certain kind of fan to the project and dissuaded others. While I believe that last effect is probably minimal with respect to the surveys, it may be more relevant to the fan diary project. Even so, it is worth noting that only one of the 15 diarists shared all the major components of my own view of Carolina basketball (as expressed in the preceding sections).

But the purpose of the diaries project is not to reflect in a statistically significant way the actual attitudes of all Carolina fans—that is a task which the 606 surveys collected for this book are better equipped to handle. Rather, the purpose of the diaries is to provide an in-depth, qualitiative look at how some fans fit following Carolina basketball into their lives, and to reveal some of the flavor and texture of what being a serious Carolina basketball fan entails.

I thus report on the activities, thoughts and comments of these 15 fans during the 2000–01 season. Given limitations of space and the desire not to abuse readers' patience, I do not report on the contents of all 300-plus diary entries: What is printed reflects a significant but abridged sample of the total data collected.

These diary entries report on the participants' self-reported behavior, attitudes, and opinions, not all of which I personally think are praiseworthy or correct. However, it is not my intent to cast judgment on the way these diarists as individuals incorporate Carolina basketball into their lives, but simply to report their attitudes and actions. The diarists themselves represent a diversity of approaches to being a fan, but all the participants in the study are intelligent, conscientious people who are also, indisputably, knowledgeable and enthusiastic Carolina fans.

While I do not intend to provide a moral or intellectual assessment of any particular diarist's habits and attitudes, the end of this chapter does contain brief interpretive remarks about the patterns of behavior reported in the diaries. We begin, however, with thumbnail descriptions of each participant in the diary project.

WHO THE FAN DIARISTS ARE

All biographical data, including ages, refer to each individual's situation as of the 2000–01 season.

Steve Andrews is a 30-year-old college tennis coach living in Fayetteville, NC. Steve graduated from UNC in 1993 with a degree in psychology and received his Master's degree in exercise science from UNC in 1998. Steve says that "the third and fourth words I ever uttered were 'Dean' followed by 'Smith.'" Steve says, "Historically, in my lifetime, UNC Basketball is a living representation of the pursuit of excellence.... It represents having the courage to admit your mistakes and to learn from them." Steve's most important UNC memory was watching the NCAA final in 1993, his senior year at UNC, and the celebrations that ensued afterward. "As a psychology major at UNC, " he recalls, "I studied Carl Jung's theories about the Collective Unconscious. I feel like I came as close as anybody could to truly feeling such a powerful force. I can still feel the collective joy on Franklin Street following the game.... It's like I could get inside the soul of every person I came in contact with, because they were feeling the exact same thing I was feeling." Due to his busy schedule, Steve is unable to make the trip to Chapel Hill for games very often, so he watches most Carolina games at home, either alone or with family members (most often his mother). Steve describes himself as slightly conservative politically (he puts himself at 4 on a 1 to 10, right-to-left scale), and estimates that at least 85% of his social life during the season revolves around Carolina basketball.

    Trip Cogburn is a 21-year-old UNC student and a very committed Carolina basketball fan. Trip attends every home game and sits in the student section near friends. When not studying or following Carolina, Trip spends time with his girlfriend or other friends, and playing intramural sports. Trip says he is slightly liberal (6) and associates Carolina basketball with the values of "integrity, loyalty, passion, courage, consistency, success." Not surprisingly, most of Trip's close friends are also Carolina fans. Asked how he would explain his Carolina passion to a stranger, Trip, who claims he became a fan at age three, wrote that "It's in my blood and a part of my life. It would be difficult to give them a single reason that is easy to understand because I don't completely understand it myself."

    Ross Cole is a 25-year-old living outside Seattle, WA. When the season started, Ross was working on staff at an outdoors camp, but when the job ended in December, he began looking for new employment—a time during which Carolina basketball became a distinctly lower priority. Ross attended UNC, graduating in '98, and went to Carolina basketball school for two summers during high school. Ross says he became a fan at age seven or eight while growing up in North Carolina. Ross describes himself as slightly conservative (4). Prior to the 2000–01 season, Ross reflected that "The fact is, Tar Heel basketball is part of my identity. Having lived about half of my life outside the state of North Carolina, watching the games and following the team has always helped me feel connected with home. When the Heels do well, I feel especially proud to be a native Carolinian." Asked to explain the origin of his allegiance, Ross noted, "It's kind of like why you love your family—because they've always been there, been a part of your life."

Jennifer Jordan Engel is a 28-year-old advertising agency creative director living in Charlotte and a 1994 graduate of UNC. Jennifer first became a fan during the 1990–91 season as a freshman in Chapel Hill, and soon became an extremely avid follower of the program. A talented writer who enjoys journaling in her spare time, Jennifer spent several seasons writing features for *Inside Carolina*. In addition to her work at Inside Carolina, Jennifer became widely known as a frequent poster on various UNC-related message boards; she now confines herself to the uncbasketball.com board and the Heel-Hoops list-serve, an email discussion group devoted to North Carolina basketball. She now attends over 20 Carolina games a year, and her family is a substantial donor to the Rams Club, sponsoring a scholarship. Jennifer considers herself a conservative politically (3).

In late November 1999, Jennifer experienced a major medical emergency while flying back from the Maui Invitational in Hawaii. On the last leg of the trip, a flight from Atlanta to Charlotte, Jennifer's liver was torn apart as a benign and previously undetected tumor ruptured. After being rushed to the hospital upon touchdown, Jennifer was in critical condition for several days after undergoing two corrective surgeries which literally saved her life. Word of Jennifer's condition spread quickly through the *Inside Carolina* and the *Duke Basketball Report* websites as well as the Heel-Hoops list-serve, and many dozens of well-wishers expressed their concerns by sending emails and flowers to Jennifer and her husband Patrick. In time, she made a complete recovery, yet she still feels grateful to be alive. Jennifer's hospital room TV was tuned to ESPN during her stay, and the first thing she said after coming to a few days after the trauma was, "Have you seen Shammond Williams' hair?" a reference to the former Tar Heel's Afro. Jennifer now says that Carolina basketball is "one of many things" she appreciates being alive to enjoy. In an arresting passage, Jennifer wrote this before the 2000–01 season: "I have to laugh when I think of myself many, many, many years down the road, still following Carolina basketball in my rocking chair, living and dying with each win and loss, trying to understand college kids that keep getting younger and younger as I age. It's a funny image, but I look forward to being the grandmother all the kids think is sooo coool!"

John Floyd is a 34-year-old stand-up comedian who now lives in Wilmington after previously being based in Rocky Mount. John frequently works on cruises which take him out of the country for extended periods during the season, meaning he is often in the desperate situation of hoping the ship satellite dish will be able to show a given game. John reads preseason magazines and follows recruiting closely through the Internet. His first memory of the Tar Heels was Walter Davis's shot to tie Duke in 1974, and he started following the team closely as a third grader during the 1974–75 season, when Phil Ford was a freshman. John made the trip to Chapel Hill for almost every home game while attending Elon College during the 1980s. John describes himself as very conservative politically (1). Prior to the 2000–2001 season, John stated, "I am definitely proud to be a Carolina fan. When they lose, I take it personally and am embarrassed as if it is my fault. I would say Carolina is one of my top priorities in life."

Chris Gabriele, a 26-year-old ad salesman, follows North Carolina basketball in White Plains, NY, just north of New York City, where he is employed by WFAN, the sports talk radio station.

Chris became a Carolina fan while growing up in Mahopac, NY. Chris frequently watched the Tar Heels play on TV, and grew to love the light blue hues of North Carolina's home floor. Chris follows other sports as well, typically flipping through several non-Carolina college games a week, and he is an avid fan of the New York Jets, attending all their home games. Chris experiences some of the annoyances familiar to many Carolina fans outside of the ACC region: Games on network television not being broadcast by local affiliates, missing part of a game while trying to get the Internet media player on his computer to work, and so forth. With a couple of early season exceptions, Chris watched every television game during the 2000–01 season and listened on the Internet to those not available locally. Chris puts himself right down the middle politically (5), but notes that he is from a Republican-leaning family.

K. Mac Heffner is a 22-year-old senior majoring in journalism at UNC who had a closer view of the 2000–01 team than any other diarist. Mac lived in Granville Towers during the school year, in the former room of UNC great Shammond Williams, and in close proximity to most of the 2001 team. Freshman and sophomore basketball players are required to live in Granville, and upperclassmen may choose to; five Carolina players lived on the same hall as Mac during 2001. Heffner, who also lived in Granville during 1999–2000, knew and spent social time with many of the players, interacting with them on a daily basis, and several players offered Mac free admission to home and away games as a player guest.* Mac, who stands 5-4, became especially good friends with 7-5 redshirt freshman Neil Fingleton. Mac, who considers himself slightly left of center politically (6), transferred to UNC from Carson Newman College in Tennessee. Mac is a regular presence on the *uncbasketball.com* board and is known as a boisterous personality and for letting his feelings be known.

William "Biscuit Dave" Jarvis is a 42-year-old endodontist in Rocky Mount, a UNC alumnus, and a lifelong Carolina fan. Dave says, "Being a Tar Heels fan and Alumnus has the same significance as my academic accomplishments (B.A., D.D.S., M.S., various honors), civic accomplishments (Eagle Scout, etc.), religious affiliation, etc. It helps define who I am." Dave attended Carolina Basketball School one summer as a kid and recalls the day his entire team got a "tour" for being late, saying, "I have rarely been late since." Dave exhibits a robust sense of humor in his written communiques, but he is entirely serious when it comes to the Tar Heels. In response to a question about what he'd be willing to miss a big Carolina game for, Dave offered farcical answers such as "To watch the replay of Al Gore inventing the Internet," but then added, "To thank Bill Guthridge for his character, loyalty and composure under fire. This one is not tongue-in-cheek. This is what being a Tar Heel is all about." Dave, who puts himself in the middle of the road politically (5), watches all the games on television while listening to Woody Durham's radio call of the games, and also reads *The News and Observer*, *goheels.com*, and *uncbasketball.com* to keep abreast of the Tar Heels.

---

*Under NCAA rules, each player is given four complimentary admissions per game, which can be given to anyone.

Roy Keefer is a 46-year-old attorney in Gettysburg, PA. He became a fan in 1979, after his parents moved to Chapel Hill. Roy describes himself as slightly right of center politically (4). Roy says what drew him most to Carolina basketball is that "they do things right." He follows as many games as possible on television, subscribes to *Carolina Blue* and also reads the Internet. He estimates that about 10% of his social life during the season is devoted to Carolina basketball. Both of Roy's sons (one of whom now plays in college) attended Carolina basketball school, and his daughter went to the UNC women's basketball camp. To Roy's chagrin, however, his youngest son remains a Duke fan.

Bill Lunney is a 59-year-old, "semi-retired" computer and law consultant in Madison, WI. Bill has been a fan since 1959, when he enrolled at UNC as an undergraduate. He received his bachelor's degree in 1963 and remained in Chapel Hill to earn his law degree in 1966. Bill describes himself as being slightly liberal (6) and has been active in working on his local county parks commission as well as with the international organization The Nature Conservancy. Bill writes that Carolina basketball "is a source of pride. I've served in elected public office and have a fulfilling family and professional life as well as working actively for environmental preservation. UNC basketball is a very significant recreational outlet." Bill adds that what most draws him to Carolina basketball is the school's "Tradition, History, Excellence, Ethics, Graduation Rate." Bill believes that the school's basketball success over the decades has had a beneficial impact on UNC's academics and the quality of its student body. Since there are few newspaper accounts of the Tar Heels in Wisconsin, Bill relies mostly on the Internet to follow the team. Only a small percentage of Bill's close friends are also Tar Heel fans, and he says that Carolina basketball occupies about 10% of his social life during the season. Bill and his wife spent much of the 2000–01 season in Tuscon, AZ, where Bill followed with interest the way local media reported on the Arizona Wildcats' roller coaster season.

Danny Mullis is a 48-year-old attorney in Charleston, SC, who now serves as the Alternative Dispute Resolution Program Director for the United States District Court in South Carolina. Danny grew up in North Carolina and says he became a fan at about age 15, but most of his attachment to the university now comes from being an alumnus in the class of 1975. Danny says his continued interest in the program can be traced to Carolina's tradition of "continued excellence with no compromise of education or 'playing by the rules.'" Danny follows the team closely through the Internet—he admits to being something of a recruiting junkie and is an active participant on the Heel-Hoops list-serve. He is also a long-standing friend of former assistant coach and player Dave Hanners, whom he holds in the highest regard. During the season, Danny, who considers himself slightly liberal politically (6), watches every game possible, and he reports that 100% of his social life during basketball season revolves around the Tar Heels. Danny uses the games as an opportunity to spend time and bond with his 16-year-old son and "best pal" Kenan. Kenan is a Carolina fan, although perhaps not quite as intense as his father, and as an ninth grader got an A on an English paper discussing Dean Smith as a "modern day hero."

Vicki Murray is a 48-year-old computer programmer in Greenville, NC. Vicki graduated from UNC in 1973. She says that the values of loyalty, integrity and honesty are what she most associates with Carolina basketball, and that while Carolina basketball cannot rank as high as family, it is close: As she puts it, "After watching a player for four years, they are 'family.'" Vicki attends at least a half dozen games a year, and also actively follows through the team on the Internet. Vicki is an active member of the Heel-Hoops list-serve. She places herself right down the middle politically (5). Asked how she might explain her Carolina addiction to a stranger, Vicki responded, "You can't explain it any more than you can explain that just thinking about walking down Franklin Street gives you goosebumps or that the leaves from that big tree in front of Hill Hall make the best jumping into pile in the world."

Julio Rojas is a 37-year-old Pacific Bell employee and father of four living in Concord, CA. Julio became a fan of the team in the mid-1970s after watching Walter Davis play for the Tar Heels on TV. He did not attend UNC and has never lived in North Carolina, and says only a couple of his friends are also Carolina fans. Nevertheless, Julio maintains his long-distance relationship with the Tar Heels through television, the Internet (*uncbasketball.com* and other Carolina sites), and a friend in Charlotte who sends him newspaper clippings. Julio also scours national magazines with his sons for articles discussing the Tar Heels. Julio says that while admiration for Walter Davis first drew him to the program, "As I got older, I respected and loved the class of the program that Dean Smith built. It is great to root for a team that shows class, graduates its players, wins and for the most part plays the game of basketball, and life, like I want my two sons to follow." Julio, who considers himself slightly conservative politically (4), adds, "UNC basketball taught me so much not only from the basketball perspective but from the perspective of doing things the right way. The story of Dean Smith going to the lunch counter in the 60's with a black man has always been a source of great pride when I talk about Coach Smith or UNC basketball." Julio's worst memory as a Carolina fan is an unusual one: In 1985, Julio and his wife were married the day before Carolina was due to play Villanova in the East Regional Final. Julio watched the game at his mother's house before leaving on the honeymoon and was very upset when Carolina lost. "The honeymoon is the only thing that helped me get over that loss," Julio recalls.

Jeffrey Stephens is a 49-year-old vice president of his family company, a small business which serves as manufacturer's representatives for a number of corporations. He lives and works in northern Chatham County 10 miles from Chapel Hill, and has been a fan since age 15. He attended UNC on a Morehead scholarship, graduated in 1973, and has attended every Carolina home game except for one since 1976. Jeffrey avidly follows the team via television, radio, the print media and the Internet. He listens to and occasionally calls the coach's radio shows and regularly visits the Smith Center in the off-season to check out pick-up scrimmages and workouts involving current and former players. He says that Carolina basketball is "a tremendous source of pride but not the be-all-and-end-all (but almost). My concern for the environment and other living creatures rank higher." Jeffrey spends a lot of his free time working outside on construction and landscaping projects, hiking, mountain biking, kayaking and observing wildlife. He often reports that the hike through the woods to and from the Smith Center on days when the weather is "Carolina blue sky beautiful" is a very enjoyable part of the home game experience. Currently he and his wife, Marsha, also a UNC graduate and big Tar Heel fan, are designing and will soon be building a custom-designed house on 10 acres of woods and streams in Orange County, 16 miles from the Dean Dome. Jeffrey considers himself a moderate/liberal (7) and says that the values attracting him to Carolina basketball are "class, integrity, good sportsmanship (with rare exception), striving for excellence, and unselfishness." He expects to follow Carolina basketball "until I die, and even then probably I still will."

Susan Worley is a 47-year-old social worker in Chapel Hill who has followed Carolina basketball since moving to Chapel Hill as a 7-year-old in 1960. Susan attended UNC, graduating in 1976, but started going to games even before enrolling at Carolina. One of Susan's biggest memories as a teenager was attending Charlie Scott's last home game in 1970 and witnessing the loud ovation Carolina's first black player received. Susan says about two-thirds of her friends are Carolina fans, and says that UNC basketball is a good "conversational ice-breaker." What has kept her interested in Carolina basketball is "the sense of community it creates among people of different backgrounds, the tradition, the beauty of seeing the game played as it should be." Susan has strongly held progressive political views (10), and says of her love of Carolina basketball, "Crazy as it seems, it does rank right up there with love of family and with political and spiritual beliefs." Susan follows the team by attending games, through the local media, as well as the Internet. So unconditional is Susan's love for Carolina basketball that when watching games she always directs her frustrations and anger at opponents and referees and never gets mad or annoyed at Carolina's players or coaches. Whenever Susan needs a chuckle, she need look no further than the wall in her Carrboro office, which hosts a caricature drawing of former President Richard M. Nixon. Beneath the picture is the following quotation drawn from a newspaper account of Nixon's visit to Greensboro during the 1960 Presidential Campaign: "And I always remember, that whatever I have done in the past, or may do in the future, Duke University is responsible in one way or another."

HOW THE DIARISTS EXPERIENCED THE 2000–2001 SEASON

What follows is a game-by-game account of how each of these diarists followed the team during the 33 games of the 2000–01 season. The entries listed here (representing roughly one half of the total entries submitted) attempt to capture both the more mundane and the more interesting or surprising elements of how these Carolina fans experienced the season. The entries also track the mood and enthusiasm of the diarists as the season went along. Most diarists entered the season with a couple of background assumptions: First, they desperately hoped that Carolina would not have as difficult a regular season as in 2000 but would instead build on their Final Four run to have a more consistent season. But at the outset, not all were convinced that this would be the case. Second, the diarists were all interested in how Matt Doherty would do as a head coach, with initial attitudes about the new coach ranging from supportive curiosity to unbridled gushing enthusiasm. Each of the diarists had more specific concerns about Carolina basketball, as well, as will become evident in the pages that follow.

November 10, 2000, Chapel Hill. North Carolina 66, Winthrop 61

- John Floyd listened to the second half of the game on the radio after getting the tip-off time wrong. He reported, "I was a little surprised and disgusted that we could only beat Winthrop by five. But I got over it pretty fast."
- Dave Jarvis listened at home on the radio.
- Jennifer Jordan Engel went to the game with her husband. Jennifer was impressed by "Doherty's intensity—I can still see him jumping around, waving his arms and acting like a true sixth man when a Carolina player trapped an opponent at our bench."
- Danny Mullis listened to the game on the Internet. "My children think it's funny that I'll sit by the computer, with headphones on, for a couple of hours...and not even be looking at the screen. There's no substitute for the familiar sound of the voices of Woody and Mick."
- Trip Cogburn attended the game at the "good old Smith Center" with his girlfriend. He was excited by Matt Doherty's early technical foul, and relieved with the win.
- Ross Cole missed the game and read about it afterward.
- Steve Andrews heard the game on the radio, and expressed "relief" with the win. The highlight for him was hearing Woody Durham's call of Matt Doherty's technical foul in the opening minutes.
- Vicki Murray drove from Greenville to see the game, arriving late because of a traffic jam, and spent two nights in Chapel Hill with her sister, who lives in town. She said afterward, "It's a little disheartening to read some of the bulletin boards, where, because we did not beat Winthrop by a large margin, people are already predicting the continuing demise of the Tar Heels. It was the first game of the season, for Pete's sake. Are these people really too ignorant to realize that both prospects and current players read these boards? How about a little positive input for a change."

November 11, 2000, Chapel Hill. North Carolina 90, Tulsa 81

- John Floyd listened to the game on the radio at his mother's place in Wilmington. "I hate listening to the radio at home. I can remember a time not that long ago when the number of games not on TV far outweighed those that were, but those days are over and I guess I have gotten a little spoiled." John also noted that he flew to New Orleans the day after the game and "rode past the Superdome. I couldn't help but think about what the Heels have done there twice."
- Roy Keefer reported, "I was in Pittsburgh to watch my oldest son play his first college games this weekend and could only get a final score and some quick highlights on the tube."

- Jeffrey Stephens as usual parked his car on Mason Farm Road and made the hike to the Dean Dome. He attended the game with his niece.
- Jennifer Jordan Engel went to the game with her husband—they had spent the night with a sister who lives in Chapel Hill and attended the Maryland football game that day. She said the highlight was "seeing Buzz Peterson and Matt Doherty clown around with each other at the scorer's table."
- Steve Andrews listened to the game on the radio at home. "I couldn't count the number of times our defense created easy opportunities on offense," Steve wrote. "That is a sound I've not heard with such regularity in a long time."

November 17, 2000, Boone, NC. North Carolina 99, Appalachian State 69

- Roy Keefer listened to the game on the Internet.
- William Jarvis watched on TV while listening to the radio. With regard to whether he made any extra effort to catch the game, he reports that he got the "kids off to bed right before tip-off. Does listening to the first five minutes with kids screaming in the background count as extra effort?"
- Danny Mullis was delighted to see the first TV game of the season, which he watched with his 16-year-old son, Kenan. Danny said that the following day "involved the usual routine: check email and websites for accounts and impressions of the game. I rely heavily on our list-serve, of which I've been a member for four or five years or more, I guess, for support and critical analysis."
- K. Mac Heffner and several friends made a road trip from Chapel Hill to Boone to see the game. Mac and company were told to sit down during the game by an elderly ASU fan, provoking an argument. Mac didn't linger around Boone after the game, making the long drive home the same night while stopping only for chicken wings.
- Trip Cogburn listened to the game on the radio with his flag football teammates in Wilmington. His team was there for a regional tournament.
- Chris Gabriele followed the game through updates on *espn.com*.
- Susan Worley listened to the game on the radio—she was frustrated that the game was not shown on television in Chapel Hill. The local newspaper had reported the game would be on, but instead the relevant cable channel showed a hockey game. She recalled how "When I was younger, most games were only broadcast on the radio and I actually would sit, with a whole group of friends, around a radio listening intently to the entire game. Our attention spans are not what they used to be. It was hard to not let my mind wander in the second half."
- Bill Lunney missed seeing the game. "I tried to get home in time to hear it on the Internet radio, but it didn't work out." Bill said he missed Carolina not being in a nationally televised Thanksgiving tournament this year. He also expressed in detail his concerns and skepticism about Ronald Curry returning from football to be Carolina's point guard.

November 29, 2000, East Lansing, MI. Michigan State 77, North Carolina 64

- John Floyd found a sports bar five blocks from his hotel in Miami (where he was staying between cruises) to watch the game. "I hate watching games in bars outside of North Carolina. I'm always afraid they'll switch the game on me."
- Roy Keefer watched the game. His conclusion: "It's going to be a frustrating year. There will be great highs but there will also be great lows."
- Biscuit Dave Jarvis reported, "The kids were in bed and Mama was reading, so ol' Dave struggled along by himself." He thought that the better team had won the game.
- Jennifer Jordan Engel watched the game at home with her husband. She reported being "irritated and upset" after the game. "I think we could have and should have been able to win this one." By a day later, her excitement had turned to the Kentucky game: "Despite last night's loss, I still think we'll beat UK on Saturday."
- Danny Mullis watched the game with Kenan, and said he was "grateful for the 7:30 p.m. start, as this assures that, regardless of outcome, I should be calmed down enough to make a normal bedtime. I have noticed, however, as I've gotten older, that I've become less susceptible to sleep disruption as a consequence of UNC basketball. I seem to have a quicker refractory period following a game: my lows and my highs, while as extreme and acute, return to baseline a bit more readily these days. This is a good thing, and comes in handy following the MSU game."
- K. Mac Heffner watched the game with friends in Granville Towers. He reported having at least 10 conversations about the game the following day on campus, and spoke with most of the players. Later in the season, Mac noted, "Every conversation on campus is about the team after a game."
- Ross Cole watched the game with a few co-workers. Ross saw the game as a continuation of the problems of the previous two seasons, and said, "My excitement over the season beginning is all but deflated."
- Trip Cogburn watched the game alone, and was very frustrated with the loss. "I was really looking forward to seeing our 4–0 team play UK at home this weekend. With no chance of that happening, it became difficult to trudge on through the week. Not to mention I was studying for an organic chemistry test."
- Steve Andrews watched the game with his mother at his place. After the game, he said, "I was reflective, and I was still trying to maintain the proper perspective. I feel like the proper perspective is that the future still looks bright for this team, this season."
- Julio Rojas wrote, "Excitement reigned all day—this is the first Tar Heel game that has been broadcast to the West Coast this year." Julio said he entered the game with low expectations and a desire to be patient with the players, but got mad at Adam Boone after about three minutes. Julio watched the game with his two sons, aged 14 and 11. "They have always enjoyed watching the games with me, but this year they watched it more intensely than in the past. I saw their impatience and told them to relax and enjoy the game. That helped me relax and

enjoy the game. I still spent about half the game on my feet, not pacing but watching intensely."

- Vicki Murray watched the game on TV by herself. She thought during the first ten minutes that "we were going to stick with them," and described herself as "disappointed but still hopeful" after the loss.

- Jeffrey Stephens watched the game on TV with his wife. He said he was "disappointed, but not overly so." He also commented, "I thought [the Michigan State fans] were Duke fan wanna-bes: bouncing up and down and organized chants. I hope Carolina fans will never imitate the Dookies with that bouncing up and down stuff."

- Bill Lunney watched the game on TV, mostly by himself, with other family members checking in periodically. He felt "even-keeled" after the game, and looked forward to the upcoming televised games against Kentucky and Miami.

- Susan Worley watched the game with her husband and daughter. After the losses, Susan described the five stages she passes through in dealing with losses, patterned after Elizabeth Kubler-Ross's work on dealing with death (see next page). She notes, "I don't always experience them in the order listed and I can go back and forth from one to another, but I always experience each stage at least briefly. And I pretty much shift from one to the other until the Tar Heels win a game."

December 2, 2000, Chapel Hill. Kentucky 93, North Carolina 76

- John Floyd watched the game at home. He wrote, "I felt sick. I hate to see my boys play so bad." John also went on the Internet and noted that, "Some idiots are already saying that Doherty has to go. Oh please!!"

- Dave Jarvis watched the first half on TV at home and the second half on the radio while driving with his wife to Raleigh for a concert. He wondered, "Are we really this bad?"

- Jennifer Jordan Engel went to the game with her mom and two posters from the *uncbasketball.com* message board, one of whom she had never met before. Jennifer had two extra tickets and sold them at face value to the message board guys. During the game, Jennifer was told by an "older gentleman" sitting behind her to sit down during the game. "My blood literally started to boil as I complained that we weren't standing up the entire game, only jumping up in excitement when exciting things happened, and that at the point he chose to get ugly about it, it was a freakin' time out!!! Was ready to engage in a battle of words, but decided against it since I wasn't sure what the policy was on standing up and I didn't want to get thrown out, plus he was around 70, so my brain reminded me to have respect for my elders. I did make a few loud comments about how people like that give Carolina the wine and cheese reputation and if they won't stand up and cheer when exciting things happen, they should stay home and watch the rest of the game on TV! I stayed in my seat for the rest of the game, however." Jennifer reported feeling "depressed" after the loss, but had a productive following day in which she "tried not to think too much about the game."

SUSAN WORLEY'S FIVE STAGES OF DEALING WITH DEFEAT, APPLIED TO THE MICHIGAN STATE LOSS

Stage 1: Deep, Dark Depression/Questioning the Point of It All. Oh God, oh God how could this have happened? What is the meaning of life? Is it really worth living? I thought we were going to see a new day with Matt Doherty and here we were, losing convincingly once again. Is the golden age of Tar Heel basketball over? And what's with Baddour firing Carl Torbush, a good guy with a sense of ethics? What has happened to my beloved university? And our country—my God! A bunch of aging fascists have found a dumb frat boy to be their puppet, stolen an election for him, and the American public calls the other guy a "sore loser." What's up with that? Is the whole world going to hell in a handbasket? What's the point of going on in a world this screwed up?

Stage 2: Self-Blame/Guilt. It's all my fault. Why didn't I wear the Tar Heel earrings when I thought about it? They could have made all the difference but, no, I was worried that people in Asheboro might think they were a little odd and I put my own feelings ahead of the Tar Heels. What kind of worthless excuse for a fan am I? Why didn't I concentrate more on the game and get my head in the right place, instead of letting myself get distracted with work stuff and election coverage? Where were my priorities? I don't deserve to go to the Dean Dome and see the Heels play Kentucky after having failed them so miserably.

Stage 3: Extreme Annoyance. Every statement uttered by my _____ (fill in the blank: husband, daughter, sister, mom, co-worker, friend, neighbor) about the game is SO ANNOYING that it takes a massive act of will power to call on all of my pacifist beliefs and not commit murder.

Stage 4: Denial/Avoidance. I *will not* think about the game. No thought of the game will ever again be allowed to enter my head. As far as I'm concerned, the Heels never played Michigan State. I will concentrate mightily on some pleasant fantasy to keep the game from entering my brain—maybe something like all of the Dook coaching staff being caught red-handed in some scandal so horrifying and humiliating that they are stripped of all their wins for the past two decades and basketball is forever banished from their institution...or some other, equally cheerful and uplifting thought.

Stage 5: Rationalization. It's still November. This game really doesn't mean much. After all, we were playing the defending national champions on their home court. "And, just think, a billion people in China don't even know we lost" (Coach Smith). Matt Doherty is just in his second year of coaching. We're still developing our point guards. It's early yet. It's March that really matters...and maybe we'll see Michigan State again then in a game that REALLY counts.

- Danny Mullis reported, "This Saturday won't wind into afternoon quickly enough. Obviously, the highlight today is at 3:50 p.m., so any activity prior to that is just 'passing time.'" After the game, he reported being "in a funk for the rest of the evening, and I find myself dangerously short-tempered with the children. I don't like this—I should be able to separate myself from losses better than this."
- Vicki Murray attended the game with her sister and mother. This involved picking up her mother in Kinston en route to Greenville, and then picking up her sister at the RDU airport before heading to Chapel Hill. Along the way, she got a speeding ticket with a fine of $250. She felt "downright disappointed" after the game, and described her Saturday as "pretty much the day from Hades." The next day Vicki "was completely useless," but talked about the game with her neighbors on a walk through the snow and made some snow angels in her yard.
- Ross Cole watched the game at a friend's house (who didn't watch). He said he was angry and embarrassed after the game. Worried, Ross asked, "Will we have to live through another sub-par season and—worst of all—two more losses to Duke?"
- Trip Cogburn attended the game with his friend and girlfriend. He confessed to being "baffled" by the game, and said he had no conversations the next day about it: "I have refused to talk about the game.... I did not want anything to do with college basketball after that game."
- Jeffrey Stephens attended the game with his 13-year-old nephew. He was disappointed in the game, and in "the 10,000 or so 'fans' that left before the buzzer." His mood was low the next day, but improved a bit after he watched the UNC women's soccer team come from behind to win the NCAA Championship.
- Bill Lunney watched the game at home with one of his sons. He said he was "slightly concerned that Doherty would not be able to 'right the ship' but actually still very confident that he would." Bill lost a bet with a Kentucky alumnus and good friend about this game, but reasoned that "I've won more than he has, so I don't feel bad."
- Susan Worley went to the game with her daughter. After the game, she "immediately entered Stage 4 (Denial), where I have attempted to stay until I had to write this up, which is quickly pushing me into Stage 3 (Extreme Annoyance—who is this Thad Williamson fellow and why is he forcing me to relive this misery?!)."

December 4, 2000, Chapel Hill. North Carolina 67, Miami 45
- John Floyd saw the score on the cruise ship where he works as a comedian.
- Dave Jarvis watched the game on TV with his wife. He said, "I think this team is headed for 20–10, 3rd in the ACC, and second or third round elimination from the NCAAs."
- Danny Mullis noted, "The tip-off at 7 p.m. is perfect timing for us. I have time to help my 12-year-old daughter, Caroline, with her math homework before the game, and then time to spend with her after the game at bedtime. Many, many times I've given her the 'goodnight, don't let the sleeping bag bed bugs bite, I love you' bedtime tuck-in during a timeout." Danny

and Kenan were pleased with the game, especially the appearance of Ronald Curry and Brendan Haywood's triple-double. He said that he planned to pass the time before Saturday "feeding that addiction to UNC sports by finding every burp and scratch that is reported on the Internet."

- K. Mac Heffner went to the game and sat in the fifth row, courtesy of Neil Fingleton. He talked to several players after the game. Mac said he was stressing out about final exams, but things weren't too bad.
- Ross Cole missed the game—he didn't even realize there was a game until his brother emailed him the score.
- Trip Cogburn, unable to get tickets, watched the game on TV. When Jason Capel took a hard fall and appeared to get injured, Trip noted, "I felt like I was going to vomit."
- Chris Gabriele watched the game on TV at home with his fiancee, and declared himself "satisfied" with the comfortable win.
- Jeffrey Stephens attended the game with his friend Martin Baucom (former quarterback for the Chapel Hill Cowboys of 1978). He got to the game 45 minutes early, saw Phil Ford in the stands, introduced himself and chatted for two or three minutes. "He thanked me for saying hello and shook my hand twice. He is such a nice guy. I couldn't help thinking that if things had worked out differently in Phil's personal life, he could very well be the head coach right now." Jeffrey watched the game on tape after getting home, causing him to be "a little sluggish" the first couple of hours of work the following morning.
- Susan Worley went to the game with "a fifth grade girl I 'mentor' through a school-based program. This was a big moment (and a big gamble) for me, because, like so many kids, she has a special radar for knowing what's important to adults and behaving obnoxiously at the worst possible moments. I knew that she might not last through the game or might not be interested in it at all. I wanted to take the chance, though, because Tar Heel basketball is special to me and because going to the Dean Dome is a pretty high-status activity for Chapel Hill kids, and I wanted her, a kid from a public housing neighborhood, to get to go to school today and brag.

  "Sure enough, at dinner before the game, she was being incredibly bratty, even claiming she was going to cheer for Miami! I was having serious second thoughts about the whole outing but, once we entered the Dean Dome, she was completely transfixed by the entire spectacle. She never lost interest and, by game's end, had become a Tar Heel fan—she's now planning to attend UNC, be a cheerleader, and is a huge Brendan Haywood fan.

  "At the end of the game, we went down to the court and ended up standing right next to Brendan Haywood. The look of absolute awe on her face was a priceless moment for me—seeing the game through her eyes reminded me of all that makes Tar Heel basketball so special."
- Vicki Murray went to the game with her sister in Chapel Hill, and stayed overnight at her sister's place. She commented, "It has been a hectic couple of weeks with so many home games. I really wish they would not schedule this many home games before Christmas. I think the rush

of the season really hurts attendance. You would think the people who plan this didn't know that half of the fans come from a distance to see these games!"

December 9, 2000, Houston, Texas. North Carolina 82, Texas A&M 60

- Dave Jarvis watched the game at home on TV. He volunteered the opinion that 7-foot high school senior and Tar Heel recruiting target Desagna Diop "will go pro. Bet on it."
- Danny Mullis watched the game on TV with Kenan. The day after, he noted, "I didn't search the Internet for as many stories about the game as I often do. That's primarily because of two reasons: the game didn't really have sufficient drama to warrant much follow-up and it was a Sunday and I had other things to do."
- Ross Cole missed the game. His morale was at a low. "In light of the MSU and Kentucky losses, I've decided not to follow the team so closely, at least for a while…I'll also be cutting back on how often I look them up on the 'net, which has been almost daily over the last year. I get so excited about UNC basketball and then we get embarrassed by a team like Kentucky, and all I feel is anger and disappointment. It's just not worth it."
- Chris Gabriele watched a movie with his fiancee at home during the game, and checked the score occasionally on *espn.com.*
- Susan Worley listened to the game at home with her husband, daughter and two out-of-town friends. "We were very disappointed that the game wasn't televised—our friends watched many games at our house back in the 70s and 80s and were hoping to relive those happy moments. Since it wasn't on TV, we ended up talking through the whole thing so I really heard very little of it." Susan added, "I'm still obsessed with the unfolding election drama…. We were all thrilled with the Florida Supreme Court's decision on Friday and then crushed by the U.S. Supreme Court's ruling. My friend said after the U.S. Supreme Court ruled that he felt the way he does when he's looking forward to a weekend of watching the Heels play in the ACC Tournament and then they get knocked off in the Friday game."
- Jeffrey Stephens listened to the game on the radio at home with his wife. A friend of his in Boone videotaped the game for him, to be seen the next weekend on a trip to Boone. Jeff admitted to feeling "a bit low and lethargic" the day after the game, but "mostly due to events having nothing to do with the game, namely presidential politics and some personal issues. The game last night was a lone bright spot."

December 17, 2000, Chapel Hill. North Carolina 95, Buffalo 74

- Dave Jarvis watched the game on TV with his wife. He reported, "We had a tornado blow within about eight miles of the house Saturday night about 1:30 a.m. I have an employee that is a single mother of two that lives in a mobile home that was directly in the storm's path, so we called her and she brought her family over to sleep. I was up the rest of the night checking weather and generally being a 'mother hen' type. So I was asleep until right before game time."

- Danny Mullis arranged to go with Kenan to the house of a doctor friend (Jeffrey Joyner) who has a satellite dish and television access to the game, as he has been doing for dish-only games for about 10 years.
- Ross Cole was looking for a new job and had limited computer access. Still determined to limit his interest in Carolina basketball after the Kentucky loss, he read an account of the Buffalo game two days later. He wrote, "My interest in Carolina basketball will be scant because of more pressing issues (e.g. finding a job!)."
- Chris Gabriele missed the game. He went to the Jets–Lions game at the Meadowlands that day instead.
- Roy Keefer missed the game, having had hip replacement surgery on December 11.
- Susan Worley watched the game on TV at home with her youngest daughter and husband. She noted, "The place I work did get tickets donated for kids, so we had fun rounding up kids to attend beforehand. I let my daughter take a friend on my ticket, because I had a lot to do to get ready for Christmas." Susan also volunteered, "I am crushed by the illegitimate election of Dubya as our president," and reported that her sister was worried that this turn of events also implied that Duke would win the national championship. "Somehow, it makes perfect sense among my family and friends that world, national, and personal events are very closely tied into Tar Heel basketball."
- Jeffrey Stephens attended the game with a friend and his friend's three-year-old son. He was happy with the game and with the 10-minute hike back to his car on a "bright, crisp and gusty afternoon with Carolina blue skies." Jeffrey's mood fluctuated the next day: He was down about the goings-on in the election dispute, but up when thinking about "yesterday's game and other positive things."

December 23, 2000, Los Angeles, CA. North Carolina 80, UCLA 70

- Danny Mullis and his family were visiting relatives out-of-state. "My family and I were in Montgomery, Alabama, for the holidays for this game. I cannot describe how agitated I was when, in the morning paper, the TV listings were noncommittal about which of the two national ABC games would be shown locally. Apparently, this agitation led to some confusion on my part, as I went to the TV room (which happens to be the bedroom of my in-laws) an hour early to try to find the game (I blame this on keeping my watch on Charleston time, although Montgomery is an hour earlier). Once *actual* game time came, I returned with Kenan to the TV room, and was buoyed when the first ABC camera shot was of the floor at Pauley Pavilion. We were, in fact, going to see UNC vs. UCLA. No bigger Christmas present could come my way. Kenan and I watched the entire game together, and various other family members wandered in and out. There are no other true basketball fans, and certainly no other true Tar Heel fans, in the house (my father-in-law went to Duke), but having been married for more than two decades, I am expected to and not overtly punished for leaving the general family activities to watch any televised UNC games while with my in-laws. It was more difficult to follow this game as closely as I normally do, since the TV room was in constant flux with people coming and going. This was not much of a problem as we extended our lead, but when things began to collapse in the second half, I was more and more tense at not being able to focus. Plus, Kenan and I were getting little sympathy when the Heels were behind from the Alabama/non-UNC crowd. Thankfully, the Heels righted the ship and were able to stage a great response to the UCLA push."

- Vicki Murray watched the game at home. "I started watching it by myself, then my husband came in about the time UCLA was making its comeback and he annoyed me. I got nervous, so I listened to Woody for the last seven or eight minutes." Vicki, who served dinner for 18 people on Christmas Eve, wrote, "This really felt like the beginning of the season for me.... The victory under those conditions should do a lot for morale and that whole never giving up thing that is so important and that Dean taught so well."

- Jeffrey Stephens watched the game at home with his wife. After listening to the radio broadcast during the game, Jeffrey planned to watch the tape again with Billy Packer's commentary for CBS.

- Ross Cole in Seattle was entertaining his parents and younger sister, who had flown in from Winston-Salem for the holiday. "We decided to work the Carolina game into our Saturday afternoon plans. By the time we did some sight-seeing, ate lunch, and got back to their hotel, the first half was coming to an end. The score said 46-30, and seeing that count was the high point of the game. The low point was... most of the second half. Even when we were ahead, and then after we reclaimed the lead, I was very negative about our play. I even found myself disappointed that we were apparently going to win. That disappointment stemmed from the idea that, as long as we win, we'll be content with the status quo—and I don't want that!" Ross added, "The outcome of the game had little, if any, bearing on my mood that day or the following. I have been absorbed with other things, plus my family was in town, so there has been little chance for basketball to sway my disposition."

- John Floyd watched the game on TV at his dad's house in Rocky Mount. He reported, "I was at a big party Saturday night and discussed the game with several people. Also, Friday night I was at a party and had a long discussion with my friend Dave. He is 10 years younger than me and grew up next door and is like my little brother. We don't see each other very often, but when we do, Carolina is ALL we talk about.... Everybody seems to agree this is a good team but not a great team, and it will take two or three more years of Matt recruiting his type of players before we will be back on top not just in the ACC, but in the nation." John was happy with the UCLA game, and with Duke's loss to Stanford that week, which inspired him to perform "this thing I do called 'the Duke Just Lost Dance'...I did that in my cabin by myself."

December 29, 2000, Charlotte, NC. North Carolina 91, Massachusetts 60

- Dave Jarvis watched the game on TV with his mother and his wife. He had several conversations about the game the following day with his mom, who is a big fan.

- Chris Gabriele checked to get updates of the game, and read six accounts of the game the following day.
- Bill Lunney listened to the game on the Internet and was pleased that Carolina showed some "killer instinct" in the second half.
- John Floyd watched the game at home by himself on Friday night. "Staying at home on Friday night—alone—is going out of my way [to see the game] I guess. But I'd rather watch the Heels in peace and solitude than sit in some smoky bar with friends checking out girls I wouldn't have the nerve to talk to."
- Jeffrey Stephens traveled with his wife to Carrboro to watch the game with three friends (being unable to get the game on TV at home). Jeffrey's experience watching the game inspired the following comments:

JEFFREY STEPHENS ON "NEGATIVE" FANS

I've always found it interesting to observe how fans cheer for their respective teams. In the case of UNC fans, I have a hard time tolerating so-called "negative fans," i.e., those that only open their mouths to be critical of our players but seldom, if ever, offer positive comments like "Nice play," "Way to block out," or "Great hustle." Last night, while watching the game with two new friends, I was fearful of having to endure one of these fans when all of two minutes into the game he was all over Brendan Haywood, excoriating him for not getting a rebound. I was bracing for a long evening, but then his girlfriend told him it was way too early to start bad-mouthing our players. I seconded her motion and the guy was fine the rest of the way, cheering positively for the Tar Heels. I'm sure it helped that we played well and won by 31 points. Later I asked him if he attends any games. He replied that he prefers watching on the tube because in his living room he can criticize and yell at our players without having to endure dirty looks or possible confrontations with other fans. I thought that was an interesting, honest perspective and kind of amusing, but apparently that is his particular style of "team support." I am critical at times (almost always stemming from personal frustration) but come from a positive perspective 90% of the time. I always draw the line at personal attacks on 18-to-20-year-old student athletes and am extremely intolerant of those fans who exhibit such low-class behavior. Fortunately, this type fan appears to be in the minority.

December 30, 2000, Charlotte, NC. North Carolina 64, College of Charleston 60

- Danny Mullis watched the game on TV with Kenan, and was relieved by the outcome. "I knew an upset by the Cougars would result in my receiving numerous phone calls from friends [who went to C of C]...just as it did two years ago."

- Bill Lunney listened to the game on the Internet with his wife. "I rigged up a connection from my computer to the family room so I could be with her while I listened to the game." He was "elated" with what he regarded as a "big win" and especially happy to see Max Owens make important contributions.
- John Floyd watched this game at home alone again. He said he wished the team "had played harder. Against a better team, that's not going to cut it."
- Vicki Murray watched the game at home by herself. She was amused at some criticism directed at Matt Doherty for reportedly breaking a chair in the locker room at halftime of the Massachusetts game, pointing out that for years Bill Guthridge and also Dean Smith had been accused of lacking fire. "It just proves unequivocally the grass is always greener on the other side of the fence." She started looking forward to the Wake Forest game coming up: "Time to go pull out all the lucky clothes and pompoms!!"

January 2, 2001, Atlanta, GA. North Carolina 84, Georgia Tech 70

- Dave Jarvis watched the game on TV, with his wife asleep in the same room on a recliner.
- Jennifer Jordan Engel watched the game with her husband. She said a dunk by Julius Peppers was her emotional high the game, combined with a "Quick prayer aimed heavenward—please let Julius stay in school!" The following day was Jennifer's birthday, and she said her mood was at a peak. "How can it not be on my birthday? After the Great Liver Blowout of '99, I'm just absolutely grateful to be alive to see another birthday."
- Chris Gabriele tried to listen to the game over the Internet, but spent the first half downloading a new audio player. He did get to listen to the second half.
- Roy Keefer was still recovering from surgery and wasn't able to see the Tech game or the two games before New Year's, though he did see highlights.
- Vicki Murray, unable to get the game on TV in Greenville, listened to it in her bedroom, alone. "At least half the second half I was hiding under the covers." She was "happy and relieved" with the victory. She added, "I remain disappointed at fan responses that I see on the Internet, the list-serve, and various fans I run into. I am weary also of the negative press Haywood continues to receive. He seems like a nice guy who really is trying and may be doing the best he can do. Let's cut him a little slack."
- John Floyd didn't get to see the game and only found out the score when he got hold of a *USA Today* the following day in the Miami airport. He then went online "to see what everybody thought."

January 6, 2001, Chapel Hill. North Carolina 70, Wake Forest 69

Brendan Haywood scored a layup with four seconds remaining to give North Carolina the win.

- Dave Jarvis watched the game on TV with his wife. He commented happily that Curry "might be 0-for-forever, but put the game on the line and he'll take the shot—and probably make it."

- Jennifer Jordan Engel attended the game at the Dean Dome with her husband and her mother; at the end of the game she felt "elated, giddy, and 10 years younger." Jennifer had the flu and napped most of the following day, but said her mood was "at a 7 [on a 1 to 7 scale] anyway, just because I was still excited about the win and being there for it."

- Danny Mullis and Kenan watched the game at home on TV. He reported that "I was so charged up by the victory that I immediately adjourned to the computer room to listen to the post-game show with Woody and Mick. Surprisingly, Kenan joined me, in a show of Tar Heel solidarity that was moving. Yes, he's coming along just fine. In several years, he'll be tearing up at 'Hark the Sound.'" Danny noted that on the Monday after the game, "As I was driving back to the office, I saw a friend whom I know to be a Wake alum walking on the sidewalk. I put down the window and yelled, 'Go Wake Forest' to him. Once he saw who it was, a sheepish grin came over his face. Not five minutes later, I arrived in my office to find the voice mail message light illuminated. My payback message for this sidewalk assault! It was grand."

- Trip Cogburn attended the game with his girlfriend. He had a little hassle securing the tickets, which were obtained from his sister and a friend of hers. He said, "I felt like I was going to vomit for most of the game. My hands were like leaky faucets. There were a couple times my stomach tried to make its way up my esophagus during intense moments and I thought this just may be the time I need medical attention during a game." He reported being "thrilled" at the end of the game, but too exhausted to partake in Franklin Street partying.

- Chris Gabriele watched the game on TV with his fiancee, then read 7–10 accounts of the game the following day.

- Jeffrey Stephens attended the game with his brother-in-law, and used the word "euphoric" to describe his feelings. The day after the game, he woke up and "immediately listened to a tape of the radio postgame. I stayed in a good mood all day and, yes, I attribute much of it to the afterglow effect of the huge win last night." Jeffrey was also pleased by Haywood's big game, writing, "Maybe his many detractors will desist for a while.... Some fans are quite irrational and mean-spirited (e.g. 'Haywood sucks') and, in my opinion, seem to hold, for whatever reason, views of players that are not based in reality. Brendan is the current favorite target of fans such as these. I cannot relate and find it difficult to understand that mentality."

- The day after the game, Roy Keefer, who saw it on TV, reported, "I slept great last night and felt wonderful all day today."

- Julio Rojas watched the game with his two sons, and said, "Our house was intense the whole game. When Brendan H. put in the rebound, it felt so good. Beating a team that is probably a bit better than you right now is a great feeling."

- Susan Worley went to the game with her oldest daughter. She said she felt "ecstatic" during the game. "I felt that, whatever the outcome, the Heels were playing intense, Tar Heel basketball and the crowd was into it." After the game, she "stayed up until 2:00 a.m., because I was too excited to sleep." She woke up just four hours later, excited to read the papers about the game. One of her big memories of the game revolved around Brendan Haywood. "I HATE it when fans are really critical of one of our players, especially considering that they are all kids and amateurs…. How satisfying for him to have played so well, how perfect that he got the game-winning basket, and how I hope he will play this way against Maryland."

- Vicki Murray watched the game at home alone. She reported feeling "on cloud nine, way up on cloud nine" after the game. She said she was "very happy for Coach Doherty and the Heels. A very nice start for the new regime and at least for a few weeks the fans won't be questioning his hiring…. I will watch this tape a couple of times between now and Wednesday. (Confession: I've already watched the end a half dozen times. I love those students storming the floor.)"

January 10, 2001, College Park, MD. North Carolina 86, Maryland 83

- Dave Jarvis watched the game on TV with his wife. He said he was "amazed" by Carolina's performance. "The game looked more like the 'old' Carolina teams than I've seen in a long time. This was an execution, not a game."
- Jennifer Jordan Engel watched the game at home with her husband. She reported being "jubilant" after the game, and noted that her excellent mood carried over into the next day.
- Danny Mullis watched the game alone while Kenan met with a study group. His wife stepped in and out during the second half. He noted, "This game was the first time this season I noticed actual physical responses to the game. I was fidgety, my pulse rate was up, my stomach ached. At game's conclusion, I was tired from the nervous energy."
- K. Mac Heffner was in a journalism class at UNC that met on Wednesday nights, but he managed to listen to the game on the radio. "I had to be sneaky with my headphones, I hid them nicely in my shirt and tried to pay attention."
- Chris Gabriele watched the game on TV alone. He said, "This was a huge win, one that has me convinced."
- Vicki Murray watched the game at home by herself. She felt "a little euphoric," after the game, "a little stunned and still wondering a little if this team is as good as they look." She added, "I went out to eat with my husband and when we got back in the car, it was nearly halftime and I think we were down four. We stopped at the coffee shop for a cup of coffee, and when we got back in the car, I think we were up around 12–14 points and Mick and Woody were a little apoplectic. We finally get back to the house, and I turn on the TV and lo and behold Maryland starts catching up. I'm thinking, hmm, should I cut off the TV and leave? Well, both the Heels and I gutted it out, them by playing stand-up and hold 'em off and me by pacing in front of the TV and going outside with the headphones on."
- Steve Andrews watched the game at home, and said he felt "exhilarated" during the contest.
- Roy Keefer watched the game and was pleased with the team's play and Ronald Curry in particular. "That was as much intensity as I have seen Carolina play with in the last 10 years or so. At least since George Lynch was on the floor."
- Susan Worley watched the game with her oldest daughter and her husband ("who for once was actually awake during the game—7:00 tip-offs are great for middle-aged folks"). Susan left

unfinished some important business at work to get home in time for the start, and was thrilled with the outcome. She said, "My happiness [at the early ACC success] goes much deeper than the wins though—there is something intangible and beyond my powers of description called Tar Heel basketball. I can't put it into words, but I know it when I see it.... Tonight's game, along with the Wake game, convinced me that Tar Heel basketball is definitely back."

- Jeffrey Stephens watched the game with his wife at another couple's house. "The high point was when our second-half run topped out with our team up 19 points and a little over eight minutes to go. We were so caught up in the action that a double take was required for it to sink in that we were indeed up 19 points on Maryland in their gym." He reported listening to Adam Gold's radio talk show the following day when a "Carolina 'fan' called in blaming the refs for the Maryland run that got them back into the game and then proceeded to bash Haywood for only scoring eight points. I was sitting here thinking 'My God, can a person like this ever be happy with a huge win like this, or do they watch these games only to be irritated, angry and bothered?' This is a rhetorical question, I know, but I will never understand or relate to their mode of thinking."

January 13, 2001, Chapel Hill. North Carolina 84, Marquette 54

- Dave Jarvis watched the game on TV with his wife. His first thought after the game was "Where are we gonna go for dinner?"
- Jennifer Jordan Engel attended the game with her mom and Jim Nichols. The following day she posted on the message board a defense of the "fatcat" alumni in the Dean Dome: "Not all alums are stoic wine and cheesers and not all students are hard-core yelling machines. It's been my experience that both sides are quite prone to sweeping generalizations when describing themselves or the opposition. It's all well and good to cry and shake your fists at the evil alums during the four years you're a student, but the sad truth is this: graduation. Happens to the best of us. And suddenly you're forced to take sides against your former comrades—the students. Just because you graduate doesn't mean you want the seats less. In most cases, you want them more."
- Danny Mullis had been out of town and away from the computer for a few days, during which he called home long-distance several times to try to ascertain the news on whether Julius Peppers would be going to the NFL and possibly leaving the basketball team. He watched the game alone, and then spent about three hours the rest of the weekend reading Internet reports about Carolina.
- Trip Cogburn attended the game with three friends. He was impressed by Carolina's intensity during a nonconference game, and at game's end was "ready for us to play again."
- Chris Gabriele was not able to see the game, because the New York CBS affiliate did not carry it. He helped his brother move, instead, and checked score updates. Chris, the Jets fan, was unhappy some of the next day because the New York Giants made the Super Bowl.

- Vicki Murray watched the game at home alone. She reported, "It has been several years since I found myself this excited about basketball. We had some great teams in the nineties, and who wouldn't enjoy watching Stackhouse and Wallace and Jamison and Carter, but I think this team is on the way to notching itself as special. I haven't seen this kind of defense since 1993."
- Roy Keefer wrote, "Great Game for Carolina. They beat a team they should have beaten in the way they should have beaten them." Roy also expressed concern for former Marquette coach Al McGuire's health. "Let's just hope that his health will allow him to see many more Carolina and Marquette games." (McGuire died less than two weeks later.)
- Susan Worley, who splits her two season tickets with her two daughters, watched this one at home. "My oldest daughter is a fifth grade teacher—she got two extra tickets and had a drawing in her class. The winners got to go to the game with her and had a blast!" Susan added, "I have no bad feelings about Marquette as a team or a school, but they were our opponent in the most heartbreaking loss of all time [in 1977]. Beating them soundly doesn't come close to making up for that game, but it feels pretty good."
- Steve Andrews watched the game while at work. He was pleased to note, "during garbage time, I noticed that even the guys off the end of the bench are moving the ball and trying hard to play stifling defense."

January 17, 2001, Chapel Hill. North Carolina 92, Clemson 65

- Dave Jarvis watched the game on TV with his wife. He called the game "another yawner."
- K. Mac Heffner listened to the game during his journalism class again.
- Bill Lunney watched the game at home alone, with family members looking on from time to time.
- Roy Keefer watched the game and expressed pleasure that 11 Tar Heels scored and that Matt Doherty lectured Brian Bersticker after a bad shot during garbage time.
- Danny Mullis watched the game alone, except for the final eight minutes or so, when his 12-year-old daughter, Caroline, "came down in the pajamas and curled up on the sofa beside me. She was a nice companion, and asked many good questions about the rules of basketball." Danny had negotiated with Caroline so that she would be ready to have him review her math homework (a nightly ritual) at halftime of the game.
- Vicki Murray went to the game with her mother. "We went all out for this one, making it a real Mother-Daughter adventure. We spent the entire day before the game shopping and then spent the night in Raleigh." As is usually the case when Vicki rides the bus to the Smith Center from the park-and-ride lot, she got into a lot of conversations about the game on the way over. Capping Vicki's high spirits the next day was an appearance in traffic court which reduced her $250 ticket from the day of the Kentucky game to just $10. Vicki wrote, "Something is different in Chapel Hill this year.... The atmosphere in the Dean Dome has never been scintillating for a Clemson game until this one. The crowd was wonderful, and the students' enthusiasm

seems to be rubbing off on the entire crowd. I think, in part, that the students and younger fans now have a coach that is 'theirs,' whereas despite great winning records and great teams, Smith and Guthridge were 'ours.'"

January 20, 2001, Tallahassee, FL. North Carolina 80, Florida State 70

- Trip Cogburn watched the game on TV at a bar on Franklin Street with friends. Trip reported a sense of fear in the bar when FSU cut the lead to three in the second half, and being relieved when the game was over. The next day, he recalled the sight of "Doherty visibly developing an ulcer on the sideline."
- Danny Mullis listened to the game on the Internet, with no local coverage available and his doctor friend with the satellite dish out of town. He wrote, "Of all recent games, and I believe this is because I could not watch it on TV, this one had the feel of 'disassociation.' I was helpless when the game tightened because I was out of my element; the lack of TV coverage was tantamount for me to being relegated to 'mere observer' status. I did not enjoy this. As a consequence, I read very little about the game afterwards."
- Bill Lunney skipped the game. It wasn't on TV, and his plans to listen to it on the Internet were foiled by a last-minute commitment. During the game, however, he "thought about the game and the fact I was missing it. I wanted to find out the score as soon as possible. If Carolina loses and I did not see the game, I'm usually pretty 'down', because I don't know why they lost and what happened—so it was nice to get the win."
- Chris Gabriele listened to the game over the Internet at home with his fiancee. He noted, "This was the first time I ever got the chance to listen to Woody broadcast a game. I have only heard clips in the past. I really enjoyed it and I'm glad I now have this option, because there are still a few more games left that aren't on TV up here."
- Jeffrey Stephens watched the game on television with "my best basketball buddy, Randy, and my wife Marsha." He was pleased by the win but "disconcerted that we were outplayed in the second half by a 5–12 team which is winless in the ACC."
- Steve Andrews watched the game on TV at his uncle's house with a cousin and his aunt. Having partied late the night before for his 30th birthday, Steve was a little drowsy during the game and went to sleep right afterwards. He reported that the milestone left him in an unstable mood much of the day. "I played a tennis match, which was fun, but then the reality of turning 30 struck me kind of hard and I wasn't a happy camper for part of the day. I looked forward to turning 30 for the most part. I thought it would be no big deal, and for the most part it wasn't, until right there at the very end of my last day as a 20-something. It was just a brief touch of reality. I'm not old, but I'm definitely not a kid anymore."
- Susan Worley skipped the game. She was in Washington, attending a protest against the inauguration of George W. Bush as President.

January 24, 2001, Chapel Hill. North Carolina 88, Virginia 81

- Dave Jarvis watched TV while listening to the radio alone. He noted that "ultra-quick teams still hurt us and Virginia was the same."

- Jennifer Jordan Engel went to the game with her mother, and reported feeling "cheery" throughout the contest. She gave herself a 5 (on a 1–7 scale) for both productivity and mood the next day. Her mood was buoyed in part by the news that her little sister, Amber, was accepted into Carolina. She also posted on a message board, "The chemistry is there. Best example was when Capel went down with a muscle cramp and three players, including Forte, rushed over to help him out with it—before the trainer could even get there! Remember that during this summer, there were rumors of Capel and Forte having some ego clashes. I don't see that anymore."

- K. Mac Heffner was at his night class again, but listened to the game on small radio headphones. Mac noted, "I feel I should attend this class because it is in my major, and I know there are students out there who would love to be in my seat at the best school in the nation." Mac was pleased the next day to get an autographed picture of Dean Smith, courtesy of Neil Fingleton.

- Trip Cogburn attended the game with his girlfriend. After feeling uneasy during the game, he was thrilled with the win. "I was also just in awe of Forte's ability to put the team on his back."

- Jeffrey Stephens attended the game with a friend. He also received an invitation from a friend to attend the upcoming game against N.C. State in Raleigh, which touched off a practical and ethical dilemma: "What should I wear, and how demonstrative should I be? Another UNC buddy of mine, Randy, advises me to wear neutral colors and to be very low key; why invite trouble? My wife tells me to wear neutral colors and cheer loudly but not vociferously. She also thinks that I need to be careful not to provoke an encounter with any State fans. My current thinking is to wear my usual Carolina basketball shirt and cheer vigorously.... I've never attended a Tar Heel game on a rival's home floor. It should be lots of fun."

- Chris Gabriele watched on TV at home alone, then read 7–10 accounts of the game the following day.

- Danny Mullis watched the game mostly by himself. Although Carolina won the game, pleasing Danny, he lost a standing bet with two lawyer friends who graduated from the University of Virginia, covering all basketball and football games between UVA and UNC. The bet involves the point spread, and because Carolina failed to cover the spread by two points, Danny found himself on the hook for two lunches for his colleagues. He reasoned that his UVA friends might find justice in the fact that missed free throws by Ronald Curry in the closing moments shrank the margin of victory, since Cavalier fans are still upset at Curry for breaking a verbal commitment to Virginia and signing with UNC in March 1998.

- Vicki Murray attended the game with her 18-year-old daughter, an East Carolina student who is a Carolina fan. They got to Chapel Hill early to go to the Shrunken Head on Franklin Street, "to get the foot put on our faces." She felt great during the game and says she "was really having a good time with my daughter." She reported that "I have taken to watching old games this year—just the latest in a long line of superstitions. Before each conference game, I watch a victory against the same team from a previous year. It seems to be working so far."

- Roy Keefer wrote "Joe Forte for President!!!" The following day, he "told everyone I saw about the game and read everything I could get my hands on. I also watched the game again on tape."

January 28, 2001, Raleigh, NC. North Carolina 60, North Carolina State 52

- Jennifer Jordan Engel watched the game at home with her husband. She said she felt "mentally drained" at the end of the game. "We would never have heard the end of it had we lost to the Wolfies." Jennifer added, "I honestly believe we are going to beat Duke in Cameron. Call me crazy."
- K. Mac Heffner was supposed to attend the game, but got to Raleigh at halftime because a friend was late. When they arrived at will call, their tickets were gone, and they had to listen to the game on the radio while driving back. Mac said he felt "stupid" and said, "I should have gone without my friend."
- Trip Cogburn watched the game on TV with a friend. His comment was, "Oh, thank God we didn't blow it." He also observed that in anticipation of the Duke game, "The excitement level here on campus is unreal. If we pull off the shocker on Thursday, this place is going to go ballistic. I'm talking about the National Guard better be on alert or there may be nothing left of Franklin Street."
- John Floyd tried to catch the second half of the game in the New Orleans airport after flying in from Atlanta. The bar he found wouldn't change one of the TVs to the Carolina game, so John called his mom and got the play-by-play over the phone. "Bless her heart, I don't think Woody has anything to worry about. It went something like, 'OK, we've got the ball and one of our guys is dribbling, he's still dribbling, now's he's moving closer to the basket, now he's further away...and well wait a minute...something just happened...I'm not sure what, but it must have been something good, because our guys are clapping.'"
- Julio Rojas noted, "This is a great week, N.C. State and Duke back to back. Super Bowl? What Super Bowl! I always enjoy the Super Bowl, but it is nothing when compared to the Duke vs. UNC game. Today I'll go to the videotape and watch one of the games from the past. Hopefully, this will be a precursor of Thursday night's game."
- Jeffrey Stephens braved enemy territory by going to the game in Raleigh with three friends. He said that, after the game, he "felt proud to be a Tar Heel, wearing my Carolina basketball sweatshirt while walking out of the arena among a sea of disappointed and angry red-shirted State fans." He reported, "When the game was over, we were walking against the grain of red shirts in the concourse and someone saw us and shouted at the top of their lungs 'Carolina sucks!' which brought applause and cheers from many. Immediately afterward, another person shouted 'Carolina is a fag school!' The four of us just walked on in a very satisfied and confident manner."

The next day Jeffrey noted, "It's pretty amazing how different fans interpret and react to officials' calls. State fans were screaming about calls all day long and acting like their players never committed any other fouls. I saw things 180 degrees different. It's just an interesting phenomenon that is brought into sharp focus in the opposition's arena."

- Steve Andrews watched the game at home with his mother. He observed, "There certainly was no love lost out there between the players! I love that!" Not for the first (or last) time, Steve recorded a Julius Peppers dunk as his highlight of the game. Steve reported being in a great mood the next day, largely because of a budding romantic relationship that had him excited.
- Vicki Murray watched the game at home alone. She wrote that this "was the ugliest basketball game I have seen all year." She noted that, with her husband out of town, "I didn't watch one minute's worth of Super Bowl hype, in my personal opinion the most overrated day of the year." Vicki added that despite the great start for Carolina in the ACC, "For some reason, I still, every single game, am waiting for the glass slipper to break, or the bomb to drop. I try to take the attitude to just enjoy it while it lasts, but then I think, 'OK, I hope it lasts one more game.'"

January 29—February 1, 2001: North Carolina vs. Duke: The Buildup

- The Monday prior to this game, Jennifer Jordan Engel's mother bid for and won two tickets in a prime location for the Duke–Carolina game in an auction to benefit the Duke Children's Hospital, sponsored by the *Duke Basketball Report*. The motivation for the bid was reported as helping the hospital. Jennifer was then told she could use both tickets and take her husband, Patrick. Jennifer had been to one UNC–Duke game before in Cameron, in 1996, and the thought of going to another one made her "excited and terrified." She then began debating what Carolina gear and paraphernalia to wear and bring to the game, hoping to find the right combination that would bring luck to the Tar Heels.
- Prior to the game, Roy Keefer asked, "Was I the only one who couldn't stop thinking about this game since Sunday? Am I the only one who will be sweaty and keyed up before the game starts? Please let me know that I'm not the only nut out there who needs to get a life!" Roy went on to repeat his dismay that his youngest teenage son is a Duke fan.
- Vicki Murray recalled, "You may not believe this, but at one time I would pull for Duke. When they had their runs in the late 80s, they had some pretty likable players like Dawkins and Amaker. They never really gave you any fuel to spark the flames of loathing. However, with the arrival of Christian Laettner on the scene, all that changed. They were no longer fresh-faced kids out having fun on the court. The excitement rapidly turned to arrogance, and the media had already proclaimed them Kings of the Basketball Universe. Never mind that we were still right up there as we always had been. They were getting to the Final Four regularly, and we had been in a Final Four drought."

Vicki went on to describe various Duke players she did not like over the years, and to critique Duke's aggressive defensive style as being dependent on getting away with a lot of fouls. Then she trained her sights on Duke's head coach, "Ruler of the Evil Empire, the man whose name I refuse to learn how to spell. Since he so glibly had the '95 losses expunged from his record, denying all association with that team and ending the career of Pete Gaudet, I have very little respect for him. From his tendency to banish four-year players to the end of the bench to the constant berating of the referees, the kneeling in prayer prior to a stream of epithets that would curl your hair and talk about 'relationships,' the man is nauseating ad infinitum."

She concluded, "So there it is, that's why the game is important. It's more than a number in the win-loss column, it's more than bragging rights, it's more than Northern bravado vs. Southern gentility. It is a battle of good vs. evil."

- Susan Worley, the progressive social worker, revealed her true feelings about Carolina's arch-rival in the buildup to the game. She recalled, "My earliest Duke-related memory is of my parents pulling into the driveway after a football game (probably 1960), leaning out of the windows, shouting and cheering, 'We beat Duke!' Early on, there were a lot of messages that beating Duke was a highly desirable outcome. Of course, my sisters, our friends, and I loved to sing 'Don't Give a Darn About Dook University' (when we were old enough, we got to sing 'don't give a DAMN about Dook'—we thought that was pretty racy!) and the Beat Dook parade was an event all the kids in Chapel Hill looked forward to each year...."

Even when Duke was not doing as well in basketball and was not as big a rival as N.C. State or Virginia, Susan noted, "Still, there was just something about Dook, the name itself, the campus, the people associated with it, that all conjured up negative feelings."

Moving on to the 1990s, Susan elaborated: "The hard thing about it is that Duke is SO CLOSE. If you're an Indiana fan, the newspaper you read and the television you watch is going to focus on Indiana and how things look from the Indiana perspective. My newspaper and my television station both come from DURHAM—AAAGHHH! Even if they're trying to be objective, they are still telling the story from both teams' perspectives. I don't want to read about Shane Battier—I want to read about Joseph Forte. I don't think the Cameron Crazies are cute—I want to hear about the new student seating at the Dean Dome. There is no escape! People have asked if I hate Duke more than I love Carolina—I hope not! Still, I've got to admit, I measure the success of our season not just on how far the Heels go, but on if we go further than Duke. I hate to admit it but, if I had a choice of the Heels going to the Final Four, losing in the semifinal, and Duke winning the national championship, or the Heels losing in the second round game with Duke losing in the first, I'd choose the latter. As painful as certain Tar Heel losses are (South Carolina in 1971, Marquette in 1977, Boston College in 1994), Duke's two national championship wins are my worst all-time college basketball moments. (Now that I think about it, they're right up there with worst all-time *anything* moments!)

"Basketball would be a lot more fun without them. In the glorious year of 1995, when they didn't even go to the NIT, all of March Madness was so much more fun than usual. We could enjoy any success that the Heels had, without having to worry about what Duke was doing. I guess the conclusion is—I HATE DOOK. I'm not proud of it, but there it is."

February 1, 2001, Durham, NC. North Carolina 85, Duke 83

Brendan Haywood's two free throws with less than two seconds remaining gave North Carolina the win.

- Mac Heffner, his roommate and a friend, Athan Vrettos, decided to drive over to Duke the day of the game. "So we go and we have a UNC flag on the car, and a CB speaker system. Athan told K-ville they should pack up and go home, because UNC was going to win. We got some dirty looks, some middle fingers, some derogatory things were said, and so forth. Anyway, me, my roommate and Athan made it back to Chapel Hill without being hurt."

- Jennifer Jordan Engel and her husband went to the game at Cameron, and reported being on a "roller coaster ride...we were so tense throughout the game that it was hard for us to even speak to each other except in low whispers." After the final buzzer, she reported "Pure, un-adulterated euphoria. This is what makes being a Carolina fan worth it. Giddy and childlike. And I think I gloated a little in everyone's general direction as we left—the old 'I'm not talking to you, but I'm speaking loud enough to make sure you hear me' trick." The next day, she read "anything I could get my hands on just to continue that feeling of 'world-beater by association.'"

- Back in Chapel Hill, Mac watched the game in Granville with friends. He called it the best night he'd had in Chapel Hill since making the Final Four the previous year, adding, "What a great feeling to be a student at UNC and feel so proud of the team." Mac said that, after the game, "we stormed the hall, caught the first two elevators and headed to the street. Police had already blocked things off and it got crazy at that point. People grabbed anything that would burn to throw into a pile for a fire.... People climbed trees, stomped cars, and then finally, flipped a car.... When we got home, no one went to bed. We all cheered when the guys got back on the hall—Holmes, Lang, Boone, Fingleton, Morrison." Mac talked to Adam Boone and Kris Lang the following day. He added, "So now, the worry I have is a letdown in the second round of the regular season. We have a large bull's eye on our chest now."

- Trip Cogburn watched the game on TV alone: "People are not looked well upon if they are down on their hands and knees screaming and gyrating in the general direction of the television. I needed to be by myself for this one."

- Chris Gabriele watched the game on TV at home alone. "What a great game," Chris noted. "The team proved that they are a legitimate national championship contender. To go into Cameron and beat them the way they did showed a lot. It was a lot of fun to watch.... Hopefully, Stanford loses tomorrow and the Heels will be No. 1, but that really doesn't matter. All that really matters is getting that No. 1 seed in the Tournament, which, if things hold up, they will get in the East region."

- Danny Mullis watched the game with his son, Kenan, at home. Per an agreement with a close Carolina friend, Wallace Dixon, he wore a North Carolina tie identical to the one that UNC Chancellor James Moeser had worn upon his introduction as chancellor in the summer of 2000. When the game ended, the phone rang immediately. It was Wallace on the line, and

TRIP COGBURN'S LATE NIGHT AT THE DEAN DOME

[After the game], I met up with a group of my friends on Franklin Street. The noise level all over town was amazing. People were just screaming with joy. We took part in the festivities on Franklin, singing, talking, high-fiving, hugging, and partying with people you've never seen in your life. It was really wild. Even the police officers seemed to be enjoying themselves, taking pictures and celebrating with all the rest of us.

In the midst of our fun, one of our friends had an epiphany. Why don't we go down to the Dean Dome and greet the players and coaches when they get back! We raced down there to find everyone leaving...apparently, the team had already gotten back and was inside. We were not going to give up. We waited with about 150 others for the team to come back out. After about 30 minutes they came, walking through a kind of human tunnel we'd formed, smiling and slapping fives with everyone. First Holmes and Bersticker, later the stars like Forte and Capel. It was a thrill to share at least some small part of the victory with them. At this point almost everyone left but about 30 of us who wanted to see Coach Doherty. We waited for another 30 minutes or so and finally, at 1:45 a.m., here he comes. He was stopped first by the only other group of people that had waited around besides my group. He shook hands and they took pictures and then they were off. That left us lurking about his car like a pack of vultures with a history of stalking. Now it's almost two in the morning, this guy is exhausted, he's just won the biggest game of his coaching life and is the darling of the college basketball world. So he just blows off six wide-eyed students without the TV cameras around right? Not quite. We shook his hand and congratulated him, told how glad we were to have him here and started off thinking we didn't want to bother him too much at this hour.

But then, amazingly, he kept talking. He wanted to know what we thought of the game, what the party was like on Franklin Street, if people were excited. He told us stories from both his playing career and earlier in the night and even told us how satisfying a win it was for him and the team. The guy was amazing. After five minutes of him talking and us being able to muster only a head nod or two, he said he needed to be getting home and that we should be as well. He reminded us to get to class the next day and told us how much it meant to him that we had come out. It was just incredible. Just as Dean was the coach of my father's generation, Matt is fast becoming the coach of mine.

they both started screaming into the phone line. By the time he hung up with Wallace, another friend had already called in and left a message. Danny "reveled" in reading post-game media coverage, but wondered, "Why can't these spontaneous victory parties occur without the inevitable vandalism and needless defacing of personal property?"

- Jeffrey Stephens watched the game at home with his wife while listening to Woody. During the game, he maintained frequent phone contact with his friend Randy in Boone, NC. Various feelings he reported during the game included "tense, nervous, angry, up, down, hopeful, uptight, happy, depressed, jubilant." In the day following the game, Jeffrey consulted a season high of 28 news accounts/commentaries about the game, and had seven different conversations about it. He also reported having a highly productive day: "Enhanced endorphin levels provide lots of extra energy."

- John Floyd reported, "I was on the ship and didn't think I would get to see it. The ship NEVER shows ESPN2. Regular ESPN sometimes, but never the deuce. They only get three channels at a time, and the way the satellite works you get all of the major networks and no cable or all cable and no networks. Figuring I had nothing to lose, I called the radio room and told them who I was and asked if they could put it on ESPN2 for a really big basketball game. He said 'sure no problem' and switched it over at about 8. He even called me back to make sure I found it. I was elated. But then about 8:20, he called back to say they had been getting complaints from guests who wanted to see 'must see TV' and he had to switch it back. I was livid—I had to sweat it out till the 11 o'clock news. The ship gets the NBC affiliate from New York. Normally they are notorious for not giving scores from any game that wasn't played in the tri-state area, but they actually showed some highlights. I was beside myself that we won and sick that I missed it. I would have killed to see Coach K's dejected look as he shook hands with Matt. He better get used to losing to him, though, because Matt is the man."

- Roy Keefer reported, "I couldn't sleep a wink last night. I had to watch the whole game over again. What a performance by the whole team!"

- Julio Rojas noted that his wife "had the house ready for the game," adding that, "she is not a fan but always hopes UNC wins for my sake." Julio's wife and two daughters didn't want to see the game, "but my two boys and I watched intensely. It's been a while since we had that much screaming, yelling and high-fiving in our house."

- Vicki Murray watched the game on TV with a friend who is "not a very big basketball fan." She says she "went to the sports bar because my nerves were too raw to watch at home alone, and I thought a couple of margaritas might take the edge off (and I'm not a lush!)." She was most thrilled by the backdoor cuts Carolina executed during the game. She added that when Mike Dunleavy made a three-point shot to tie the game with five seconds to go, "My brain was screaming 'no! no! no!' Actually, my mouth was screaming it too." After the game, she reports, she was "giving high fives with strangers all around the bar." The following day, Vicki felt both "on top of the world" and "as useless as any human being could possibly be."

February 3, 2001, Chapel Hill. North Carolina 82, Georgia Tech 69

- K. Mac Heffner watched the game alone in Granville Towers, and talked about it with Joseph Forte after the game.

- Chris Gabriele listened over the Internet by himself. It was a busy sports-watching week for Chris, as he caught parts of four other college games on TV, as well as the Super Bowl, the Pro Bowl, and the debut of the XFL (which he hated).
- John Floyd got to see the game at a friend's house, noting, "We talked too much to really concentrate on the game as I much as I would have liked to."
- Danny Mullis watched the game on his doctor friend's satellite dish, accompanied by Kenan and his friend Wallace Dixon. He wrote, "I cared only that we won, and was willing to accept a below par performance so long as, when the clock expired, we were ahead."
- Roy Keefer wrote, "What a great week for basketball. The Heels beat Duke at Cameron, they score 23 points in a row to beat Tech. My son's ninth grade team beats their archrival by 21. Not to brag, but my son, the Duke lover that he is, got 22." Roy missed the Tech game but saw the highlights.
- Susan Worley attended the game with her oldest daughter and reported, "The emotional high of the Dook game continued." Following on the Duke game, Susan had several comments about the communal aspects of being a UNC fan.

"One of the things I love about Carolina basketball is that people from diverse backgrounds embrace it. Someone I know moved to Chapel Hill from Charlottesville a few years ago and was shocked that grocery store clerks and fast food cashiers who'd never attended UNC all referred to the team as 'we.' He said that in Charlottesville there was a real division between the town and the university, with many townspeople strongly disliking the university. In Chapel Hill, and other parts of the state as well, there are plenty of Tar Heel fans who have no official connection to the university. I always notice, when there are celebrations on Franklin Street after big wins, that reporters always seem surprised to interview people who aren't students—you'd think they'd have figured it out by now, Tar Heel basketball belongs to everyone!

"In 1993, I paid a visit in my job as a social worker to the home of an African-American, single mom, who lived in a public housing neighborhood and had a serious drug problem. Such visits can be pretty awkward, but before long we discovered that, not only were we both big Tar Heel fans, but that we had both headed straight for Franklin Street after the national championship win. That bond was enough to break the barriers between us and ease any initial feelings of awkwardness.

"All day on Friday, I saw and talked to people decked out in Tar Heel paraphernalia, with UNC flags on their cars and joyous expressions on their faces. With all the differences that often seem to separate us, it's great to have a happy reminder of what we share—that's one of the great things Tar Heel basketball brings to the community."

February 6, 2001, Winston-Salem, NC. North Carolina 80, Wake Forest 74

- K. Mac Heffner attended the game using a ticket donated by Neil Fingleton. Mac said he most enjoyed "The look on Wake's fans' faces after the game, people headed to the exits before the game ended, and singing the UNC Alma Mater in the parking lot. My friend has a PA in his car, and we turned up the volume and we belted it out as loudly as possible."

- Jennifer Jordan Engel watched the game at home with her husband. After her dog was hit by a car the day before the game, she spent a lot of time at the vet's and had to rush back from the vet's to catch the game starting on time. Right after the game, she felt "fantastic," but the pleasure from the win was muted the following day by concern for her dog. She also got into a long discussion on a message board about players' comportment on the court and various accusations of unsporting gestures made by Haywood and other players. She argued that "street/playground culture" is "an inherent part of the game and to ask the kids to play without this bit of culture is boring and ridiculous."

- John Floyd was at sea again and saw the score on the ship's news channel at 2 a.m. "Wow—four games in 10 days in which three were on hostile away floors, and we win all of them. Matt sure isn't afraid to go into somebody else's house and just put his feet up on the furniture. I like that."

- Roy Keefer watched the game and described it as "an excellent college basketball game." He was pleased that his son would be applying to attend Carolina Basketball School in the summer, but felt more ambivalent about his son's intent to also go to the Duke basketball camp.

- Danny Mullis listened to the game on the Internet with Kenan. He noticed with special interest during the week a two-page color photo spread in *Sports Illustrated* focusing on the North Carolina bench at the moment Brendan Haywood shot his free throws to beat Duke. He was impressed that "Our entire coaching staff looks to be sitting in church, which is in stark juxtaposition to the complete and total eruption of emotion from the players and fans behind the bench."

- Vicki Murray watched the game alone at home. She said her low point during the game was "Haywood woofing at the fans."

February 10, 2001, Chapel Hill. North Carolina 96, Maryland 82

- K. Mac Heffner attended the game using a ticket donated by Jonathan Holmes. He enjoyed seeing the mascot get ejected as well as an emphatic dunk by Jason Capel. "The players seem to have a new-found swagger to them and it is scary!"

- Trip Cogburn attended the game with his family, in town for their first game of the year. He wrote, "It's almost surreal at this point. Every time I say 'Well, we can't possibly get through this week undefeated,' we do it."

- Roy Keefer wrote, "If I'm dreaming, please don't wake me up.... How excited am I about the way the Heels are playing? I just spent the last half hour on the 'net trying to price tickets for the East Regional finals in Philly. Is $400 a seat too much to pay for three games?"

- Steve Andrews watched the game at home. He wrote, "This basketball team is special. They keep demonstrating that game after game. Julius Peppers! That's what I'm talking about, you know!"

- Danny Mullis watched the game at home with Kenan. Danny was one of many diarists to remark upon the Carolina mascot's ejection from the game, a historic first, and speculated, "Perhaps Matt used this as a rallying point for the team in his halftime remarks: 'Let's win one for Rameses!'" Later in the week, Danny commented on the mild media uproar when it was reported that Matt Doherty had referred to Duke cheerleaders as being "ugly" in a team huddle during the Duke game. Danny's take was "It strikes me as more than a little ironic that it is the Dookies who are feigning offense over this episode. What Matt said was done in the privacy of his team's huddle, which should be sacrosanct; the Crazies routinely far exceed comments like this, and always in the name of 'team support' and always in a very public manner."

- Jeffrey Stephens attended the game with a friend. He reported feeling "emotionally high and full of energy" after the game, and added that "the hike through the woods back to the car under the completely cloudless Carolina blue sky was mighty fine." Reflecting on the game, Jeffrey wrote, "Having been a part of every home game crowd [except for one] since 1976, I'd have to say that the group in the Dean Dome for the Maryland game was one of the very best in terms of game-long proactive cheering and enthusiasm. It was quite loud for just about the full 40 minutes and downright raucous on many occasions." On an even more optimistic note, Jeffrey wrote, "The lessons learned from last year's struggling regular season—among them that we should never take winning for granted—in combination with how very hard and well this year's team is playing have yielded a genuinely appreciative, compassionate and well grounded attitude among those of us who pull for Carolina. I just sense that this attitude is here to stay under Coach Doherty. A loss or two will test this idea, I suppose, but I feel the days of wine and cheese may finally and happily be over. Hallelujah!"

- Chris Gabriele watched on TV with his fiancee. He noted, "I'm starting to get a special feeling about this team. They are rising to every challenge. I'm just not worried that they will lose like I was in '98–99, '99–00 and the beginning of this year. I feel more confident in this team than any other since '92–93."

- John Floyd was happy to finally get to see a game at home alone with no distractions. He was pleased with the win and also Duke's loss the following week to Virginia. "Twice in two weeks I've gotten to do my 'Dook just lost' dance."

- Ross Cole watched the game on TV, and was thrilled with Carolina's performance. "This team is 'special.' I hate to use that word, because it's so frequently and frivolously used that it doesn't mean much anymore, which is truly ironic. But I have to use it, because it describes the way this team performs, as well as the feeling I have about them. Joe Forte has exuded 'specialness' since the first shot he took as a freshman—a nothing but net three from the left wing in Hawaii. It took a season and a month to do, but I think he's infected the entire team."

- Dave Jarvis watched the game at home on TV with his wife. He advised Julius Peppers to "give up the football gig and play roundball."

- Vicki Murray went to the game with her sister and mother. Right after the game she felt "Happy, happy, happy. It was a beautiful day to be in Chapel Hill. The sky was indeed Carolina Blue." She added, "This sure is fun, hope they can keep it up!"
- Susan Worley attended the game with her eldest daughter, and reported, "There was such a positive energy at the Dean Dome...everyone seemed to be having a great time throughout. Saturday was one of those unseasonably warm, Chapel Hill days with a Carolina blue sky and the Heels playing fantastic basketball—times that make you believe that God really must smile down on our little neck of the woods." Susan also chose this time to provide a thorough discussion of a topic of great importance to Carolina fans not previously discussed in this book: superstitions.

SUSAN WORLEY'S GUIDE TO CAROLINA SUPERSTITIONS

I think superstitions play a major role in the lives of Tar Heel fans. Everyone's superstitions are different but just about all of us have them, and we all have an absolute bedrock conviction, whatever our superstitions, that there is a set of deities known as the basketball gods that determine our fate. Fans find it funny when athletes or coaches call on God or thank God for their success, because we know that God doesn't bother with this stuff—instead, God assigned it to those capricious basketball gods. Every superstition has at its root the desire to appease the basketball gods. These guys are not at all like the fair and loving New Testament God that people have learned about in Sunday School—they bear a much closer resemblance to Greek gods who will strike mortals down on a whim and without a second thought. One little misstep from a Tar Heel fan and the next thing you know, George Karl is stepping out of bounds at the end of the State game, or Kenny Smith is breaking his wrist.

Tar Heel fans were always secretly amused that Dean Smith, bless his heart, didn't believe in superstitions. Because we love him so, we let him go on believing, all those years, that Carolina's success rested solely in HIS hands and those of his players. Little did he know how much help his teams were getting from fans all over the country! In fact, I've always tried to remain modest about this, but it hasn't failed to escape my notice that I became a fan the VERY SAME YEAR that Dean Smith became a coach—all you have to do is take a look at the record since then to see what kind of effect I've had.

Last year, many people I know felt as if they were no longer able to affect the Tar Heels' fortunes. It was a very scary feeling. One person I know even speculated that there may have been a single individual who, unknowingly, was the conduit for all superstitions and that person had died, severing the connection between fans and the team! Whatever the cause, the connection was restored when the Heels went to the NCAA tournament and we were able to help them get all the way to the Final Four.

Just about everyone is superstitious about what they wear on game day. Someone I know recently e-mailed me for a ruling on whether or not she should wear new, Carolina blue underwear on the day of the Wake game. With a new coach, I'm much more reckless than I used to be, and told her to go for it, but she ultimately decided that she couldn't take the chance.

What people eat or drink can affect the fortunes of the Heels. Coca-Cola, of course, has played a major role in the Heels' success over the years. In 1975, in what could have been the Heels' last chance to defeat David Thompson, I smuggled a small, 6 oz. bottle of Coke into Carmichael (no food or drinks were allowed) and surreptitiously sipped it at key moments. If memory serves, there were 17 minutes left in the game when we went to Four Corners—my Coke and Phil Ford and Brad Hoffman all helped pull out one of the great, all-time wins for Carolina.

Some poor souls cannot watch or listen to games, because they bring bad luck to the Heels. Some of them sit in other rooms of the house while family members report to them on the Heels' progress. My 78-year-old mother is one such person—a big contribution my sisters and I have made to UNC over the years is making sure our mom is informed about when the games are on so that she will be sure not to turn on her television during that time. A lot of people remember the Cincinnati game in the regional finals in 1993 when, with a tie score, Dean Smith diagrammed a perfect, game-winning play at the end which got the ball to Brian Reese for a dunk...and somehow he missed it! It was actually all my mom's fault—her curiosity had gotten the better of her and she turned on the TV to see how the Heels were doing, JUST as Brian Reese got the ball. Luckily, she quickly realized her error and turned off the TV, and the Heels went on to win in overtime, advance to the Final Four, and win the national championship.

Where people sit to watch the games at home is also critical—a lot of people switch seats when things aren't going well. For many years, we had a houseful of people whenever the Heels were playing (unfortunately, they've all moved away). After the championship win in 1982, we all agreed that the places we were sitting that night would be our permanent seats from then on. Even though a lot of folks had to sit on the floor, no one wanted to take the chance of changing. For several years, my younger daughter wouldn't move during the games. She had to sit in the same, cross-legged position throughout. When Jeff Capel got that three (the one we've all seen approximately 7,137 times on highlights even though THEY DIDN'T WIN THE GAME) to send the Dook/Carolina game into a second overtime in 1995, I looked over and saw huge tears streaming down my daughter's face. She wasn't just crying because the Heels might not win, but because her legs were cramped from not moving for so long.

February 18, 2001, Clemson, SC. Clemson 75, North Carolina 65

- Bill Lunney listened to the first half on the Internet, and followed the score on the radio while driving to a social engagement. He reported being "amazingly calm" despite the loss. "It seemed that the Heels were starting to get a bit cocky and this loss hopefully returned them to the reality that there are no easy games in the ACC."

- Vicki Murray "watched until I couldn't stand it anymore, then went in to the bedroom and listened to Woody. In other words, I went where I go and did what I did." She reasoned that "sooner or later, it was bound to happen." Vicki was upbeat the following day and said she "got over it pretty quick."

- Ross Cole listened to the game on the Internet. He was angry right after the game, but then wrote an article posted on *uncbasketball.com*, the first of several contributions he made to that site, expressing the idea that a loss wouldn't be such a bad thing for Carolina at this point of the year. He noted in the article, "Part of being a follower of the boys in sky blue is weathering that one game when the jumpshot stars align for the opposing players, and threes rain down like manna." He added that, with regard to the future, "the reality of this Carolina team will cut through our perceptions, for better or worse."

- Danny Mullis and Kenan watched the game together, and were also looking forward to the Daytona 500 and a replay on ESPN classic of the Carolina–Duke game. "Kenan and I settled onto the couch for what was certain to be a satisfying day of sports viewing. We couldn't have been more wrong." Danny reported being stunned by the loss to Clemson, and went outside and took a walk after the game. He did not learn until several hours later that Dale Earnhardt, his favorite driver, had been killed from a seemingly mild wreck at Daytona. He wrote, "A real loss occurred today in sports, and, even in my Carolina Blue world, that loss was not the game at Clemson."

- Jeffrey Stephens watched the game on television with his wife while listening to the radio. After the game, he said he "wasn't looking forward to the anti-Carolina factions' inevitable flaming or for that matter the negative irrational reactions of that element of Carolina fans who think the world's coming to an end and will bash some of our players.... Very shortly after the game it was announced that Dale Earnhardt had died in a crash on the last turn of the Daytona 500. That sobering real-world news certainly put our loss in perspective. It just didn't seem to matter as much any more."

- Chris Gabriele listened to the game on the Internet by himself. He said, "I admit I was worried heading into the game, but I really never thought they would lose. I thought Carolina was too good and Clemson was too bad. I guess I was wrong."

- Julio Rojas couldn't get the game over the Internet, so he took a nap during the game. "When my son woke me up to tell me they had lost, I couldn't believe it. He was more disappointed than I was. He doesn't see that, long-term, this may help the Tar Heels. His perception is that all losses hurt and none of them can be redeeming."

- John Floyd missed the game while on the ship, but heard about it on a local sports newscast. "After hearing about the death of Dale Earnhardt, I realized that one basketball game doesn't mean much in the great scheme of things."
- K. Mac Heffner listened to the first half of the game, then saw the end of it with an assortment of people, including Neil Fingleton. As soon as the game was over, he reported that his phone began to ring. "Duke fans, State fans, etc. I had to ignore that ringing in my ears. It was the wake-up call I didn't want to hear." Mac, the journalism major, expressed some satisfaction at having used the Internet to "break" the story that Adam Boone had sprained his ankle during the week.
- Dave Jarvis missed the game due to a meeting. He noted that "Clemson called a timeout, ahead by 10, with five seconds left—really. I'd like to see those guys again."
- Roy Keefer was busy and only caught the halftime score, but after getting home and turning on ESPN, "All I saw was the Earnhardt story. Finally, they flashed the score at the bottom. I said a bad word, but you know what, it's not so bad. This has been a great season so far..."

February 22, 2001, Chapel Hill. North Carolina 95, Florida State 67

- John Floyd was on the ship and missed the game, but was pleased with the lopsided win.
- Vicki listened to the game at home on the radio, and later watched a tape of the game sent to her by her sister. She felt "more relieved than overjoyed" with the win.
- Susan Worley attended the game with her youngest daughter. Susan wrote additional comments talking about what a thrill it was to see "history in the making" in the form of Matt Doherty and her pleasure at Carolina appearing to have reclaimed the mantle of local superiority from Duke. But then she added, "As successful as we have been so far this season, in a lot of ways it almost becomes meaningless if we are knocked out of the regional early on. The good ole Durham paper was kind enough to point out that the other two recent times that we lost to Clemson we went on to lose early in the NCAA's to Boston College and Weber State...I keep thinking back to that amazing win against Dook in 1992 and how important it seemed at the time, but how it all paled in comparison to the unthinkable horror of Dook winning the national championship that year. Surely history will not repeat itself!... I'm trying hard to convince myself that all that we've accomplished thus far will stand no matter what happens the rest of the way."
- Jeffrey Stephens attended the game with a friend. He was especially pleased with two jumpers in the lane by Ronald Curry. After the win, they immediately started talking about the upcoming Virginia game.
- Danny Mullis listened to the game on the Internet. Danny was among many diarists who watched with dismay Duke's last-second win over Wake Forest the following Saturday.

February 25, 2001, Charlottesville, VA. Virginia 86, North Carolina 66

- Julio Rojas taped the game (which began at 10:30 a.m. Pacific time) and watched it after returning from church. "I came home from church, rewound the tape to the end just to see the score before I watched it in its entirety." Despite the losses, Julio noted, "Overall this season has been a great ride with a team that has overachieved a bit."

- John Floyd again had no luck in the New Orleans airport—the TVs at the bar didn't get ESPN2. He called a friend in Wilson, NC, who gave him the play by play from the last four minutes of the first half through to the second half. This play-by-play was "better than my mom's version, because he at least knows the players' names, but it was still hard to tell what was happening. It was something like, 'OK, Forte's got it, bringing it up and…[expletive!].… Now Virginia's coming down and…[expletive!]' When we went down by 19 with about 12 minutes to go, I'd heard enough and went back to the ship."

- Vicki Murray watched the game alone "until I couldn't stand it anymore." In contrast to the 10–15 commentaries she reads after wins, she mostly avoided news accounts of this game. She noted, "I guess the basketball woofing gods got me back for being happy that Duke lost to UVa."

- Danny Mullis watched the game at home with Kenan, and said, "It's tough not to be disappointed and even scared by what Kenan and I saw.… The team very well may be on a downward slope of confidence.… I hate to think that perhaps we've seen the best our team has to offer." Danny added that he found it difficult to follow media coverage of the game, "primarily because the reports are full of negativity. Writers (and bulletin board posters) are analyzing comments and actions of the players immediately following the game, and the 'spin' being put on all this is that a crack is appearing in the heretofore very strong UNC veneer.… This is a delicate and critical time for the coaches, and we must keep in mind that Matt is working without the benefit of a significant 'history' with these players. Since this season has been so overwhelmingly positive, Matt and the team have had little adversity to react to. We know that the team endured a great deal of adversity last season, but Matt was not with them during that. So, there's a certain lack of 'common experience' at work currently.… I would think this is the time when we'll see how effective Matt is as a coach—can he find the way to right his very formidable ship?"

- Susan Worley watched the game at home with her husband and oldest daughter. She said she felt "absolutely horrible" watching the game, and mentioned, "it is too terrible to contemplate that it was Matt Doherty's birthday." She also reported eating lunch with someone who said, "I like to see them lose a couple at this time of year—it keeps them from getting cocky." Susan wrote, "Oh, how I would love to have such a mature and healthy attitude."

- Jeffrey Stephens watched on TV with his wife while listening to it on the radio. He said he felt "strangely calm during the game," but opined, "It seemed to me that Forte forgot he had teammates in the ensuing possessions and put up a number of bad shots which snuffed the rally."

- Trip Cogburn watched the game on TV alone. "I watched it locked up in my room, which was a good thing, considering the performance." He said he felt "anger leading to disillusionment and disappointment" during the game, and just depressed afterward.
- K. Mac Heffner missed the game while he was asleep, catching up on some badly needed rest. He said, "I just woke up and looked on the web for the score. It was pretty sad, but I didn't jump off the band wagon and won't like some people."
- Bill Lunney watched the game on TV with his son, having made sure his schedule for the day was clear. His observation was that "UNC played Virginia's brand of basketball and we do not have the capacity to do that." He said he was "nervous and frustrated to see Carolina get sucked into the run and shoot offense that nullifies the Carolina big men to a great extent."

February 28, 2001, Chapel Hill. North Carolina 76, North Carolina State 63

North Carolina clinched a tie for the ACC regular season title with this win, the first regular season title for UNC since 1995.

- Dave Jarvis expressed concern for N.C. State coach Herb Sendek's job security, and added the comments, "Forte looks a little tired to me" and "No matter what happens the rest of the season, this team had a really good year."
- Trip Cogburn went to the game with five friends and said he was "thrilled to be ACC Champions!" Trip appreciated a drive to the basket by Curry for a three-point play in the first half: "One thing I love about Ron is his even-keeled demeanor at all times, but it was fun to see him show some emotion." But he criticized the student section for chanting "NIT!" at State before the game, which he thought might have provided the Wolfpack extra motivation.
- K. Mac Heffner did not attend the game, after his friend Neil Fingleton needed to give his complimentary tickets to visitors from out of town. Instead, he watched the game with a UNC freshman on a "first date," and reported, "It was fun even though we didn't go, because I got to hang with her." After the game, Mac and his new friend hung out with his stepbrother and his date's brother, who happen to be teammates on their high school wrestling team and were in Chapel Hill for the game.
- Susan Worley went to the game with her oldest daughter. Susan has a daughter who goes to NCSU, and she remarked that this fact "changes my attitudes toward some of the cheers. I really didn't appreciate the 'If you can't go to college, go to State' chant!" The day after this game, Susan went to see the live broadcast of Matt Doherty's weekly radio call-in show at "23," Michael Jordan's restaurant on Franklin Street. She got there two and a half hours early and found the "place was packed with Tar Heel fans, all in excellent moods. The mood in Chapel Hill has been incredibly positive for most of the season. It may be because it's Doherty's first season, but there seems to be much less pressure than in the past." She was really impressed with Doherty and his manner at the show.

- Chris Gabriele watched the game at home by himself. He said he was "still not as confident as a few weeks ago, but they did play better than against Virginia."
- Bill Lunney watched the game with his wife in Tucson, having chosen to skip out on "other entertainment that evening." Bill was happy with the win, but added that it was "not a fun game to watch. I'm beginning to worry that the Heels are not playing as well and have lost some confidence, which can be deadly in college basketball, particularly as the tournament approaches."
- Jeffrey Stephens attended the game with his nephew. He was pleased with the win and said, "I cheered extra loud at this game, in part for the benefit of the numerous State fans in our section." Jeffrey went on to observe, "State fans are an interesting bunch. There is a large element that hates Carolina with such intensity that all rationality goes out the window. On the other hand, there is the group that cheers loudly and loyally for their team regardless of how dismal a season the Pack may be having. Both were on display at the Dean Dome last night." He also noted that for his 13-year-old nephew, David, "This was the first rivalry game he has ever attended. David said that at least half his schoolmates (he lives in Cary) are State fans, maybe 20% UNC fans, and the rest don't care; Duke fans are hard to find.... Needless to say, he was actually looking forward to going to school today with bragging rights in hand.... I'm going to call him this evening for some day-after analysis and to see how his school day went."

March 4, 2001, Chapel Hill. Duke 95, North Carolina 81

- Dave Jarvis watched the game at home with his wife, noting, "I would have cancelled my own funeral to see this." Continuing the morbid theme, Dave compared his mood after the game to a wake.
- Roy Keefer noted, "When Battier blocked Forte's dunk, the whole game ended. It was as if Battier snatched the game, the seeding, and the player of the year all in one move. You have to give him credit, it was one heckuva play, but that doesn't make this any easier to swallow."
- K. Mac Heffner watched in Granville Towers, having "turned down a ticket so that a UNC fan could see his first game in the Dome! Sounds crazy, but I got to watch the game in my room with a female I have taken a liking to. She is cute, and I ticked her off because I wouldn't talk to her during the game. She finally got mad and left, and I had to call and say I was sorry! But, oh well, I was upset."
- Susan Worley watched the game at home with her husband, having let her two daughters use the tickets. She reported feeling very upset in the second half, and "indescribably bad" after the game. Having avoided all news accounts and conversations about the game the following day, she wrote 24 hours later, "I am trying hard to put it out of my mind forever." After being quite down in the dumps all day, she perked up a little with the thought that maybe Carolina could win the ACC Tournament.

- Danny Mullis and Kenan watched the game at home, and after a good deal of fist-fiveing during the first half, "During the bulk of the second half, we mostly sat quietly in each other's presence." He said, "I don't expect to read a lot of news articles this week.... We'll have more vultures flying slow, lazy circles over the team this week than last week, which had more than the week before. Our guys will be severely tested during the week.... They'll be asked questions with negative connotations and will be backed into defensive positions. Their reactions to this may go a long way in determining how many more games they actually get to play."
- Jeffrey Stephens attended the game with a good friend. He reported being "a little angry, quite disappointed, and somewhat depressed that we were out-hustled and out-played. Basically, I felt bummed out." He noted, "After each time-out, I kept expecting a surge of some sort, but it continued to be the same-old, same-old." The next day, he wrote, "Immersing one's self in work and other activities after a bad loss can be emotionally and mentally therapeutic."
- Ross Cole found himself in a pessimistic frame of mind again after the game. "The helpless feelings of being dominated by Duke the last two years have re-surfaced because of how thoroughly they crushed us."

THE POST-SEASON

"March is the best month of the year, and it is also the worst." —Roy Keefer

"If only I really could control the world, or at least the NCAA Tournament." —Susan Worley

March 9–11, The ACC Tournament, Atlanta, Georgia. North Carolina 99, Clemson 81

- Dave Jarvis took a couple of hours off from work, cancelling his last patient of the day, to watch this Friday afternoon game at home. He said he wished Carolina had scored 100, and added, "Matt D will get you—maybe today, maybe tomorrow, but he'll get you."
- Jeffrey Stephens watched the game on TV while listening to the radio. Battling the flu, Jeffrey wrote that he was "satisfied that the team played well and with energy." He said, "Being sick during the ACC Tourney is no fun. On the one hand, it is nice to have the basketball diversion, but on the other hand, it is hard to enjoy the games as much."
- K. Mac Heffner had a Portuguese class at 1 p.m. during which "we were supposed to have a quiz. So I watch the first 40 minutes of the game at noon, then grab my headphones and head to class. To my shock, only six people show up, and the teacher says she couldn't give a quiz because of the game. YES! So she lets us go and I get to watch the rest of the game. The weekend is off to a great start." Mac then watched the Friday night games with a friend before driving home from Granville Towers at midnight.
- Danny Mullis reported, "We have a tradition here in Charleston for Friday afternoon of the ACC tourney which also is observed by many, many of my lawyer buddies. One fellow, many years ago, started having a group of the college basketball zealots to his house at noon on ACC

tourney Friday, and this group, composed of fans of various ACC schools, watched the afternoon games together and generally harassed the 'opposition' which meant every other school but one's own allegiance. I've been doing this for well over a decade, and the same guys show up every year. It truly is one of the anchor events of the year for me. It gives me a chance to see some of my closest friends and it provides some of the best laughs I have all year. If McCormack ever failed to phone to remind me of his gathering, I'd still show up at his house at noon on the Friday of the ACC tourney, like a Capistrano swallow following genetic instinct.

"The gathering at McCormack's house this year would be an especially tense one for me, I anticipated, since UNC played in the noon game against Clemson. While our group generally did not include many ardent Clemson supporters, it ALWAYS contained a surplus of ABC'ers. So I knew that I'd be in a distinct minority in pulling for the Heels in their opening game. And I was right on target: We had one UNC fan (me), one Clemson fan, and the remainder of the group that varied between 10 and 15 as the afternoon progressed were ABC'ers. I thought, this gathering was probably very much a microcosm of the Georgia Dome itself at the same time.

"Anyway, while it wasn't particularly pretty, the Tar Heels did grab a victory, and I was able to survive the McCormack gathering without ego diminution."

North Carolina 70, Georgia Tech 63

- Dave Jarvis wrote that "Neither team played well. You gotta win one like this sometimes in a tournament, and a few in a season.... Now it's time to concentrate on Duke. I wonder how much they've got left in the tank after the Terps?"
- Roy Keefer watched the game and said, "Two down and one to go.... On to Duke Part III. I'm really selfish. If Carolina is in the East, I may be able to see them in Philly. My youngest wants to know how come we won't go to see Duke if they are there. He's not a very bright kid, is he?"
- Susan Worley watched the game at home with her husband and daughters. She was excited by Brendan Haywood's big game and held out hope he might be named the tournament MVP if Carolina won in the final. "One thing I keep noticing about him," she added, "is that he is a great interview. He always has insightful and funny quotes after the game. Only white guys or white-acting black guys ever seem to be considered great interviews. Too bad the reporters' bias prevents them from seeing what an interesting and witty guy Brendan Haywood is."
- Danny Mullis reported, "This entire morning, it seems that all I'm doing is treading water, awaiting the real reason for living this day: the ACC Semifinals. I find myself pondering this question: At 48.5 years, am I the oldest person in the world wearing a 'Doherty's Disciples' t-shirt?" Danny watched the game with Kenan, and then both missed the second half of the Maryland–Duke semifinal to attend a wedding. "It goes without saying that if the Tar Heels had been playing the second game, the newlyweds would have had one less witness to their vows."
- Mac Heffner was at home and watched with his family. After dinner at his grandparents', he talked with another Carolina fan Saturday night, who concurred with him that "Duke is going to kill us."

- Vicki Murray attended the ACC Tournament, and a picture of her and a friend, Jimi Harrison, wearing Carolina gear and with the Heel painted on her face, ran in the Raleigh *News and Observer* on the Saturday of the tournament.

Duke 79, North Carolina 53

- Dave Jarvis watched the game at home. When Carolina fell behind by 15 points, he started doing some chores around the house. His comment was: "We quit! We quit! We quit!" Dave added, "We won't make the Sweet 16."
- Jeffrey Stephens watched the game by himself at home. He said he felt "resigned to the fact that we played a terrible game. There were virtually no bright spots in this game." A day later, he added, "We did not play with the heart or toughness so characteristic of that which is North Carolina basketball. Any hope for an extended NCAA run seems to lie in lessons learned from last year when many thought we might not make the NCAA field, let alone the Final Four."
- In Seattle, Ross Cole reported, "As I started the car to go to church, the radio came on playing a sports radio station. Before I could turn it off (I didn't want to know what was going on until I watched the tape), I heard the score was 45–27. I turned it off quickly but it sounded like the announcer was going to say 'North Carolina,' so I got excited at the thought that we were leading. That was the high point. Little did I know...." A day later, Ross reported that his brother in North Carolina had passed along rumors regarding internal strife among the team, which concerned him. "Nonetheless, I still think if we can get our ego stuff straightened out, we'll do great in the tournament."
- Danny Mullis watched the game at home with Kenan. He said it "likely will be very difficult to recover from the way this season ended, and the pounding in today's finals was the worst of the worst.... This week, I'm certain there will be nothing positive written about our team. In a tournament of sharks, we'll be seen as a hemorrhaging participant. Questions will be asked about our heart, about our abilities, about our coaches, about our team spirit. This will be the most difficult period yet for these young men, and for those just slightly less young coaches."
- Susan Worley watched the game at home with her husband and oldest daughter "for a while." Susan added, "In an unprecedented move, my daughter became so upset that she left in the middle of the first half. I found out later that another family member gave up as well, turning off the television in the first half. It must have been the way the planets were lined up or something—Tar Heel fans and players were giving up all over the place!" A day later, Susan was a bit more philosophical, and reported, "As always, I'll pick the Heels to go all the way in my office pool." She added, "It's funny in the world of sports how quickly people (especially the press) completely change their feelings about a team. These are the same young men and the same coaches that everyone was raving about a month ago, going on and on about how well they get along and what great friends they are. Now, in four short weeks, we are to believe that suddenly they can't stand each other. It IS a game and it's played by human beings. We all

DANNY MULLIS ON THE HEEL-HOOPS LIST-SERVE

Just as it provides community celebration following a victory, the Tar Heel list-serve to which I belong provides community support following a loss. Today, the day following the Duke loss, I am being supported by my friends on the list-serve. Although I've never met any of the members, strangely I feel as though I know many of them. The email addresses, which is how I identify most of the members, have individual personalities. It's much like a real family, except that this one exists only in cyberspace. As with a "real family," I know which member's posts will be humorous, which will be blowing off steam, which will be giving analysis that would make a SportsCenter reporter jealous. I've belonged to this list-serve since its inception. I don't recall how on earth I happened to be lucky enough to get in "on the ground floor," but that event, and my years of belonging to this community of Tar Heel brethren, has meant more to me than many of my blood relationships. Were I to find myself no longer receiving the wonderful emails generated by this affiliated gathering of UNC basketball nuts, my enjoyment of that wonderful thing we share—love for our university and especially its basketball program—would be diminished greatly. I feel their excitement, I feel their love, I feel their sorrow. And they feel mine.

have had our fair share of bad days that we just can't explain. Why are we so quick to overanalyze when a sports team performs poorly?"

- Chris Gabriele watched this game (as he had the entire tournament) at home with his fiancee. He said he felt "sick" watching the game and "sicker" when it was over. He wrote, "I was absolutely embarrassed by this game" and that he had "zero confidence entering the tournament." Chris went on to spill out a series of observations, mostly negative, about the game, before closing on an upbeat note. "In 1991 Carolina beat Duke by around 20–25 points in the ACC title game, but Duke went on to win the NCAAs. Hopefully, we'll see the same thing out of Carolina." What is interesting about Chris's comment is that former North Carolina coach Dean Smith made exactly the same point in an Internet chat the Sunday night after the Duke game hosted by the web site *finalfour.net*.

- Mac Heffner watched at home, and was disheartened to see Carolina lose on his 23rd birthday. "On my 21st birthday, we lost to Weber State. I am not sure which loss was worse, but both were tough on me. Sunday night I went out with my family for a birthday dinner, and luckily there was a TV in the bar area. I caught the selection show and saw how we got seeded. I came home to a barrage of emails about the game—UNC fans mostly just mad about the loss. Then I go to the UNC bulletin boards (on the Internet) and was shocked to see people just blasting Joe and the rest of the team. What a bummer. I posted once just to take up for Joe and decided not to bother with it anymore." Three days after the tournament, Mac learned that his father had been laid off from his job as a supervisor after eight years with the same company. "Whoever expects that to happen?" asked Mac, adding, "It has been a strange week for me."

March 16 and 18, 2001, NCAA Tournament South Regional, New Orleans, LA.
North Carolina 70, Princeton 48

- Roy Keefer noted, "CBS is terrible. After watching the Heels get off to a 25–8 lead, CBS cut to the Notre Dame game. That game wasn't any closer or more interesting than the Heels. Why can't ESPN do the tourney again?" He added, "In the last two weeks, I've seen Penn State blow a 20-point halftime lead to lose to Ohio State, beat Michigan State, and lose by 20 to Iowa. Nothing that happens Sunday will surprise me very much." Roy was glad that the game would definitely be shown in its entirety in Pennsylvania, however. Roy later wrote in and said, "Next to losing to Duke, and facing my son, losing to Penn State would be the worst. There are tons of Penn State rooters and grads around here. It's amazing how many of them came out of the woodwork these past two weeks or so."

- Jeffrey Stephens watched the game with his wife, alternating between Billy Packer's TV commentary and the UNC radio broadcast. He reported being "quietly confident and pleased with our intelligent play." Jeffrey said he watched parts of 30 different first-round NCAA games besides the Carolina game.

- Susan Worley watched the game with her husband and youngest daughter. She wrote, "My mood is really on hold for this whole weekend—watching basketball, and waiting, waiting, waiting for 5:00 p.m. tomorrow, when the mood of the week ahead and possibly the entire spring and summer will be determined. Playing the last game is very tough!"

Penn State 82, North Carolina 74

- Jeffrey Stephens watched the game at home with his wife, and said he had a "que sera sera" attitude during the game. He confessed to mixed feelings after the game. "On the one hand, I was frustrated and disappointed with the 22 turnovers and what seemed like mediocre defense. On the other hand, I felt relief that the season was over after enduring .500 ball for the last month. We just could never regain the magic of the 18-game win streak."

- Roy Keefer: "I am so disappointed…. It's a shame that a team with this much talent let the season end this way. For the last month, North Carolina has been a team on the skids…. Maybe Carolina needs to recruit less superstars and more guys like Titus Ivory who play with heart and aggressiveness. The best team did not win this game but the team that played the hardest did."

- Julio Rojas noted that "Except for 1993 and 1982, every season has had this bit of disappointment to deal with. While every season has had that feeling, they have also had different degrees of disappointment…. The sudden loss to Penn State was a week too early, I thought they would make it to the regional final and face Michigan State. The tourney just isn't the same once UNC is out. It is still great, but not the same." Julio added, "On days like Sunday, Sports-

ROSS COLE'S INNER STRUGGLE WITH BEING A CAROLINA FAN

I always debate with myself about whether or not following Carolina basketball is "time well spent." One can argue that, just like any leisure activity or interest, it has its time, place, and value. It provides enjoyment, and there's a lot to be said for engaging in enjoyable pastimes. On the other hand, I take Tar Heel basketball so seriously at times that I have a hard time justifying the undue stress I undergo during and after the games—specifically the losses. I'm not the kind of fan who can just enjoy the victories, write off the defeats, and move on. The anguish I experience after a loss is disproportionate to the satisfaction of a win—except, of course, when the win comes against Duke or some other highly ranked opponent. In those cases, I felt truly elated.

Had I foreseen the bitter note(s) on which the season would end, I certainly would have remained more emotionally removed from the team's mid-season success. As a matter of fact, after our pathetic showing against Michigan State and Kentucky at the beginning of the year, I made the decision to step back and observe only from a distance. I didn't see any point in agonizing over every game if we were going to struggle like last year. But slowly, as our play improved and our wins began to pile up, I got "sucked in" by the success. I started caring again. I allowed myself to reattach. Looking back, I honestly don't think it was worth it, considering the disappointment of the last five weeks of the season. I started resting my hopes on another win over Duke, another Final Four appearance, maybe even a national championship—none of which materialized. Frankly, I think the season would have been less disappointing if we'd gone 10–6 in the ACC, gotten a lower seed in the NCAA tournament, and bowed out more expectedly. With a new, inexperienced coach, instability at the point guard spot, and the loss of Jason Parker, we would have had plenty of excuses for that kind of year. The mid-season run just made the late-season skid that much more painful.

center is not watched, nor is any sports segment. The paper is not read for a few days. It is a great time, but lessened without the presence of the Heels."

- Ross Cole watched the game at home—he had to put up with only seeing score updates most of the afternoon, but then CBS showed the last eight minutes of the game in Seattle. Ross said he felt "sarcastic" after the game. Ross noted that after a season in which Carolina looked "terrible" at the beginning and the end but brilliant in between, "Emotionally speaking, I almost wish we had been mediocre all season." He also expressed concern that Matt Doherty "doesn't burn himself out due to how much of himself he puts into the job."

- Susan Worley watched the game with her husband and daughters at home. She said the low point was near the end of the game. "When things were looking bleak but we still had a slim chance, the TV cameras zoomed in on Matt Doherty and his assistants. For just a moment, the thought flashed through my mind, 'Who are these people whose names I don't even know, with no connection to Tar Heel tradition, and how has it come to pass that they hold our fate in their hands? Where, oh where, is Dean Smith?!' It was just a moment, but definitely a low." After the game, Susan allowed, "My reaction was not one of my more mature or prouder moments." Susan was unable to even make herself go to work the following day (Monday) until the afternoon and felt miserable all day.

- Chris Gabriele watched the game with his fiancee at a sports bar. "I think the game was on TV here in New York, but I went to the four tourney wins last year and the other night, so it was more a superstitious thing, but I guess that's over with." After the game, he reported feeling "disgusted." "The Tournament is my favorite time of the year, but when they go out like this, it completely ruins it for me. I'm not sure if I'll watch any more games."

The Immediate Aftermath

- After the game, Jeffrey and Marsha Stephens had dinner together, then watched "The Sopranos" on HBO and then the movie "Mission to Mars," while ignoring the ringing phone. Jeffrey avoided the media the following day until Monday night, when he "made the half-hearted plunge into media accounts and reactions to the game."
- Meanwhile, in Fayetteville, Steve Andrews put on a 10-song guitar concert for about eight of his friends in a gathering at his house, which he said helped let off some of his steam after the game.
- After watching the game with a friend and UNC graduate in Raleigh, K. Mac Heffner drove back to Chapel Hill and Granville Towers. When he got back, "I had to field all these questions from people who just couldn't understand how we had lost to Penn State. Then the players got back at some point and it was really strange. It was almost like they were glad it was over.... Our guys were burned out, and they weren't happy they lost, but it happened." Mac later noted that after the loss, "People on the hall like me were kind of shocked. But we all dealt with it.... Campus was very quiet that next Monday. People were either over it or blasted our guys."
- The day following the game, Jeffrey Stephens reported, "The pall around Chapel Hill is palpable today. The loss permeates the atmosphere. Some folks want to vent, while others are depressed and do not want to even think about it. For myself, as philosophical as I try to be, it is hard to escape these feelings of emptiness and dispiritedness that go hand in hand with the end of any Tar Heel basketball season." Jeffrey said, "I know of no Tar Heel fan who believes the Heels played particularly well since February 12. So my feelings right now are mixed, with a distinct bias to the negative side. These feelings will abate with time, but for today, the 22 turnovers against a Penn State team that applied little defensive pressure still have a way of invading my thought process."

SUSAN WORLEY SUMS IT UP

Shortly after the Penn State game, Susan Worley offered a lengthy set of comments reacting to the loss and trying to put it in perspective.

You would think that 27 consecutive trips to the NCAA tournament would have taught us that the season usually ends with a painful loss—but every year, March rolls around, and every year I'm thinking.... This is the year! Two glorious times in those 27 years, we have won the whole thing. But, once those other 25 seasons have been put behind us and time gives us some perspective, we can see that these years have a lot of special memories too.

Susan went on to put the game in an even broader perspective:

When you think of all the people who have lived on this planet through the ages, slaves in ancient Egypt, people eking out a living on the banks of the Amazon, subsistence farmers in China, you realize how incredibly fortunate we are to have been born into this time and this place, living the easy life. Along the same lines, I sometimes think how lucky I am to have lived in Chapel Hill and to have been a Tar Heel fan for these past 40 years. I came to this town because my dad got a job teaching here. I remember him getting job offers from Tempe, Arizona and Columbus, Ohio— I'm sure there were others. We could have ended up in one of a dozen college towns; I could have grown up an Ohio State or Arizona State fan! Maybe I would have had the great, good sense to recognize Tar Heel basketball as something special, like those people you hear about who have never set foot in the Tar Heel state but, with no ties to the school at all, become Tar Heel basketball fans, but it's pretty unlikely.

Chance brought me here, to a place I love intensely. And a variety of random circumstances brought amazing people like Frank Porter Graham and William Friday and Dean Smith here. Those random circumstances converged to create a unique and special place whose spirit somehow seems to be embodied, year after year, by a group of kids with a basketball. People sometimes refer to Carolina fans as being arrogant and I'm always surprised by that—first, because I always think we are the underdog and I never bring a trace of overconfidence to any game, but mostly because I am so completely humbled to be a Tar Heel fan. I could have ended up anywhere in this world, but here I've been for 40 years, enjoying the incredible privilege of being a fan of one of the great programs in college sports. It's a privilege that I never take for granted. As hard as it is to see the season end this way, it's absolutely worth the price we pay in heartache to experience this privilege and to be a small part of this proud and storied tradition.

Continuing, Jeffrey reflected, "The home game against Maryland on February 10 remains, perhaps, the highest point of the season. That was our 18th straight win and our second week at No. 1 in the land, a ranking of which we were very deserving. That day is etched vividly in my memory. I can still feel the euphoric sensation upon leaving the Dean Dome and being greeted by beautiful Carolina blue skies. The walk through the woods to the car among like-minded Tar Heel fans was surreal, like walking on air—a peak experience if there ever was one."

POSTMORTEMS AND MOVING ON

The Week After

Two days after the end of the season, the diarists were asked to respond to two questions: First, did they think that the time they spent following Carolina in 2000-01 was worth it? Second, would they have behaved the same way if they had known all along Carolina would lose in the second round of the NCAAs?

- In response, Roy Keefer wrote, "I guess at the end I felt a little bit like Matt Doherty did, ready to cry a few tears for what might have been. Was it all worth it? Yes. Would I do it again? Yes, in 2002."
- Jeffrey Stephens wrote, "Time spent following Carolina basketball this year, as every year, is always time well spent. It does not matter whether we bomb out in the first round (or the second like this year) of the NCAAs or go to the Final Four. Carolina basketball must be followed. The pull of Tar Heel Hoops is inexorable.... I have never reflected back on a season wishing I had devoted more time to other endeavors. This latest season just ended is no exception."
- K. Mac Heffner wrote, "If I answered 'no' to this, I wouldn't be a real fan. If UNC wasn't in my blood, then maybe I could say that no, I would not have put my heart into this team, but I can't because I love this team and this school. Anyone who expects to be playing later in March every season should look at changing teams every so often, but at UNC, we seem to always be there. This season we just didn't get it done and man, did it hurt."

*

In early April, several days after the tournament ended and Duke defeated Arizona to win the 2001 NCAA Championship, the diarists were asked to respond to a final set of questions:

1. *How much of the rest of the NCAA Tournament did you watch after Carolina lost? How long did it take (or may still be taking) before you began resuming your usual media habits with regard to Carolina basketball or college basketball in general?*
2. *Which did you find most painful/bothered you most about the end of the season? a) Carolina losing the two games to Duke handily; b) Carolina losing early in the NCAA Tournament or c) Duke winning the NCAA championship. Which of these three events would you change if you could (and could change only one)?*

3. *Are you more or less optimistic about the future of Carolina basketball than you were six months ago? You can answer with respect to either a) on-court success or b) all the off the court stuff associated with UNC basketball (i.e. the values it represents, etc.).*
4. *After Carolina lost to Penn State, did you do anything special to cheer yourself up or otherwise help cope with the loss? Did your family members or friends try to help you get over it (or vice versa)?*
5. *Are there any activities or endeavors (including following other sports teams) that you plan to undertake more of during the off-season to fill the gap in the time you devoted to Carolina basketball, now that the season is over? Do you plan to use your free time significantly differently in the offseason than you did during the season?*
6. *Finally, having kept the diary all season and having had the chance to think about the year, are you happy with the role being a Carolina basketball fan plays in your life?*

- John Floyd said he watched a fair amount of the rest of the NCAA tournament, "But after the Heels were knocked out my heart was never completely in it again." John reported no change in his media habits after the loss, and noted, "This is the time of year when all attention turns to recruiting, which is fun." John said Duke winning the NCAA title was the low of the season for him, that he found their victory "sickening," and that the fact that Coach K has more titles than Dean Smith "means there is no justice in the world." John volunteered, "I had a late show on the ship after the game and a good bit of my act was ripping on Duke," including jokes about the kind treatment Shane Battier and Duke were perceived to receive from the officials in the Final Four. John noted, "I took a survey and probably 95% of the audience said they were not happy Duke won." John, who found another crew member from North Carolina with whom to commiserate about Carolina's NCAA loss, said he would play golf over the summer and follow the Boston Red Sox and the PGA tour, but that, "I'm always counting the days until October 15th," the first day of college basketball practice. Looking to the future, John said he foresaw a brief rebuilding process of a year or two for Carolina followed by a return to ACC dominance under Matt Doherty, but added, "I just hope he continues the Carolina tradition of recruiting good kids, not just good players. I don't want a bunch of thugs wearing Carolina blue." He concluded that he was very happy with being a Carolina fan. "It is my No. 1 passion. I can't think of life without it. I get more into it every year. God bless my Heels!"
- Roy Keefer reported that he watched a lot of the rest of the NCAA Tournament, including the final, and that if he could change one thing about the season it would be the loss to Penn State. Roy said he didn't do anything special to cheer himself up after the Penn State loss, although he did have to endure some local Penn State fans as well as his son (the Duke fan) rubbing it in. He said he had become more optimistic about Carolina basketball and said, "Matt has brought the joy back to Carolina basketball." Roy said his free time becomes more focused on his kids' activities during the off-season: His daughter is playing high school soccer, and his youngest son, who plays high school basketball, had already begun early-morning workouts

for next year. And Roy has a one-year-old grandson to keep him busy. Roy concludes, "I am happy with the role that the Heels play in my life. Maybe I am too into it during the season, but writing this diary has helped to keep things in perspective. When I take my son down to camp in June, I am looking forward to shopping on Franklin Street, eating at '23,' and seeing the new basketball museum. How can life be any better than that? As James Taylor sang, 'In my mind, I'm going to Carolina.' "

- Biscuit Dave Jarvis said he watched the Final Four, with hopes of seeing Maryland or Arizona beating Duke, and criticized the officiating in those games. He said the most disappointing part of the end of the season was the loss to Penn State: "We were a tired team, and we weren't going to win it all. But Penn State?" David said he cheered himself up after the loss by absorbing himself in information about recruiting and that he was especially pleased that UNC got a commitment from high school junior Raymond Felton. He also said the season had made him more optimistic about Carolina's on-court future. In typically flippant style, Dave wrote, "Matt Doherty is an excellent recruiter. I'm not sure how good a bench coach he'll be, but Mike Krzyzewski isn't any brain surgeon and he got pretty good after Dean beat his brains out for a decade or so." Dave said he planned to spend more time playing his guitar in the off-season and was looking forward to going to a guitar camp in Tennessee for a week in June.

  In conclusion, Dave added, "I couldn't get through the winter without the Heels...I'm not a winter person (short days, cold, dreary, gray) and I always enjoy the other three seasons more (more sun, more color, outdoor activities, etc.). So you would think I'd be in high spirits after the conclusion of basketball in the spring, right? Not so. I think it goes beyond basketball and touches how I feel about the calendar beginning to roll around at a pretty fast rate. The end of basketball really demarcates the end of the year, seasonwise. Spring starts everything anew. When you think about it, we're not here for too many springs/summers/falls/winters, so the passing of each set should touch us. I guess I just feel it most at the end of the season (both winter and basketball) because it is so definitively the end, unlike the end of other seasons, which blend into one another."

- Steve Andrews watched the rest of the NCAA tournament "diligently," and even got excited about Maryland making the Final Four. He said he started back into checking Carolina web sites and so forth immediately, waiting for news on whether Joseph Forte would go pro. Steve said that while he thought the two losses to Duke were the most painful parts of the season, if he could change one thing it would be for Carolina to have at least made the Sweet 16 of the NCAAs, "because this group really did deserve that. They had a great season, they just had it too early." Steve said he was optimistic about Carolina's on-court future, largely because of Matt Doherty's recruiting ability, but that he thought it "remains to be seen" whether Doherty could continue Carolina's tradition off the court. Steve said that he didn't do anything special to try to cheer himself up after the loss to Penn State, and that he really didn't even talk to many people about the game. Steve added that while he planned to watch the NBA playoffs, he would be using his free time differently in the offseason, playing as much tennis as possible. "Overall," Steve reports, he is happy with the role Carolina basketball plays in his life. "I pay such close attention to the team that I am usually ready for what comes (even the bad stuff). That gives me a certain inner peace. Furthermore, even people around Fayetteville I'm associated with who are from Europe, for example, have all identified me as a Carolina Fan. I think these people sense in me the strength and the genuineness of my association with Carolina and ACC hoops, and they really respect it."

- Julio Rojas said he followed the rest of the tournament pretty closely, though he said, "I couldn't read the newspapers for a few days after the UNC loss, and I still haven't read my *Sports Illustrated* with Duke on the cover. I'll never read the cover article." Julio said if he could change one thing he would undo Duke's title, and added that he had done nothing to try to cheer himself up after Carolina's loss, "Because there is nothing that will give me solace at that time. Once the tourney is over, the healing begins." Julio said he was more optimistic about Carolina's future on the court and that "without a doubt" Matt Doherty would uphold Carolina's standards of the past 35 years, pointing to his hard work as a recruiter. Julio said he would watch baseball and the NBA over the summer, and also continue to check *uncbasketball. com* every day. He concluded by saying he was very happy to be a Carolina fan: "I'm not sure that being a fan has changed my morals or the way I look at life, but I do know that the UNC program is in step with the values I hold. It is good to teach my kids certain things and to be able to use sports (which they love) to reinforce some of those values."

- Trip Cogburn might have taken Carolina's downturn at the end of the season harder than any other diarist. Trip reported that he watched much of the rest of the tournament, "with the exception of Carolina's bracket. It would have been a little too much to watch Penn State and Temple battle for a spot in the Elite Eight." Trip soon resumed looking at media outlets, but with an emphasis on recruiting and the future, saying that regarding "information on the current team, I pretty much stay away from that. It's still hard to get excited about anything that's going on with that bunch." Trip said the two losses to Duke were the most painful parts of the season, but that if he could undo one event it would be Duke's national title. Trip said his parents called him almost every day in the period after the game to try to cheer him up, and that he "threw myself into competition, playing tons of basketball and soccer to try to let out some of the frustration." Looking to the future, Trip thought Carolina would be in for a lean two or three years but would be back after that, and he was optimistic that "Carolina will continue to represent the character we love and respect them for." Trip concluded, "I truly love being a Carolina fan. I have to admit that earlier today, while eating my lunch, I was thinking about how it was truly a blessing to be born in North Carolina and brought up a Carolina fan. To be born into a great family, in the best state, of the world's most incredible country...and be associated with Carolina on top of it all: WOW."

- Bill Lunney wrote that the ups and downs of the season had done nothing to shake his appreciation for North Carolina basketball and what it has meant to him over the years. "Although sometimes my comments seem a bit critical, I fully support the UNC basketball program from top to bottom. It has been a wonderful source of pride and recreation for me for over 40 years. It is so unusual in sport (maybe even unique) to have a college program maintain such high levels of accomplishment within the rules and with class for such an extended period of time. The program has adapted to the rapidly changing environment of players' circumstances—early exits, television demands, higher fan expectations and pressure from all sides without sacrificing its basic principles."

- Chris Gabriele said that he was surprised at how many tournament games he watched after Carolina lost, and that he "was back checking the Carolina websites a few days after the loss." Chris said the loss to Penn State was the most painful event, but that if he could change one thing about the season it would be Duke winning the NCAA title, reasoning that the pain of a Duke title and Carolina defeat would have been hardly less if Carolina had advanced farther before losing. Chris, who said writing his diary entries helped him get over the loss, said he was just as optimistic about the future as before the season. He also credited Doherty's recruiting ability and said that Doherty would grow from what happened in 2001. Chris said he would turn his attention to baseball and the New York Yankees during the summer, and then to the New York Jets in the fall, and he reckoned that the net time he spent watching sports would not change (four or five hours a week) as the seasons shifted. Commanding his immediate attention, however, was Chris's preparations for his wedding, upcoming in May, and a honeymoon in Aruba. Chris said he was happy with how UNC basketball fits into his life. "I enjoy the time I spend following them and think I always will.... One of these years, they will win [a championship] again, and if they don't, I'll still be along for the ride because it's the journey that's special to me. When people hop on teams' bandwagons, they don't enjoy the championships as much as a real fan."

A FEW INTERPRETIVE REMARKS

This chapter closes with a few rather straightforward observations about the fan diary material.

First, for most of these fans, Carolina basketball is an intrinsically social activity—even if some, like Trip Cogburn, needed to be alone to watch big games on television and even though some of the diarists watched most of the games by themselves. But even those diarists reported talking or at the least electronically communicating with others about the games. Most diarists constantly referred to other people in reporting their own experience of the game, from Danny Mullis watching games with his son, to Vicki Murray's mother-daughter trips to games, to Bill Lunney hooking up his computer so that he could listen to a game on the Internet while being in the same room as his wife. Being a Carolina basketball fan, by and large, is not a lonely activity.

Second, in general the experience of the season reported by those who lived in Chapel Hill or in North Carolina seemed to be more intense than it was for those who followed the team from long distance. That should not be surprising. Interestingly, however, whereas the Internet is often seen as the best friend of the long-distance sports fan (such as some of the diarists here), it was in fact consulted more intensively by fans like Jeffrey Stephens and Jennifer Jordan Engel, who were located in relative proximity to Chapel Hill.

Third, as we might expect and as other sociologists of sport have found, the diarists' moods did improve after wins, especially big wins. Productivity also seems to be higher for Carolina fans when Carolina wins. And fans are likely to read more articles and talk more about games after wins than losses. But only a few Carolina wins over the course of the 2001 season produced across-the-board positive effects on the diarists' mood and productivity. (On the other hand, almost all of the losses produced across-the-board *negative* effects.) In most instances, a Carolina win was just one factor in predicting well-being.

Fourth, as Susan Worley put it, no matter what is going on with the Tar Heels, "Real life is going on all the time." People get sick, lose jobs, go on first dates, have surgery, get speeding tickets, go see their kids play for school teams, and follow current events just as much between early November and early April as in the rest of the year. The difference is, for these fans at least, events in real life tend to become intertwined with Carolina basketball, so that life events and the outcomes of games become markers for one another.

Fifth, many of the fan diarists were very aware—and concerned by—the presence and behavior of other Carolina fans. Over half the fan diarists, including almost all who live in North Carolina, criticized either directly or obliquely habits and attitudes they saw in other Carolina fans. For these fans, Carolina losses are often doubly painful: The loss in painful in itself, and so is listening to the response of fans after the losses. But for long-distance fans such as Bill Lunney in Wisconsin and Arizona or Chris Gabriele in New York, how other fans behave appeared to be a non-issue.

Sixth, following Carolina basketball was the cause of very little overt conflict for the fan diarists (at least based on the evidence submitted) during the season, although evidence of some fan-related tension was reported. The diarists in general appeared to be in situations where 1) they could pursue their desired activities as a fan unconstrained by family, spousal, or relationship obligations; 2) their family and/or spouses directly shared in and encouraged fan-related activities; or 3) the diarists had long before worked out a set of expectations with their families/spouses whereby their commitment to following the team could and would be accommodated. Even so, however, it is worth pointing out that there was considerable variation among the diarists as to willingness to miss parts or all of non-essential games for social or family-related activities.

Seventh, just as many non-Carolina fans no doubt suspect, the fan diarists' love for Carolina is very much mixed in with feelings of superiority to fans of other schools, particularly Duke, N.C. State and Wake Forest. These Carolina fans all truly think that it is a much better thing to be a Carolina fan than to be a supporter of another school. The diarists varied, however, in the degree to which they expressed sympathy or empathy for fans of other schools. Again, these feelings of superiority to fans of rival schools seem to be most strongly present among the diarists in closest proximity to the ACC, with the exception of extreme antipathy toward Duke, which crossed geographical boundaries in this sample of Carolina fans.

Eighth, and perhaps most significant, almost all of the diarists are unequivocally happy with the role Carolina basketball plays in their lives. Only one diarist, Ross Cole, expressed serious doubts during the year about whether being an intense fan is worth it. The overwhelming majority are prepared and expect to follow the team as closely in 2002, the year after that, and the year after that, and the diarists have a variety of a coherent explanations about why they are convinced being a Carolina fan is a really, really good thing.

Ninth, none of the diarists offered any serious speculation or consideration about whether they'd be better off doing something else besides spending time on Carolina basketball. There was little evidence that the diarists would be starting new community groups or engaging in political and civic activities if only Carolina basketball were not taking up so much time. Some of the diarists reported being very active socially and belonging to groups such as churches throughout the season, and some did not, but there is little to suggest that following Carolina closely makes much difference one way or another.

Tenth, it is obvious that if North Carolina basketball were to disappear, it would leave a big hole, a gaping void in these diarists' lives. The role that North Carolina basketball plays in these fans' lives represents a source of meaning and, often, a way of making sense of and marking time in their own lives, that is simply not convertible to other forms of belonging that a social scientist or political theorist might consider more praiseworthy (such as membership in a political organization). To these diarists, Carolina basketball is a constitutive part of their identities, not an activity that can be tried out and abandoned as one finds convenient, such as a bowling league or a crafts club.

Many of these interpretive observations about the fan diary material can serve as working hypotheses to be further tested in Chapters Six and Eight, which analyze the attitudes and habits of over 600 North Carolina fans. At a certain level, however, the fan diaries and the stories they tell speak for themselves, and I invite readers to draw their own conclusions about the evidence presented above. Indeed, while the habit of social scientists is to focus on generating and empirically supporting generalizations about a class of people, what the fan diary material should make clear is that each fan, and each fan diarist story, is unique. No social science theory in the world could have predicted that somewhere out there, there would be a Carolina basketball fan who had worked out a theory of the stages of dealing with a loss in a basketball game based on Elizabeth Kubler-Ross's work on death and dying or that a 34-year-old man would have invented his own special dance to perform every time Duke University lost a basketball game. There are common patterns of behavior that hard-core Carolina fans tend to exhibit in following their team, but there is also an unfathomable array of highly unique ways individual fans follow North Carolina basketball. Hopefully, the fan diaries project has helped convey both the commonalities and the uniqueness of North Carolina basketball fans.

6

The North Carolina Basketball
Fan Survey: Part One

Americans hate surveys. They hate the idea of the phone ringing during dinner time, or just when they're sitting down to turn on the television and exhale after a long day, and having someone conducting a marketing poll make a claim on 45 minutes of their time. Yes, it might be fun to do once or twice, but that's about it. In fact, Americans' response rates to polls of various kinds have been falling precipitously in recent years—to the point that some political scientists and other scholars who rely on survey research have become very worried about whether surveys will survive as a viable research tool.

But even though Americans dislike surveys, from time to time they make exceptions. In the case at hand, more than 600 fans spent up to an hour answering a range of questions, some of them quite personal, about their relationship with UNC basketball. Their collected responses form this book's last major piece of evidence about how Carolina fans think, feel, and behave.

This book has proceeded from autobiographical material providing a detailed account of how one person grew up as a Carolina fan, to an account of how a small group of fans experienced the 2001 season, and finally to a broader account of the basic tendencies of Carolina basketball fans in general. The strength of this survey data is that it allows one to make meaningful generalizations about Carolina fans with some confidence. The weakness is that the surveys cannot probe any particular individual's beliefs and motivations quite as deeply as the autobiographical material or the fan diaries can. However, that weakness is offset to some degree by the numerous insightful and interesting comments provided by the survey respondents in the course of their answers, many of which are cited here.

This survey material is presented in three chapters: Chapter Six focuses on how and why people became serious Carolina fans, how they experience watching the games (with special attention to how they handle losses), and how being a Carolina fan affects friendships, families and other relationships. Chapter Seven briefly describes Carolina fans' attitudes toward Duke University. Chapter Eight discusses what Carolina fans do when they are not watching the Tar Heels play, their interactions with UNC players and coaches, their attitudes toward college basketball in general, and their thoughts on "what it all means."

These topics are interesting in themselves, and I hope that readers will be interested in seeing what Carolina fans have to say about them. But at the end of the day, I doubt many readers will long remember many of the facts and figures contained in these chapters. What is more important is that these chapters provide a chance for big Carolina fans to look in the mirror and reflect on some of the really big questions discussed in these chapters: "How important is being a Carolina fan in my life? How important should it be? Would it make any difference if I invested more or less energy into it?"

Whatever the value of the North Carolina Basketball Fan Survey as a piece of social science, it will be a success if it can inspire readers to reflect upon those questions.

HOW TO READ CHAPTERS SIX AND EIGHT

Chapters Six and Eight report in substantial detail the findings of the North Carolina Basketball Fan Survey. The following data analysis is not pitched at a very elevated level by social science standards—it is intended to be accessible to all curious readers, whether or not they have a strong background or interest in statistics. Nonetheless, some readers may not be interested in tracking each of the nuances in the following analysis and may prefer instead to simply get the "big picture."

These chapters are designed, then, to make the basic findings available to readers in four ways. First, one can choose to read the chapters as written, including all the tables and all of the data analysis. Second, one can choose to simply flip through these pages and look at the tables to find answers to the individual survey questions that interest them most. Third, one can flip through these pages and read only the quotations (set off in bullet points) from North Carolina fans about various issues. Fourth, one can turn to the end of both Chapter Six and Chapter Eight to find a brief, bullet point summary of the main highlights of the data analysis. I hope that readers not inclined to follow every step in the following analysis will find at least one point of interest among the tables, the quotations, or the chapter-ending summaries.

DESCRIPTION OF THE DATA

The following description of the habits and values of North Carolina basketball fans is based on 606 responses to an 86-question survey designed by the author and distributed via *uncbasketball. com*. (See Appendix Two for a copy of the survey questions.) The survey responses were completed over a six-month period from October 2000 to May 2001, with the vast majority of surveys returned by mid-January, 2001.

Not surprisingly, given the method in which the survey was distributed, the responses to the Fan Survey primarily reflect a particular demographic group that is probably not fully representative of the countless thousands of persons who consider themselves UNC basketball fans. The median fan in this survey is a 30-year-old white male who started following the team at age 10. Over 90% of the fans who completed the survey are under age 50: The "Big Ram" set that occupies the lower level of the Smith Center is under-represented (though not wholly absent) in this sample. There are, however, a sufficient number of older fans in the sample for inferences to be made about how the habits of older people differ from those of younger people.*

Table 1. Age of Survey Respondents

11–17	8.4%
18–25	21.5%
26–35	39.1%
36–50	22.4%
51–60	7.1%
61 and over	1.5%

Average age: 32.1. Median age: 30

Similarly, male fans are over-represented. Women constitute just under 10% of the sample—a far smaller proportion than the number of females in the Smith Center for any given home game. On the other hand, it may well be that women constitute no more than 10% of the population of fans who regularly visit UNC Internet sites, the pool of people from whom this sample draws. In any case, however, there are enough women in this sample to make at least some tentative observations about the extent to which female fans behave or think differently than male fans.

Table 2. Gender of Survey Respondents

Male	90.8%
Female	9.2%

The third and most serious way in which this sample of fans differs from North Carolina's overall fan base is its under-representation of racial minorities. African-Americans constitute just 2.8% of the sample. Given the racial composition of both UNC–Chapel Hill and the state of North Carolina, a conservative estimate of the percentage of all human beings who consider themselves Carolina fans who are African-American would be 15%–20% (and the actual number, while unknowable, may be even higher). The sources of this relative absence of African-Americans in the sample can probably be traced to racial differences in Internet access and use: the most recent government survey tracking Internet use between 1998 and 2000 found that white households were

---

* Numbers in the tables in Chapters Six, Seven, and Eight may not always add up to 100% due to rounding and/or omitted responses. For ease of presentation, phrasing of questions in the tables may vary from the exact text of the questions on the actual survey. See Appendix II for the verbatim text of the survey.

KEY TERMS USED IN THE FOLLOWING DISCUSSION

For the benefit of readers without any background in statistics, it will be helpful to define the following five basic terms which are used frequently in the following discussion:

Correlation between two characteristics means that the two characteristics tend to go together. For instance, there is a correlation between being male and having facial hair, and a correlation between being older and having gray hair. Correlation between two characteristics, however, does not necessarily mean that one characteristic is the *cause* of the other.

Statistically significant means that there is at least a 90% probability that an observed relationship between two variables—such as a correlation—is not simply accidental, but reflects a real world relationship between the two variables.

Sample refers simply to the set of surveys collected and used in this data analysis, which is considered a "sample" of all Carolina fans.

A *variable* is simply a term describing the thing that is being measured in a specific discussion—for instance, the degree to which UNC fans get mad at referees during the game.

The *median* of a given variable is the exact point that is above one half of the sample and below one half of the sample. For instance, if the median number of Carolina games attended by UNC fans is 18, that means that half the fans have gone to more than 18 games, and half have gone to fewer than 18 games. The *median* is often significantly different than the *average* for a given variable.

twice as likely as African-American or Hispanic households to have Internet access. This sample reflects that bias. Unfortunately, the small number of racial minorities in this sample means that making meaningful inferences from this data about how race may or may not affect the experience of being a fan is essentially impossible. (For this reason, I also omit the race of the respondent when quoting fans in the following pages, unless knowledge of the fan's race is important in understanding the content of the comment.)

Table 3. Race of Survey Respondents

White	93.7%
African-American	2.8%
Asian, Hispanic, or Native American	3.5%

Having noted these disadvantages of the current sample, it should be pointed out that using the Internet to gather survey responses also had very significant advantages compared to plausible alternative methods. For instance, if the surveys had been distributed to fans attending games at the Smith Center, or to donors to the Rams Club, or to an alumni mailing list, the resulting samples would have lacked the diversity of the data at hand: Younger fans, fans who have no formal connection to the university, and fans who cannot afford or do not wish to contribute financially to UNC athletics would have been largely absent. Out-of-state fans would also likely have been severely under-represented.

Table 4 shows the great geographical diversity of North Carolina fans, and if taken literally, indicates that about half of all serious North Carolina fans live outside the state's borders. Table 5 describes the leading occupations of survey respondents, showing that a variety of walks of life and stages of life are represented in the sample, although there is almost certainly a bias toward middle-class professionals among these respondents. Blue-collar workers are poorly represented, even though North Carolina has a greater percentage of its labor force employed in manufacturing than any other state. Table 6 illustrates the diversity of political views present among North Carolina fans.

Table 4. Where The Survey Respondents Live

1.	North Carolina (outside Chapel Hill/Carrboro)	41.9%
2.	Chapel Hill (includes Carrboro)	7.4%
3.	Virginia	6.6%
4.	Georgia	5.8%
5.	New York	4.1%
6.	California	3.3%
7.	Texas	3.1%
8.	Maryland/District of Columbia	3.0%
9.	South Carolina	2.6%
10.	Pennsylvania	2.3%

Forty of the fifty states are represented, as well as Benin, Bosnia, Canada, Germany, Hungary, Japan, and Puerto Rico.

Table 5. Leading Occupations of Survey Respondents

1.	Student	19.3%
2.	Computer/information technology-related	6.4%
3.	Lawyer	5.8%
4.	Sales/Retail	5.6%
5.	Teaching/Scholarship	4.8%

Table 6. Political Beliefs of Survey Respondents

Based on Reports of One's Political Views on a 1–10, Right-to-Left Scale.

Very Conservative (1 or 2):	14.5%
Moderate Conservative (3 or 4)	28.7%
Middle of the Road (5)	18.7%
Moderate Liberal (6 or 7)	21.4%
Very Liberal (8 or 9)	14.6%
Left-wing Radical (10)	2.1%

Average: 4.98. Median 5.00

The only way to obtain a relatively pure scientific sample of all Carolina fans would be to have the General Social Survey or another large, ongoing survey of all Americans identify who is a North Carolina fan and who is not, and then have those people claiming to be fans answer the 86 questions of this survey. Failing that, a researcher is left with a choice among imperfect methods of data collection. Given the resources available, making the survey available to anyone with Internet access and the inclination to spend 30 minutes to an hour answering questions about UNC basketball was almost certainly the most efficient method for gaining in-depth information about hardcore Carolina basketball fans. Even so, it is important to keep in mind the biases in the sample produced by the medium used to collect these surveys.

This survey then, is best understood as reflecting the views and experiences of individuals with Internet access who are strongly enough attached and identified as Carolina basketball fans to volunteer to spend half an hour to an hour answering questions about their attachment to the team. The respondents, simply by virtue of taking the time to do the survey, all qualify as serious North Carolina basketball fans. But as we shall see, the survey respondents differ among themselves in many respects, including the overall importance they place on being a fan.

HOW PEOPLE BECAME FANS

Perhaps the best place to launch this description of North Carolina basketball fans is at the beginning—how did these 606 people begin following Carolina basketball in the first place?

As Table 7 shows, there are four major ways survey respondents developed allegiance to North Carolina basketball: Being an alumnus (the most common method), being a North Carolina resident (slightly less common), being influenced as an out-of-stater by a family member who was already a Carolina fan (often alumni themselves), or simply choosing to follow Carolina despite living out of state. That nearly 20% of hard-core Carolina fans fall into this last category speaks volumes about the national visibility and appeal of North Carolina basketball. Chapel Hill residents or natives constitute about one-fourth of all non-alumni North Carolinians who follow the team, but the number of fans who (like the author) have Chapel Hill roots as their sole connection to the team is relatively small. Numerous fans, however, have multiple sources of allegiance, being both Chapel Hill and North Carolina natives and also alumni of the university. (All such cases are counted as "alumni.") Just under 1% of respondents cited a personal relationship with a Carolina player as the source of their allegiance to UNC.

Table 7. How Did Carolina Fans Become Carolina Fans?

What is the Primary Source of Your Allegiance to North Carolina Basketball?

Alumnus	37.6%
North Carolina Resident	26.3%
Chose to Become a Fan From Out of State	19.1%
Chapel Hill Native or Resident	8.2%
Influence of Family Member	
While Living Out-of-State	8.1%

Note: All alumni were reported under "alumnus," even if they grew up in North Carolina and were fans before attending UNC. Similarly, all non-alumnus North Carolina residents or former residents are reported as "North Carolina residents," even if they cited a family member as the main reason for becoming a fan.

Compact Summary:

Alumnus	37.6%
Live or Lived in North Carolina	34.5%
Out-of-State Fan	27.9%

That many alumni became fans at a much younger age is shown by looking at how old most fans were when they became attached to the Tar Heels. Nearly 75% of fans started following the team by age 12, and almost 90% of fans followed the team by the end of high school. The average alumnus, in fact, started following the team by age 12. However, Chapel Hill natives, North Carolina natives, and people who became fans through family members all started even earlier, by age 9. Even out-of-state fans with no other connections on average started following the team by age 11. These figures will probably not surprise many readers, yet it is a little startling to think that a decision made at age 9, 10 or 11 could have such a lasting impact on individuals' lives.

Table 8. Get Them While They're Young

Age at Which Respondents Became North Carolina Basketball Fans

From the Cradle (0–4 Years Old)	13.7%
Kindergarten Carolina Fever (5–7 Years Old)	21.3%
Elementary School (8–12 Years Old)	38.6%
Secondary School (13–17 Years Old)	15.2%
College Age (18–22 Years Old)	6.1%
Young Adult (23–29 Years Old)	4.3%
Adulthood (Over 30 Years Old)	0.8%

Average Age: 10.4 Years. Median Age: 10 Years Old.
Oldest Age at Which Anyone Became a Fan: 37 Years Old.

WHY PEOPLE ARE FANS

"It is a heartfelt love that supercedes reason."

—*Julia Peterson, 60, elementary school teacher, Clinton, NC*

"Losing would be easier than a bad reputation."   —*Colby Weikel, 25, financial analyst, Charlotte, NC*

Family ties, geographical proximity, school pride and simply being impressed by North Carolina basketball based on their national television appearances all constitute mechanisms by which people become fans. But these factors do not necessarily explain *why* people choose to be fans, decade after decade: Many things people are introduced to as children are put aside later (including sometimes sports allegiances). Likewise, while the origins of many fans' allegiance are non-rational, some fans can and do try to think through just why they are fans—even if, like the following fan, they are simply acknowledging that their attachment to UNC at bottom cannot really be explained in rational terms.

- "It is the one source of irrational passion for me. I am passionate about many things, but they all grow out of my personal ideology. The appeal of Carolina basketball exists for me solely on an irrational and emotional level—I could construct it via a logical argument, but the logic would arrive post facto. I would compare my following of UNC basketball to people who speak in tongues, riot at soccer games, or otherwise let emotion win out over reason. It is a passion." —Tommy Ross, 23, graduate student in New York

One way to get at why Carolina fans stay fans is to ask what is the main thing that draws them to Carolina basketball. Over two-thirds of the respondents mentioned the word "tradition" in answering that question—either the tradition of consistent winning, or the perceived off-the-court tradition.

- "The tradition of Carolina basketball and the family bond players and coaches have from the past to the present [is the main thing]. You hardly see something like it in life let alone in sports. It is very special." —29-year-old supervisor in New York

Others fans go even further in explaining why they are attached to Carolina basketball, as the following two statements show:

- "I see UNC basketball as more than just a sport or an entertainment; it has moral and historical importance in our society. I think my life would be somehow lacking without my love for UNC basketball." —Craig Gourley, 36, schoolteacher in Texas

- "It is very difficult to put your finger on why Carolina basketball is different from every other sports fan's allegiance to their team. But it is different. It involves pride in national championships and graduation rates; Dean the coach, and Dean who protested the war and who [helped integrate Chapel Hill]. It is the multi-millionaire pros who come back to get their degrees because they believe they are role models and they must act accordingly. It is about much more than winning, but it is also about a program that is all these other things and still wins."

—Ronald Fritts, 55, North Carolina native living in Atlanta

Survey respondents were asked to further specify what they saw good in Carolina basketball by listing the values they think Carolina basketball stands for. Table 9 shows the responses to this question.

Table 9. Top 15 Values Associated With Carolina Basketball by Fans

Based on First Value Mentioned by Each Respondent.

1.	Integrity	13.2%
2.	Loyalty	12.5%
3.	Class	8.9%
4.	Honesty	7.9%
5.	Teamwork	4.3%
6.	Family	3.5%
7.	Tradition	2.8%
8.	Sportsmanship	2.6%
9.	Hard work	2.5%
10.	Excellence	2.1%
11.	Honor	2.0%
12.	Pride	1.8%
13.	Discipline	1.7%
14.	Clean program	1.5%
15.	Respect for others	1.0%
	No response:	8.4%

Clearly, North Carolina fans associate many positive values with the basketball program—less than 10% of respondents omitted answers to this question, and only two respondents attributed negative values to Carolina basketball. Whether or not the Carolina program deserves to receive such unmitigated praise is, for the moment, beside the point: What is important is that so many fans strongly believe that the program stands for all these desirable human qualities. Indeed, some fans explicitly say that these values are more important to Carolina basketball than the wins and losses.

- "I would be ashamed if UNC athletes routinely embarrassed the university with their conduct on or off the court. The winning means very little by comparison."

  —Craig Gourley, 36, schoolteacher in Texas

- "I believe that some coaches teach their players to cheat if they can get away with it, e.g., grab an offensive rebounder's wrist when the arm is down by his side to prevent them from getting a rebound, bump the hip slightly while a player is in the air to gain an advantage, touch the ball after it goes through the hoop after every made basket. (Duke does this every time and it burns me up!) I sincerely believe that DES never did this and I hope that Carolina continues to follow his example. I would rather lose the game (or all the games) than cheat!"

—Terri Tarheel, 45, paralegal in Jacksonville, NC

MATT DOHERTY ON NORTH CAROLINA FANS

"I think they all want to win, but they want to win with class and integrity, which is what they have come and grown to expect. They appreciate teamwork, they appreciate a lot of little things that Carolina fans have grown accustomed to, whether it be an unselfish play, hustle, all those kinds of things. They want to win, sure, but I think they don't want to sacrifice anything for that. They want to make sure we do it the right way."

That these feelings are very, very widespread becomes clear when we consider Carolina fans' responses to this question: "Can you imagine ever no longer following the Tar Heels?" Table 10 reports the response to that query. What is striking and obvious is that, of those fans who could imagine themselves losing interest, the overwhelming majority cited changes in the character of the program. Less than 2% of respondents said an extended period of losing or mediocrity would cause them to lose interest or stop supporting the team, a remarkably low number.

Table 10. Would Carolina Fans Ever Stop Following the Tar Heels?

Can You Imagine Ever No Longer Following UNC Basketball?

1.	No, never	66.9%
2.	Yes, if the program lost its values or became a win-at-all costs program	13.2%
3.	Yes, if the program had a major scandal	6.8%
4.	Yes, if the program hired Mike Krzyzewski or another unwanted coach from outside the program*	4.4%
5.	All other "yes" responses	8.7%

*Krzyzewski was specifically mentioned by 2.6% of respondents. Among the other individuals named: Rick Pitino, Bob Knight, Billy Packer, Jerry Tarkanian and Steve Wojciechowski.

A natural question to ask is whether seeing these qualities in Carolina basketball actually impacts the way fans live their own lives. No specific question addressing this point was asked on the survey, but a number of fans volunteered a positive answer.

- "I think I am probably a better person because of it, thanks to Dean and the way he ran the program. It has been a real life lesson."   —Phil Stowe, 58, salesman in Pinehurst, NC

- "My mother knows the family of Bill Chamberlain, and when his wife passed away a few years ago, she saw Coach Smith and Guthridge attending the funeral and supporting a former player. She shared that story with me and my siblings to tell us about being loyal and supporting your family in a time of need. I have always had great respect for Coach Smith. My mother adores him, and since she is the best judge of character that I know, she would not steer me wrong."   —Sheronda Harris, 30, social worker in Greensboro

- "I hope that all of my family and friends understand that all I did in my life I learned from the example set by this outstanding program."
                                            —Paul Wilmoth, 35, sports supervisor in Richmond

- "I grew up with Carolina basketball not being a pastime, but a very integral part of my existence. It also teaches a person about good qualities that far outlast any game or season. Carolina does things the right way, and that is why it is so dear to so many people."
                                                —Dan Smith, 29, marketer in Greensboro

PRIDE AND PREJUDICE

"To me, I guess, it's more than a game."   —*Patrick Michel, 27, graduate student in Florida*

The preceding section discussed how North Carolina fans feel about the program, what they see in the program that draws them to remain a fan. This section asks a slightly different question: How do the respondents feel about being a fan? How important, really, is it in their lives?

One way to answer that question is to consider how much time fans spend following the team, and the degree to which Carolina basketball games take precedence over other activities. As Table 11 shows, for over a quarter of the survey respondents, Carolina basketball games absolutely take precedence over other activities during the season. Over 80% of all fans say they largely shape their schedules around the team's.

Table 11. Degree to Which North Carolina Fans Schedule Their Life Around the Games During the Season

Fans Were Asked How Much Their Schedule Is Shaped by Carolina Games During the Season, on a Scale of 1 to 10.

Not Very Much (1–3)	5.4%
A Moderate Amount (4–6)	12.1%
For the Most Part (7–9)	55.1%
Completely (10)	27.4%

Average: 8.0.   Median 8.0

A second way to address this question is to consider what respondents said when they were asked whether being a fan is a matter of personal pride. Table 12 reports the responses to this question.

Table 12. Most Carolina Fans Say They Are "Proud" To Be One

Is Being a UNC Basketball Fan a Source of Personal Pride?

Yes, It Is Important	92.5%
No	7.5%

An overwhelming majority of fans say that being a fan is a source of at least some personal pride, and over half of all respondents noted that it plays an "important" part in their life. The following quotes from fans can speak for this majority:

- "The only thing that means more to me than Carolina basketball, football, baseball and any other sport is my family, and they are barely ahead in the standings."
  —Tom Hicks, 46, Chapel Hill native and UNC alumnus

- "I would rather Carolina beat Duke than get an A on a test. I know that seems silly, but I can't help it." —22-year-old college student from Hope Mills, NC

- "My idea of heaven would be going to see the Tar Heels play every day and winning."
  —Tim Hauser, 49, retired alumnus living in Wilkesboro, NC

- "I wish there were 25 hours in the day so I could more fully speculate on who will replace Ed Cota." —Zachary Wyrick, 28, law firm employee in Austin, Texas

Other fans added that Carolina basketball provides a cathartic experience in terms of being an important emotional outlet.

- "Very rarely in our lives do we get to scream and holler and get very, very excited about things, and Carolina basketball is one means of expressing these kinds of feelings."
  —Jason Knott, 22, alumnus and law student in Cambridge, MA

- "I probably show more emotion regarding UNC athletics, and basketball in particular, than I show in any other area of my life." —Jonathan Hornaday, 24, venture capitalist in Charlotte

Many of the most interesting comments came from respondents who placed less importance on being a fan, or expressed ambivalence about the depth of their attachment to the team. Consider these statements:

- "It's important in the way that only something ultimately unimportant can be—maybe at times a substitute or outlet for other feelings that are too real to focus on. My family, my career, and my community are more important, but in the realm of the actually unserious, nothing else is as important."   —Ed Cone, 38, journalist in Greensboro

- "I still love UNC hoops, but it's just a game, you know? And the players are just kids. I worry about the pressure put on them. Being a fan (short for 'fanatic') of anything is kind of silly, but it can be fun. It ranks pretty low in the grand scheme of my life, but I still enjoy it a lot."
  —Greg Bower, 35, computer systems analyst in Durham and Chapel Hill native

- "UNC doing well in basketball is very important to me, but I think it's a bad move to place too much importance on something you have no control over. As sad as this is going to sound, it's probably the most important thing to me that I don't have any control over, and although I realize the hollowness of that statement, I don't see that changing anytime soon."
  —Aaron Fox, 25, software engineer in San Diego

- "It is important because of the community of followers and the sense of well-being that the program generates. Overall however, these things are not very important because they are far removed from one's personal achievements."
  —Lee Robinson, 58, real estate developer in Hendersonville

- "As I have matured, I have realized that I have taken many lessons from watching Dean Smith's teams play on the floor that I have used in my life. I have also realized that I shouldn't put too much time and energy into it, because it pales in comparison to other things in life. It is hard not to get caught up in it though."   —Lee Hardee, 22, software engineer in Charlotte

We will shortly return to the question of whether there is any evidence that being a more ambivalent fan, or a fan who self-consciously recognizes that basketball is only so important, is a healthier attitude than making one's attachment to Carolina basketball an extremely high priority. For the moment, it is worth noting that, for both more and less rabid fans, becoming self-conscious about the role being a fan plays in one's life can be a breakthrough in itself: Consider this statement by a fan describing his "worst memory" as a Carolina supporter:

- "When I realized that I took it personally when the team lost—kind of an embarrassing revelation, and yet, a liberating moment."
  —Harrison Braxton, 30, mental health counselor from Virginia

Finally, it is also worth hearing directly from the 7.5% of survey respondents who said that they take no pride in being a fan. Many of these respondents pointed out that they are not the ones playing the games. Others argued alone these lines:

- "Being a fan is not something to be proud of. Any bozo can be a fan. There are quite a few UNC fans that I find somewhat embarrassing, by association."
  —Mike McCann, 43, computer tech in Clemmons, NC

THE EXPERIENCE OF WATCHING THE GAME

Watching the basketball games is the principal activity involved in being a fan; and most fans watch the majority of games not in person but on television. As Table 13 shows, most fans watch the game with other people at least some of the time, but it is noteworthy that for nearly one-third of Carolina fans, watching the games is a solitary activity, whether by circumstance or choice.

Table 13. Carolina Basketball on TV: Solitary or Shared Consumption?

Do You Watch the Games on TV Alone or With Other People, or Does It Not Matter?

Watch Games Alone	31.7%
Watch With Others/Doesn't Matter	68.3%

Many of the fans who watch alone volunteered specific reasons why they prefer to be by themselves during the game, most of which reflect that the fans are so involved in the game that they are at higher-than-normal levels of stress and irritability. Consider these explanations for watching the game alone:

- "I get nervous and hate other people's reactions, even if they are UNC fans."

  —Derek Croxton, 31, historian in Michigan

- "I don't like to be messed with during the games. I don't like discussing Heels basketball with neophytes and I don't like explaining the 'situation' while the game is being played."

  —Jake Dickens, 28, business owner in Greenville, SC

Whether fans watch alone or with other people, however, almost all fans devote maximum attention to the game while the ball is in play, as Table 14 shows.

Table 14. Glued to the TV: How Carolina Fans Watch the Games

When Watching Games on TV, Do You Watch Every Moment Attentively, or
Do You Go In and Out of the Room and/or Combine Watching the Game With Other Activities?

Watch Every Moment Attentively	95.9%
Go In and Out, or Combine With Other Activities	4.1%

Emotions are high for serious sports fans while the games are being played. But to what extent do those emotions translate into expressions of anger, anger directed at the players and coaches one is cheering for, at the opposition, or at third parties (such as the referees or the media)? Table 15 shows the propensity of Carolina fans to get mad at Carolina's own players and coaches during the game, and also shows the effect of being an older fan or being female on experiencing these angry emotions. Table 16 reports the propensity of Carolina fans to get mad at referees, opponents or their fans, and television commentators.

Table 15. The Emotions of Watching the Game, Part One

Frequency With Which Carolina Fans Report the Following Emotions While Watching Games, on a Scale of 1 (Never) to 10 (All the Time).

Getting Mad at North Carolina Players	*All fans*	*Women*	*Over 40**
Never (1)	4.3%	7.1%	10.2%
Occasionally (2–3)	30.7%	39.3%	43.1%
Sometimes (4–6)	39.1%	34.0%	29.9%
A Lot (7–9)	23.3%	16.0%	16.8%
All the Time (10)	2.6%	3.6%	0.0%
Average:	4.8	4.3	3.9
Median	5.0	4.0	3.0

Getting Mad at North Carolina Coaches	*All fans*	*Women*	*Over 40*
Never (1)	14.7%	21.4%	16.8%
Occasionally (2–3)	36.8%	37.5%	40.1%
Sometimes (4–6)	29.4%	28.6%	29.2%
A Lot (7–9)	16.5%	10.7%	11.0%
All the Time (10)	2.6%	1.8%	2.9%
Average:	4.0	3.5	3.8
Median:	3.0	3.0	3.0

*Throughout these chapters, this category includes fans aged 40 and above.

Table 16. The Emotions of Watching the Game, Part Two

Getting Mad at Television Commentators	*All fans*	*Women*	*Over 40*
Never (1)	7.9%	8.9%	13.1%
Occasionally (2–3)	9.4%	5.4%	12.4%
Sometimes (4–6)	21.6%	19.6%	16.1%
A Lot (7–9)	39.0%	34.0%	32.1%
All the Time (10)	22.1%	32.1%	26.3%
Average:	6.8	7.3	6.5
Median:	8.0	8.0	8.0

Getting Mad at Referees	*All fans*	*Women*	*Over 40*
Never (1)	5.1%	0.0%	10.9%
Occasionally (2–3)	15.4%	14.3%	25.6%
Sometimes (4–6)	30.3%	28.6%	24.8%
A Lot (7–9)	33.9%	37.5%	24.8%
All the Time (10)	15.3%	19.6%	13.9%
Average:	6.2	6.6	5.3
Median:	6.0	7.0	5.0

Getting Mad at Opponents'	*All fans*	*Women*	*Over 40*
Players, Coaches, or Fans			
Never (1)	9.6%	3.6%	10.9%
Occasionally (2–3)	13.9%	3.5%	19.8%
Sometimes (4–6)	28.1%	28.6%	35.0%
A Lot (7–9)	30.1%	42.9%	21.9%
All the Time (10)	18.3%	21.4%	12.4%
Average:	6.1	7.0	5.3
Median:	6.0	7.0	5.0

Looking at the evidence from both tables, what immediately becomes evident is that all Carolina fans are less likely to get mad at Carolina's own players and coaches than at outsiders. Moreover, the basic tendency is more pronounced among female respondents: Women are less likely than men to get mad at Carolina players and coaches, but *more* likely to get mad at opponents and at television commentators, and slightly more likely to get mad at referees.

Older fans show a different pattern: Fans over 40 are less likely to get mad at Carolina players and coaches than other fans, but they are also less likely to get mad at referees or opponents. The percentage of older fans saying they *never* get mad at players or at referees is strikingly high compared to all fans. One group not spared from the wrath of older fans, however, are the poor television commentators: Apparently, all groups of fans are likely to be irked by Billy Packer's criticisms of UNC tactics or by Dick Vitale's frequent praise of Duke. Anger at actual participants in the games (including referees) tends to mellow as fans get older, although not to an overwhelming degree.

Two further observations about these answers are in order: First, very few fans reported never or almost never getting mad at *anyone* during the games. Only 2.1% of all respondents have an average "getting mad" response of 2.0 or less for all five categories. Similarly, only 3.0% of respondents had an average "getting mad" response of 9.0 or higher for all five categories. The great majority of fans fell in the middle (with an average of 5.6). In short, very few fans are hotheads who are mad about everything all the time, and very few fans never get their capacity for anger or irritation aroused during games.

Second, it should be noted that the fans differ among themselves in the target of their anger: 78% of all fans, including 89% of all women, are more likely to get mad at outsiders than at Carolina players or coaches, but a notable minority (18%) tend to focus their anger on Carolina's participants. (4% of fans get equally mad at Carolina players and coaches and at outsiders.) Persons with more conservative political views are slightly more likely to fall in this latter category: there is a small but consistent correlation between being more liberal and being less likely to get mad at a Carolina player or coach. However, there is little or no correlation between being more liberal and one's likelihood of getting mad at the television, the refs or the other team.

Carolina fans will probably be happy to learn that most of their brethren are substantially less likely to get mad at their own players and coaches than at the opposition. Whereas a fan's anger at

DEAN SMITH ON WATCHING THE GAMES AS A FAN

Q. Has there been a big difference for you in retirement, watching the games as a fan?

A. Oh yeah, it's terrible. That has been a revelation to me. When you're sitting there involved you're calm, most of the time. You're thinking ahead, if I got annoyed by a call I might say something, but still I'd be thinking about the next player, or how much time. In a game a long time ago in Carmichael, some doctors put me on a heart thing, and it didn't change much during the game. But now, I'm a nervous wreck! I'm not superstitious, but I just get up to stretch and maybe it'll change things (chuckle). It's horrible, I can see what fans go through.

an outsider, even if it persists after the game is over, in all likelihood will have little or no real-world effect on the targets of that anger, if Carolina fans get angry at a Carolina player or coach, stay that way, and then vocalize their feelings, it can have a damaging effect on morale and create a negative climate for participants and fans alike.

This data does not allow us to specify with any certainty whether folks who tend to get mad at participants during the games are also more likely to vent criticisms of players and coaches on Internet message boards or call-in radio shows—but it is hard to believe that there is no correlation. That's why it is good news that, while the average Carolina fan does sometimes get upset with Carolina folks, only a minority says they get angry at Carolina participants and their efforts most or all of the time.

HOW NORTH CAROLINA FANS DEAL WITH LOSSES

After the game is over, Carolina fans experience either the satisfaction of victory or the disappointment of defeat. This survey sought to probe North Carolina fans' attitudes toward and experiences of defeat in two ways: first, by asking fans how they process losses after a defeat, and second, by asking how long fans thought about losses after the game was over.

Table 17 shows that most fans have both an analytical reaction and an emotional reaction to losses. Fans who reported having only an analytical reaction outnumbered those who reported having only an emotional reaction by a more than 2-to-1 ratio. Carolina fans are more likely to greet losses with a search for what went wrong, where the game was won or lost, and how it might have turned out differently than to be consumed by emotion. Moreover, as Table 17 also shows, older fans are slightly more likely than younger fans to have an analytical reaction to losses. Most Carolina fans of all ages, however, have doses of analysis and heartbreak in their post-defeat tonic.

Is there a relationship between how mad fans get during the game and how they react after the game? Yes, there is. As Table 17 also reports, fans who react analytically to losses are also about

20% less likely to get mad at anyone during the contest (whether from UNC or not), compared to those who react emotionally.

Table 17. How North Carolina Fans React to Losses

Fans Were Asked If Their Response to Losses Was Typically to Analyze What Went Wrong, React Emotionally, or Both.

	Average age	*Mad at UNC During Games**	*Mad at Others During Games***
Both (62.1%)	31.8 years old	4.6	6.6
Analyze (27.1%)	33.2 years old	3.9	5.5
React Emotionally (10.8%)	30.6 years old	4.9	6.9

* Average response for getting mad at a UNC coach and getting mad at a UNC player.
**Average response for getting mad at an official, getting mad at the other team, and getting mad at television commentators.

How long does the taste of defeat stay in the mouths of hard-core fans? As Table 18 shows, a large majority of fans think about losses for at least a day, but most get over it within a week. Very common responses to this question included "until the next game" or "until the next win," meaning three or four days in most cases.

Table 18. Dealing With Disappointment: How Long Carolina Fans Think About Losses

At Least Until the Next Day	82.7%
Longer Than 24 Hours	70.1%
One Week or More	17.2%

This question about how quickly fans process defeat generated numerous interesting responses. A common theme among respondents who elaborated upon their answer to this question was that they have learned to take losses better over time. Consider these quotations from fans describing how long they think about losses:

- "Less as I grow older. I'm more philosophical and recognize the youth of the players and the limitations of a coach. Up until seven or eight years ago I'd have said until after the following day. Now I think I've shrugged it off after the first shudder in the morning."

    —Alan Palisoul, 54, lawyer in Maryland

- "Over time I have learned to let go of the disappointment of losing games, particularly important games. I take them to bed with me but when I wake up the next morning it's over and I'm on to whatever I'm doing . . . I have friends however who want to rehash and overanalyze the games, which I try to tolerate to a point."

    —Jay Barnes, 55, businessman in Dallas

- "During a game, it is the most important thing in my life. Over the last 10 years, I have tried to separate my identity and ego from the team, because losing was such a personal and destructive experience. Instead of live and die, I now am able to recover (respond to and communicate with others, and think about non-game topics) from the critical injury of a loss, after several hours."   —Brian Taylor, 39, computer programmer in Chapel Hill

- "I try to keep things in perspective; basketball is just a game, no matter how all-consuming and intensely important it may seem at the time. Life goes on, even if you miss a game and even if we lose. It has taken around 50 years to become so philosophical."
                                                      —62-year-old attorney in North Carolina

- "In my younger days, I would get really emotional over it. I would be emotionally down for a couple of weeks over an NCAA loss, especially in the Final Four. I found out years later that many of my college friends got really tired of hearing me talk about UNC and Dean. Luckily, they didn't hold it against me. I've learned through experiencing life that there are a lot of things that are really important and sports is not that high on the list. It's not good to put so much emotion into something that makes you unhappy as often as it makes you happy. I enjoy it a lot more with a moderate approach."
                                       —Michael Bailiff, 39, North Carolina native and Georgia resident

This theme of learning to take losses better as one gets older is evidenced in the aggregate statistics as a whole, which show a clear, albeit weak, relationship between age and likelihood of dwelling on a loss for longer than a day. Fans in this sample who don't think about losses for more than a day are nearly two years older on average than those who do.

Interestingly, however, there is no apparent correlation between age and thinking about losses for a *very* long time—i.e. a week or more. In fact, fans who think about the losses for over a week are slightly older on average than fans who think about the game between one and seven days. In short, older fans are more likely than younger fans to be found either among those who get over losses very quickly, or among those who dwell on losses the longest. Thus, while the quotations just noted indicate that numerous fans have managed to process the losses more quickly as the years go by, the aggregate data suggests that many others have not, or at least not yet.

Taking losses hard is correlated with several other fan characteristics, some of which will be noted in subsequent discussion. Two quick observations are in order here. First, it should be noted that there is a robust positive correlation between thinking about losses for at least a day and getting mad during the games, suggesting that those who think about losses until the next day are 24% more likely to get upset for some reason while the game is being played than those who do not. Second, there is a strong positive correlation between whether one thinks about losses for over a day and whether one takes being a fan as a matter of personal pride; being a proud fan makes one 25% more likely to need 24 hours to get over a loss. Just as one might expect, more intense fans have more intense reactions to losses.

FAMILY TIES, RELATIONSHIPS AND INTERPERSONAL STRAINS

We now turn from the dismal subject of dealing with defeat to a substantially rosier question: How does being a Carolina basketball fan affect important relationships in fans' lives? This section considers the impact of Carolina basketball on friendships and family relationships, and on conflicts in interpersonal relationships.

Friendship

"Without friends," wrote Aristotle, "no one would choose to live, though he had all other goods." But as Yale political scientist Robert Lane has pointed out, numerous forms of human companionship, especially frequent visiting with family members and neighbors, have been gradually declining in the United States in the past generation. Fortunately, visiting with friends has largely resisted this downward trend. Even so, given the larger context of growing individualism and increasing social isolation, any activity that has the capacity to generate new friendships should not be sneered at. For a very substantial number of fans, North Carolina basketball appears to have precisely that effect of encouraging new relationships and strengthening old ones.

Over half of all survey respondents say they have made a friend and/or a business contact through Carolina basketball. Several respondents elaborated on this issue in a telling fashion:

- "I am always introduced by my clients as 'Susan who loves sports and don't say anything mean about Carolina.'"   —Susan E. Harper, 26, event planner and alumna in Chicago

- "I have found throughout my life that other Heels fans give preferential treatment to other Heels fans. For instance, I received a 40% discount from a moving company whose entire family are alumni/fans and knew that I was a fan, and when I meet someone who is also a Carolina fan, it definitely influences my opinion of them. So I think the answer here would have to be yes."   —Terri Tarheel, 45, paralegal in Jacksonville, NC

Ninety percent of respondents said they had at least one close friend who is a Tar Heel fan. Only 30% of respondents, however, said that half or more of their close friends are also Carolina fans. Most fans have a few friends with whom they can share Carolina basketball, but many more friends who don't follow Carolina. Perhaps surprisingly, there appears to be no significant correlation between advancing age and having a smaller number of friends who are Carolina fans. There is, however, a modestly strong relationship between being male and having a higher percentage of Carolina fans among one's friends.

Table 19. Friendship and Carolina Basketball

Percentage of Respondents Who Report They Have Made a
New Friend or Business Contact Through North Carolina Basketball

Yes	56.5%
No	43.5%

That Carolina basketball is in general an experience fans share with other people is further illustrated by the fact (see Table 20) that 78% of all fans communicate with friends or family members after games; it is a safe bet that most of these fans do not telephone their friends to talk about most sitcoms or other TV shows that they have just seen. Interestingly, 72% of those fans who regularly watch the game alone communicate with other people after the game (compared to 81% of those who watch the games with others at least some of the time). All told, only about one-eighth of Carolina fans watch the games by themselves and talk or otherwise communicate with no one about it afterwards.

Table 20. Did You See That? Propensity of Carolina Friends to Communicate With One Another After Games

Percentage of Carolina Fans Who Say They Regularly Communicate With Friends or Family Members About the Games After They Are Over

Yes	78.3%
No	21.7%

This bring us squarely to the issue of family ties and Carolina basketball, a subject that evoked a number of interesting responses. Before turning to some of those reports, the basic facts are worth noting, because they are rather surprising. Some 77% of all fans say they have another Carolina fan in their immediate family. But fully 51% of Carolina fans say they have to contend with a fan of another school in their immediate family: the experience of Roy Keefer, the fan diarist with a Duke-loving son, is not at all uncommon, although the data does not allow us to know anything about the intensity of the allegiances to other schools in these "mixed" families.

The relationship between family and Carolina basketball is, not surprisingly, somewhat tighter for North Carolina residents than for others: just under 90% of Chapel Hill and North

---

DEAN SMITH ON LOCAL RIVALRIES

"What happens here, and it's so unique, is that say we work together, you're a lawyer and I'm a lawyer, and you're for State—and State was the big one in the 70s, nobody talked about Carolina-Duke—and if Carolina won, I couldn't hardly wait to get to the office, ready to needle my buddy. Then just wait, and we get beat, and here comes the needle back. I think that created more than anything this following of one versus the other, and it's really so we can needle our buddy. That's why I used to joke at Foundation meetings, I'd say, 'Well, we had a good year,' but when we win, just say, 'You all played well,' so they won't come back at you the next year when they beat us. The fact is that it's on television and they're all watching, so that after a rival game, everyone tells me that in the offices of any business, they're talking about the game."

Carolina residents in the survey say they have other Tar Heels in the family, and nearly 45% of North Carolinians say they have a non-Carolina fan in the immediate family. The reasons why fans living out of state might have non-Carolina fans in their family are not hard to deduce. That so many in-state fans also have "mixed" fan families speaks to the fact that rooting for North Carolina is not the only available option for in-state residents. It also suggests that for a surprising number of fans, winning and losing can at least some of the time be an especially intense experience. Watching Carolina lose and then having a sibling offer not consolation but instead rub it in has to be difficult, and this data suggests that phenomenon is probably more common than one might have guessed.

Table 21. Family Ties

Percentage of Fans With Another Carolina Fan in Their Immediate Family

Yes	77.0%
No	23.0%

Percentage of Fans With a Fan of Another School in Their Immediate Family

Yes	51.0%
No	49.0%

Breakdown of Presence of Other Fans Within Respondents' Immediate Family

No Carolina fans and no fans of other schools	7.3%
Carolina fan(s) and no fans of other schools	41.8%
Fan(s) of other schools and no Carolina fans	15.5%
Carolina fan(s) and fan(s) of other schools	35.4%

For many Carolina fans, family relationships have played a central role in their experience as a fan. Numerous respondents spoke of relationships with fathers in particular as being among their most cherished memories of being a Carolina fan, while others spoke of the family bonding benefits of Carolina basketball in a more general way. The intensity of some of these anecdotes defies description. Consider these comments:

- "Some of the greatest moments I spent with my dad revolved around Carolina Basketball.... Shortly before he died, Carolina ended a losing streak against Duke at the Smith Center, I don't remember the year, but Laettner missed a shot at the buzzer. The next day, my dad and I watched him miss that shot every 30 minutes on CNN Headline news. Greatest day of my life!

   "Carolina basketball serves as a link in my family. It has always been something that I could communicate with my father, my brothers, and my own children about. I truly can't imagine what would have taken the place of Carolina basketball over all these years."

   —Richard Hickman, 45, teacher in Ocean Isle Beach, NC

- "In 1990, my then-husband received four tickets from a UNC-alum physician he worked with who wouldn't be attending the game. My father (who passed Carolina Fever to me genetically) was virtually a hermit at the time. I had tried to get him to go with me to other events I knew he liked (e.g., a boxing event only six or seven miles from his home), but he wouldn't. He was a rather stoic, undemonstrative man. When we received the tickets, I called my father to see if he and my mother would go with us (since he was the biggest fan besides me I knew). I had hardly got the words out of my mouth when he asked me what time we'd be leaving for Chapel Hill! After being a fan for probably 50 years, this was the first game he'd have a chance to attend. We went and he waved the pompom left in the seat; he even did the wave. I was in utter shock at his behavior, but loved it. (We won the game, 71–63.) He had a WONDERFUL time. He died seven months later, not having attended another game; at his funeral, I put his ticket stub for the game—his ticket to 'Blue Heaven' in his shirt pocket. I will never be able to thank that doc enough for getting me those tickets."

—Terri Tarheel, 45, paralegal in Jacksonville, NC

- "While my Dad has been dead for the past 17 years, his allegiance and our shared love for UNC basketball remain one of my most poignant, frequent, and cherished memories. UNC basketball has definitely played a tangible role in my life."

—Keith Lane, 33, budget analyst in Hillsborough

- "It's the one big thing my Dad and I could share equally and agree on always. How can you beat that?" —Steve Stover, 37, Chapel Hill native living in Los Angeles

- "My grandfather was a huge UNC fan and had a particular affinity for the underappreciated players. The year before, he kept telling everybody who would listen that some kid from Garner—Donald Williams—was going to be a hell of a player.

  "Two days after UNC smoked Rhode Island in the tournament [in 1993], my grandfather died. I had the honor of giving his eulogy. In the eulogy, I mentioned how he loved UNC hoops and particularly underappreciated players like Donald Williams, because my grandfather really respected those kinds of players. To make a long story short, I firmly believe that my grandfather had something to do with Donald's performance in the Final Four that year."

—Jason Jenkins, 30, consultant in Conshohocken, PA

- "Before my father died, he would occasionally mention that he wanted his ashes spread around the campus, but would especially mention the Dean Dome floor. A few months after his death, my sister and I began to spread his ashes and started in the Dean Dome. There was a cheerleading competition (of all things) among young girls from around the state, so I had to get creative. I needed to get down to the floor, so I used one of my kid's Happy Meal toys that remotely resembled a camera. I walked confidently up under one of the goals, kneeled down, acted like I was taking a picture, and poured a small vial of his ashes under the goal....

  "Putting some of my father's ashes on the Dean Dome floor was powerful. As a young man, the whole NC Basketball aura seemed so much larger than life. My father introduced me to NC basketball, it provided a unique way for us to bond. He had an extremely confident manner and would walk right out on the floor during warm-ups to meet/see the players and coaches. He would take me down with him at times to show me how big the players were, atmosphere on the floor, etc. It was extremely exciting for a kid to walk with the big guys. I will do the same with my son when he is older."   —Scott Ashcraft, 33, archaeologist in Asheville

Nearly half of Carolina fans, in fact, report that their parents had a role in their becoming a fan. And like Scott Ashcraft, most Carolina fans intend to at least try to pass their fanhood on to their children, as Table 22 reports.

Table 22. The Generational Transmission of North Carolina Basketball

Percentage of Fans Who Say Their Parents Played a Role in Their Following Carolina

Yes	46.3%
No	53.7%

Percentage of Fans Who Say It Is Important That Their Children Become UNC Fans

Yes	71.9%
No	28.1%

The responses to these questions were often interesting, even poignant. Many of those who said "no" to the question about passing on fanhood to children mentioned that children should have their own choice about whom to follow, and some volunteered the view that trying to make their children fans would in fact be counterproductive. But most respondents said it would be important for their children to become fans—although many of these, too, said it would not be the end of the world if that didn't happen. Other fans said they didn't care if their children became Carolina fans or not, just so long as they didn't become Duke fans.

Consider this sample of responses to survey questions about passing Carolina hoops from generation to generation:

- "Watching the games with my parents was always fun. Even when I went through the difficult teen years and 'hated' them, we could always watch games together.... [As far as my future kids are concerned] I just hope they have something to follow as much as I do UNC."
  —Mike p. Burton, 31, comic in New York

- On her children growing up Carolina fans: "They will. Oh yes, they will. Their baby formula will be mixed with water from the Old Well!" —Susan E. Harper, 26, event planner in Chicago

- "We will fail to bond on some fundamental level if they [my children] do not share my love for the Heels."   —Jeff Langenderfer, 38, college professor in Rome, Georgia

- "They already are fans, or they don't eat."
  —Troy Hazzard, 39, elementary school counselor in Delaware

- On whether having his children become fans is important: "Not really. I will try to teach them loyalty, professionalism, and trust, and that will make them Carolina fans eventually."
  —Jose Llavona, 38, stockbroker and businessman in Puerto Rico

- On whether her children will become fans: "Unless they wanted to become street urchins, yes." —Karen Lee, 39, UNC alum in Greenville, NC

The notion that spectator sports are often a vehicle for shared family relationships, particularly father-son relationships, is well established in the sociological literature on sports and well attested by common observation. Stories like the ones told above by North Carolina basketball fans—including the common expectation that Carolina fanhood will be passed on to the next generation—are probably not all that exceptional compared to what a study of fan allegiances for another team would show. Nonetheless, the tangible role sports often play in helping bond families across generational barriers is a morally important fact that should not be taken lightly or for granted.

DEAN SMITH ON FAMILY TIES

"The best thing about television that I've gotten a sense of from the retirement letters, is that a guy will write about how his father and grandfather had him watching the game at 10, and then his whole family was together. It served as a group outing, to watch the game. I still get so much mail now from people who want me to sign a picture to send to his 80-year-old grandfather, or his 80-year-old father, who got them started in Carolina basketball. So television served a family purpose for a change! I was really amazed at how many times that happened."

Relationships, Conflict, and Carolina Basketball

As noted in Chapter Four, however, some critics of America's passion for spectator sports point to the role that sports can play in causing conflict within relationships, particularly within marriages. Although no specific question in this survey asked about the impact that being a fan had upon one's marriage or relationship, several fans volunteered telling responses indicating that passion for Carolina basketball is indeed often a strain on male-female relationships. Consider these comments:

- "Believe me, I have had lots of feuds with significant others over the love of UNC hoops."
  —28-year-old fan in New Jersey

- "I have dumped more than one girlfriend because she tried to change my viewing habits of UNC." —28-year-old engineer in Hickory, NC

- "All girlfriends and family members have known that they may not interfere unless emergency requires it." —26-year-old fan in Michigan

- "There have been times in my life when, before the start of the season, I've told myself that I should not worry about the season so much. I shouldn't forego other plans just to watch the games. I could never do that, however—it was almost impossible for me to miss any game. I've actually turned down going out on dates to watch games. It's hard to put a finger on the force that drives me to do that. I think I just get excited about seeing how returning players have improved, and, of course, it's always exciting to see the new players."

  —Matthew Pruden, 26, law student in Winston-Salem

By reporting these anecdotes, I do not mean to cast judgment on the people who made these very honest comments. In fact, I know firsthand the tension involved in being in a relationship with a non-sports fan who cares little or nothing for Carolina basketball: In 1993, my then-girlfriend asked me to pick her up at the airport at 9:45 p.m. the night of the national championship game against Michigan. I offered to pick up the bill for a cab, but we broke up less than a month later. I'm pretty sure I would make that same decision again, but there were other moments of basketball-related strain in that relationship that I am less proud of. Following Carolina basketball is not an inherently selfish activity, but under certain circumstances placing consumption of Carolina basketball above someone else's desires and needs is bound to inspire conflict.

I strongly suspect, however, that this particular tension is most strongly felt by singles in their 20s like the ones quoted here, and that eventually most hard-core fans will successfully find ways to accommodate their passion for UNC within their longest-lasting relationships. No one in this sample, at least, volunteered the information that their marriage had broken up over conflict resulting from Carolina basketball.

Moreover, the picture with respect to male-female relationships and Carolina basketball—even among 20-somethings—is not entirely bleak, as the following quote illustrates:

- "The further I get from Chapel Hill (both in distance and years), the more basketball I watch. It's a way to keep in touch with my alma mater, and feel connected to campus. Also—and this is a big part of it—my boyfriend is a big sports fan. I don't really like any of his sports, but having *Sports Illustrated* and a sports fan around the house has encouraged my enthusiasm. He's happy to watch any sports with me, so we watch UNC basketball."

  —Joan Petit, 27, UNC alum and graduate student in Bryson City, NC

It would be naive to think, however, that a passion for Carolina basketball cannot put a strain on even the closest of relationships. This survey asked three questions intended to measure the degree to which Carolina basketball was a source of conflict in fans' lives. First, fans were asked whether being a fan had ever put a strain on a relationship with a friend or family member. Second, fans were asked if they had ever gotten into a passionate face-to-face argument with another Carolina fan about Carolina basketball. Third, fans were asked if they had gotten into an argument with a fan of another school over Carolina basketball.

Responses to the first question show that just over two-fifths of all hard-core Carolina fans report that being a fan has been a source of conflict within a relationship. Table 23 shows the relationship between having had a conflict and several other fan characteristics. Women are less likely to have experienced a relationship strain as a result of Carolina basketball, and people who live in North Carolina are somewhat more likely than out-of-state fans to have had a conflict.

One of the more interesting findings is that whereas living in North Carolina but not in Chapel Hill is associated with higher rates of relationship strain, fans who live in Chapel Hill or Carrboro actually have experienced strains less often. That finding may be puzzling at first, given that one would think that the closer one is to the epicenter, the more intense one's experience of being a fan is likely to be, which in turn could create greater potential for conflict in relationships. That appears to be true for North Carolina residents in general—why isn't it true for Chapel Hill residents, too? The most likely explanation is that because UNC basketball is such a dominant strain in the culture of Chapel Hill, big fans who live in the town are less likely than fans who live elsewhere to have important relationships with people who don't care at all about Carolina basketball.

Table 23. Carolina Basketball and Relationship Strain

Has Being a Carolina Basketball Fan Ever Put a Strain on a Relationship?

	All fans	*Women*
Yes	41.6%	33.9%
No	58.4%	66.1%

Fans Who	*Think About Losses For at Least One Day*	*Do Not Think About Losses For at Least One Day*
Yes	45.2%	26.0%
No	54.8%	74.0%

Fans Who	*Think Mostly About Losses in Remembering the Past*	*Think Mostly About Wins in Remembering the Past*
Yes	63.1%	35.7%
No	36.9%	64.3%

Fans Who	*Regularly Get Mad at Carolina Players or Coaches*	*Always Schedule Their Life Around Games (10 on 1–10 scale)*
Yes	48.4%	50%
No	51.6%	50%

Fans Who	*Do Not Say Being a Fan Is a Source of Personal Pride*	*Have Made a Friend Through Carolina Basketall*
Yes	29.5%	48.7%
No	70.5%	51.3%

Fans Who	*Live in Chapel Hill/Carrboro*	*Live Elsewhere in North Carolina*
Yes	37.8%	49.6%
No	62.2%	50.4%

The most striking and important finding, however, is the strong, significant connection between how long one thinks about losses and the likelihood of having had a strain on a relationship. Fans who are able to stop thinking about losses by the end of the day on which the game was played are 42% less likely than fans who do think about losses until the next day to have experienced a relationship conflict on account of Carolina basketball. Similarly, fans who, in thinking about the past, focus heavily on wins (7–10 on a 1–10 scale from always thinking about losses to always thinking about wins) are 59% less likely than those who focus mostly on losses (1–3 on the 1–10 scale) to have experienced a relationship strain.

A significant connection also exists between experiencing conflicts and taking being a fan as a matter of personal pride. Additionally, those fans who get mad at Carolina players or coaches during the game on a very regular basis are slightly more likely to have experienced conflicts than other fans. Finally, fans who say they *always* schedule their life around the game are substantially more likely to experience a conflict than other fans. Fifty percent of such fans have had conflicts, compared to 41% of fans who answered the schedule question with an 8 or 9 on the 1–10 scale, and 35% of fans who answered 7 or less on the 1–10 scale.

These findings suggest that certain fan habits which might be thought to be undesirable, or at least questionable, tend to run together: Taking being a fan very seriously, dwelling on losses, getting mad at participants during the games, always scheduling one's life around the games, and having one's passion for basketball induce a conflict in a relationship all run together. In addition, fans with these characteristics have a substantially higher chance of being among the 57% of fans who have gotten into an argument with another UNC fan or the 83% of fans who have gotten into an argument with a fan of another school (see Table 24). With one exception, each of the seven variables measuring these characteristics has a positive, statistically significant correlation with one another. (Being proud to be a fan is not significantly correlated with getting into arguments with other Carolina fans.) Those fans who exhibit each of these characteristics might be termed "Overcommitted Fans."

Table 24. Propensity of Carolina Fans to Get into Arguments About Basketball

Have you ever gotten into a passionate, face-to-face argument about
UNC basketball with another Carolina fan?

Yes	57%
No	43%

With a fan of another school?

Yes	83%
No	17%

Three caveats are in order at this point, however. First, it is fairly likely that propensity to experience relationship strain pertaining to Carolina basketball is also affected by factors not measured here: such as, fundamentally, how happy one is with one's personal life and/or family situation.

More detailed information about these respondents would be required to ascertain whether happiness in one's personal life is connected in a consistent way with either propensity to dwell on losses or one's likelihood of having experienced a conflict pertaining to basketball.

Second, the number of fans who completely match all seven aspects of the Overcommitted Fan is small. In fact, just 13 fans, 2.1% of the total sample, exhibit all seven traits.

Substantially more fans do not regularly get mad at Carolina coaches or players (defined here as averaging 7.0 or higher on the 1–10 scale for anger during games), but do exhibit the other six characteristics of the Overcommitted Fan: pride in being a fan, thinking about losses at least one day, always scheduling one's life around the game, arguing with Carolina fans, arguing with other schools' fans, and experiencing a conflict in a relationship. Thirty-eight fans, or 6.3% of the sample, fell into this category. The 51 fans—8.4% of the total—who exhibit these six characteristics noted above will be referred to as "Overcommitted Fans" in subsequent discussion, whether or not they also often get mad at Carolina players and coaches. These 51 fans are demographically quite similar to the rest of the sample, with the exception that they are on average about 15% more conservative politically than the sample as a whole.

While the total number of Overcommitted Fans is small, the number of fans who exhibit *none* of the seven characteristics noted above is even smaller: Just three fans out of 606 are not proud about being fans, get over losses by the end of game day, don't always schedule life around the games, have never argued with Carolina fans or other schools' fans, have never experienced a conflict in a relationship, and don't get mad at UNC coaches and players. That number increases to 61, 10.2% of the sample, if we include respondents who are proud to be fans and have gotten into arguments with either other Carolina fans or fans of other schools, but do not exhibit any of the other characteristics of Overcommitted Fans. About 8% of fans, then, fall into an Overcommitted Fan category, and perhaps 10% of fans are in a Lower Intensity Fan category. But the great mass of fans—over 80% of them—fall somewhere in the middle. Most Carolina fans are not intemperate fanatics; nor do they take an approach of serene, conflict-averse moderation in being a fan.

The third major caveat is that while being an Overcommitted Fan is correlated with some unpleasant things, it is also correlated with good things—such as the likelihood one has made a friend through Carolina basketball. Some 75% of Overcommitted Fans have made a new friend through Carolina basketball, a much higher ratio than the sample as a whole. In contrast, only 46% of Lower Intensity Fans have made a friend through Carolina basketball, a lower-than-average ratio. In short, the story here is not that all less-pleasant parts of being a fan (conflicts, arguments) go together to the exclusion of good things about being a fan (making new friends). Fans who take pride in their fan status and devote more time and emotion to being a fan are more likely to experience both the negatives and positives of being a fan than those who do not. Indeed, as Table 23 indicated, there is a strong, statistically significant correlation between having made a friend through Carolina basketball and having had a strain placed on a relationship.

Even so, if we take making a new friend as one of the highest goods that being a Carolina basketball fan can produce, and having a strain put on a relationship as one of the least desirable aspects of being a fan, are there people who somehow manage to have the good part without the bad? The answer, as Table 25 illustrates, is yes, quite a few do. It should be taken as good news that fans who have managed to make a new friend without having a strain put on a relationship outnumber by 2-to-1 fans who have had the precise opposite experience.

Table 25. Friendship Without Strain

On Account of Carolina basketball I....

Have not made a new friend and have not had a strain on a relationship	29.3%
Have not made a new friend and have had a strain on a relationship	14.2%
Have made a new friend and have had a strain on a relationship	27.5%
Have made a new friend and have not had a strain on a relationship	29.0%

What this section has established, then, is that greater intensity in following Carolina is in fact associated with greater likelihood of having certain negative experiences. But it is also associated with at least one really good experience, making a new friend; and it is true that being an intense fan does not guarantee that one will have a conflict in a relationship. The relationship between fan intensity and relationship conflict is only a tendency, and does not determine how it will go for every single person. Moreover, it needs to be stressed that having had a strain placed on a relationship in the past does not mean that one cannot be a healthy fan or that one's usual experience of being a fan is riddled with such conflicts. Even so, it is surely useful to be aware that certain kinds of fans—in short, the less intense fans, and especially those who can process losses quickly—are less likely to experience such conflicts.

SUMMARY OF MAIN FINDINGS OF CHAPTER SIX

- About half of hard-core North Carolina fans now live outside the state of North Carolina. Over 70% of fans either attended UNC or grew up in North Carolina. The average Carolina fan has been following the team since age 10 or 11.
- An overwhelming majority of North Carolina fans associate the program with positive values such as loyalty, integrity, honesty and teamwork. Most Carolina fans say they cannot imagine no longer following the team. Those who can cite a change in the character of the program or an NCAA scandal as the most likely reasons they would lose interest.
- Most Carolina fans orient their schedule around the basketball team's during the season. Over 90% Carolina fans say being a fan is a matter of personal pride, and over 80% of Carolina fans need at least one day to get over losses.
- Nearly 80% of North Carolina fans are more likely to get mad at a referee, opponent or TV commentator than at a UNC player or coach while watching games.
- Over three-quarters of Carolina fans have another Tar Heel fan in their immediate family. About one-half have a fan of another school in their family, however. Nearly one-half of the

fans say their parents played a role in their becoming a fan, and over two-thirds of the fans expect to encourage their children to become Carolina fans.

- Just over one-half of Carolina fans have made a friend through Carolina basketball. More than 40% of fans say that being a Carolina fan has caused a strain in a relationship. Over half of Carolina fans have had a passionate argument about Carolina basketball with another Carolina fan, and over 80% have had an argument about basketball with a fan of another school.

- Fans who take losses harder, devote more of their schedule to UNC basketball, and say being a fan is a matter of personal pride are more likely to have been in an argument with someone else about UNC basketball, or to have experienced a strain in a relationship on account of UNC basketball. However, these more intense fans are also somewhat more likely than other fans to have made a friend through Carolina basketball.

7

A Few Words (Including Some Kind Ones) About Duke

In February 1988, President Ronald Reagan paid a brief visit to Duke University for a panel discussion about fighting drug use in America. Fred Kiger arranged for our American History class at Chapel Hill High to zip over to Durham to get a glimpse of the Commander in Chief as he arrived by helicopter. As we milled around in the crowd waiting for President Reagan to land and wave at us, Danny Ferry and the Duke basketball team walked by our class and stood in the crowd. Standing about 15 feet away and in something of a punchy mood, I shouted out one or two mildly derogatory comments about Ferry. Ferry was certainly within earshot, but pretended not to hear anything—but then I noticed that Mike Krzyzewski was looking at me. I smiled a little sheepishly and said with a shrug of the shoulders, "We're from Chapel Hill." He responded with a knowing grin, and I stopped yelling at Ferry.

That exchange represents the sum total of my interaction with Duke's head basketball coach. But by then I had already formed an impression of Duke basketball: They were the archrivals, and they stood for different things than what Carolina stood for, and I liked (and still like) what Carolina stood for better, on the whole. But I also thought that there was indeed something powerful about Duke basketball, specifically the relationship between the team and the student body. Going to two games in Cameron with a friend during the 1987 season had shaped that impression, and returning in 1999 to watch from press row as Carolina tried to upset the Blue Devils confirmed it. Shortly after that game, I wrote an article titled "The Virtues of Duke Basketball," which tried to make the point that perhaps there are some admirable things about the phenomenon of Duke basketball. The article provoked more reaction than any other piece I published in five seasons at *Inside Carolina,* from both Duke fans (who were mostly thrilled by it) and Carolina fans (most of whom appreciated it, some of whom definitely did not).

Writing that piece was informed not just by the visit to Cameron, but by an earlier, conscious decision, a decision made when it became quite evident that Duke had assembled a nucleus in the late 1990s that would likely be top five nationally for several years running. The decision was simply that I would not let whatever Duke did or didn't do affect my perceptions of how well Carolina was doing (except, of course, when the schools met head to head). And at the end of the 2001 season, the issue of how Carolina fans would deal with Duke's fantastic success came to the fore again, in the strongest possible fashion: Mike Krzyzewski won his third national title, surpassing Dean Smith's two titles, and looked likely to win at least another one at some point before retiring. After Matt Doherty coached Carolina to a famous win in Cameron in January, Duke took the once No. 1 Tar Heels to the cleaners twice in a week in March, adding to the hurt. And Krzyzewski looked like he might even be able to break Dean Smith's record for all-time wins, if he wanted to. All those considerations led some to conclude that maybe Duke had really pulled away from Carolina in terms of on-court success.

Whether that is true over the long term remains to be seen. (I wouldn't bet the house on it.) But the possibility that Duke may have claimed, and be in a position to maintain, local and national superiority opens again one of the central questions raised by this book: What does it really mean to be a Carolina fan? Is it fundamentally based on being No. 1, or on being better than all rivals? Or is it based on identification with certain values, certain conceptions of what a college basketball program should look like, even certain conceptions of what a university is for? For fans who fall in the latter camp, Duke's success need not be a major source of jealousy (although, naturally, perhaps a little angst!). These fans can respond to any and all Duke triumphs simply by saying, "Yeah, but I'd rather be a Carolina fan and lose in the NCAA second round than be a Duke fan and win the whole thing," not as a saccharine rationalization for tournament failure, but as a sincere statement that one is a Carolina fan for reasons that transcend whether the Tar Heels beat Duke or go farther than the Blue Devils in the tournament.

How then, do Carolina fans view Duke basketball? And how do they view Duke University? The North Carolina Basketball Fan Survey asked precisely those questions, questions which generated not only some interesting aggregate findings but also inspired a number of interesting observations by Carolina fans.

Table 26. Carolina Fans' Appraisal of Duke Basketball

	All Respondents	Fans Over 40	UNC Alumni
Positive	37.8%	46.0%	34.1%
Mixed	22.5%	21.2%	23.1%
Negative	39.7%	29.9%	42.8%

Given all the media hype surrounding the Duke–North Carolina rivalry, the story told by Table 26 may be a bit surprising: Carolina fans are evenly split in their evaluation of Duke's basketball program. Carolina fans aged 40 and over, however, are more likely to have a positive rather than a negative appraisal of Duke basketball, indicating that the rivalry may be felt most intensely among the younger fans. UNC alumni are also more likely than other Carolina fans to take a harsh view of Duke basketball.

To be sure, the finding that almost as many Carolina fans have a positive appraisal of Duke as a negative appraisal understates Tar Heel antipathy toward the Blue Devils: A very common response to this question was, "I hate them, but I respect their program," an answer which was recorded as a positive appraisal. Answers recorded as "mixed" were those that included positive comments as well as specific negative comments about some aspect of Duke basketball (e.g., "their coach uses bad language") beyond simply saying one disliked the team. Answers recorded as "negative" were those that were entirely negative in tone.

The following quotations from Carolina fans are representative of those fans who had a predominantly negative appraisal of Duke basketball:

- "In a nutshell, my hatred for Dook is like the burning intensity of 10,000 white hot stars. If Dook played a team called Satan's Minions, I'd pull for Satan."

  —Mark Lavender, 30, accountant in Apex

- "Intellectually, I respect their success. Emotionally, they are the enemy and must be mocked and destroyed."   —Cassandra Sherrill, 30, graphic designer in Winston-Salem

- "Dean never would have petitioned the NCAA to take losses from his record."

  —Preston Humphreys, 24, accountant in Atlanta

- On Duke: "Apparently, according to my wife and her family, they sacrifice children before the games."   —30-year-old lawyer in Atlanta who became a fan through his wife and in-laws

But, as noted, over 60% of Carolina fans had a more nuanced reaction to the invocation of Duke basketball. Consider the thoughtful comments by these fans:

- "I don't ever want to see [Carolina] play Duke in the NCAA tournament. The pressure leading up to the game, the stress on me, their fans as well as the players and coaches would be too much. Even if we won, I would not want to see that. It's not worth the risk. I really have thought about it for years, and have not changed my thoughts on it at all. Even if we beat them 20 straight times afterward, it would still never be enough."

  —Jon Sasser, 28, television producer in Virginia Beach

- "What would Carolina have been without Duke for the past 15 years? The ACC would have been much less interesting."   —Scott Ashcraft, 33, archaeologist in Asheville

- "Many, many people take Carolina, and especially Carolina vs. Duke, far too seriously in this area. The rivalry is fantastic, but the kids who represent each school are often friends off the court, and fans lose that type of perspective. I love UNC basketball (and football) as a hobby, and for fun. I wish all Carolina and Duke fans could say the same."

  —Tom Wilson, 25, Chapel Hill resident

Steve Hale scores on a lay-up against Duke in the opening game of the Smith Center, 1986

To what extent does antipathy toward Duke basketball spill over into antipathy toward Duke University as an institution? Table 27 provides an answer to that question.

Table 27. Carolina Fans' Appraisal of Duke University as an Educational Institution

	All Fans	*Fans Over 40*	*UNC Alumni*
Positive*	79.2%	81.2%	75.7%
Mixed /Don't Know	10.4%	9.8%	13.7%
Negative	10.4%	9.0%	10.6%

*21.9% of predominantly "Positive" appraisals of Duke University also claimed that it has important drawbacks, such as being overrated, too expensive, mainly for rich kids, or snobby.

Only 10% of Carolina fans offered a thoroughly negative assessment of Duke as a school. One way to interpret that finding is that about 90% of Carolina fans are not so blinded by their dislike of Duke basketball that they fail to recognize that Duke University does some good things. In fact, most Carolina fans specifically credited Duke as a good educational institution, or praised the Duke Hospital, or expressed admiration for Duke Chapel. Another way to interpret the data is to credit Duke University with having done a spectacular public relations job, such that 80% of its archrival's fans think of it highly. I doubt that similar numbers would emerge if you asked Alabama fans their views about Auburn or Texas fans about Texas A&M.

However, a substantial portion of fans gave "mixed" reviews of Duke University, saying that while the school was good, it had significant drawbacks, and over 20% of those fans who had a mostly positive appraisal of Duke tossed in a negative remark (such as that Duke students are snobby or that Duke is overrated by the media). The following quote is a good example of a Carolina fan praising Duke, but not without taking the chance to get a couple of jabs in:

- "Excellent school. Of course, one must ignore the fact that the architecture is faux Princeton (itself faux Cambridge), and that all its money came from hawking a highly addictive carcinogenic substance to people...."
                    —William Knorpp, 38, professor of philosophy at James Madison University.
            (Professor Knorpp went on to add that he has great respect for Duke as a school.)

Critiques of Duke University by Carolina fans often come from opposite political perspectives: A liberal critique of Duke, for instance, is that it caters to rich students, is snobby, lacks the public mission of a UNC, and is not well-integrated into the Durham community. A conservative critique of Duke holds that it is too liberal and politically correct, that it caters to elitist Northerners, and that it is located in Durham, with "Durham" understood in a pejorative sense. Both the left and the right critique of Duke often express the view that the school is too expensive, especially compared to Carolina.

The following quotations give a good sense of how these more critical Carolina fans feel about Duke University:

- "They represent the rich, elitist, success, and ego-driven Republican world I abhor."
                    —David Russell, 25, Peace Corps volunteer in Benin

- "I don't like Duke. I often find the team smug and elitist. I don't care for Coach K (partially because of his politics)."   —35-year-old college professor in North Carolina

- "Most of the Dook fans that I have met have what I would characterize as 'ego' and 'insecurity' issues."   —30-year-old alumnus in Raleigh

- " [Duke education] is good, in a carpetbagging sort of way."
                    —Terri Tarheel, 45, paralegal in Jacksonville, NC

What are we to make of these comments, about both Duke University and the Duke basketball team? Carolina fans really do feel that UNC is in some moral sense more laudable than Duke. For some, this is because they like Dean Smith liberalism and UNC's public mission better than Coach K's Republicanism. For others, it is based on a claim that Duke basketball is not run with as much class or as selflessly as Carolina. Many Carolina fans point to Mike Krzyzewski having losses removed from his coaching record from the 1995 season, or the way certain Duke seniors at times have disappeared on the bench at the end of their careers, as actions that "Dean would never have done." Others attack the composition of the Duke student body, based on their income levels and geographic origins. Still others claim that Duke is arrogant and haughty beyond its merits. And, above all, many Carolina fans point to the behavior of Duke's student body at basketball games as rude and undignified.

Whether these claims by Carolina fans about Duke are valid or not is beyond the scope of this chapter (although if I were answering the survey, my evaluation of Duke basketball would have been "mixed" and my assessment of Duke education "positive"). What is important are the twin observations that first, many Carolina fans' antipathy toward Duke basketball is intertwined with complex and sometimes contradictory social and political critiques of Duke as a private educational institution, and second, many Carolina fans are in the habit of pointing out Duke's supposed faults as a way to articulate why they think Carolina is better.

In my judgment, Carolina fans are correct to think that UNC basketball has over time stood for something somewhat different than Duke basketball, and they are also justified in preferring Carolina's distinctive virtues to Duke's. But those beliefs about what UNC basketball is about do not and should not depend on viewing Duke as unambiguously evil or the "enemy."

Go into a Duke locker room and talk to their players, and you will see young men who are just as impressive and likeable as their counterparts in Chapel Hill. In terms of the basic function of promoting self-discipline, good habit formation and a sense of team, and from those three building blocks promoting personal growth for the players in the program, Duke basketball seems to be very successful, indeed. One may not like aspects of Duke's overall coaching philosophy, and that's O.K. Even so, I see little reason that a preference for Carolina's historic philosophy should lead one to begrudge Duke's players whatever success they earn.

Moreover, Carolina fans should be aware that broad-based swipes at Duke such as those taken in some of the quotes noted above (and many others not reported here) can be a double-edged sword. An additional research strategy for this book might have been to ask other Big Four fans what *they* thought about Carolina fans, as a complement to Carolina fans' self-reported attitudes and habits. I did not carry out such research. But it is a good bet that a survey of non-Carolina fans living in the state of North Carolina would say that UNC fans are arrogant, spoiled, and full of themselves—many of the same criticisms that Carolina fans level at Duke supporters. And I'm not sure that such a characterization of Carolina fans by rival fans would be entirely without basis. This observation is simply by way of noting that Carolina fans might do well to keep their criticisms of Duke and its fans largely to themselves, on the "don't throw stones in glass houses" principle.

The final point to make in this brief chapter is this: It can be a liberating moment for Carolina fans to say, "Even if Duke wins five straight national titles and beats Carolina more than their share, my opinion of Carolina basketball will not change, and I'd still rather be a Carolina fan."

How many Carolina fans can with total honesty make that kind of statement is unclear, but the survey data suggests that at least a substantial portion can.

Or to put the principle more simply, one might say the following: "Like one's adversaries in politics, Duke is always going to be there. Why let its proximity to and competitiveness with UNC become a source of anxiety and pain, in which one is constantly comparing UNC to Duke? Why not instead let the rivalry be a source of pride and a chance to express appreciation for Carolina basketball's own distinctive values—secure in the knowledge that no matter what happens on the court on a given night or in a given season, those values will still be there?"

As in so many other areas of fanhood, Carolina supporters have the ability to make conscious choices about how to think about Duke. Those choices are likely to substantially affect the extent to which they can enjoy UNC basketball—and also the extent to which love of UNC basketball plays a healthy role, not a destructive one, in the lives of both individual fans and the communities to which they belong.

8

The North Carolina Basketball Fan Survey, Part Two

CAROLINA FANS AND THE GAME OF BASKETBALL

"I know this sounds weird, but I have found in pickup games that you can take two UNC fans who may be complete strangers against two non-UNC fans, and the UNC guys can play together as if they had been doing it for years. I mean they'll have an idea of what passes and moves and cuts their partner is going to make beforehand. I think this comes from years of watching the same UNC system of basketball. I think this is a phenomenal aspect of the Carolina/Dean Smith impact on basketball."

—Craig Partin, 40, hospital employee in Clayton, NC

"I think for the most part our fans are very knowledgeable when it comes to the game of basketball and how we play, how we play as a team, how we like to play defense. I think our fans are really aware of how important an assist is, how important a screen, a block-out, something like that is." *—Phil Ford*

We now turn to a rather different subject: The relationship between North Carolina fans and the game of basketball. The point may, upon reflection, be obvious, but what this data shows loud and clear is that the preponderance of hard-core fans of Carolina basketball love the game for its own sake, and have or have had a relationship with it apart from watching North Carolina play. As Table 28 shows, roughly three-fifths of fans currently play pickup basketball, a figure that surely reflects the relatively young demographic of the survey sample. But three-fifths of fans also report having played on a school team, and there is only a modest negative correlation between age and having played for a school team. Nearly 75% of these fans have pretended to be a Carolina player while shooting baskets, and nearly half (including three-fifths of those age 30 or under) have been to basketball camp. Nearly two-fifths of the respondents have coached basketball at some level, although that figure might be an overestimate. (Some rather young fans claimed to have experience in "coaching," which could be well true in the sense of giving informal instruction.) Yet even if we discard the teenagers claiming coaching experience, some 35% of the sample reports having been a coach.

Table 28. Personal Involvement of Carolina Fans With the Game of Basketball

Currently Play Pickup Basketball
Yes   58.9%
No   41.1%

Have Played Basketball on a School Team
Yes   59.4%
No   40.6%

Have Attended a Basketball Camp
Yes   48.5%
No   51.5%

Have Personally Attended UNC Basketball Camp
Yes   20.0%
No   80.0%

Have Pretended to Be a Carolina Player While Shooting Baskets
Yes   74.6%
No   25.4%

Have Coached Basketball, At Any Level
Yes   37.3%
No   62.7%

By any measure, these Carolina fans are quite involved with the game of basketball, and most have had significant experience in the sport as participants. One question I had in constructing the survey was whether people who had played basketball at a formal level or who had experience coaching would be more or less likely to get angry at North Carolina players and coaches during the games. For coaches, the answer is a bit surprising: people who have coached are somewhat more likely than other fans to direct their anger at Carolina players and coaches rather than at outsiders. This is not because being a coach makes one more likely to get angry at what UNC is doing wrong, but because coaches are about 10% less likely than other fans to get worked up about the officials, the TV guys or the opponents. Overall, however, coaches do follow the general trend of directing more anger at referees, opponents and TV commentators than at Carolina representatives, but in a less pronounced way. People who have played for a school team are also slightly more likely than other fans to direct their anger at Carolina players and coaches during a game, but the relationship is much weaker than is the case with coaches.

Do coaches and school players get over the losses faster than other fans? Both coaches and players are very slightly less likely than other fans to say they can get over a loss by the end of the day, but the effect is small and statistically insignificant. Most of the respondents who have "coached" are not full-time basketball coaches (although a few are), and most of those who have played for a school team never played in college (although a few have). Making strong generalizations about how being a full-time coach or a big-time player affects the way one sees and processes the games is beyond the capacity of this data. That fact, however, makes it all the more remarkable that there is such a robust relationship between having tried to coach basketball and being less likely to be perturbed by the opponents, the referees or the TV commentators during the game.

Participation in basketball is quite high among Carolina fans. So is consumption of basketball played by teams other than North Carolina. The survey asked fans how many college basketball games a week they watched, apart from the ones Carolina played in. Table 29 reports the results. The median fan watches three non-Carolina games a week, which, assuming they also watch two Carolina games, makes for a total of 10 hours a week spent watching college basketball. Women watch fewer non-Carolina games than male fans, and fans who watch more are also slightly more likely to say they have experienced a strain in a personal relationship resulting from basketball. While those findings point in an unsurprising direction, they are weak and of somewhat questionable statistical significance.

Table 29. College Basketball Junkies, or Just Carolina Basketball Junkies?

Number of College Basketball Games Not Involving Carolina
Watched In Typical Week During the Season

Zero	3.0%
0.1 to 1.5	20.0%
2.0–2.5	24.0%
3–3.5	13.3%
4–4.5	10.0%
5–9.5	20.2%
10 or more	9.5%

Average: 4.0   Median: 3.0

CAROLINA BASKETBALL FANS AND OTHER SPORTS

This leads us to the next topic: To what degree are Carolina basketball fans involved as spectators and participants in sports besides basketball? We can start answering this question by looking at how much Carolina men's basketball fans care about two other prominent sports played at UNC, football and women's basketball. Most Carolina men's basketball fans at least have a moderate interest in the football team. But if we assume that all of the respondents who took 45 minutes to fill out a survey on *uncbasketball.com* would say that their interest in Carolina basketball ranks "10" on a scale of 1–10, less than one-quarter of these basketball fans have an equal passion for football. Nor did any respondent say, "Well, I'm really more of a Carolina football fan, but basketball is not bad for the winter," or anything like that. Even so, about half of these basketball fans could be safely classified as pretty big Carolina football fans. Not surprisingly, interest in football is significantly higher among alumni.

As to women's basketball, a majority of fans confess minimal or no interest in Sylvia Hatchell's troops (although one male survey respondent did list being at the 1994 women's national title game as his all-time greatest moment as a Carolina basketball fan). Only 10% of men's basketball fans consider themselves big fans of the women's team. Interestingly, female fans were no more likely than male fans to follow the women's team; and female fans were just as big football fans as the men.

Table 30. Fans of Carolina Sports, or Fans of Just Carolina Basketball?

Survey Respondents' Interest in North Carolina Football, on a 1–10 scale

	All fans	*UNC Alumni*	*Women*
Little Interest (1–4)	26.5%	15.8%	26.8%
Moderate Interest (5–7)	25.6%	21.0%	30.3%
Heavy Interest (8–9)	24.1%	29.9%	17.9%
Hard-Core Interest (10)	23.8%	33.3%	25.0%
Average:	6.6	7.6	6.6
Median:	7.0	8.0	7.0

Survey Respondents' Interest in North Carolina Women's Basketball, on a 1–10 Scale

	All fans	*UNC Alumni*	*Women*
Little Interest (1–4)	59.2%	55.1%	64.3%
Moderate Interest (5–7)	31.1%	32.1%	26.8%
Heavy Interest (8–9)	7.8%	10.2%	7.1%
Hard-Core Interest (10)	2.0%	2.6%	1.8%
Average:	4.1	4.5	3.9
Median:	4.0	4.0	3.0

Do Carolina fans follow other sports teams not associated with UNC? As Table 31 shows, most, but not all, do. The average Carolina fan follows between one and three other teams. Frequently mentioned teams include the Atlanta Braves, the Dallas Cowboys, the Washington Redskins, the Carolina Panthers, the Boston Red Sox, various soccer teams and "any NBA team with a Carolina player on it." Many fans who said they followed specific teams added that they do not follow those teams with the same intensity as they follow Carolina basketball, although a handful said that other teams had an equal or higher place in their heart. Carolina basketball is clearly the main sports attachment for most of these respondents, but most find other sports teams to follow when basketball season is over.

Table 31. Ties to Other Sports Teams

Number of Non-UNC Sports Teams Followed By Carolina Fans*

Zero other teams	19.5%
One	31.9%
Two	21.0%
Three	16.9%
Four or more	10.7%

Average: 1.8 teams   Median: 1 team

*Some respondents said "all other ACC teams" or "any NBA team with a Carolina player on it" without mentioning any specific teams. Responses of this kind were counted as equivalent to cheering for one non-Carolina team.

We have already noted that some three-fifths of fans in this sample play pickup basketball. The survey also asked whether fans get exercise in ways besides playing basketball. As Table 32 shows, the vast majority do: 92% of all survey respondents get regular exercise, including 79% of those age 40 or over. Whatever else you say about Carolina fans, you can't say that watching basketball has turned them into couch potatoes.

Table 32. Sports and Exercise: The Athleticism of Fans

Number of Fans Who Play Pickup Basketball

Yes	58.9%
No	41.1%

Number of Fans Who Play Some Sport Besides Basketball
(Including Working Out, Jogging, Etc.)

Yes	86.6%
No	13.4%

Total Number of Fans Who Play Either Basketball or Another Sport

Yes, at least one	92.2%
No, neither	7.8%

Carolina Basketball and Other Activities

We have established that most Carolina basketball fans follow other sports, and that most participate in basketball or other sports. But what do they do—if anything!—besides sports? This is an important question not just because of its intrinsic interest, but because some social scientists, as discussed in Chapter Four, have worried about whether being an intense sports fan crowds out other, more desirable activities.

Obviously, the limitations of this survey make it impossible to make many finely graded judgements on this matter. The data here lacks the highly detailed information on personal habits and social and civic attachments which informs most contemporary "social capital" research. But the data does permit making the rough judgement that even these hard-core North Carolina basketball fans are not significantly worse off with respect to their ability to generate "social capital" than the average American—nor are they any better. At the same time, however, this does not mean that at least some of the enormous amount of time these fans sink into participating in and watching sports might not be better used in other pursuits or activities. Indeed, as Table 33 shows, sports-related activities were mentioned by over half the respondents as their primary free-time activity.

Table 33. How Do Carolina Fans Use Their Free Time?

Based on the first activity named by survey respondents in response to this question

1.	Sports (undifferentiated)	15.1%
2.	Basketball	12.4%
3.	Reading	11.4%
4.	Golf	9.9%
5.	Time With Family/Children	8.3%
6.	Assorted Sports*	4.8%
7.	Computer/Internet	4.6%
8.	Music	4.4%
9.	Outdoor Sports**	3.7%
10.	Time With Friends/Socializing	3.6%
11.	Coaching Sports	2.4%
12.	Movies/Films	2.2%
13.	Running/Jogging	2.0%
14.	Working Out/Weightlifting	1.9%
15.	Watching Television	1.7%
16.	Biking	1.4%
17.	Playing Tennis	1.2%
18.	Church/Volunteering	1.2%
19.	Gardening/Yard work	1.0%
	All Sports-Related Activities:	54.8%
	Everything Else	45.2%

*Includes Football, Soccer, Softball, Baseball, Karate, Judo, Horses, Lacrosse, Rowing, Rugby, Swimming, Boating, Skiing, Surfing, Volleyball, Wakeboarding and Walking.
** Includes Fishing, Camping, Hiking, Backpacking and Hunting.

It should be noted that many respondents listed more than one activity, sometimes including both sports-related and non-sports-related activities; and we cannot conclude from this data that the fans actually spend over half of their collective free time on sports (although it seems quite plausible that they in fact do). But the data does show that "sports" is what comes to mind first for most fans when they think of what they do with their free time, a finding which is telling in itself, whatever the actual distribution of time between sports and non-sports activities may be.

Another interesting finding from the data on fans' use of free time is that Carolina fans seem to be quite a literate bunch, with reading proving to be the third most popular free-time activity. (The 67 fans who listed reading first among free-time activities are significantly older, more liberal and more likely to be female than the rest of the sample.) Most fans also read the newspaper—not including the sports section—on a regular basis, as Table 34 shows. Studies have often found that regular newspaper readers are more involved and knowledgeable citizens than non-readers, and indeed, newspaper readers in this sample belong to substantially more organizations than do non-readers. Interestingly, though, there is no discernible correlation between saying one reads a paper and one's attitudes toward and experiences of Carolina basketball, with the exception that newspaper readers are slightly more likely than non-readers to have made a friend through Carolina basketball. But for the most part, it appears that you don't need an editor to know which way the ball bounces.

Table 34. Newspaper Readers

Percentage of Carolina Fans Saying They Read a Newspaper
(Not Sports Section) at Least Four Times a Week

Yes	75.7%
No	24.3%

Fans were also asked how many organizations they belong to, defining organizations as inclusively as possible (including, for instance, sports teams). As Table 35 shows, this sample tracks rather closely results from a recent national survey of nearly 30,000 individuals conducted by the Saguaro Seminar on Civic Engagement in America at Harvard University. The main difference is that these basketball fans appear more likely than the national sample not to belong to any organizations.* The basketball fans are also slightly less likely to belong to five or more organizations than the national sample.

In short, it appears that while the Carolina basketball supporters profiled here may be somewhat less likely to join organizations than other, these fans by and large mirror the larger society in their joining habits. That suggestion is consistent with earlier research on sports fans and social capital (discussed in Chapter Four) which suggests that there are some civic benefits from being a sports fan, but that devoting a great deal of time to spectator sports (especially watching them on TV) does not increase one's likelihood of being involved in the community. In any case, because

---

*The finding in Table 35 that 20% of respondents belong to no organizations may be a mild exaggeration (probably no greater than 1–2%) as it counts all non-respondents as belonging to zero organizations. For more information about the Harvard survey, see *www.ksg.harvard.edu/saguaro*.

the demographics of this sample of North Carolina fans differ in numerous important ways from the national sample of Americans in the Harvard survey, we cannot conclude with any certainty that being a Carolina fan *in itself* affects the likelihood one will join an organization.

Table 35. Joiners or Couch Potatoes? Organizational Ties of North Carolina Basketball Fans

Number of Organizations North Carolina Fans Report Belonging to

Zero	20.0%
One or Two	24.9%
Three or Four	29.9%
Five or More	25.3%

Average 3.1 Median 3.0

Number of Organizations Respondents in Saguaro Seminar Survey Report Belonging to

Zero	12.4%
One or Two	30.9%
Three or Four	24.8%
Five or More	31.9%

Table 36 describes the philanthropic habits of North Carolina fans, both for the sample as a whole and for older fans who, naturally, are more likely to have given money to organizations. The basic story is that fans are about twice as likely to have given money (in any amount) to an organization other than the University of North Carolina than to have given money to either the Rams' Club or UNC's academic programs. Most people who have been generous in giving to the university also have been generous outside the university: Nearly 90% of Rams Club donors in this survey, for instance, report giving money to organizations outside the university, as have 92% of donors to academics at Carolina. It is also worth nothing that 79% of Rams Clubs donors have also given money to academics at Carolina. In fact, only 4% of Rams Club donors say they give money to neither UNC academics nor other organizations. The vast majority of donors to UNC athletics also find other endeavors worthy of philanthropic support, just as the majority of hard-core Carolina fans think that non-UNC-related endeavors need their support more than either Carolina athletics or UNC academics.

Table 36. Carolina Basketball Fans and Philanthropy

	All Fans	*Fans Over 40*
Have You Ever Donated Money to UNC Athletics?		
Yes	37.5%	54.4%
No	62.5%	45.6%
To UNC Academics?		
Yes	41.7%	61.8%
No	58.3%	38.2%

To Any Other Organization Besides UNC?

Yes	75.6%	91.9%
No	24.4%	8.1%

Tickets, Books, and Videotape

This section takes brief note of three sorts of fan activities, all of which are likely to affect how fans perceive North Carolina basketball and to influence their views of the coaches and players. Tables 37, 38 and 39 describe how many games these hard-core fans have seen live, how many books they have read about Carolina basketball and whether they ever watch games on videotape after they are over. The vast majority of fans have seen a game in person (although the numbers of games attended varies widely), have looked at a book about Carolina basketball and do watch games on tape from time to time. Only about 2% of fans have *not* done any of those things.

Even so, it is worth reflecting upon that portion of these hard-core fans—12.7%—who have not yet participated in the fundamental fan activity of going to a game. Not surprisingly, those fans who have not attended a game are on average five years younger than the rest of the sample, although some 20% of these fans are over age 35. The other notable observation is that most of the people who responded to this survey—no doubt because of their relatively young aggregate age—have never known any building other than the Smith Center as Carolina basketball's home, a fact which at some level strikes the author as incredibly sad.

Table 37. Live and in Person: Attendance at UNC Basketball Games

Number of Games Attended at Carmichael Auditorium, 1966–1986

None	61.3%
1–5	18.0%
6–20	6.8%
21–49	7.9%
50 or More	6.0%

Average: 9.6 games. Median: 0 games

Number of Games Attended at the Smith Center, 1986–Present

None	28.8%
1–5	19.5%
6–20	21.3%
21–49	13.4%
50–99	11.0%
100 or More	6.0%

Average: 21.8 games. Median: 7.0 games

Number of Games Attended at Away or Neutral Sites

None	26.0%
1–5	41.6%
6–20	25.8%
21–49	4.9%
50 or More	1.7%

Average: 6.6 games   Median: 3.0 games

All Games Attended

None	12.7%
1–5	19.2%
6–20	22.0%
21–49	20.8%
50–99	15.1%
100–199	6.9%
200 or More	3.3%

Average: 38.0 games   Median: 17.0 games

Table 38. Is Your Library Carolina Blue?

Number of Books About Carolina Basketball Read by Carolina Fans

None	26.4%
One	22.2%
Two	15.9%
Three or Four	20.7%
Five or more	14.7%

Average: 2.2 books. Median: 2 books

Table 39. Repeat Viewing

Percentage of Carolina Fans Saying They Sometimes Videotape Games
To Watch Again Later

Yes	74.7%
No	25.3%

Interactions With Players and Coaches

We now turn to a discussion of how often Carolina basketball fans have not only seen their heroes play in person, but had a chance to meet them in real life. Table 40 reports the number of fans who have had interactions with a Carolina player or coach, or who know a player or a coach. The basic story is that while only a minority—albeit a quite significant minority—of fans personally know a player or coach, a great many fans have had a chance to *meet* a coach, or even more likely, a Carolina player, at some point.

Table 40. Fan Interactions With Carolina Players and Coaches

Personally Know a Current or Former UNC Player

	All	Live in Chapel Hill	Live in NC (not Chapel Hill)
Yes	27.1%	42.2%	31.1%
No	72.9%	57.8%	68.9%

Have Met a Current or Former UNC Player

	All	Live in Chapel Hill	Live in NC
Yes	78.4%	91.1%	87.4%
No	21.6%	8.9%	12.6%

Have Spoken For At Least 10 Minutes With a Current or Former UNC Player

	All	Live in Chapel Hill	Live in NC
Yes	46.9%	57.8%	52.0%
No	53.1%	42.2%	48.0%

Personally Know a Current or Former UNC Head or Assistant Coach

	All	Live in Chapel Hill	Live in NC
Yes	13.4%	22.2%	14.2%
No	86.6%	77.8%	85.8%

Have Met a Current or Former UNC Coach

	All	Live in Chapel Hill	Live in NC
Yes	56.4%	75.6%	63.4%
No	43.6%	24.4%	36.6%

Most fans who have met Carolina players and coaches have come away with a favorable impression (though a few fans say they have had a bad experience with a player refusing to sign an autograph, etc.). Getting to meet a player or coach—or even to simply exchange eye contact and a wink—has counted as a very memorable experience for many fans. Moreover, numerous fans cited being very impressed by the elephantine memory of Dean Smith, or by the friendliness of Bill Guthridge, Phil Ford or other coaches and players. The following quotes provide a good sample of the range of interaction fans have had with figures in UNC basketball, as well as how they feel about it.

- "When I was in the sixth grade, I was planning on writing a paper for school on the history of UNC basketball. I wrote to Coach Smith asking him for information. He sent me the current media guide along with a letter wishing me luck on the paper. Three months later, I went to his camp and brought the book with me. At one point during the week, I asked him to sign it for me. As he was signing it, he asked me where I had gotten it. I reminded him of the paper and he said, 'oh, okay,' and finished signing the book. As I walked away, I glanced down to see that he had written 'Best wishes to John, Dean Smith.' A few seconds later, I realized I had never told him my name. He remembered it from the letter I had written to him three months earlier. I will NEVER forget that." —John Floyd, 34, comedian and fan diarist

- "Every time I meet a player or coach, I instantly become a little kid. I put them all on a pedestal. No matter how old I get, I still look at these 18- to 22-year-olds as my heroes. Maybe that's wrong, but I feel good about it." —Jon Sasser, 28, television producer in Virginia Beach

- "The first and only time I met Dean Smith, I was shocked at how nervous and flustered I was." —Bradley Coxe, 32, attorney in Wilmington

- "I am friends with very close friends of Bill Guthridge and have met him through them. He is one of the nicest human beings in the world. In his first year as Carolina coach, he took time to write—handwrite—a note to me after my dog died. (Daisy was a little terrier in a Carolina t-shirt who was in an issue of *Carolina Blue*.) His kindness was stunning. I showed the note to several close friends here who are basketball fans, and each of them was literally speechless, and could think of no other person in his position who would take the time for such kindness." —Peggy Heilig, realtor in Champaign, IL

- "Coach Smith used to come into the video store I worked for in college. He was very gracious and very quiet, didn't want to talk about basketball. I respected his wishes and never said one word about ball, just movies. It helped me realize that he and other sports figures are people also. They have lives, families and also enjoy their down time." —Ben Moore, 29, technical director for a TV station in Charlottesville

- "I met Phil Ford at a Lowe's store when he was signing autographs about six years ago. I was so impressed with him. I had a high school friend (Freddie Kiger) who teaches in Chapel Hill and was there at the same time I was there. He used to keep stats for the Heels and Phil knew him and we shared some info on Freddie. But what impressed me the most was Phil's candidness about his problem with alcohol (he brought it up) and the true love he had for Dean Smith and the UNC program. Phil was open with me (a stranger) about his problem and told me he had to deal with being an alcoholic on a daily basis and how hard it was, but that he had tremendous support from his fellow coaches. There was total sincerity in what he said, and I felt so much for him when it was announced that he had had the DUIs, because I believe he was really fighting against what I believe is a terrible disease that not everyone can control." —Tim Hauser, 49, retired from Lowe's in Wilkesboro, NC

- "In the late fall of 1974 (when I was 12), when Phil Ford was beginning his freshman season, the Heels came to my hometown of Asheville. I was getting some autographs, and Bill Guthridge, having recognized me from the prior summer's basketball camp, asked me if I was coming back to camp the next year. I was shocked that he would have remembered me. Needless to say, I was one of the few who had no criticism of Coach Guthridge when he was head coach." —Ben Baldwin, 39, lawyer in Charlotte

- "I met Phil Ford at an Atlanta alumni function. My wife and I were impressed with his love for Carolina and his outgoing manner. He and I share a battle with alcohol, and he is in my prayers daily. Very few have done more for our school."

  —David Potts, 58, salesman in Atlanta

- "I've always told my friends that I beat Rasheed [Wallace] in a game of one-on-one. And I did, down in the Student Union in the arcade. Needless to say, he is just as animated playing video games as he is playing real ball."   —Chris Everhart, 26, disc jockey in Salisbury, NC

- "I sat next to Bill Guthridge on a plane once—he was so friendly and willing to talk to a fan. I have so much respect for him and all of the coaches."

  —Caroline Goodwin Wilson, 27, alumna and business owner in Raleigh

- "When I met Brendan Haywood, I got a picture with him and he lifted me up and stuff. And I went to Jason Capel and Kris Lang's dorm and gave their roommate a shirt to sign, but they weren't there. I gave them my address and about two months later I received a package in the mail and they signed my shirt. I was so surprised and happy because I didn't think they would spend the time to send me the shirt. They must be really nice people."

  —Carl Richburg, 14, fan in Mason, Ohio

- "When I was in Chapel Hill two summers ago my father introduced me to the secretaries in the basketball office whom his father had become very good friends with over the last 10 years or so. The way they treated me was outstanding. They made me feel like part of the family. I got to talk to players and coaches alike. It was an awesome experience."

  —Brian Bibey, 20, student in Pittsburgh

- "Dean Smith was sitting with my mom at a UNC dinner and Mom mentioned that his daughter, Sandy, was my day camp counselor and a lovely person. Dean noted that she got her looks from her mother, then said, 'But of course, she can't do this'—and stuck his tongue out to touch the end of his nose. I always thought that story showed that Coach Smith didn't take himself too seriously."

  —Peter Cashwell, 38, teacher in Woodberry Forest, VA

The dynamic of interactions between well-known people and fans who have their posters on the wall is a subject unto itself. What is interesting to note here is that while UNC basketball has had a reputation of not being very open or forthcoming with the media, of keeping problems or conflicts in-house as much as possible, and of carefully parceling out media access, the human beings inside the program, starting with the coaches, are all quite open to interactions with fans and well-wishers—at least to a certain extent. Carolina's players and coaches are not remote, unreachable rock stars protected from the public by layers of security, and most hard-core Carolina fans have gotten the chance firsthand to see that the objects of so much media attention and hype are, in the end, just people. Moreover, a significant number of hard-core fans have had

Sam Perkins signs an autograph for Joan Williamson in 1982. At left is Chris Brust.

more than just fleeting interactions with players and coaches and report that they know at least one as a friend.

Does simply having met a Carolina player or coach have any discernible effect on one's habits as a fan? The short answer to this question is, probably not. It is true, however, that people who have at least met a player or coach are likely to be more intense fans than those who have not: Meeting a player or coach is positively correlated with being proud to be a UNC fan and with scheduling one's life around the team. Overcommitted Fans, as described in Chapter Six, are substantially more likely to have met or to know a coach or player than are other fans. However, there is no clear reason why we should think that in most cases simply having met a player *causes* this increased intensity in fan behavior. The more probable explanation is that being an intense fan helps put one in a position to bump into a player or coach.

We might think that people who have met players or coaches might prove to be more sympathetic toward their efforts in games than those who have not. This does not appear to be the case. People who have met players are no more or less likely than other fans to get mad at players during the games. And people who have met coaches are in fact slightly more likely than those who have not to get mad at both coaches and players, although the effect is small.

What about people who not only have met coaches and players, but who also know them in an ongoing way? A more involved relationship with a coach or player is, interestingly, not correlated with thinking longer about losses or being "proud" to be a fan, but it does make one slightly more likely to schedule one's life around the games. And, people who know players are more likely to have had a strain in a relationship on account of UNC. (This is not the case for those who know coaches.)

How do people who personally know a player or coach react to the games themselves? It turns out that these people are no more or less likely to get mad at a UNC player or coach than are other fans. Interestingly, however, they are slightly more likely than other fans to get mad at an outsider—a TV commentator, an official, an opponent. This seems to indicate that people who know participants directly do get wound up by the games more than other fans, but they direct their excess anger at people not involved with UNC.

The safest summary statement, however, is that meeting or even knowing a player or coach does not tend to have a very powerful impact on fans' habits. But interactions with Carolina players or coaches do count as important, constitutive moments for many individual fans, moments that can be referred back to in reflecting upon or explaining why one is a fan; or put another way, moments that one can brag about to one's friends.

As for those who have admired their heroes only from afar, this data suggests that, in time, most will indeed have a brush with someone associated with Carolina basketball—especially if they happen to live in North Carolina.

Q. How does it make you feel when you meet fans who say you are a really important person in their life?

A. I know I'm not important, and they think so sometimes. And sometimes, it's just very normal, I cheer for Carolina, great. I'm always happy to see a Carolina fan.... I don't think it should be so [important], nor is it, it's just another human being meeting another human being. —Dean Smith

Q. When someone comes up to you for the 5000th time and pats you on the back and says hello, does that still mean something to you?

A. That means a lot. Any time I'm asked for an autograph, I'll sign my autograph and at the bottom say "thank you," and I really mean that. You think of all the young men that play basketball in the United States, for me to have the opportunity to play at the University of North Carolina, which I consider the best school in America—I'm sure I'm a little prejudiced to that—to be recognized by our fans, who I think are fairly knowledgeable as to the game of basketball, is just an unbelievable feeling.

—Phil Ford

Michael Brooker signs an autograph for a young fan at Dartmouth College, December 1998.

How Fans View the Past

I suggested in Chapter Four that an important part of the art of being an intense fan while not letting other people's achievements dictate one's life is the ability to maximize identification with the team during good times while maximizing one's separation from the team when they suffer defeat. Perhaps paradoxically, however, this book has also suggested that part of being a *good* fan is an ability to empathize with and appreciate participants when they put in what turns out to be a losing effort.

Another important fan skill, one would think, is being able to derive more pleasure from the wins than pain from the losses—even though almost every fan who has been around the block a couple of times understands that pain is part of what makes the pleasure of winning so overwhelming. So an important question to ask of Carolina fans is how they view the past. Do they think about wins more than losses when reflecting upon the past?

The survey asked that last question directly. Do Carolina fans look back and think, "Wow, this has been a pretty amazing run," or do they say, "A bounce here or a bounce there, and we could have had so many more national championships"? As Table 41 shows, hard-core Carolina fans in the aggregate do lean to the bright side, with older fans having slightly sunnier memories than other fans. Survey respondents were four times more likely to say they remembered mostly the wins than to say they remembered mostly the losses. But the majority of Carolina fans lie right in the middle, thinking about wins and losses in about equal measure.

Table 41. Is the Past a Happy Memory?

When Thinking About Past Carolina Games, Do You Focus Mostly on Wins or Mostly on Losses? Answer On a 1–10 Scale

	All Fans	Fans Over 40
Fans Who Think Mostly About Losses (1–3)	9.4%	9.6%
Fans Who Think About Both (4–6)	53.0%	47.0%
Fans Who Think Mostly About Wins (7–10)	37.6%	43.4%
Average	5.8	6.0
Median	5.0	6.0

That is an interesting finding, especially if we combine it with the plausible assumption that most hard-core, long-term fans view attachment to Carolina basketball as a positive thing in their lives. To recall, fully two-thirds of these fans can't imagine no longer following the Tar Heels, under any circumstances. But whatever it is that makes Carolina basketball a good thing in their lives, it's not, on the whole, the fact that by virtue of cheering for a winning team, fans have unambiguously happier memories since they have more wins than losses to reflect upon. In reality, the losses are all the more intense for being few, or for frequently occurring just one or two steps short of the national championship. One might make a good case for why fans *should* think much more about the wins and just forget the losses, but this data shows that the majority of fans don't do that.

It should be added, however, that, this finding does not mean that there are not very real psychic benefits from cheering for a winner. But the benefits of winning don't appear in the sense that Carolina fans have more happy memories than sad ones. Carolina fans do focus their memories more on wins than losses, but as Table 41 shows, only to a slight degree overall.

Rather, the benefits from cheering for UNC appear to be connected to first, ongoing satisfaction with Carolina's long run of consistently good teams, and second, peak positive experiences that Carolina fans have experienced: in particular the thrill of winning the national championship. The overwhelming majority of survey respondents indicated that they thought about Carolina's past national titles on a periodic basis (and only a tiny handful said they "never" did). Carolina winning the title stands out as important markers in many of these fans' lives, and thinking back on the past titles provides a window for thinking about where one was and what was going on in one's life when it happened.

National titles are not the only memories important to Carolina fans, of course. Table 42 provides a list of the best memories of hard-core Carolina fans. And there are bad memories, too,

North Carolina fans inside the New Orleans Superdome celebrate the 1982 NCAA Championship.

which Table 43 lists. But my strong suspicion is that, for the average fan, the peaks of the highest highs really do exceed the lowest lows—even though one may spend nearly as much time remembering the lows as the highs.

One final point: the fact that fans spend almost as much time recalling disappointments as they do triumphs indicates that fans are attached to Carolina for reasons distinct from and not reducible to the "psychic benefits" wins provide. One might assume that, since Carolina is a proven winner, there are many fans who jump on bandwagon-style because they like winners. But that phenomenon is a fairly marginal one among the fans portrayed in this survey, who cite everything from family ties to ethical values in explaining why they are fans, and who frequently claim that they don't want to cheer for a win-at-all-costs team and that they would not abandon ship if the team started losing. Psychic benefits from reflecting on winning surely help explain part of the loyalty of hard-core Carolina fans, but those benefits are simply not powerful enough to explain all and probably not even most of it. Carolina fans remain Carolina fans, even when they expect to be thinking about losses almost half the time.

Table 42. Best UNC Memories of Survey Respondents

All Fans

1.	1993 National Championship	22.1%
2.	1982 National Championship*	21.6%
3.	2000 South Regional Championship	5.4%
4.	1974 home win over Duke	4.6%
5.	1998 home win over Duke	4.2%
6.	1995 away win over Duke	3.4%
7.	Dean Smith's 877th win to gain all-time record, 1997	2.9%
8.	1993 home win over Florida State	2.5%
9.	All wins over Duke	2.2%
10.	1983 home win over Virginia	2.0%
11.	Dean Smith	1.9%
11.	1957 National Championship	1.9%
13.	Phil Ford	1.2%
14.	1979 away win over North Carolina State	1.0%

Fans Age 40 and Over

1.	1982 National Championship*	34.3%
2.	1974 home win over Duke	13.4%
3.	1957 National Championship	8.2%
4.	1993 National Championship	5.2%
5.	Dean Smith	4.5%
6.	1979 away win over North Carolina State	3.7%
7.	Phil Ford	3.0%

*Includes those who listed both 1982 and 1993 as their best memory.

Table 43. Carolina Fans' Worst Memories

All Fans

1.	1999 Loss in NCAA Tournament to Weber State	13.7%
2.	1994 Loss in NCAA Tournament to Boston College	10.3%
2.	All Losses to Duke	10.3%
4.	1998 Loss in NCAA Tournament to Utah	10.1%
5.	Dean Smith's retirement	6.9%
6.	1984 Loss in NCAA Tournament to Indiana	6.3%
7.	1977 Loss in NCAA Tournament to Marquette	4.6%
8.	Makhtar Ndiaye incident at 1998 Final Four	2.9%
9.	2000 Regular Season	2.5%
10.	1981 Loss in NCAA Tournament to Indiana	2.2%
11.	1991 Loss in NCAA Tournament to Kansas	1.9%
11.	1995 Loss in NCAA Tournament to Arkansas	1.9%
13.	1971 Loss in ACC Tournament to South Carolina	1.5%
14.	Roy Williams Remaining at Kansas in 2000	1.2%
14.	1972 Loss in NCAA Tournament to Florida State	1.2%
16.	1994 Season as a Whole	1.0%

Fans Age 40 and Over

1.	1977 Loss in NCAA Tournament to Marquette	11.9%
2.	All Losses to Duke	10.4%
3.	1984 Loss in NCAA Tournament to Indiana	9.6%
4.	1971 Loss in ACC Tournament to South Carolina	6.7%
5.	1972 Loss in NCAA Tournament to Florida State	5.2%
5.	Dean Smith's Retirement	5.2%
5.	1981 Loss in NCAA Tournament to Indiana	5.2%
5.	1999 Loss in NCAA Tournament to Weber State	5.2%
9.	1994 Loss to NCAA Tournament to Boston College/ 1994 Season as Whole	4.4%
10.	Makhtar Ndiaye incident at 1998 Final Four	3.6%

HOW CAROLINA FANS VIEW THE COLLEGE GAME

Four questions were asked which bear on how North Carolina fans view the state of college basketball and its future. The questions were simple:

- How corrupt do you think college basketball currently is?
- Do you think players get too much attention?
- Would you support players being paid?
- How different do you think college basketball will be in 20 years?

Tables 44, 45, 46, and 47 describes Carolina fans' responses to those questions. The basic story is that fans are split right down the middle on these issues with most fans having pretty moderate views about the state of college basketball. Just 16% of fans think dramatic changes in college basketball are likely to emerge in the next 20 years, and only one-quarter of fans were willing to portray college basketball as mostly corrupt. Fewer than half support players being paid, and about 25% say basketball players get too much attention (answering 7 or higher on a 1–10 scale.). Less than 5% believe all of the following: College basketball is very corrupt (7 or higher on a 1–10 scale), players get too much attention, and players should get paid.

Table 44. How Corrupt Is College Basketball?

	All Fans	Fans Over 40
Pretty Clean (1–2)	5.0%	6.6%
A Few Problems (3–4)	31.2%	37.9%
Somewhat Corrupt (5–6)	38.1%	29.2%
Very Corrupt (7–8)	22.5%	22.7%
Morally Bankrupt (9–10)	3.2%	3.6%
Average	5.2	5.0
Median	5.0	5.0

Table 45. Do College Basketball Players Get Too Much Attention?

	All Fans	Fans Over 40
Not at all (1–2)	25.5%	20.6%
A Little Too Much (3–4)	25.8%	19.1%
A Bit Much (5–6)	23.5%	19.1%
Too Much (7–8)	17.8%	27.2%
Much Too Much (9–10)	7.4%	14.0%
Average	4.5	5.3
Median	4.0	5.0

Table 46. Should College Basketball Players Be Paid?

	All Fans	Fans Over 40
Yes	43.3%	48.9%
No	56.7%	51.1%

Table 47. Into the Crystal Ball: How Much Will College Basketball Change?

Survey Respondents' Views on What College Basketball Will Look Like in 20 Years, Based on 1 (Radically Different or Non-Existent) to 10 (No Change) Scale

	All Fans	Fans Over 40
Radically Different (1)	3.4%	5.2%
Big Changes (2–3)	12.7%	15.5%
Moderate Change (4–6)	44.5%	39.3%
Little Change (7–9)	36.8%	38.5%
No Change (10)	2.7%	1.5%
Average	5.7	5.5
Median	6.0	5.0

These different measures of fans' discontent with the structure of college basketball are correlated with one another, but only imperfectly so. People who believe that the players get too much attention and that the game is corrupt are more likely to think that big change is on the way in the next generation. But believing the game is corrupt is not significantly correlated with support for one specific oft-proposed change—paying players. Similarly, more liberal fans are more likely than others to say college basketball is corrupt and that players get too much attention, but liberalism has no evident effect on the likelihood that a fan would think players should be paid.

Older fans differ from younger fans with respect to two of these issues. Older fans are much more likely than younger fans to say that basketball players get too much attention, which is not surprising, and they are somewhat more likely than younger fans to support paying players, which is a bit surprising. But age has little or no effect on the likelihood of a fan making the diagnosis that the game is corrupt, and it has little or no effect on the likelihood that a fan would think big changes are in sight in college basketball.

Finally, more intense fans do not differ from less intense fans in any substantial or consistent way in their assessments of college basketball. Those Carolina fans who do think the college game has serious defects or commands too much attention are in general no less likely to be intense, involved fans than those who are not very worried about such issues. For instance, if we consider the 8% of fans who meet the criteria of being an "Overcommitted Fan" (see Chapter Six), 28%—for all the time they spend on basketball—substantially agree (7 or higher on 1–10 scale) with the statement that college basketball players get too much attention, compared to 25% of the sample as a whole. True, the small minority of fans who say they are not "proud" to be fans are substantially more likely than most fans to also think college basketball is corrupt. But for the most part, having the view that something is rotten in the state of Denmark with respect to basketball, or the view that college basketball and athletics command too much public attention, does little to dilute the intensity of the Carolina fans who responded to this survey.

On the other hand, scheduling one's life around the games and thinking about losses for a long time are both substantially connected with the belief that college basketball will not change so much over the next 20 years. Overcommitted Fans, however, are only slightly more likely than other fans to think that few changes are on the horizon.

To put it one way, the appeal of Carolina basketball is so strong to most hard-core fans that awareness of problems with college basketball is not nearly enough to drive them away from the game. To put it another way, it is not the case that involved, intense fans all mindlessly turn a blind eye to these issues. Many fans think there is something wrong with college basketball and worry that it gets too much attention, but love it anyway.

WHAT FANS WOULD CHANGE IF THEY COULD

Survey respondents were asked what one change they would make to Carolina basketball, given the opportunity. Notably, only a very small number of respondents, on the order of 1%, mentioned issues pertaining to the structure of college basketball in answering that question. Not many Carolina fans made this sort of comment in discussing what changes they'd like to see:

- "I work at UNC–Asheville, and I love that athletics is not emphasized like it is at UNC. Athletics can really detract from what should be a school's mission. UNC–A supports its athletes, but they're not worshipped. That's a much healthier attitude."
  —Stephen Brooks, 30, library assistant at UNC–Asheville

Instead, Carolina fans in overwhelming numbers said they wanted to see the Smith Center become a more student-dominated, electric environment for home games. Some changes in that direction certainly took place during the 2000–01 season, but even respondents who answered the survey during or after the 2001 season mentioned that issue more than any other.

Table 48 shows all the leading changes favored by Carolina fans—some of which are simply unattainable wishes. It is also worth noting that a significant percentage of North Carolina fans— nearly 10%—specifically said they wouldn't change a thing about Carolina basketball. Consider, for instance, this statement:

- "There are seasons when UNC had great teams but failed to win an NCAA championship that I of course would like to change. However, that is a selfish, short-sighted shallow fan tendency, in stark contrast to the values of Coach Smith and his honorable attempts to teach us and his players to put less emphasis on winning just to be No. 1."

—David Russell, 25, Peace Corps volunteer in Benin

Table 48. What Would Carolina Fans Change About Carolina Basketball, If They Could Change One Thing?

1.	Better Seating for Students in the Smith Center	21.8%
2.	Louder Crowds in the Smith Center	11.1%
3.	Nothing	9.7%
4.	More NCAA Titles	7.1%
5.	Dean Smith Still Head Coach	4.4%
6.	Better, More Supportive Fans	3.8%
7.	Always Beat Duke	2.9%
8.	No More Players Going Pro Early	2.7%
8.	More Athletic Players	2.7%
10.	More Intensity and Emotion	2.4%
10.	Better Ticket Availability	2.4%
12.	Bring Back Pressure Defense	2.0%

FANS ON OTHER FANS

The first two items listed in Table 48 refer to the Smith Center crowd on game night. The third most popular item was fans who said they didn't want any changes, and the next two items are a wish to have won more NCAA titles in the past and a wish to have Dean Smith still be the head coach, wishes that by their nature cannot be fulfilled. The sixth item mentioned most frequently by fans is a desire that Carolina have *better* fans—more supportive, more appreciative, less spoiled. (Only one respondent out of 606 expressed a desire that Carolina have *more* fans.) Beyond the Smith Center atmosphere issue, then, the second most salient issue bothering Carolina fans is the subject of the rest of this chapter: the behavior of *other* Carolina fans.

Survey respondents expressing unhappiness with other Carolina fans were often harsher on fellow Tar Heels than any Carolina-hating fan of a rival school could be. But some fans also argued that most Carolina fans are good fans. Consider this range of comments—as we see here, numerous fans specifically mentioned treatment of Bill Guthridge as an example of Carolina fans at their worst.

- "It bugs me that many fans do seem spoiled by being successful for so long. We don't appreciate what it takes to maintain the level of play from year to year, and Guthridge never got enough credit for what he did. I hope that is fixed as the years pass."

  —Jason Bates, 30, former *Daily Tar Heel* writer living in Washington

- "Some fans think that Carolina will naturally win all the time and don't seem to understand how hard it is to consistently win today."   —Peggy Heilig, realtor in Champaign, IL

- "Over the years, I've been a little disappointed in the lack of loyalty and class of the UNC fans. I hated the way they treated Guthridge—and I really hate the way they criticize players. Like the way they've treated Haywood."   —41-year-old marketing director in Greensboro

- "Bill Guthridge being disrespected over the last three years" is [my worst memory]. "The man went to two Final Fours and was instrumental as anyone else in the family of building the dynasty. The treatment he got by the press and Wal-Mart fans was reprehensible."

  —Ben Moore, 29, technical director for a TV station in Charlottesville

- "If you're going to sit in the lower level, stand up and cheer and don't socialize about how much money you made today or who you bribed to get the Ram Road built. The games are primarily for the undergrad students to enjoy—it de-energizes the arena to have the people who run North Carolina business and industry and their junior-league wives sit there to see and be seen. If they're gonna do that, do it on the mezzanine level. I don't care who fronted the money to build the arena. You could probably propose a bond statewide to improve the Dean Dome and it might pass (even though I don't think that should happen)."

  —Ramsay Hoke, 28, public health worker in Durham

- "I'm proud of [Carolina basketball], but also ashamed. Because most people associate Carolina basketball with being uppity and spoiled. And, unfortunately, most UNC fans don't do anything to shed that stigma. For those of us who don't want to be known that way, it's hard."

  —Wilson Hooper, 19, UNC student

- "I believe Coach Gut was treated very poorly by the press and the fans. I thought the fans were ridiculous ingrates. Gut was a great man who gave so much to Carolina basketball. I was very saddened by his decision to retire . . . He deserved far more respect and appreciation. No wonder Roy Williams decided to stay in Kansas."

  —Sharon Hodge, 39, doctoral student in Durham

- "I hate the bad rap our fans get, when I know so many who bleed Carolina blue. I am proud that I am not a fair weather fan!"   —Virginia Raby, 42, church employee in Raleigh

To be sure, while the vast majority of references to UNC players and coaches were positive in tone, a small handful of fans (about 2–3%) did offer specific criticisms of the abilities of individuals connected with Carolina basketball. (No survey question specifically asked fans to evaluate any particular individual associated with Carolina basketball, but there was plenty of room for fans to say anything they wanted over the course of the survey.) But such critical comments were outnumbered by comments, like some of those just reported, in which respondents expressed dismay at the way other fans have berated figures associated with Carolina basketball in the recent past.

Indeed, not a single respondent wrote that North Carolina fans are too soft on coaches, that they tolerate losses too much, or that they don't care about winning enough. On the other hand, not a single fan said, "I really don't care about the university or the kids or the values or any of the rest of this as long as they keep winning games." Yet, unless we are to believe that the fans who delivered criticisms of other Carolina fans like the ones made above are talking about figments of their imagination, attitudes like that do exist, and they do bother other Carolina fans. Unfortunately, while this survey does allow us to probe the degree to which Carolina fans exhibit certain undesirable behaviors and attitudes, it does not allow us to specify just how many Carolina fans are among the "ridiculous ingrates" referred to above.

But the overall force of this data suggests that the number of North Carolina supporters who thoroughly deserve the label of "ridiculous ingrates" is probably only a minority of fans. The values Carolina fans mention as a reason for supporting the team transcend issues of winning and losing. The scenarios which Carolina fans most often cite as a reason for no longer following the team have to do with issues of integrity. Most Carolina fans do not report getting very angry at UNC coaches and players during the games. And as we have just seen, a substantial number of Carolina fans hate the fact that any of their number could express ingratitude or shallow fan attitudes.

Even so, the fact is that Internet message boards—24 hours a day, seven days a week, all year long—are full of discussion about Carolina basketball, some of which reflects minimalist, win-at-all-costs attitudes toward being a fan. Talk radio in North Carolina is filled with similar perspectives. And when losses mount—whether it's Carolina having a four-game losing streak in January 2000 under Bill Guthridge or Carolina getting thumped by Duke twice in March 2001 under Matt Doherty—the outpouring of emotion and reaction from fans is undeniably negative and unpleasant. Quite obviously, the number of human beings actually posting negative messages or calling into talk radio shows to criticize is small. The real question is whether that small number of human beings is truly representative of most Carolina fans' attitudes.

The data presented here strongly suggests that it is not. Most Carolina fans support and appreciate the UNC program for stable, long-term reasons that are not easily shaken by the latest win or loss. In fact, this data has spotlighted seven identifiable forms of fan identification with Carolina basketball present among Carolina fans. Table 49 provides my best informed guess as to how many Carolina fans in this sample adhere to each type of fan identification.

Table 49. Seven Forms of Fan Identification With Carolina Basketball

	Estimated Percentage With Form of Identification
Personally Know Players and/or Coaches	30%
Admire the Political Values Associated with Dean Smith	30%
Part of My Community Identity/Connection With School I Attended	75%
Something I Share With My Family and Friends	85%
Admire the Values It Stands For	90%
Like the Way They Play the Game	95%
Like Them Because They Win	100%

Most Carolina fans have a more elevated sense of why they are Carolina fans beyond the fact that their team wins games, and also identify as Carolina fans for one of the other reasons. This does not mean that some of the people who are most vocal in attacking players or coaches or acting like "ridiculous ingrates" do not also hold one of the more elevated forms of fan identification. But it does mean that much of their speech reflects only the baseline concern with winning, not the loftier reasons for being a Carolina fan with which most hard-core fans at least partly identify.

If this conclusion is right—that the loud voices on the Internet and the talk radio shows are not a fair sample of how most Carolina fans think and behave—then there is good reason to be more optimistic about Carolina fans than the harsh assessments by some of Carolina's own fans suggest. And there is also good reason for seeing extreme negative utterances on the Internet and the talk radio in a rather different light: not as representative of all UNC fan opinion, but as a form of pollution produced by a certain kind of fan which, far from being representative of what the typical serious fan thinks, is often despised by many (though certainly not all) serious fans.

A second and perhaps more important conclusion, however, is to simply recognize once again the potential conflict between these forms of identification. Carolina fans like the Tar Heels because they win; they like them because they are seen as a class act that plays the game the right way; they like them because of the values associated with the program. When Carolina is winning night in and night out as they did for a long stretch of the 2001 season, all these reasons reinforce one another, and everyone's happy. When Carolina is not so successful, these forms of identification may conflict—both within individual fans and the fan base as a whole.

How both individual fans and fans as a whole negotiate such conflicts speaks volumes about whether Carolina's fans talk about values and so forth is in the end just so much hot air. And if Internet message boards after losses were one's only barometer, one might indeed conclude that all the lofty talk must be just hot air. This data suggests, however, that such a conclusion would be a big mistake.

WHAT IT ALL MEANS

"It would be my biggest dream come true to have anything to do with UNC."

—*Michael Hemphill, 17, high school basketball player in Brevard*

We have now looked in considerable detail at the habits, values, hopes, and attitudes of hard-core North Carolina basketball fans. In the conclusion of the book, I turn to the central question stated at the outset: What does it really mean that so many people are so heavily invested in North Carolina basketball?

But as a last step before taking up that question, I wish to turn the floor over to North Carolina fans themselves, many of whose thoughts on the subject are eloquent, insightful, and on occasion provocative. Consider these comments:

- "Dean Smith brought a sense of class, dignity, and decorum to the world of sports that so often lacks those very qualities. From what I can gather, Smith is a humble, flawed, giving teacher who treats those around him as though they are family. These are the qualities I most admire in him. More often than not, Carolina basketball makes me proud and gives me joy and what more can you ask for in today's world."

  —Brian Evans, 26, information architect in Lititz, PA

- "We live in a difficult world. Loyalties change, family values are not what they used to be, and it's harder for people to both figure out and do the right things in life. It's nice at times to have an emotionally safe haven where you can see these values in action, while at the same time enjoying the on-court success of a great sports program."

  —Jim Papajesk, 32, loan officer in Michigan

- "I can count on UNC basketball to be successful, year-in and year-out. It's consistent in an ever-changing world. I guess even bleeding-heart liberals want some things not to change."

  —Stephen Brooks, 30, library assistant in Asheville

- "It embodies what I think is important in life, and it is so much fun, to boot. It really has enhanced my life, led to friendships, helped me learn to deal with disappointment. It's just so many things."   —Jason Orndoff, 26, UNC Law School graduate

- "In all of the pressures that come with running a business and raising a family, UNC basketball has always given me a sense of comfort in a chaotic world."

  —Ty Stone, 32, alumnus living in Savannah, GA

- "At age 45, I realize that following the Tar Heels is one of the enduring themes of my life—one of those things that the man of 45 still has in common with the boy of 12."

  —Oren Coin, 45, office manger in Franklin, NC

- "To me, a very, very large chunk of what's important about Carolina comes from Dean. Despite his control freakishness and other minor negatives, I think he's an extraordinary person who has done so much good in NC that it's hard to even contemplate. My optimism about Carolina Hoops' future stems from the belief that future coaches will try to follow his example."   —David Spence, 42, college professor in Austin, Texas

- "In Buddhism, we know everything is connected. Carolina basketball is a way of life or a big part of one's life. It embodies all that 'good' character, teamwork, cooperation, leadership, results, etc. It's a way to be connected to fellow classmates, parents who are deceased, the beauty of Chapel Hill, the feeling of being with a winner."
  —Steve White, 35, retail manager in Atlanta

- "I love Carolina hoops because it represents everything that is best about college athletics, and, of course, because of its association with the university. As much as I love the program per se, I guess UNC hoops mostly has a grip on me because it represents something about the university itself. Dean built something really great there, something that is bigger than basketball and bigger than winning. I know it can't last forever...eventually, the crass desire to win will overpower Dean's vision of a program that puts honor and the good of the players first. But getting Matt and keeping the coaching job 'in the family' is a good step, and I'm just going to enjoy it as long as it lasts."
  —William Knorpp, 38, professor of philosophy, James Madison University

- "Americans are crazy, but it is better for them to watch basketball than to bomb innocent people."   —Patrick Minges, 46, publications director for Human Rights Watch, Washington, DC

These statements point to a number of different themes: the value of stability and consistency in a changing world, the role of a sports team as a unifying theme in one's life narrative, identification with specific values associated with Carolina basketball thought to be rare in the larger society, appreciation of the uniqueness of Dean Smith, and a sense that even if basketball-watching isn't the best thing Americans could be doing with their time and their passion, it isn't the worst thing, either. All of those themes, in my view, have some merit in coming to a tentative assessment of what the significance of Carolina basketball really is for its fans, but they need to be further developed and worked out. That task will be taken up in the last chapter, by way of coming to a conclusion.

SUMMARY OF KEY FINDINGS OF CHAPTER EIGHT

- A majority of Carolina fans have been or currently are involved in basketball at some level as a participant. Roughly 90% of Carolina fans report either playing basketball or participating in some other sport as exercise.

- Participating in or watching sports is the preferred free-time activity of over half of all Carolina fans. The average Carolina fan watches three college basketball games a week in which UNC does not play.
- Three-quarters of all Carolina fans read a newspaper, and about 80% of all Carolina fans belong to at least one organization. The organizational membership patterns of Carolina fans roughly correspond to national patterns.
- Nearly 90% of Carolina fans have attended at least one Carolina game in person. Over 70% have read at least one book about UNC basketball, and about 75% of fans videotape the games.
- The majority of all fans have met either a player or a coach at some point, and about 30% of fans report knowing personally a participant in Carolina basketball. Meeting or knowing a player or coach appears to have a minimal effect on one's attitudes or habits as a fan, in most cases.
- Carolina fans have mixed views on the issue of how corrupt college basketball is, whether players should be paid, and whether big changes in college basketball are likely. About one-quarter of Carolina fans feel that college basketball players get significantly too much attention.
- Carolina fans are somewhat more likely to reflect upon wins than to recall losses when thinking about the past, but most fans think about wins and losses in roughly equal measure. North Carolina fans' best memories tend to be national championships, wins over Duke, and particularly remarkable comebacks; their worst memories are losses in the NCAA Tournament.
- If Carolina fans could change one thing about the program, it would be to continue to improve student seating in the Smith Center and to have a louder home court environment.
- Numerous Carolina fans say they have been frustrated by the attitudes of other Carolina fans, and think that too many Carolina fans are spoiled and ungrateful.
- Many Carolina fans say that Carolina basketball plays a unique and irreplaceable role in their lives, citing the consistency and stability of the program, the values associated with the program, and the belief that they have learned important life lessons from following Carolina basketball.

Conclusion

This book has been informed by several key premises. One premise is that attachment to sports teams is a major part of American culture, and that the role it plays in our lives is worthy of serious, critical reflection. A second premise is that there are better and worse, healthier and less healthy, ways to be a sports fan. A third premise is that part of what makes Carolina basketball interesting and different from many sports teams is that its fans strongly believe that the program has "moral and historical significance in our society," as one survey respondent put it. A fourth premise is that, with the retirement of Dean Smith and then his lieutenant, Bill Guthridge, it is an open question whether *that* part of Carolina basketball—the part that is more than just winning—will continue indefinitely, or whether over time Carolina will gradually become just another college team. A fifth premise is that the attitudes and behavior of Carolina fans have the capacity to influence the future—and that fans now have more potential influence, in fact, than they ever had during the Smith era.

This book has used several different kinds of evidence to illustrate the role attachment to Carolina basketball plays in many people's lives: autobiographical evidence, diary evidence and survey evidence. I have also offered, in Chapter Four, an ethical assessment of the pros and cons of being a serious Carolina fan, as well as several observations about what being a good fan does and does not involve.

Now it is time to tie the evidence examined in Chapters Five, Six, and Eight back in with the theoretical discussion of Chapter Four, and return to some of the basic questions posed at the outset. We have already learned over the course of this book a great deal about *why* North Carolina basketball means so much to so many people, and also *how* Carolina supporters fit the activity of following the team into their own lives.

But something more still needs to be said about two further questions: In what respects is the attachment of Carolina fans to their team a good thing, and in what respects is it not such a good thing? And, finally, what can this in-depth investigation into the relationship between North Carolina fans and their basketball team, tell us, if anything, about the society in which we live?

IS BEING A CAROLINA BASKETBALL FAN A GOOD THING?
TWO ALTERNATIVE ASSESSMENTS

The evidence presented about Carolina fans in this book lends itself to multiple interpretations. Readers are certainly invited to form their own conclusions about what the diary entries and the results of the North Carolina Basketball Fan Survey show. In this section, I boil down a range of possible interpretations to two stylized views: an optimistic assessment of Carolina fans, and a pessimistic assessment. After exploring both points of view, I go on to offer my own synthesis.

AN OPTIMISTIC VIEW OF CAROLINA FANS

North Carolina basketball fans have richer, more interesting lives on account of following the team. Following Carolina basketball provides rare emotional peaks, and stirs up passions and feelings not usually present in everyday life. It provides an opportunity for parents to bond with children. Many fans make new friends through Carolina basketball. Following the team also provides lessons in how to deal with disappointment.

More than this, fans find through Carolina basketball a way to make sense of the "narrative unity" of their own lives: As one survey respondent put it, the memory of following the team becomes something the man of 45 has in common with the boy of 12. For many fans, being a Carolina basketball fan literally is a constituent part of who he or she is as a person, who one's self is. It need not be the only or the most important part. But having an attachment, something one cares about deeply, is generally a good thing in itself. It is part of being human. And having attachments, things that one cares about deeply, is in large measure what separates people with rich, strong characters from empty, vacuous people who float through life without meaning or purpose.

The benefits of Carolina basketball do not flow to individuals alone. In fact, the phenomenon of Carolina basketball has created a *shared* community of memory among fans. Carolina basketball is meaningful to fans precisely *because* so many other people find it meaningful. While everyone has his or her own personal experience of being a UNC fan, no one can appropriate UNC basketball wholly to himself or herself. It is a pure public good, open to everyone. But unlike a public beach, having more and more people partake of that good doesn't spoil everyone else's experience: in fact, it adds to it. In a society not noted for its sense of sharing and community, following the Tar Heels provides a new set of shared experiences every season for its fans. Those experiences might be shared in the form of two family members who have traded observations about Carolina basketball for 25 years having one more thing to talk about. Or they might be shared when two perfect strangers, both Carolina fans, meet on a playground and take joy in being able to play the game the right way together. Or they might be shared when strangers suddenly start hugging each other after a particularly dramatic event in the Smith Center. Carolina basketball has the potential to form a common bond that breaks down the separateness of individuals.

Moreover, Carolina basketball differs from many other sports teams in that its fans identify it with a set of values, a way of doing things. Carolina fans are proud of the program's reputation, and think that it reflects well on the university. Most are not interested in a win-at-all-costs program. In fact, many of them explicitly say that the program has been an inspiration to them in their own lives. Most Carolina fans express very high levels of respect for the people in the program as well, and systematically direct their basketball-related frustrations away from Carolina's own players and coaches.

Finally, many Carolina fans, as they get older, learn how to put the game in its proper perspective, how to accept the losses better, how to enjoy the basketball without being consumed by it, how to share the emotional journey of any given season without letting that journey disrupt one's central relationships and commitments. In short, cheering for Carolina counts as a major plus in many fans' lives, and the contribution it makes is deeper than just the transient pleasures of winning: Following the team closely can help shape fans' own characters, in a healthy direction. And even if this happens only for a minority of fans, that is still a very impressive accomplishment, indeed.

A PESSIMISTIC VIEW OF CAROLINA BASKETBALL FANS

Tying one's emotions to something one does not control is fundamentally irrational. And too many Carolina basketball fans substitute basking in the reflected glory of Tar Heel wins (or in the "reflected virtue" of the Carolina program) for substantive accomplishments in their own lives. Look at fans who say that being a Carolina fan is more important than their job, or doing well in school. That is crazy!

Similarly, many Carolina fans substitute the type of community that comes from endless discussions of Carolina basketball for deeper kinds of community, such as the kind of community found in undertaking a shared task together or in a church or even (at its best) in politics. Look at all the hours these people spend following Carolina basketball: Two Carolina games a week during the season, plus an average of three non-Carolina basketball games, plus time spent reading articles and talking to other people and cruising the Internet. The average fan may easily spend 10–15 hours a week during the season on UNC-related activities. That amounts to 150–200 hours over the course of the season. Some of that time would be better spent doing other things!

Moreover, nearly half of these fans say that their passion—addiction?—to the team has been the cause of a conflict in a close relationship. Young men say they'd dump their girlfriends over Carolina basketball. Most of these fans get into arguments at some point about basketball with other people. Over 80% of fans say it takes them at least until the next day to get over a loss.

Carolina fans are also spoiled by their success. They think their association with the team reflects well on them, even though they had nothing to do with it! They arrogantly lord Carolina's success over neighboring fans, and some fans spend more time bragging about Dean Smith's good deeds than trying to emulate them. They forget that every Carolina victory is someone else's pain and act as though they are entitled to win.

To make it worse, some Carolina fans aren't even grateful for what they have! At the first sign of distress or the first run of losses, you hear self-identified Carolina fans whining about the coaches, the players, the recruiting. Carolina fans say that "loyalty" is important, but some of them don't think that means *they* owe anyone any loyalty. Instead, they seem to think that the players and coaches are there to entertain them, and that if they don't, then they should be subjected to fan abuse. Carolina fans are in fact so arrogant that they think every time they lose, it's because a player or a coach must have committed some mortal blunder. Some of them can't ever accept that the other team was just better.

The enormous amount of energy sunk into Carolina basketball by hard-core fans is mostly a waste of time. They spend hours and hours debating the nuances of decisions and circumstances they know very little about and can have no real influence over, instead of spending those hours and hours creating their own accomplishments. A game played by other people should not become one's central free time activity—there's so much more to life, so many other sources of joy, so many other worthwhile things to do, so many things that desperately need to be done, and these hard-core Carolina fans aren't doing them (or doing as much of them as they could).

CAN THESE VIEWS BE RECONCILED? WHICH IS CORRECT?

Both the optimistic and pessimistic assessments of North Carolina basketball fans and their activities have plausibility. Both assessments can be supported empirically, at least to a degree. But which, on the whole, is a more accurate picture, given everything we've learned about Carolina fans in this book?

The only honest answer the author can provide at this point is: I still don't know—or at least don't completely know. We do know from Chapter Six, however, that only a small minority of fans report across-the-board fanaticism at levels that are likely to be disruptive to relationships and to consume other parts of one's life. And we also know from Chapter Six that hardly any fans are able to completely avoid all the potentially unpleasant parts of fandom and simply follow the team in a spirit of Socratic moderation.

What that means, then, is that most Carolina basketball fans fall somewhere in the middle, between life-absorbing fanaticism and cool, utterly detached enjoyment. And given that most fans are in the murky middle ground, it is not safe to draw sweeping generalizations about whether, for most fans, following Carolina basketball plays a healthy or an unhealthy role in their lives. (Note carefully: The relevant question here is not whether the fans *enjoy* being fans—unless we think that these hard-core fans are masochistic or irrational, they certainly do—but whether the manner in which they are fans is on balance *good* for them, or for society.)

In any case, what is more important than any sweeping generalizations about Carolina fans is the reader's own assessment about whether one recognizes more of himself or herself in the optimistic view or in the pessimistic view.

I can safely say, however, that it is abundantly clear to me that following Carolina basketball—passionately—*can* be a healthy *part*, even a valuable part, of a well-lived life. The sample of Carolina fans who responded to the Fan Survey included people engaged in meaningful work of all kinds—lawyers and businessmen, philosophy and history professors, social workers and pastors, artists and writers, elementary school teachers and high school coaches, physicians, political advocates and even one Peace Corps worker. For many of the fans we have heard from, Carolina basketball is a recreational activity, but one that provides not just pleasure but inspiration. Seeing the team do well provides a boost and excitement that one can carry back over into the grind, into day-to-day work. Moreover, identification with the specific values that fans associate with Carolina basketball may carry over into the workplace, or the family, or other areas of life. But being a fan doesn't become a substitute for one's own accomplishments and pursuits. It becomes a supplementary, not a primary, activity. One may follow it with passion and vigor, but one's passion for being a fan is balanced by one's passion for other things.

However, I think I can also safely say that it is possible for Carolina basketball to assume an unhealthy role in one's life—and that this can happen in a countless number of ways. While the North Carolina Basketball Fan Survey does not allow us to pinpoint with any confidence an estimate of how many fans have a positively unhealthy attachment to Carolina basketball, it does allow us to point to certain characteristics and behaviors of fans which make undesirable outcomes more likely. The single most important finding in this vein is that one's likelihood of experiencing a conflict related to Carolina basketball is strongly tied to one's capacity to get over losses. People who have a harder time getting over losses are more prone to conflicts with other people, more prone to arguments and more prone to get mad at participants. Misery in the wake of defeat is the mother of a thousand ills: conflicts with family members and loved ones, days spent unhappily, getting angry with (and in some cases publicly attacking) Carolina players and coaches, arguments with North Carolina fans, arguments with fans of other schools.

One piece of encouraging news, however, is that older fans do appear to get somewhat better over time at dealing with losses, and it's not too hard to understand why: Handling defeat is presumably something one gets better at with practice, and as one learns how to confront the adversity and disappointments that "real life" so often dishes out. Moving into adulthood also makes it more likely that one will acquire the kinds of commitments which might moderate the degree to which one follows a sports team—such as children. But the data has also shown that fans do not *necessarily* take the losses better as time goes on. And while moving through the life-cycle often influences how fans take losses, just as important may be moments of realization that fans do or do not have along the way, moments where they say, "Hey, I don't need to take this quite so seriously." It seems to me that moments like that can happen just as easily at age 21 or 25 as at age 46.

Dealing with losses well is also connected to a second major ill pointed to by the pessimistic view (and discussed in greater detail in Chapter Four): the air of entitlement assumed by some Carolina fans, who act as if players and coaches owe it to them to win so many games, who look for scapegoats when wins don't happen, and who on occasion have displayed profound ingratitude toward the very people who created and sustained the Carolina basketball tradition. But in this case, taking losses badly probably does not so much create this sort of attitude in fans as reflect the fact that a mindset of entitlement was already there.

Being able to deal with losses well goes a long way in making sure that being a basketball fan plays a healthy role in one's life. Many of the ills pointed to by the "pessimistic" view of Carolina fans relate to that issue, as well as to the issue of fans feeling "entitled" to bask in reflected Tar Heel glory.

Two other specific issues raised by the pessimistic view merit additional discussion. First, it should be noted that if someone cares about Carolina basketball more than his or her job, that may say more about that persons' job than it does about the individual. This is not to say that it is not possible or desirable to take pride in doing well in all kinds of endeavors, but it is worth observing that, for many Americans, their employment is not a central focus of who they are as individuals: it's just a "gig," to quote the title of a recent book on work in contemporary America. Similarly, I hesitate to cast too much judgment on a secondary school student who says, "To me UNC basketball is more important than school," without taking a couple of moments to recall the day-to-day drudgery of junior high and high school. In general, it is probably a mistake to judge too strongly individuals who have what may appear to be an excessive attachment to their chosen team, without knowing the specifics of what's going on in that individual's life. Life is difficult for a lot of people, and I would be the last to begrudge anyone going through trying times the moments of joy and inspiration that following North Carolina basketball from time to time provides.

Second, as to the issue of the sheer amount of time Carolina fans spend following their team, a critical distinction must be made: Is the relevant standard for ethically assessing the 150–200 hours an average fan spends over the season directly following Carolina basketball what they *should* have done with that time instead, or what they *would* have done with that time? One could make the argument that Americans in general should be spending much more of their free time helping the poor, writing letters to Congressmen, organizing community groups, mentoring troubled youth, or on countless other activities, and that if some of the time Americans now spend on sports (or watching television in general) were re-directed to these other activities, an enormous amount of good could be done.

I'm quite sympathetic to that argument, with the proviso that human beings are not under an ethical obligation to burn themselves out by pushing themselves past the breaking point, and that everyone is entitled to some leisure. But I'm not sure that the "Shouldn't they be doing something better?" question provides the only relevant standard of assessment in this case. Perhaps a more useful question to ask is, do the 10–12 hours a week a fan spends on the Tar Heels serve as the primary source of leisure during an otherwise busy week, a week that perhaps includes time doing things on behalf of other people? Or does that time come on top of many other hours consuming sports or other forms of entertainment? What one should think about the sheer amount of time any given fan spends on the Tar Heels depends greatly on the answer to those questions.

Even so, it is worth pressing on to ask: If these fans were not watching Carolina play, what else would they likely be doing?

Studies of time diaries by John Robinson of the University of Maryland have shown that media consumption—particularly television watching—occupies nearly 40% of Americans' free time, dwarfing all other leisure activities. Given that finding, the safest bet about what Carolina fans would do without Carolina basketball is that they would spend more time watching televison or using the Internet, perhaps to follow some other sports team. Probably a fraction of that newfound time would go into increased participation by fans in playing basketball or other sports, and maybe some of it would go into reading, socializing or another activity not related to sports.

But there's little evidence that Carolina fans have a lot of pent-up social justice and community-building energies that would be unleashed on the world, if only their attachment to Carolina basketball were not holding them back. The reality is rather that many and probably most fans do *not* have those kinds of energies and inclinations. If one thinks that Carolina fans should be more active in the community and the world, the smart strategy for persuading them to do so would be not to take away Carolina basketball and assume fans will do something better with their new free time, but rather to try to encourage and stimulate such inclinations directly. Indeed, one might boldly point out that engagement in the world and activism are wholly consistent with the historic ethos of Carolina basketball. But if someone is already determined to change the world, I doubt that having a strong attachment to Carolina basketball is going to seriously impede that person's efforts. In fact, it might even help, especially in the department of keeping the spirits up: After all, Carolina has a better won-loss record than do activist political movements.

But beyond the role Carolina basketball may play in cheering up hard-working activists, there is also a deeper connection between following the Tar Heels and a sense of idealism. This connection can be described in the following audacious (but, I think, defensible) claim: North Carolina basketball has demonstrated over the past four decades that it is possible under certain circumstances for flawed human beings operating within a very flawed society to build and sustain something in the world which is, on balance, *good*. It is true that from a certain perspective, what has been built, a basketball program, is in itself rather trivial; but the lesson that program has set about the possibility of doing good in the world is not.

WHAT ALL THIS SAYS ABOUT AMERICAN SOCIETY

It's worth returning again to the optimistic portrait of Carolina basketball fans noted above. I believe that much of that portrait is justified, at least for some fans. But it's time to venture a few answers to this question: What does it say about American society that so many people can have such loyalty to a basketball program and see so much good in it?

One possible answer is that fans see and appreciate things in North Carolina basketball that they don't see very often in the rest of the society, and that fans' attachment to Carolina basketball can also be understood as an implicit critique of American society. To be sure, a lot of the values that fans say they associate with North Carolina basketball are quite widely celebrated in American life. For instance, the basic concepts of teamwork and selflessness have been spun and presented a thousand different ways by corporate management gurus and organizational consultants, even though those words are often facades and hollow in many organizations that preach them. Similarly, many fans associate UNC basketball with hard work, self-discipline and respect for others—again, values that almost no one opposes in the abstract, but values that many (from all stripes of the political spectrum) feel are denigrated in contemporary American culture.

But other concepts associated with Carolina basketball are nowadays almost downright countercultural—such as stability and loyalty to individuals over a long period of time. Not too long ago, many major companies at least honored the notion that these were good ideas, as firms such as IBM had lifetime employment arrangements for many of its employees. That concept is pretty much a thing of the past in the corporate world, however—and a new wave of corporate-minded leaders in academia are trying their best to dilute the concept of tenure in universities and colleges, too. The overwhelming message of the larger society at present is that places and persons can be thrown away and replaced when they no longer generate an optimal return, or any time there is a downward tick in the three-month quarterly report. Indeed, my great fear is that this sort of thinking will one day be applied to Carolina basketball itself. Already we've seen intimations from some fans that they could stomach that happening.

What the throw-away mentality forgets is that human beings need stable touchstones, things that stay the same over time, in order to make sense of their lives and to be able to relate to their community in a coherent way. Just as constant insecurity in one's job or relationships is a recipe for stress and unhappiness, everything changing all the time is a recipe for disorientation. (Serious conservative political thinkers have always understood and emphasized this point.) What Carolina fans see most in North Carolina basketball is not just the pleasure from the last great victory, but an ongoing source of stability. A constant theme in the survey responses of fans age about 25 and up was that "Carolina basketball has been there for me for my whole life."

And the good news is, it will almost certainly continue to be there in some form or another, for a very long time to come. The University of North Carolina is not going to move to Mexico, or threaten to pick up and leave if the state doesn't pick up the tab for refurbishing the Dean Dome some day, or anything like that. And one can pretty safely bet that for as many years on the Earth as people are reading books at UNC, they'll be dribbling basketballs, too. The real question is what the character of the UNC program will be in the future. Will it be guided by the same values and exhibit the same stability it has over the past 40 years? If it does not, the evidence collected here strongly suggests that the meaning Carolina basketball bears for many fans will change, and not for the better.

Other values that fans have seen in North Carolina basketball are even more countercultural in contemporary America than the ideas of loyalty and stability: for instance, the notion that while being No. 1 from time to time is nice, it's not the main reason to have a basketball program, or the main measuring stick for it. Dean Smith was directly responsible for deliberately cultivating that idea (although he, too, often admitted he struggled to truly place playing well above winning). Matt Doherty became head coach in July 2000 and promptly announced that his goal as head coach was to compete for the national title year in and year out—and there is nothing wrong with that goal, as stated. Dean Smith and Bill Guthridge certainly competed for national titles, too. What would mark a change in the character of the program is if fans, administrators or even coaches were to make winning a title such a high priority that they sacrificed other important qualities just to win—or if winning the whole thing comes to be seen as the sole measuring stick for Doherty and subsequent coaches. It took Dean Smith 21 years to win a national title, and Carolina fans prior to 1982 were remarkable in their near-unanimous support for Smith (much as Kansas fans are today in their support of title-less Roy Williams). Would today's Carolina fans be willing to wait 20 years to see Matt Doherty win a national title the right way, if that's how long it takes (indeed, if it ever happens at all)? I'm not sure I want to find out.

Yet whether or not the values of loyalty, stability and not acting as if being "No.1" were everything continue to characterize Carolina basketball in the future, the fact is that those values remain very important to many, many Tar Heel fans at this point in time. One broad conclusion we can draw from this inquiry, then, is that Carolina fans recognize in the basketball program certain values not widely present in the larger society, values that they wish were more widespread.

A second and related observation is that Americans are starved for meaningful moral leadership, for good examples, for exemplary characters to learn from. I don't mean starved in the sense that, "They need good moral leadership, they just don't know it," but in the sense that, "They do know they want better examples for themselves and their kids, and they don't see it in very many places." Many Carolina fans have found a good deal of it in UNC basketball over the years. That they could find it in a sports program is ironic, given the competitive basis of sports and given that competition makes almost everyone in sports at one time or another act in ways they are not proud of. As discussed in Chapter Four, it may well be that being a proven winner is a prerequisite for being taken seriously in American society. Americans don't mind a Dean Smith or someone else preaching selflessness or a certain way of doing things as long as the results show that it works. If Smith hadn't won so many games, probably the attention paid to his other good qualities would have correspondingly declined.

But that irony does not dilute the substance of the moral leadership role Carolina basketball has played for many of its fans. The degree to which this leadership has made individuals any more virtuous, any wiser, than they might have been otherwise is impossible to gauge, although as noted in Chapter Six, some fans report that being a Carolina fan has indeed helped make them a better person in various ways. And apart from Carolina basketball's impact on individual fans, I would suggest that it also has had a tangible impact on North Carolina culture as well. Not many individuals who stay in the public eye over a long period clearly stand for values larger than themselves, larger than their careers or the office they are seeking or the CD they are promoting. Those who do have an elevating effect on the culture—and it's hard to deny that Dean Smith is one of those people.

For some readers, especially fans of other schools, that assessment may invite cynicism. Take, for instance, Carolina fans' near-reverence for Dean Smith and their habitual willingness to recite chapter and verse his good works. No one could be that good! Smith's tangible *moral* impact on so many North Carolina fans, just now alluded to, must be the result of an illusion or just good marketing.

Such skepticism is understandable, to a degree, especially if testaments to Smith's character and impact come from UNC fans who are all too happy to lord Carolina's on-the-court success over neighboring fans. But it also reflects, at bottom, a deep cynicism toward the possibility of anyone truly having sincere moral convictions and a giving character.

The fact is, it *is* possible for human beings to live lives with moral meaning. Dean Smith is but one example of what is possible when a human being's habits of dealing with other people are formed in a certain way, when an individual has strong, lifelong moral convictions that guide behavior, and when an individual happens to find an absolutely perfect fit between his or her own talents, capacities, and interests and an occupation, a fit that permits full human flourishing. The reason so many people have been touched by interactions with Smith is that thoughtful actions are so habituated in the man that, to him, such responses are simply second nature. To deny that this is possible is to put too low a ceiling on what human nature can accomplish, and indeed to let *ourselves* off the hook in taking responsibility for what kind of people we are and the kind of life we lead. There will probably never quite be another "Dean Smith" as a basketball coach, at North Carolina or anywhere else. But there could be many, many more Dean Smiths in countless other walks of life—and there needs to be.

> "The most important reason for all the success of Carolina basketball, and nothing else is close, is Dean Smith: what he stood for, the way he handled himself, the way he treated the people he surrounded himself with as players, coaches, and secretaries, the stance he took on social issues. There isn't anything else that comes a close second."
> —Bill Guthridge

MORE THAN A GAME?

This book closes with one final, obvious observation: A lot of people—fans who have grown up with Carolina basketball and come to understand it as an integral, important part of their lives—have a lot invested in the future of Carolina basketball. If something should go seriously awry with the program in the future, it would be incredibly painful for many fans. In my more optimistic

BILL GUTHRIDGE ON THE FUTURE

Q. What's your fondest wish for what Carolina basketball will be like 20 years from now?

A. I hope that 20 years from now Carolina basketball remains at the top, continues to have the family atmosphere, and the success. By that I mean winning 75–80% of the games, having some ACC championships, being a contender for the national championship most every year, and then continuing to produce people who are going to be successful in their chosen field, whatever it is.

Q. What if there is a bump in the road along the way—a year where Carolina has injuries and things just fall apart, and Carolina has a losing season. How should fans react?

A. The odds are that something like that could happen. It could have happened while Dean Smith was coaching or it could have happened when I was a head coach—there's a fine line between winning and losing. The streaks of 30-plus years never finishing lower than third in the ACC, winning 20 games every year, never losing to Clemson in Chapel Hill, going to the NCAA Tournament every year, those are going to be stopped somewhere along the line, because of the competitiveness of our league. When that happens, it's not the end of the world. It is going to happen, and it's important to understand that it's going to happen, although hopefully it won't happen soon. If it does happen, I don't think it will be a trend, but a one-time thing, and things will proceed and go on from there. I don't foresee us having what would be considered a bad year at other schools, but those streaks are bound to be stopped. When they do, I think Carolina fans just should be appreciative of all the years we had that success. But a lot of people will be disappointed, and naturally everybody associated with the program is also going to be disappointed. There'll never be a run of those type of statistics again in college basketball at any school.

moments, I think that maybe Carolina fans would be able to handle an interruption of the on-court success, that they wouldn't fall to pieces and create a negative climate that would condemn Carolina's first two decades after Dean Smith to look something like UCLA's unsettled first two decades after John Wooden. Unfortunately, I have received far too many emails from professed Carolina fans ripping on players and coaches in the most unrestrained manner to feel 100% confident about what might happen in that circumstance.

But an even worse scenario would be if something dramatic happened which substantially impacted UNC's reputation in a negative way. That would break the heart and shatter the dreams of Carolina's very best fans, and at the deepest possible level. This seems to me very unlikely to happen. But leaving the basketball aside, at that level alone—the level of doing things right and maintaining integrity—Matt Doherty has assumed a pretty awesome responsibility.

No reasonable person can or should expect that Doherty will be all the different things Dean Smith was for Carolina fans in the latter part of Smith's career, or make the same large mark on the culture of North Carolina. Moreover, it's worth remembering that, as Smith's own career showed, for college basketball coaches establishing a foundation and track record of competitive success is a prerequisite for gaining any sort of larger stature, either within the game of basketball or beyond. Even so, as time goes on, the character of the basketball program and what it means to people will inevitably reflect Doherty's own personality and his own manner of treating people and doing things.

Carolina fans will have relatively little direct say on the tone that Doherty sets for his regime, the everyday decisions on which a program is built and sustained. The focus of this book, however, is on what fans *can* control: the way they think about Carolina basketball, the attitude they take toward disappointments, how they balance being a fan against other priorities, and what they expect to get out of being a fan. Of particular importance, too, is the manner in which fans choose to treat players and coaches when things don't go so well. How fans think about each of those matters will go a long way toward determining just how long Carolina basketball remains something special, something not simply reducible to brilliant basketball and great wins.

The central irony is this: North Carolina fans truly believe that Tar Heel basketball represents more than just a game—and they have plausible reasons for thinking that. For decades, Carolina coaches openly declared that basketball was not life-and-death, but merely a tool in the service of broader purposes. Those purposes can neatly be separated into three parts: First, providing a meaningful educational experience for the athletes that helps make them better people; second, making a contribution to the life and reputation of the University of North Carolina; and third, setting an example to the larger society about how to do things the right way. Carolina basketball has been more than a game precisely because Dean Smith, the relentless competitor, so often reminded us that it was only a game.

Similarly, North Carolina basketball can mean "more than a game" to fans precisely to the extent that they treat it as just a game in their own lives. If what you derive most from Carolina basketball is a strong sense of the values of loyalty, self-discipline, never giving up, not making excuses, and working unselfishly with other people, then even the biggest on-court disappointment experienced by the Tar Heels can only be a relative one. But if one's enjoyment and appreciation of Carolina basketball can be summed up by only the pain or the joy of the last defeat or victory, then Carolina basketball indeed becomes nothing more than a game; and one must seriously question why so many people could stake so much emotional energy on something as capricious and morally arbitrary as who wins a basketball game.

I think the former orientation is a much better way to be a fan: healthier for the fan, healthier for society and better in accord with the historic ethos of North Carolina basketball. Many Carolina fans, including a good number of those we have heard from in this book, agree with that conception.

But in 2001, it's no longer a conception that can be taken for granted. UNC basketball gains thousands of new fans every year—the eight- and nine-year-olds in North Carolina who start paying attention to the ACC, the new freshman class at UNC every fall, the many people scattered around the country who become fans via national television. These new fans aren't likely to share in this deepest sense of why being a Carolina fan can be special—at least not right away. If the reasons why Carolina basketball, at its best, has meant something "more than a game" are to endure, they will have to be expressed, articulated and sometimes even argued for, by way of passing the torch from generation to generation.

I hope that this book has stimulated and even entertained readers, but I will be happiest if it contributes in some small way to that ongoing task.

Appendix I

The Fan Diary Project Questionnaire

Below is a copy of the form the fan diarists were asked to use as a basis for tracking their experiences following the team during the season.

Name:

Game:

Initial Reactions

1. Did I attend, watch, listen to, or skip this game?
2. Who did I attend, watch, or listen with? Where?
3. Any extra effort to watch, hear, or attend this game?
4. What was the emotional high point of the game for me?
5. What was the emotional low point of the game for me?
6. How did I feel during the game?
7. How did I feel right after the game?

Next Day Reactions

1. How many news accounts/commentaries about the game did I look at today?
2. How many conversations with other people did I have about the game today?
3. 24 hours later, what are the two or three things I remember most about this game?
4. Did I have a productive day today (defining "productive" anyway you want), on 1–7 scale? (4 being average)
5. How positive/happy/energized/good moodish did I feel today on 1–7 scale? Did my mood fluctuate over the course of the day?

Other Information (Report This After Every Other Game)

1. How many other college basketball games did I watch/see/listen to since last report (for first report, say, how much in the last week), besides Carolina games?
2. Did I watch/see/listen to any other sporting event during that time? How many?
3. How much time did I spend in total in informal or formal social gatherings outside of work (anything from dinner with friends to religious service) since last report? Give your best estimate.
4. Is there anything else you would like to add to your diary at this time? (i.e. I had a great conversation with someone about the game, I got into a flame war on the bulletin board, I saw a cool article, I bumped into a player, etc, etc.)

Appendix II

The North Carolina Basketball Fan Survey

1. How long have you followed UNC basketball? From what age?
2. What is the source of your allegiance to UNC? (Alumnus, student, local resident, etc.)
3. How many games a year do you see in person?
4. How many games a year do you watch on TV?
5. Where do you live now? Have you ever lived in the Chapel Hill area? Elsewhere in North Carolina?
6. Describe all the ways you follow the team now (watching games, reading news accounts, Internet, participating in message boards, etc.).
7. What proportion of your close friends are also UNC fans?
8. Are other family members big UNC fans?
9. Is UNC basketball a frequent source of conversation with other family members?
10. During basketball season, what proportion of your social life revolves around UNC basketball?
11. Do you regularly communicate with friends or family by phone or email after games?
12. If you watch the games mostly on TV, do you prefer to watch alone or with others, or does it not matter?
13. Do you watch attentively every play, or do you wander in and out or combine watching with other activities (reading, talking, etc.)?
14. Do you schedule your life around seeing the games? Rate the extent to which this statement is true, on a 1–10 scale.
15. Has being a UNC basketball fan helped you make new friends? New business contacts?
16. Has being a UNC basketball fan ever put a strain on a friendship or familial relationship?
17. How long do you think about losses after the game is over?
18. After a loss, is your initial reaction to try to analyze what happened, or to react emotionally? Or both?
19. Do you ever get mad at UNC players while watching games? Rate your frequency on this between 1 (never) and 10 (cursing at every missed shot).
20. Do you ever get mad at UNC coaches while watching games? Again use the 1–10 scale.
21. Do you get mad at television commentators? 1–10 scale.
22. Do you get mad at the referees? 1–10 scale.
23. Do you get mad at opponent's players, coaches, or fans? 1–10 scale.
24. What is the main thing that draws you to UNC basketball?

25. Is being a UNC basketball fan a source of pride? Where does it rank compared to other attachments in your life (important, not-so-important, trivial)? What other attachments do you place at the same or higher level?
26. What other teams (beside UNC in other sports) are you a fan of? Are you a fan at the same intensity level as UNC basketball?
27. After a game, what are the chances that you will have a face-to-face conversation with someone else about it within the next 24 hours? Answer on 1 (never) to 10 (always) scale.
28. What is your favorite memory related to UNC basketball?
29. What is your worst memory related to UNC basketball?
30. Do you personally know any current or former UNC basketball players?
31. Have you ever had a conversation exceeding 10 minutes with a current or former UNC player?
32. Have you ever met a current or former UNC player?
33. Do you personally know any current or former UNC coaches?
34. Have you met any current or former UNC coaches?
35. Has any interaction with a current or former UNC coach or player had a particular impact on you or anyone you know? If so, please elaborate and explain.
36. Is there any memory—not necessarily your favorite—regarding UNC basketball that for any reason strikes you as of particular emotional importance? If so, please elaborate and explain.
37. What is your age, race, gender?
38. What is your occupation?
39. What are your primary free time activities?
40. Do you read a newspaper (non sports section) 4 or more times a week?
41. How would you describe your political views, on a scale of 1 (very conservative) to 10 (radical)?
42. What values do you associate with UNC basketball?
43. Is it possible to conceive that you would ever stop following UNC basketball? Under what circumstances or for what reasons?
44. What are your main sources of information about UNC basketball? How much weight do you give each source?
45. Describe your feelings (in brief) regarding the Duke basketball program.
46. Describe your evaluation of Duke University as an educational institution.
47. Have you ever gotten into a passionate, face-to-face argument with another Carolina fan about some aspect of UNC basketball?
48. Have you ever gotten into a passionate, face-to-face argument with a fan from another school about some aspect of UNC basketball?
49. During the season, how many other college basketball games a week do you watch on average besides UNC games?
50. Have you ever played basketball for a school team?
51. Have you ever attended a basketball camp?

52. Have you ever coached basketball at any level?

53. Do you play pickup basketball regularly?

54. Have you ever pretended to be a Carolina player while shooting baskets by yourself? Who?

55. Do you participate in some other sport regularly (including jogging, working out, etc.)?

56. What other schools have basketball programs that you respect?

57. Do you think college sports is fundamentally corrupt? Answer on a 1 (clean as a whistle) to 10 (simmering cauldron of hypocrisy) scale.

58. Do you think college players should be paid?

59. Do you ever videotape games so you can watch them again later?

60. Do you think college basketball will be recognizably the same as now in 20 years? Answer on 1 (radically different or non-existent) to 10 (everything same) scale.

61. Name as many activities or reasons (other than personal or family emergency) as you can think of (up to 10) that you would be willing to miss seeing North Carolina play against Duke or in the NCAA Tournament for.

62. If you have children or are planning to, is it at all important that they eventually become Carolina fans?

63. Were your own parents an influence in becoming a UNC fan?

64. Do any members of your immediate family actively root for another school?

65. How many games have you ever been to in the Smith Center?

66. How many games did you attend in Carmichael Auditorium?

67. How many times have you traveled to see UNC play at an away or neutral site?

68. What is the most memorable game you have attended and why?

69. If you have never attended a UNC game, have you ever been to Chapel Hill?

70. Have you or anyone you know ever attended UNC basketball camp? When?

71. If so, what is your biggest single memory?

72. Do you watch the weekly television highlights show regularly even if you've already seen the games it reviews?

73. How much do you pay attention to the UNC women's team? Answer on a 1 (don't care) to 10 (follow closely and watch and/or attend games when possible) scale. How much do you pay attention to the UNC football team? Answer on 1 to 10 scale.

74. How many books have you read about Carolina basketball? Which ones?

75. Do you remember where you were and who you were with when UNC won the national championship in 1957, 1982, and 1993? How often do you think about those occasions?

76. Do you remember where you were and who you were with when Dean Smith's retirement was announced? Who did you speak to about it within 24 hours?

77. Do you agree that college athletes get too much attention/public acclaim? Answer on 1 (disagree) to 10 (agree) scale.

78. If you graduated from UNC five or more years ago, are you a bigger fan now than when you were a student?

79. How many organizations do you belong to (can be anything from sports team to a church)?

80. Do you or have you ever financially contributed to UNC athletics in any amount? Do you or have you ever financially contributed to UNC apart from athletics? Do you financially contribute to any other organizations (answer yes or no)?

81. When you think about past seasons and games, how much time do you spend thinking about losses as compared to wins? Answer on 1 (only think about losses) to 10 (only think about wins) scale.

82. If you could change one thing about UNC basketball, what would it be?

83. If you had to explain to a stranger from another country why you spend so much time following Carolina basketball, what would you say?

84. Would you be willing to be contacted for follow-up questions about these answers?

85. Are you willing to be cited by name in connection with any of these answers? Please answer, "yes," "no," or "please contact me again to get permission—I want to know how it's going to be used."

86. Is there anything else you want to say about what Carolina basketball means to you?

Acknowledgments

From the outset of this project, I knew that putting together the envisioned book in the desired time frame would require significant help from other people. But the number of assists I've received over the past 12 months far exceeds what I could have reasonably expected, so much so that I almost feel like I know what it would be like to play on the same team with Ed Cota or Phil Ford. It also has been a joy to come into contact with so many new people through the project. The least I can do now is to run back down court and try to point out all the people who have helped make this book possible.

What got this book off the ground was the fantastic response to the North Carolina Basketball Fan Survey. The 600-plus people who filled out the survey provided priceless information. The knowledge that another interesting story, quote, or insight might lie in the next response made the work of processing and analyzing the surveys a pleasure. I especially appreciate those fans who agreed to be quoted by name in this book.

My thanks also go to Ben Sherman and Michelle Hillison, then of *uncbasketball.com*, who readily agreed to cooperate in posting the survey and helped create a usable online form. I also would like to thank Steven Sullivan and his family for sharing with me his inspiring story, as first reported in a February 2001 article for *uncbasketball.com* and as recapitulated in Chapter Four.

The 15 North Carolina fans who faithfully kept diaries over the course of the 2000–01 season can be considered almost as contributing authors to this volume. The diarists, all volunteers, put up with all my requests and reminders, and persevered through losses to Duke, an unexpected March ending and even one computer mishap to provide a wonderful and telling collection of material.

A quick word on sources is in order. The narrative account provided in Part One of the book is based on my own memory and experiences of growing up with and then covering Carolina basketball. I did not rely upon the many previously published accounts of the teams and seasons referred to in Part One in constructing the narrative, although, inevitably, there are likely to be points of overlap between those accounts and the account offered here. I did, however, frequently consult past editions of UNC media guides, Charlie Board's online ACC Stats Archive, and (with the help of Lexis-Nexis) many newspaper and wire service accounts of games in fact-checking and correcting details.

Numerous people read parts or all of the manuscript at various stages and provided very helpful feedback, including Ned Foster, Ben Sherman, David Daly, Danny Mullis, Jay Barnes, Steve Andrews, Jeffrey Stephens, Pearl Seymour, Dan Broun, Tom Williams, Tamar Bland, David Moreau, and Duncan Murrell. An additional word is needed to describe fan diarist Susan Worley's contribution: After the conclusion of the 2001 season and the fan diaries project, Susan read the manuscript literally as it was produced and provided detailed comments as well as lots of enthusiastic encouragement, even going so far as to dig into her own archives of Tar Heel memorabilia to help confirm several ancient events.

Another person who made an extraordinary contribution to the book is Tim Houk of Burbank, California. Tim, a UNC graduate, volunteered at an early stage to provide copy-editing assistance with the book. He ended up doing much more, providing a detailed, knowledgeable read of the book with many excellent suggestions as to both content and style. Without his help, finishing this book would have been impossible.

Both the writing of the book and the finished product benefitted invaluably from the opportunity to interview Dean Smith, Bill Guthridge, Matt Doherty and Phil Ford. The day I went in for the interview with Smith, he had just finished a meeting pertaining to his work in opposition to the North Carolina lottery, his next meeting was with former player Joe Wolf, and he had just said hello to Shammond Williams in the hallway, who helped him sidestep a group of high school students who were touring the building. To be a part of a day that was almost a microcosm of what Smith is all about is something I will remember and appreciate long after this volume is consigned to the dustiest of bookshelves. Many thanks to each of the coaches, and thanks also to Steve Kirschner, Linda Woods, Jennifer Holbrook, and Angela Lee in the basketball office for helping arrange the interviews.

Quite obviously, this book could not have been written without having had the chance to cover the Tar Heels as a journalist, and I remain grateful to the former owner of *Inside Carolina*, David Eckoff, for that chance and for being a friend during and after my time with the magazine. I also owe a debt to the three dozen or so current and former North Carolina basketball players I have interviewed since 1995. To most of those players, I was just another nameless journalist, and my interaction with them ranged from brief one-time conversations to repeated interviews over a number of years. Even so, I learned something from each interaction that helped shape my understanding of Carolina basketball.

Thanks also to the staff and editorial collective of *Dollars and Sense Magazine*, which enthusiastically supported the writing of this book and accepted the proposal to publish it. I always have thought that there were ways that my writing about Carolina basketball could be connected to my writing and work on political and economic justice issues, but I never imagined it happening quite like this!

Sheila Walsh, designer for *Dollars and Sense*, did a superb job with the layout. Alison Strickler of New York City provided the cover design. Marie Michael and Tami Friedman from *Dollars and Sense* assisted in thinking through the publication plans, and Michelle Hillison and Ben Sherman, now with a refurbished *Inside Carolina*, assisted mightily in brainstorming distribution and advertising.

How does one appropriately thank one's own family in a public context? Suffice it to say that the support of my parents, siblings, and wife were absolutely essential to sustaining this project amidst a very busy academic year and summer. My parents, Sam and Joan Williamson, and my sister Treeby Williamson Brown, each successfully pulled off the difficult task of providing numerous suggestions and helping correct my memory without telling me what I should or shouldn't say. Meanwhile, my brother-in-law, Robert Brown, was (as usual) willing to discuss with me any and all aspects of Carolina basketball during the writing of the book, and my niece Frances Brown provided further inspiration.

My brother, George Williamson, had an even more involved role. The writing of this book coincided with George's sabbatical year from teaching at the University of Alabama, which he spent doing research at Harvard. His close proximity both permitted and fueled dozens of conversations about the themes of this book; but even more important than our discussions and his many comments on both the organization and the details of the book was his underlying encouragement that this book was worth writing and that it was worth the investment of my time to write it. And George's presence also provided what I suspect will be my own lasting memory of the 2001 season: both of us excitedly standing up in front of the televison set at the very end of the Duke-Carolina game in Cameron, George agitated that Brendan Haywood had made his second free throw instead of deliberately missing, me suppressing my worries and saying that it would be O.K. Our underlying dispositions while the game is being played may not have changed so much in 20 years, but at least now we're more than happy to watch in the same room together.

Finally, my wife and colleague Adria Scharf pushed her already heroic tolerance of Carolina basketball to unimaginable levels during this past year, and lived with me through the many ups and downs involved in putting this together and seeing it through to completion. An underlying theme of this book has been the importance of gratitude, but some forms of gratitude, like the gratitude I owe to Adria, cannot be expressed adequately in words.

About the Author

Thad Williamson is a doctoral student in political theory at Harvard University and a consultant to the National Center for Economic and Security Alternatives in Washington, DC. A graduate of Chapel Hill High School, he received an A.B. in Religious Studies and History from Brown University in 1992 and an M.A. in Christian Ethics in 1998 from Union Theological Seminary, New York. Williamson has written on issues ranging from economic policy to disarmament for over a dozen publications, including *The Nation*, *Tikkun*, and *Dollars and Sense*, and has completed two other books, *What Comes Next? Proposals for a Different Society* (National Center for Economic and Security Alternatives, 1998), and *Making a Place for Community: A Policy Primer for the 21st Century* (Routledge Press, 2002), co-authored with David Imbroscio and Gar Alperovitz. Williamson, who has written about North Carolina basketball since 1995, lives in Cambridge, Massachusetts with his wife, Adria Scharf.